1

Prayer Man

More Than a Fuzzy Picture

Bart Kamp

Book Cover by: Bartolomy.

Back cover photograph: Peter Gallina.

Back cover text Alan Dale.

First edition 2023.

Table of Contents

Lee Harvey Oswald

- Stood on the upper west side of the steps at the entrance of the TSBD when JFK was assassinated.
- Was not encountered by Roy Truly and Marrion Baker in the second-floor lunchroom after the shooting.
- Was the first one to leave the TSBD after the police made their entrance and locked the building down. His details were taken upon his departure.
- Said the revolver was tossed at him in the Texas Theatre at the time of his arrest.
- Was frisked three times in a 2.5-hour period and during that final search 5 bullets were 'found' in his pants' front pocket.
- Had his authentic alibi destroyed during his first interrogation.
- There was no Hidell ID among the evidence laid out on the table in the Homicide & Robbery Bureau on November 22nd.
- Did not get his phone call to contact a lawyer for almost 24 hours.
- Marina Oswald did not recognise the rifle on Friday evening.
- All the fingerprints and the palm prints were taken away by the FBI and had to be done again at about 01:00 on November 23rd.
- There was no palm print underneath the rifle barrel on November 22nd.
- The nitrate test results were not known until November 23rd and even then, they produced no conclusive evidence of Oswald firing a rifle.
- By the time he was 'arraigned' for the murder of the President the DPD had no evidence at all to tie him to the alleged murder weapon.

Don't believe me?
Read on.*
Don't want to believe me?
Then close this book.

*For all sources I refer to the numbers in brackets that correspond with all audio, photographs, documents, videos & websites that are used as supporting evidence at prayer-man.com/misc/the-book/

Foreword

When Bart Kamp sent me his draft manuscript, I printed all its pages out and labelled the file as follows: "Bart's Monumental Effort." Now, because of this "monumental effort," you the reader may discover, at last, a true representation of Lee Harvey Oswald's final hours.

I met Bart at a UK JFK Conference in April of 2016 and my first impression was of a tall brooding guy, somewhat overconfident in his beliefs. Later, I came to realise that first impressions really can be misleading. Martha Lane Fox, a successful entrepreneur, defined success recently: "Determination is not enough, neither is hard work...what it really takes is persistence." If ever there was an accurate description of Bart Kamp, then it is here in those few words; head down, keep going, never give up, and above all do not be thwarted.

I remember mentioning to Bart that I had some audio tapes from the Harrison Livingstone archive and he offered to digitise them, little realising that the number of items was actually in the hundreds. Nonetheless, he took on this challenge and not only processed the audio tapes, but also a large number of video (VHS) tapes as well.

Whenever Bart visited me, I often gave him documents which I personally thought were interesting which he then posted on his website. When my family and I moved house, home and possessions, all of my documents plus the (Harry) Livingstone Archive ended up being stored in a building I owned in the market town of Tetbury in Gloucestershire.

Soon after, Bart visited the Tetbury building and decided to digitise the entire Livingstone paper archive (which was a major commitment). As he got into that process, my personal archive got his attention and he suggested that he should digitise those documents also once he finished with the Livingstone Archive (1001).

Now after years of hard work and great persistence Bart is finally completing this mammoth task. Because of Bart's labours many useful documents from my archive (1002) have now been used to good effect and are a part of what the reader will now see in this book. Furthermore, these records and many others, amounting to roughly 165,000 pages in 25,000 PDFs, are freely available for those that are interested in them.

This colossal effort by Bart has produced the most accurate and enlightening description of Lee Harvey Oswald's treatment within the Dallas Police Department over the weekend of the assassination. We can see how this bewildered young man was shuttled from pillar to post, and how he was railroaded and framed for the murders of Officer Tippit and President Kennedy. The official version of Oswald's time in custody by the Dallas Police Department is a travesty of the truth.

In the aftermath of the assassination, November 24th 1963, FBI director J Edgar Hoover stated that, *"the thing I am concerned about, and so is Mr. Katzenbach, is having something issued so we can convince the public that Oswald is the real assassin."* Deputy Attorney General Nicholas Katzenbach stated one day later, *"the public must be satisfied that Oswald was the assassin; that he did not have confederates who are still at large; and that evidence was such that he would have been convicted at trial."*

Thus, we have the simplistic narrative of Lee Harvey Oswald the lone nut commie replayed over and over by a compliant main stream media. In lockstep with their drivel was the portrayal of a heroic Dallas Police Department out of its depth but doing their best in impossible circumstances.

Over these many years the JFK research community has suffered from much misdirection from within and without. It suffered heavily as its credibility was challenged. The danger for all researchers/authors especially those of us investigating the JFK assassination is the *confirmation bias* trap where information suiting our own research is included but information to the contrary is excluded.

Bart Kamp is meticulous in this regard and that is why this book stands head and shoulders above anything thus far produced on the TSBD employees, the alleged second floor lunchroom encounter and Lee Harvey Oswald's interrogations. This body of work is a rare beast, chock full of little-known important facts which are themselves backed up by a multitude of hard-to-find documentation.

Bart's huge effort has produced the ultimate reference point for future authors and researchers working on this aspect of the Kennedy assassination.

Malcolm Blunt – April 2023.

Introduction

It was 1977, during the House Select Committee on Assassinations (1003) hearings, when at the age of eleven I saw a documentary on TV which showed b&w footage of the Orville Nix film (1004). I remember a close-up of the film sequence that focused on a possible shooter's position near the grassy knoll where JFK was assassinated in Dallas on November 22nd 1963. The fact that there were many witnesses present, and quite a few films and photographs of the graphic and horrendous murder, fascinated and amazed me. Whenever there was an article about the JFK assassination in a magazine or newspaper, I would be reading it.

Then in early 1992 I saw Oliver Stone's film, JFK (1005). It was in the American Cinema in Vienna, as I lived and worked there for a brief period as a professional photographer. After my return to the Netherlands, I saw the movie again and followed that by watching the director's cut on VHS tape. Now more than 30 years later it is easy to point out the mistakes in the film, but it was based on the information that was available at that time. More importantly, this film was responsible for the creation of the JFK Records Act in 1992 (1006) and the Assassination Records Review Board (1007), which got a lot of documents released to the public long before they were scheduled to be declassified. There are not many films that have generated such an achievement.

Books are always more detailed than a movie, and a friend of mine had Jim Garrison's book, On the Trail of the Assassins (1008), which he lent to me. Then I got hold of the second book that was used as a source for the Stone film, Jim Marrs' Crossfire (1009), to get even more acquainted with the material at hand.

The internet beckoned. My first ever search was either "Fletcher Prouty" or "JFK Assassination" in 1995 thru the Excite search engine (1010), a few years before there was a thing called Google.

Since I was a professional photographer, I happened to be mostly interested in the photographs and films taken that day, but at that time they were difficult to check due to connectivity issues while having a 56K modem. Social Media and YouTube did not exist at that time either.

Then in 1997 I decided to walk away from it all. The baseless *for and against* chatter, *"I believe this...," "I think that...,"* bored and angered me. Without evidence, you only get just another so-called *'expert's opinion,'* which is why you will have a hard time finding such opinions in this book. I prefer the gathered evidence to do the talking.

I did nothing further until 2008 when I shot a 12-page fashion story entitled "Pax Americana" (1011) for a magazine which involved an amazing looking Chinese female sniper, American looking officials, and a youthful patsy. All that *'conspiracy stuff'* was good for something!

It took another three years until I regained interest at a time when I had stopped using some social media channels and started to read about 20 books on the JFK and RFK murders instead.

At the same time, I had been involved with interactive technology for about 5 years. Then in 2013 I was at first involved with a 3D project and the RFK assassination which was set in LA's Ambassador Hotel's kitchen pantry. When that project fell through, I ended up creating a JFK Assassination multitouch applications suite (1012) just before the 50th anniversary of the assassination. This applications suite enabled me to interact and present a lot of big data in the shape of PDFs, photos and videos.

During that same year I came across the work of Sean Murphy with a subject matter that interested me, it was *Prayer Man*. After seeing the still photograph and the supporting evidence laid out, I was of the opinion that if anything could solve an extremely crucial element of this case, Oswald not guilty of shooting the President, it was *Prayer Man*. Had there been no *Prayer Man,* I would have most likely folded my activities there and then.

In late 2014 I joined the ReOpenKennedyCase forum (1013). This small forum posts a lot of evidence-based material and discusses it in depth. I also became a member of Dealey Plaza UK (1014), a British research group, founded by the late Ian Griggs. At that time, we got together regularly at bi-monthly meetings in Finsbury, London.

The following year, 2015, I started to dig in the few archives that were available online. The first was the Harold Weisberg archive at Hood College (1015). I spent almost the whole year ploughing through it. The JFK Assassination archives at Baylor College were next. It was the documentation that helped me in painting a clearer picture of a situation that showed there was a lot of evidence that contradicted the official story.

As a first public outing of all my research, I posted a video on YouTube (1016) that featured a 98 min presentation of all evidence I had gathered, at that time, in early December of 2015.

In 2016, I had put a decent amount of material together for my first presentation at the Dealey Plaza UK seminar in Canterbury (1017). I had to rush through the material even though I had a two-hour slot.

At that seminar, I finally met the great JFK documents expert, Malcolm Blunt (1018). I knew of his involvement with various researchers in the US and had watched some videos (1019) of him being interviewed by Alan Dale, who ended up producing an excellent book on these interviews.. It was at that same Canterbury conference that I ended up interviewing (1020) him myself.

Later that same year I released my first research paper, *Anatomy of the Second Floor Lunchroom Encounter,* for which I managed to receive two awards. Just before Christmas 2016, I started to work on my second paper, *Anatomy of Lee Harvey Oswald's Interrogations*, which was a humongous task of trying to piece together the puzzle of his last 48 odd hours. Something that no one ever did before. It took me two years before I released the first volume.

In 2018, Malcolm Blunt invited me over to his place to help him with digitising part of a fellow researcher's archive that he had acquired. While staying over, I got to see some of his own files which made me realise that they would be of tremendous help to me and the four research papers I was working on. This meant that I would have to wait at least another two years before I could release them. His archive was that vast and I needed to go through all of it!

The four final papers were released in June 2022, and just after that, Malcolm quipped to me, *"You should do a book."* Producing a traditional book was something I had decided against, at first.

I consider myself at best a non-writer. English is still a second language to me even though it has become my primary one. And since I was working professionally in digital technology, I had no intention of following a traditional publishing route with endnotes where the sources are mentioned at the very end. The whole going back and forth in a book to check sources has been a pet hate of mine.

In the original papers I inserted images and documents for the reader to see right there on that page what I was referring to. However, that increased the page count significantly, and I opted to change to the traditional way to share my work.

There are many, many discrepancies in the official evidence as has been pointed out from the moment the WR was released in September 1964.

What I believe in is trying to get as much evidence as is available together to build a picture that explains what actually *did* happen. The Warren Commission WC left out a truckload of evidence in their final report (1021), which, btw, is not a legal document.

With the release of a lot of documents in 2017-18, and my involvement with the creation of the Malcolm Blunt archive (1022), I managed to gather a lot of never-before-seen material that enabled me to present a much more detailed story.

I would like to thank Malcom Blunt for his generosity of time and his archive that enabled me to produce this book in far greater detail than I ever could have hoped for. Alan Dale (1023) for his advice and support. William Matson Law for the many chats. The ROKC forum gang consisting of Greg Parker, Ed Ledoux, Stan Dane, Mick Purdy, Vinny and Terry Martin. The Dealey Plaza UK crew, especially Barry Keane for telling me to write it down. Rick Bucciarelli for transcribing some of the audio interviews, Russell Kent (1024) for his valuable publishing info. And last, but not least, my partner, Terri, whose patience and understanding enabled me to do this in the first place.

Bart Kamp – May 2023.

Chapter I

Prayer Man

Intro

Prayer Man, a name given by researcher Sean Murphy, is the male figure seen standing in the shadow on the upper left side of the Texas School Book Depository front steps while JFK is assassinated. He seems to have something in his hands or holds his hands together as if in prayer. PM is featured in two films. One is shot by Dave Wiegman (1025) for NBC and very shortly after he is captured again by WBAP (an NBC affiliate) camera man, James Darnell (1026).

I started looking into *Prayer Man* shortly before the 50th anniversary in 2013. I began at the JFKAssassination forum (1027), where the subject was ridiculed and deleted. At about the same time, a thread was made at the Education Forum (1028). Sean Murphy's observations were very interesting and this thread yielded a lot of new information and, above all, new perspectives in this case, and that is something that hasn't been repeated on a revelatory scale since.

I myself did not really get actively involved in the discussion until January 2015 at the ReOpenKennedyCase Forum (1029).

During our internal discussions at ROKC around May 2015, Stan Dane shared that he was going to do a book which, at that time, I thought of doing as well. Stan was going to do a book that would take all the juice exclusively from that important thread at the Education forum, *"Oswald Leaving the TSBD."* I then knew my approach would differ from Stan's. I suggest you read his work, *Prayer Man: Out of the Shadows and Into the Light* (1030) It is a very good book which details the pivotal parts of that ED forum thread in 2013 and a little after. Sadly, the thread was turned into a troll fest and it has remained locked ever since.

I personally am not keen on the name *Prayer Man*, but when that name was created by Sean Murphy it was based on a lower resolution image than the one that emerged later in 2015 and in the years following.

Prayer Man was captured by Dave Wiegman, and James Darnell, but not many people were aware of the shadowy figure on the Texas School Book Depository front steps. It was a different still photo that drew the attention to the people on those steps initially.

Altgens 6

It starts with the Altgens 6 photograph (1031) taken by AP photographer James 'Ike' Altgens (1032). This photograph was published in various newspapers across the world on the day of the assassination. The release of the Altgens 6 photograph raised the question whether a man who is visibly sticking his head out from the doorway in the background is Lee Harvey Oswald.

That question has been answered. The figure, frequently referred to as 'Doorman,' or 'Doorway Man,' has been definitively identified as a TSBD employee named Billy Lovelady (1033). The FBI showed up on his doorstep (1034) with a large print of the shot that same evening and he confirmed it was him. This was also confirmed by Roy Truly (1035) and Bill Shelley (1036).

The debate about Oswald being Doorway Man was settled a long time ago, although some zombie conspiracy theorists refuse to believe it and come up with all sorts of fakery just to keep it 'alive' (1037). There is a good article on the Altgens 6 photo and the Lovelady "discovery" in the New York Herald Tribune, Sunday Edition from May 24th, 1964, by Dom Bonafede - *The Picture With A Life Of Its Own (1038)*.

Dave Wiegman

The Altgens photo made a few researchers look for alternative angles on Doorway Man to determine whether it was Oswald or Lovelady. The Wiegman film (1039) confirmed that it was Billy Nolan Lovelady. But what the film also did was bring another person to our attention. Someone who was not visible before due to the opposite angle of the Altgens 6 photo: A man standing in the shadow of the northwest top corner of the TSBD front steps.

Dave Wiegman, before becoming an NBC cameraman, was a watchmaker from Baltimore who was assigned to Camera Car 1 (1040) in Dallas on November 22nd 1963. This was the first of the camera cars in the procession, and the 10th vehicle (the Presidential Limousine being the 2nd) in the motorcade. The car, a yellow 1964 Chevrolet Impala Convertible, carried six occupants, only three of whom were cameramen. David Wiegman Jr of NBC, Thomas J Craven Jr of CBS, and Thomas Atkins of the White House. The other three were the driver, Texas Ranger John Hofan, an NBC sound engineer, and Cleveland Ryan, a lighting technician.

Cam Car 1 is captured in a photograph by Jay Skaggs on Houston St (1041) Dave Wiegman, wearing his fedora hat, has his hand on the handle already. By the time of the third shot he was already out of the car and running down Elm St, and the camera was rolling for the whole duration. This particular sequence (1042) is often used in documentaries about the assassination of JFK. Wiegman shot this entire sequence with a Filmo (made by Bell & Howell) movie camera, using a 10mm lens. What isn't shown very often is the sequence just before his run, where Wiegman's camera, while on Houston St, is panning to the right and captures the front entrance and steps of the TSBD on two occasions. The first sequence is from further away and shows the entrance and the steps quite small, but it also shows the spectators alongside Elm St about 30 feet in front of the steps. The second time Wiegman's camera swerves he captures the employees on the front steps from about a forty feet distance and only just before he departs from the car.

The glimpse of *Prayer Man,* seen in Wiegman, is dark and blurry, and the films that have been available are several generations removed from the original. The original is shelved in NYC at NBC. But, we can see a male human form there in the background of the landing and also a reflection, which is from a glass bottle. Careful study of the film sequence shows that this man is drinking and holding a bottle which is illuminated due to the man's position and the sunlight being reflected in front of him.

In Richard Trask's *Pictures Of The Pain* (1043) Wiegman talks to the author on the phone: *"We were in that straight-a-way heading down to what I now know as the Book Depository, and I heard the first report and I thought like everybody that it was a good size firecracker---a cherry bomb. Then when I heard the second one, the adrenaline really started pumping because there was a reaction in the motorcade, I was sitting on the edge of the (car door) frame, which I sometimes did. I keenly remember right after the incident that my feet were on the ground during one of the reports. I don't think I was fast enough to react to the second, but I think on the third one I was running.*

The car had slowed down enough for me to jump out. I swung my leg over and jumped while the car was still moving, but it was very slow. I jumped and I remember running and I remember the third shot.

When I got out, I knew I better get around the corner. The car was stopping. I'd better run around there and see what was happening. I knew the reaction was to run forward. I'd done this before in other motorcades because a lot of times the President will stop and do something. He might just shake a hand. He might look at a sign. So

21

you're doing no good sitting in your car, and you can always retrieve your car as it goes by....It was a technique I've used and I've gotten some good pictures that way. That may have been built in to get out and run and get up there and see what the heck's happening. The motorcade has stopped, plus you heard a report I don't think I thought on the first or second (shot), but when the third one went off, I really thought I felt the compression on my face.----I really thought I felt it. Then I thought "Somebody is shooting."

The idea of turning on the camera, I don't know where that came from. I've turned in some real sloppy work over the years that went into editing because I believed that sometimes you're not photographing what's happening as much as the moment. It's a slice of time. And something told me, "Hey look, what have I got to lose? I've got a full spring and just turn it on." I can't stop and plant my feet, so I put it against my chest because you can't run with a Filmo up to your eyes. So, I just slid it down under my chin and looked forward and ran as fast as I could and took in everything I could."

James Darnell

Darnell filmed a lot of major news stories from the 1960s to the 1990s (1044), including the JFK assassination. James Darnell's film snippet of the front entrance of the TSBD is part of the reason I got involved researching *Prayer Man*. Darnell rode in Cam Car 3 (1045) along with Malcolm Couch (1046), Tom Dillard, Bob Jackson and James Underwood. The schematic is wrong on Darnell's and Couch's positions inside Cam Car 3. They should be swapped. Couch's arm can be seen in the Darnell film to his left (1047). From all his recollections, be it private or to the FBI, there is no mention of him shooting the part where his camera pans when Marrion Baker storms towards the TSBD building (1048). Darnell was not called up to testify in front of the WC. He only gave a statement to the FBI (1049), on December 11th 1963, in which he states that he never looked at the TSBD.

Darnell's film was not admitted into evidence by the WC. Here is Baker's run segment from a 1964 screening (1050). Three decades later, this sequence of Baker's run got more exposure with the documentary *"Beyond JFK, The Question of Conspiracy" (1051)*. It was the first time I was introduced to this footage.

We cannot see Baker going up the steps as the camera is panning back towards Elm St The last frames of Baker is when he is about to set foot on the pavement in front of the building which is at least 10 feet in front of the steps. Darnell's footage is clearer compared to the Dave Wiegman film. But it is also blurred due to the rapid sweep of his camera. The film sequence does provide some insights as to the steps' occupants compared with the slightly earlier shot Wiegman film. It shows some TSBD workers have left (Lovelady, Shelley, Jones and Williams) and at the same time also two women have joined the occupants on the bottom right of the steps.

In 2016 I emailed and phoned Jimmy Darnell and after a few tries I managed to get hold of him, but he did not want to talk about it. I did squeeze in one quick question as to where his original film was and he said that he didn't know. And that was that.

Darnell passed away on September 29th 2017, and two years later I was successful in contacting and communicating with his daughter, Nelly. We exchanged messages and she shared some photographs with me. Then in 2021, I was contacted by her again and received a digital copy of a document with her dad's story typed out from 1964 where he described, in his own words, the happenings of that weekend and also the Jack Ruby trial. The document can be viewed online (1052). This is a great read as it gives the best insight into his thoughts about his movements and interactions during that weekend. I would like you to especially read pages 2, 3 & 4 which deal with when the shots were fired.

On page 3, Darnell relays Bob Jackson's observation and saying, *"there's a gun,"* yet he only *seems* to remember that it was said, after which it seems he never gave it another thought. Amos Euins, who had described the shooter as coloured, is mentioned in it as well. A side scribble states, *"wrong suspect"* next to it. Why?
In December 2021 I got hold of some snippets of film sequences which I had not seen before. Some of the footage shows Darnell filming while getting out of the car, filming the press bus and bystanders on Main St and running and stopping on the way down Elm St I have posted these still shots at the Darnell page (1053) on my website. These frames give a good view as to what he did from the second he left the car until he crossed the road to go up the Plaza steps and film behind the picket fence. There are also a few frames of the TSBD steps' occupants that have slightly better definition and enabled me to differentiate the added occupants a little better that were not present in the Wiegman film.

Malcolm Couch

Malcolm Couch (1054) was a part-time TV cameraman for WFAA. He started his journey just like Wiegman and Darnell, at Love Field. He is seen (1055) when the President and the First Lady are entering the limousine. Couch sat next to James Darnell and Bob Jackson, and once the vehicle stopped in front of the TSBD building he decided to stay inside the vehicle. Then Cam Car 3 continued down Elm St towards the triple underpass. Like Darnell, Couch managed to capture DPD patrolman Marrion Baker as he ran towards the TSBD building (1056), but he swerves the camera back to aim at what is going on in the grassy area down Elm St The actual film sequence (1057) starts right at the beginning and runs until 0:09. There is a GIF that blends both the Darnell and the Couch films (1058) while Marrion Baker runs towards the TSBD. The result is a visually interesting comparison between the two films. Couch's film does not capture *Prayer Man*, but it deserves to be included. It shows a few TSBD employees, having left the steps after the shots were fired, are moving towards the railroad yard or down Elm to get a better look at what happened.

Darnell left the car, as seen in a still shot from Couch's film (1059), and ran down Elm on the main grass area. Couch on the other hand, along with Bob Jackson, stayed behind in the car (1060) and went down Elm first and then left the vehicle and walked back towards the TSBD.

The Couch film gave us more info on the crowd along Elm and what was happening in the far distance of the grassy area. Notice Wiegman filming the Hesters. Some of the occupants of the steps had by this point left their places and were making their way to get a better view of what had happened: Jones, Shelley and Lovelady are all recorded by Couch much more clearly in the Darnell film. Billy Lovelady's and Bill Shelley's departures (1061) are discussed in detail in an article (1062) I published in December 2015.

Malcolm Couch's testimony (1063) was taken by the WC. His film footage was not entered into evidence, and yet, Couch's WC testimony shows how eager David Belin was in ascertaining any info regarding the front steps of the TSBD as seen on pages 6, 7 and 8 (1064) Couch and two others were interviewed and 'dealt with' by the Commission within a two-hour window.

History of Prayer Man Research

The research into *Prayer Man* started roughly five years after the big event. In the late 1960s the first person heavily involved researching this was Richard E Sprague. Sprague, a specialist on photography and computers, corresponded with Harold Weisberg (1065), Howard Roffman (a protégé of Weisberg), and Richard Bernabei, a professor at Kingston University (1066). It was 1968 when *Prayer Man* was first introduced as, *"The Man in the Shadow."*

This research was the result of work being done on Doorway Man (Billy Lovelady) in Altgens 6. Sprague and Bernabei wanted to look at Doorway Man from a different angle, and it was the Wiegman film that gave them that opportunity to do so. Sprague was an avid collector of the films of the assassination. He managed to buy a copy of the Couch film for $ 60.00 and got a copy of Wiegman via Fox Metrotone. NBC had sold a copy to them. When I contacted Fox Metrotone in 2018, they stated they did *not* have a copy.

The July 9th 1968 letter from Sprague to Bernabei (1067) is a gem and contains some really good info on Wiegman's film and its history. Furthermore, it brings to light how many generations are involved in the copying process combined with gradual quality deterioration before Sprague got his hands on his copy. Wiegman, during a phone interview with Sprague, stated he had never seen the film himself!

I managed to get hold of some great info from Bernabei's archive at Kingston's University (1068). He was quite a talented sketch artist, plus he made a very good diagram of the men and women on the TSBD steps (1069).

Richard E Sprague lent Bernabei some copies of his Wiegman film, so that he could study them and subsequently made sketches here and here (1070) of the *"Man in the Shadow."* Bernabei also had some slide copies of that film himself. I have these, but sadly these copies are too dark and have too much contrast to be of value (1071). And then this topic went dormant and became quiet from 1969 through and beyond the millennium. At least I did not come across any new research until 2005.

In that year, 2005, Charles Wallace posted about Oswald standing outside the TSBD (1072) on one of the JFK Assassination online message boards. These posts were based upon his observations of the Wiegman film. This by itself is quite a discovery due to the fact of the poor quality of the Wiegman film frames making the rounds at that time.

The only half-decent copy of the Dave Wiegman film in the public domain around 2005 would have been that of Robert Groden's DVD, *The Assassination Films* (1073). Wallace also refers to the Malcolm Couch film (1074) in that very same post and observes before anyone else that Billy Lovelady and Bill Shelley had left the TSBD steps and made their way towards the railroad yard. This observation came seven years before Gerda Dunkel made it in 2012 on the Education Forum. I do not agree with some of Wallace's other findings, but he deserves the credit for noticing some details before anyone else did. The responses to his findings are more of disbelief than actual co-research.

In 2007 Sean Murphy and Chris Davidson were in contact with each other (1075). Davidson, who had extracted still copies of the Wiegman segment from the *Death in Dealey Plaza* DVD (1076), shared his findings with Sean Murphy.
It is possible that Murphy picked up on Wallace's post and followed this with his discussion with Chris Davidson. Then, Murphy started to create some posts on the now defunct JFK Lancer forum (1077). I have not been able to find any posts related to *Prayer Man* or when exactly he created that name due to the fact that the forum got hacked and it was never reinstated. There are only a few pages visible through the Wayback Machine.
Then in 2010, a forum post (1078) was made with the Altgens/Wiegman/Darnell images by Colin Crow and Sean Murphy, both trying to find out more about the man circled in red. The post on the first page of this thread is the first verifiable mention of *Prayer Man* by Sean Murphy.

In the 2010-13 period this particular Darnell frame was used in the *"Oswald Leaving the TSBD"* (1079) thread at the Education Forum created by Bill Kelly. It was also used in the May 2010 thread of the JFKAssassinationforum, *"Where's Wesley?" (1080)* by Colin Crow.

And in 2013, the JFKAssassinationforum had a thread started by Ian Kingsbury which was originally called, "You Ain't Got a *Prayer Man*," (1081) but was changed to *"Who is Prayer Person?"* by administrator Duncan MacRae. The entire thread was then later on deleted by MacRae shortly before his forum *'blew up!'*

Subsequently, Sean Murphy entered into the debate on the Education Forum thread started by Bill Kelly (1082), in which Kelly posted the same Darnell shot. This kicked off a serious debate which, regrettably, got turned into a troll fest in later years, and resulted in getting the thread locked down by the administrators.

Murphy resigned from posting his research on November 22nd 2013, the 50th anniversary of the assassination. He has not been seen or heard of ever since. But, by that time, he and a select few other researchers had put forward a very compelling case.

The ROKC forum carried the torch from there on and has been going strong in its research ever since. The WEBS forum (1083) and the Forum

Notion forum (1084) are both filled to the brim with very informative postings.

In 2015, Stan Dane produced a book called, "*Prayer Man: Out of the Shadows and Into the Light*" (1085). This book is solely based on the key findings in that thread started by Bill Kelly at the Education Forum. It shows the research on key TSBD employees and their movements inside the TSBD just before, during, and a little after the JFK Assassination. The power of deduction applied in these postings already makes it extremely difficult *not* to point to Lee Harvey Oswald as being *Prayer Man*. It is only in the following years from 2015 forward, that slightly better images were provided by Robin Unger, Mick Purdy, Stan Dane and myself.

The Search for the Darnell & Wiegman Films

I and a few others regard the films as the 'cherry on top' of all research done. And the search for a better quality, higher resolution copy of the Darnell and Wiegman films has been an ongoing mission and then some. First research pointed out that the original films were sent to NBC in New York.

The main problem with the Darnell and Wiegman films' reproduction that are available is the issue of resolution. These copies are also littered with artefacts from their transfer (from film to video tape) decades ago. At this point what is available is at a resolution of just 654 x 480 pixels. This is not a lot to get on with in this digital era, especially when we are trying to identify the people in that blurred film segment.

From 2012 onwards some people were being recognised in the films and the search for better copies was on. Around that time some documentaries had been released in HD format and I ended up pulling screen shots of the clips in those films. Those still shots helped me and others, especially Linda Giovanna Zambanini, to identify several people of the TSBD and the DPD.

The late JFK researcher turned curator of the Sixth Floor Museum (1086), Gary Mack, had access to unedited Couch and Wiegman films. Read all about it, starting at the bottom of page two, in a 1982 issue of his Cover Ups 'zine (1087).

While watching a tribute to Mack, posted on the Sixth Floor Museum's YouTube channel (1088), I came across commentary from Megan Bryant of the SFM, and Brian Hocker, VP – Programming, Research and Digital

Media at NBC 5 / KXAS-TV, (1089). He gave an extensive talk about remembering Gary Mack, who passed away on July 15th 2015 (1090).

According to Hocker, (at 30:40) Gary Mack catalogued all the films of WBAP/KXAS/NBC5, some of which are seen in the basement in this NBC5 video (1091). I posted an article (1092) about my search for the films and included this segment. That project took place in 2013. Where is that catalogue? Hocker mentions that they had many conversations about what they were going to do and he ended up working hard with Gary Mack to be able to preserve these films, and get them to a good safe home, but there is no mention as to how and where they are being kept.

Gary Mack can be seen 'down in the bowels of NBC5' in *this video* from 2015 (1093). The film reels are in cardboard boxes. At least they have been kept in a cool dark basement.

Then there is this video (1094), and Brian Hocker carefully explains how they collaborated with the University of North Texas when it came to digitising their archival collection.

It can be assumed that the JFK Assassination material is to be included within that historic archive. Or will it not? Not really, no. I got in touch with UNT and they had trouble telling me what was supposed to be the case. I emailed Megan Bryant of the Sixth Floor Museum as well and she told me that the material in question can be viewed HERE (1095). But this is 1970's 3/4" video tape and is so fuzzy that detailed scans are not worth the bother. I would like digital copies of the reels that Gary Mack had in his hands and that have been documented to be stored in boxes in the basement of NBC5.

I emailed Brian Hocker asking what had happened to these films. After a few weeks he responded and I was not much the wiser. Apparently, Gary Mack, when it came to the films, was his 'crutch' and was the person with the greatest knowledge of the films. Gary Mack told two different individuals, Vanessa L (1096) and Darren H (1097), about the Darnell film via private messages at the Education Forum and via email. This was quite a few years before the Sixth Floor Museum went public about its ownership of that Darnell first generation copy.

In 2005, the Sixth Floor Museum did not hold a copy of Wiegman, as per Gary Mack's communications, and when they tried to source the film for the Death In Dealey Plaza DVD (1098), they had to go to the Hearst Corporation [which had acquired a copy soon after the assassination] as they were not able to source it through NBC.

Harold Weisberg had a print of the Wiegman frame (1099) from the Sprague materials clearly showing Billy Lovelady.

Meanwhile, fellow ROKCer Ed Ledoux was in contact with NBC trying to source the original films. Not much came out of that other than the acknowledgement that they admitted to having the films. I quote from a reply on June 3rd, 2015 by Meg Nakahara to Ed Ledoux:

Thank you so much for your patience. Unfortunately, I have some bad news. I just received a call from the powers that be and sadly they do not want to authorize any film transfers from the original footage. They are pretty protective of the original and hence the reason we have the dubs that we are able to license from.

In November 2015 one of our ROKC research team, Terry Martin, went to The National Archives to nose through Richard E Sprague's archive in the hope of obtaining better still scans of the film. The collection of films of the Richard E Sprague collection were only available on VHS tape; there was no sign of the original reels. I later found out that they are supposedly being kept at Georgetown University in Washington, but since then I have been told that none of Sprague's films are kept there, only documentation.

Terry managed to find three 5x4" b&w repro negatives. Richard E Sprague used a professional photographer to reproduce three images that Sprague had cut out of his copy of the Wiegman film. These negatives were reproduced by Terry on a flatbed scanner. This produced a better image for *Prayer Man* at position No. 1 (1100) than in all previously available copies. Then the discovery of Bill Shelley (No. 3), who by the looks of it has moved more to the centre and is in the process of following Billy Lovelady (No. 2) down the steps.

In November 2018, during an appearance at the JFK Lancer Conference (1101), Alan Dale managed to ask Stephen Fagin of the Sixth Floor Museum (1102), "*What is happening with the Darnell film?*" Fagin answered that they have a 2K digital version of this film available in their research room and were going to go public about this in the near foreseeable future. These days the film can be viewed by making an appointment to see it in the Reading Room at the Sixth Floor Museum. I have asked whether I could have a still, but I have had no success in getting one so far. I intend to go and check this copy out myself at some point within the foreseeable future.

Then, in March of 2019, while digitising Dealey Plaza UK's founder Ian Griggs' archive, I learned about a source that may have a good copy of the Wiegman film. They were said to have a 16 mm newsreel and claimed they could deliver something that would surpass my expectations, a *5K resolution digital copy*. The only thing holding it back from a quality POV, would be the loss of generations with this particular newsreel. But I was wrong, in part, about that. From comparing the images, I think the loss of detail is due to the fast-copying process used at that time to make these newsreel prints. Here, the Sprague 5x4" negative on the left and, on the right, a sample of the 5K film (1103) for comparison. The Sprague shot remains the best copy of Wiegman available today. His purchased reels of the films have not yet turned up.

After turning the 5K sequence in question into a set of still frames it became clear that the majority of the frames were mostly blurry. Of all the so called Wiegman TSBD front steps close-up shots, there are only one or two frames that could help with the ID of that male individual. The frame that I considered to be the best quality is the same image Richard Sprague enlarged to a 5x4" negative.

In July 2019, Denis Morissette pointed me to two videos of Jimmy Darnell being interviewed. He spoke in May 2000 while being interviewed from the basement of KXAS. These days, KXAS is known as NBC5. These videos have been recently released via the UNT site (1104). This material is part of the collection that NBC5 shared with UNT for digitising. In the first clip (1105), you can see Darnell looking at a strip of 16MM film on a reel. This strip is of the front of the TSBD segment. Now this may not even be his film, it is made by Dave Wiegman instead!

I am a little astonished that he is looking at this film, and does not realise it is *not* his own. This Wiegman film, that no one can locate, is the one Gary Mack had issues with obtaining as mentioned before with the *Death in Dealey Plaza* DVD. And this Darnell interview happened five years prior! By the looks of it, from this segment and the next, the copy they have digitised for these video reports looks to be of decent quality. The question is, at what resolution did they digitise the film? And how could Gary Mack have missed this? And where is it now?

In the second clip (1106), skip to 01:40, Darnell provides a narration of himself running, *'this is where I bail,'* while the Wiegman film is playing on the monitor. It was Dave Wiegman who ran on the pavement on the right (north) side of Elm St, whereas Jimmy Darnell ran on the grassy left (south) side of Elm where he eventually is seen filming as the press bus passed in front of him. This is repeated in a third clip (1107). I report about this interview on my website (1108) in more detail.
In December 2021 I was contacted by someone who handed me a clip of Darnell footage. The exposure is in some cases better than what has

been around and that does help in differentiating a few people on the steps, but it still suffers from blurriness and low resolution. The overall quality is not great. But there is extra footage present some of us may not have seen before. Darnell sat in the middle of the backseat of Cam Car 3 and he films himself passing behind Malcolm Couch to help himself out on the left side of the car. He films the press busses that stopped on Houston St to let reporters off, and subsequently films the people on the south side of Elm St. There are still shots of this on the Darnell page (1109). He then starts his run on the lawn on the south side of Elm St passing the cop on the left (1110). He is then captured by Wilma Bond from behind while filming as the press bus (1111) drives past in front of him while he makes his way up the Plaza steps and starts filming behind the picket fence (1112).

Marrion Baker's Run

DPD patrolman Marrion Baker's dash going in the direction of the front steps of the TSBD was captured partially by Malcolm Couch (1113) and James Darnell (1114). It is about 10 seconds after the final gunshot. Marrion Baker was the one who allegedly saw Oswald in the second-floor lunchroom together with the building's superintendent, Roy Truly, 75-90 seconds after the attack. This so-called event will be brought up while I am going through the building in this book.

Here is Ed Ledoux's blend of both films based on Gerda Dunckel's GIF from 2012 (1115). It shows that Couch did not follow Baker with his camera as much as Darnell did. Couch pulled his camera back and aimed down Elm St for a few seconds. These two films give the viewer a panorama of people in front of the TSBD and the direct aftermath on the knoll only seconds after the bullets had been fired.

While Baker is running in the direction of the building, he passes TSBD's superintendent Roy Truly, who states in his first affidavit that day to Nat Pinkston (1116): *"He saw an officer start towards the entrance of his building and he came in with the officer just a few seconds after the shots were fired."*

In another affidavit to the FBI on November 22nd 1963 (1117): "*He (Truly) then noticed a Dallas City Police officer wearing a motorcycle helmet and boots running toward the entrance of the depository building and he accompanied the officer into the front of the building.*" Roy Truly's statement to the DPD, November 23rd 1963 (1118): *I saw an officer break through the crowd and go into our building.*

Truly's statement to the FBI on November 23rd 1963 (1119): *He saw a police officer in uniform approaching the building and realized he probably knew nothing of the building and therefore Truly ran into the building with him.* His Secret Service statement from December 4th 1963 (1120): *"I heard three shots fired and moments later a man who I believed to be a motorcycle policeman came running up the entrance of the building and I accompanied him inside."*

Roy Truly's WC testimony (1121):

Mr. Truly. But as I came back here, and everybody was screaming and hollering, just moments later, I saw a young motorcycle policeman run up to the building, up the steps to the entrance of our building. He ran right by me. And he was pushing people out of the way. He pushed a number of people out of the way before he got to me. I saw him coming through, I believe. As he ran up the stairway, I mean up the steps, I was almost to the steps, I ran up and caught up with him.

The Darnell film shows that Baker had a clear run for most of his dash, even though he is seen emerging from a group of people, it does not show him pushing anyone.

In CE 3035, Truly's FBI statement taken on September 23rd 1964 (1122), he says: *"I entered the building with a Dallas police officer after some shots had been heard coming from the general vicinity."*

In *The Girl on the Stairs* (1123), by Barry Ernest, Truly, who was interviewed in 1968 is asked (page 67): *"How quickly did Officer Baker enter the building?" "Very quickly,"* Truly responded. *"We were actually pushing people out of the way."* Sadly, there is no footage confirming this, nor are there any statements from the steps occupants and those ascending them confirming this.

Buell Wesley Frazier, who stood on the landing on the top of the front entryway steps, did not see Truly go in and for that I refer to his WC testimony (1124):

Mr. Ball – Did you see anybody after that come into the building while you were there?
Mr. Frazier – You mean somebody other than that didn't work there?
Mr. Ball – A police officer.
Mr. Frazier – No, sir; I stood there a few minutes, you know, and some people who worked there; you know normally started to go back into the building because a lot of us didn't eat our lunch, and so we stared

back into the building and it wasn't but just a few minutes that there were a lot of police officers and so forth all over the building there.

Mr. Ball – Then you went back into the building, did you?

Mr. Frazier – Right.

Mr. Ball – And before you went back into the building no police officer came up the steps and into the building?

Mr. Frazier – Not that I know. They could walk by the way and I was standing there talking to somebody else and didn't see it.

Roy Edward Lewis, whose position was marked as inside the vestibule (1125), confirmed this in his March 1964 FBI statement (1126). He has been recognised as being behind Buell Wesley Frazier in the Darnell film (1127), meaning right in front of the door opening, made no mention of Baker or Truly rushing past.

He has also been interviewed, on August 16th 2018, by Ed Ledoux and when asked whether he saw Truly and Baker run into the building his reply to Truly's statement was: *"Now he said that, but if he had run into the building we wouldn't have been there."*

Joe Molina, who stood there as well, did not see Marrion Baker enter as he states in his WC testimony (1128):

Mr. MOLINA. Well, I just stood there, everybody was running and I didn't know what to do actually, because what could I do. I was just shocked.

Mr. Ball. Did anybody say anything?

Mr. MOLINA. Yes, this fellow come to me-Mr. Williams said, somebody said, somebody was shooting at the President, somebody, I don't know who it was. There was some shooting, you know, and this fellow said *"What can anybody gain by that",* he just shook his head and I just stood there and shook my head. I didn't want to think what was happening, you know, but I wanted to find out so I went down to where the grassy slope is, you know, and I was trying to gather pieces of conversation of the people that had been close by there and somebody said *"Well, the President has been shot and I think they shot somebody else",* something like that.

Mr. Ball. Did you see Mr. Truly go into the building?

Mr. MOLINA. Yes.

Mr. Ball. Where were you when you saw him go into the building?

Mr. MOLINA. I was right in the entrance.

Mr. Ball. Did you see a police officer with him?

Mr. MOLINA. I didn't see a police officer. I don't recall seeing a police officer, but I did see him go inside.

Mr. Ball. Did you see a white-helmeted police officer any time there in the entrance?

33

Mr. MOLINA. Well, of course, there might have been one after they secured the building, you know.

Mr. Ball. No, I mean when Truly went in; did you see Truly actually go into the building?

Mr. MOLINA. I saw him go in.

Mr. Ball. Where were you standing?

Mr. MOLINA. Right at the front door; right at the front door.

Mr. Ball. Outside the front door?

Mr. MOLINA. Yes, outside the front door I was standing; the door was right behind me.

Mr. Ball. Were you standing on the steps?

Mr. MOLINA. Yes, on the uppermost step.

Mr. Ball. You actually saw Truly go in?

Mr. MOLINA. Yeah.

Mr. Ball. You were still standing there?

Mr. MOLINA. Yes.

Mr. Ball. How long was it after you heard the shots?

Mr. MOLINA. Oh, I would venture to say maybe 20 or 30 seconds afterwards.

Molina repeats this during his HSCA testimony in 1978 (1129):

Q: Now at the time you were standing on the front door of the Texas School Book Depository, did anyone come out of that building?

A: No.

Q: Shortly after the shooting?

A: No. There was nobody that came out of the building, there was somebody that went in to the building.

Q: Was that a person standing on the front steps also?

A: No, it was — it was Roy Truly who was the supervisor, you know Mr. Shelley's supervisor, Roy Truly. He is the only person that I can recall that went into the building while I was standing there.

And then add George & Patricia Nash's (1130) article where Molina states that Truly went past him *alone*.

Perhaps Molina's statement to BL Senkel (1131) helps a bit....or not. You be the judge:

"Mr Truly went back into the building and stayed on the first floor."

Again, Molina makes no mention of a cop going in with Truly, always seeing Truly going in by himself.

Staying on the first floor is of course a deathblow to any second-floor altercation. What also deserves a mention is that this document was created on February 18th 1964 but is from notes taken on November 23rd 1963.

TSBD employee Pauline Sanders states in her FBI affidavit of November 24th 1963 (1132) that *"She said in a matter of 10 seconds a uniform police officer in a white helmet ran into the building, but she did not observe him any further and could not state where he went in the building."* There is no mention of Roy Truly at all. Sanders' overall story recounting Reid's observation is at best hearsay and nothing more than that.

Marrion Baker's first affidavit on November 22nd 1963 (1133): *"I decided the shots had come from the building on the North East corner of Elm and Houston This building is used by the Board Of Education for book storage. I jumped off my motor and ran inside the building."*

Baker's November 29th FBI statement (1134) comes in two versions (1135), both by SA Vincent Drain (unsigned by Baker, btw):

ML Baker, patrolman, Dallas Police Department, Dallas, Texas that he went into the building of the Texas School Book Depository shortly after President Kennedy had been shot on November 22 1963.

Baker testified in front of the WC (1136), whose testimony went five times off the record, the following:

Mr. Baker. As those shots rang out, why they started running, you know, every direction, just trying to get back out of the way.
Mr. Dulles. For the record, by this area right here, you have that little peninsula between the Elm Street extension and the building?
Mr. Baker. That is right. This little street runs down in front of the building down here to the property of the railroad tracks and this is all a parkway.
Mr. Dulles. Yes. I just wanted to get it for the record.
Mr. Belin. You then ran into the building, is that correct?
Mr. Baker. That is correct, sir.

In his FBI statement from September 23rd 1964 (1137), Baker states: "I had entered the building, in an effort to determine if the shots might have come from the building."

In Larry Sneed's *No More Silence* on page 124 (1138) Baker states: *"I remember one woman standing on the corner screaming Oh, they shot that man! Oh, they shot that man! I didn't know what man they shot. I was assuming. So I ran into the building and at that time it seemed like everybody else was, too."*

Gary Savage's book "*First Day Evidence*" (1139) where Baker (named officer Y) states: *"So, I headed there, got off my motor and entered the building (TSBD). It took a while because of the crowd; they had started moving in every direction. The man who said he was the building superintendent and was outside and met me at the door and went in with me."*

Bob Prudhomme had a good hunch in the middle of 2015 when he was questioning whether Baker actually ascended the steps at the very end of the Darnell film. The subject was discussed at ROKC as well in a thread called 'Baker's Run' by Stan Dane (1140). The camera does not stay on Baker long enough to see him actually go up on the steps. He is actually about ten feet short of the steps as Baker's last filmed shot going forward has him lifting his leg to step up on to the pavement. These Darnell frames (1141) are the final images before the camera is panned back, but a close-up (1142) frame shows that Baker's shadow appears just before the end of that sequence on the curb's edge.

If you watch the Darnell film in normal speed (1143), one might easily assume that he goes directly towards the front steps. But consider a 3D setting becoming a 2D one coming into play. Closer inspection shows that Baker is veering to the right and not going straight forward to the steps. Furthermore, study and compare the direction the TSBD employees walk, who make their way back toward the steps.

This video sequence of the Darnell film (1144) shows that he goes past the front by veering to the right of the steps and not directly up to them! See also how Baker blazes past Roy Truly who turns around to his right (centre of image in black jacket and hat).

Time Difference between the Wiegman and Darnell Films

We see *Prayer Man* in both films. And we also notice certain occupants leave the steps and certain others arrive at them. I am trying to find out how much of a time difference there is between the films of Dave Wiegman in Cam Car 1 and James Darnell in Cam Car 3. The Malcolm Couch film is of great use since Couch swerved his camera back sooner than Darnell did and he shot down Elm St whereas Darnell left the car at the same time. Wiegman is shortly after the final shot captured in the Couch film, this gives us a great reference point and helps us with the time that has passed between Wiegman and Darnell.

By looking at the film sequence of Wiegman (1145), getting out of Cam Car 1 and running down Elm St, subsequently filming the Hesters going for cover in the pergola, a rough timing of 17 seconds can be ascertained. Six seconds later, at the 0:30 mark, Wiegman has then turned around and films his own Camera Car 1 approaching slowly towards him. You can subtract about 5 seconds of that by looking at the Malcolm Couch sequence (1146) of Baker racing towards the TSBD building, drawing back the camera and pausing for a view down Elm seeing Wiegman filming the Hesters. The motorcycle policeman in the bottom left corner is a great visual anchor point to measure Baker's run starting roughly 5 seconds before. So, this then gives us a time frame of roughly 12 seconds after the final shot. It could be even shorter as Wiegman stated in his interview with Richard Trask that he felt the force of the third in his face when he had already left the car. We should also take into consideration that Baker had parked his bike already and was running in the Couch sequence. My money is on 6-10 seconds.

In the end there was only one car length in between Cam 1 & 3 and these cars followed each other closely.

The TSBD Building

The Texas School Book Depository is a seven-floor building facing Dealey Plaza in Dallas, Texas, United States. Located 411 Elm Street on the Northwest corner of Elm and North Houston Streets, at the western end of down town Dallas.

In 1898, the Rock Island Plow Company (1147) constructed a five-story building for its Texas division, the Southern Rock Island Plow Company. In 1901, the building was hit by lightning and nearly burned to the ground. It was rebuilt (1148) in 1903 in the Commercial Romanesque Revival style, and expanded to seven stories.

In 1937 the property was acquired by the Carraway Byrd Corporation, and after the company defaulted on the loan, it was bought at public auction July 4th, 1939 by D Harold Byrd (1149). Byrd's career included co-founding the Civil Air Patrol. During Byrd's ownership the building remained empty until 1940, when it was leased by a grocery wholesaler, the John Sexton & Co.

Sexton Foods (1150) used this location as the branch office for sales, manufacturing and as a distribution warehouse. The building was referred to at that time as 'The Sexton Building'. Following the departure of the Sexton Company the building was empty for a few years and had renovations before the building became the Texas School Book Depository.

The Texas School Book Depository (1151) was a privately-owned company charged with fulfilling book orders from schools all over the Southwest. Books were kept in boxes and were spread out over the first floor and fourth through seventh floors. There is pictorial evidence showing boxes stored on the second-floor landing, but that floor was assigned predominately for office use and a closer look at these boxes indicates that this was the company's stationary.

In 1963, shortly before the assassination, the TSBD consolidated most of its operations in this building, employing 33 workers, including 19 warehouse men, of whom four remained at the old warehouse a few blocks north at 1917 N Houston Street. Most Depository workers used the parking lot of this smaller warehouse.

The Front Steps

The steps and the landing we are talking about is a relatively small area. The FBI made drawings of the steps from a topside view (1152) in early December of 1963. These show the measurements of the landing, the steps and the front. The landing was not even 4 ft deep in 1963. Nowadays the entrance is a fire exit and where the front door originally was, has been moved further inward.

Only in the last decade were serious efforts undertaken to identify the stairs' occupants.

Ruth Dean

Ruth Dean (1153) has been mistaken for Sarah Stanton for years. It was established in 2018 that Ruth Dean is the lady in black on the steps. This came about when Linda Giovanna Zambanini recognised her in an aftermath picture taken by Jim Murray (1154) which I had shared through my website a few years prior.
The first statement from Ruth Dean was taken by the FBI on November 25th 1963 (1155). In it she states that she heard three shots and that JFK reached to the back of his neck just before he slumped down. *"When she realized the shots came from above, she ran out into the street, but did not look up at this time."* Isn't that the most contradicting sentence? She then returns to the steps and then, together with Maddie Reese, goes to the National Bank of Commerce, making a deposit. After viewing photos of Lee Oswald she states not recalling ever having seen him.
From the Gannaway/Revill list of TSBD employees (1156) it can be derived that they even have a file on her, just like they have one on Joe Molina. What is up with the fact that she was a person of interest?

Dean is also interviewed in February 1964 by the CID (1157), and in it she states that she did not personally know Lee Oswald, but assumed she had seen him as she had been to the first floor of the TSBD. One month later she is re-interviewed by the FBI for CE 1381 (1158). She was not acquainted with Oswald, and she left the building at 2 PM. Her banking trip with Reese is omitted.

In Larry Sneed's *No More Silence* (1159) Ruth Dean tells her story:

I was the bookkeeper and cashier for the MacMillan Publishing Company in 1963 here in Dallas. Our offices were located on the third floor at the Texas School Book Depository. I think there were about seven or eight publishers that were in the building then, but there were other publishers who had their books there but did not have offices in the building. If you wanted the Texas School Book Depository to handle all your shipping for you, you deposited your books with them, when we had sales, and they did the shipping for you. I had advanced knowledge of the President's visit, but I had not planned to watch the parade. I had seen President Roosevelt probably in 1936 or '37; seeing President Kennedy just didn't mean anything in particular to me.
At lunch-time, one of the ladies in the office and I were going to lunch and were going to stop by the bank and make the deposits for the day. We just happened to be standing on the steps of the Texas School Book Depository when the parade came by. I was standing there with Madie Reese and Billy Lovelady and several other employees. I remember Billy being there because we were joking before the motorcade arrived. Lee Harvey Oswald was not there on the steps, as some people have claimed [this is in relation to Doorway Man-BK].
The motorcade, of course, came down Houston Street and then made a left turn onto Elm. The view where we were was very good. But the motorcade went a little bit beyond us before the shooting started. I heard three shots with two being close together and one a little further apart. They weren't evenly spaced. I remember seeing Jacqueline Kennedy climb over the back seat and on to the turtleback of the car, and the Secret Service man jumped up and made her get back into the car. That's about the most vivid recollection I have of it. I was able to see that reasonably clearly from where I was standing, although when the President was hit, apparently, I wasn't able to see that because some of the tree trunks were at that point. I wasn't able to tell where the shots were coming from. The sound seemed to reverberate from the buildings around that particular location. I remember saying at the time, "Oh, somebody's going to get into trouble." It sounded like firecrackers, and Mrs. Reese, who was standing next to me said, "No, that was a gunshot!" We continued to stand there because it was so quick when all three had been fired, and then we decided we needed to

hurry on because the bank was going to be closing. So, we went on to the bank, made the deposit, had our lunch, and came back. But we did talk about it.

As far as the employees of that building, very few of them really knew Lee Harvey Oswald. He stayed to himself. He did not carry on conversation with the people. The only time I ever saw him was when we went from the third floor to the fourth floor in the freight elevator which he was operating for us to pick up some of our books to be shipped from our office. He didn't operate the elevator on a regular basis. We usually just called down to the Depository and said we needed an elevator. Since it was just a short period of time that he had been there, we felt sure that it had all been prearranged. After that Sunday morning when he was shot, we just felt like we probably would never know exactly what took place or who really was behind all of it. I don't know all of the theories, but I think that it all originated from the Depository.

Buell Wesley Frazier

Buell Wesley Frazier (1160) drove Oswald to work that morning.

In the Wiegman film he cannot be seen, and only in the Darnell film, after Bill Shelley and Billy Lovelady have gone and are on their way towards the railroad yard has Frazier shifted more forward on the landing and is seen standing next to Joe Molina.

Frazier does not see Marrion Baker go up the steps and get inside the building. That by itself is odd since he is seen in Darnell right in front of the entrance while Baker is allegedly about to storm up those steps as per his WC testimony (1161):

Mr. Ball - What time did you knock off for lunch?
Mr. Frazier - 12.
Mr. Ball - Did you eat your lunch?
Mr. Frazier - No, sir; not right then I didn't. I say, you know, he was supposed to come by during our lunch hour so you don't get very many chances to see the President of the United States and being an old Texas boy, and (he) never having been down to Texas very much, I went out there to see him and just like everybody else was, I was standing on the steps there and watched for the parade to come by and so I did and I stood there until he come by.
Mr. Ball - You went out there after you quit work?
Mr. Frazier - Right, for lunch.
Mr. Ball - About 12 o'clock?
Mr. Frazier - Right.

40

Mr. Ball - And you hadn't eaten your lunch up to that time?

Mr. Frazier - No.

Mr. Ball - Did you go out there with somebody?

Mr. Frazier - Yes, sir; I did.

Mr. Ball - Who did you go out there with?

Mr. Frazier - I stayed around there pretty close to Mr. Shelley and this boy Billy Lovelady and just standing there, people talking and just talking about how pretty a day it turned out to be, because I told you earlier it was an old cloudy and misty day and then it didn't look like it was going to be a pretty day at all.

Mr. Ball - And it turned out to be a good day?

Mr. Frazier - Pretty sunshiny day.

Mr. Ball - Warm?

Mr. Frazier - Yes, sir; it was pretty warm.

Mr. Ball - Then let's see, there was Billy Lovelady and you were there.

Mr. Frazier - Right.

Mr. Ball - Anybody else you can remember?

Mr. Frazier - There was a lady there, a heavy-set lady who worked upstairs there whose name is Sarah something, I don't know her last name.

Mr. Ball - Were you near the steps?

Mr. Frazier - Yes, sir; I was, I was standing about, I believe, one step down from the top there.

Mr. Ball - One step down from the top of the steps?

Mr. Frazier - Yes, sir; standing there by the rail.

Mr. Ball - By steps we are talking about the steps of the entrance to the building?

Mr. Frazier - Yes, sir.

Mr. Ball - Shown in this picture?

Mr. Frazier - Yes, sir.

Mr. Ball - Which is Commission's Exhibit No. 362. Can you come over here and show us about where you were standing?

Mr. Frazier - Yes, sir. Like I told you this was an entrance right here.

Mr. Ball - Yes, sir.

Mr. Frazier - We have a bar rail running about half way up here. This was the first step and I was standing right around there.

Mr. Ball - Put a mark there. Your name is Frazier, put an "F" there for Frazier.

Mr. Frazier - O.K.

Mr. Ball - In the picture that would show you about there, would it?

Mr. Frazier - Yes, sir; you can see, just see, the top, about the top rail there, was standing right in there.

Mr. Ball - Right in there?

Mr. Frazier - To be frank with you, I say, shadow from the roof there knocked the sun from out our eyes, you wouldn't have any glare in the eyes standing there.

Mr. Ball - There was a roof over your head, was there?

Mr. Frazier - Right.

Mr. Ball - Did you stand there for 30 minutes or--tell us how long you stayed there?

Mr. Frazier - Well, I stood there until the parade come by.

Mr. Ball - Did you see the President go by?

Mr. Frazier - Yes, sir; I did.

Mr. Ball - Did you hear anything?

Mr. Frazier - Well, I say, just right after he went by he hadn't hardly got by, I heard a sound and if you have ever been around motorcycles you know how they backfire, and so I thought one of them motorcycles backfired because right before his car came down, now there were several of these motorcycle policemen, and they took off down toward the underpass down there, and so I thought, you know, that one of them motorcycles backfired, but it wasn't just a few seconds that, you know, I heard two more of the same type of, you know, sounds, and by that time people was running everywhere, and falling down and screaming, and naturally then I knew something was wrong, and so I come to the conclusion somebody else, somebody was shooting at somebody and I figured it was him.

Mr. Ball - You figured it was who?

Mr. Frazier - I figured it was somebody shooting at President Kennedy because people were running and hollering so I just stood still. I have always been taught when something like that happened or anywhere as far as that it is always best to stand still because if you run that makes you look guilty sure enough.

Mr. Ball - Now, then, did you have any impression at that time as to the direction from which the sound came?

Mr. Frazier - Well, to be frank with you I thought it come from down there, you know, where that underpass is. There is a series, quite a few number of them railroad tracks running together and from where I was standing it sounded like it was coming from down the railroad tracks there.

Mr. Ball - Were you able to see the President, could you still see the President's car when you heard the first sound?

Mr. Frazier - No, sir; I couldn't. From there, you know, people were standing out there on the curb, you see, and you know it drops, you know the ground drops, off there as you go down toward that underpass and I couldn't see any of it because people were standing up there in my way, but however, when he did turn that corner there, there wasn't anybody standing there in the street and you could see good there, but after you got on past down there you couldn't see anything.

Mr. Ball - You didn't see the President's car at the time you heard the sound?

Mr. Frazier - No, sir; I didn't.

Mr. Ball - But you stood right there, did you?

Mr. Frazier - Right. Stood right where I was.

Mr. Ball - And Mr. Shelley was still standing there?

Mr. Frazier - Right.

Mr. Ball - And also Billy Lovelady?

Mr. Frazier - Yes, sir.

Mr. Ball - The three of you didn't go any place?

Mr. Frazier - I believe Billy and them walked down toward that direction but I didn't. I just stood where I was. I hadn't moved at all.

Mr. Ball - Did you see anybody after that come into the building while you were there?

Mr. Frazier - You mean somebody other, that didn't work there?

Mr. Ball - A police officer.

Mr. Frazier - No, sir; I stood there a few minutes, you know, and some people who worked there; you know normally started to go back into the building because a lot of us didn't eat our lunch, and so we started back into the building and it wasn't but just a few minutes that there were a lot of police officers and so forth all over the building there.

Mr. Ball - Then you went back into the building, did you?

Mr. Frazier - Right.

Mr. Ball - And before you went back into the building no police officer came up the steps and into the building?

Mr. Frazier - Not that I know. They could walk by the way and I was standing there talking to somebody else and didn't see it.

Mr. Ball - Did anybody say anything about what had happened, did you hear anybody say anything about the President had been shot?

Mr. Frazier - Yes, sir; right before I went back, some girl who had walked down a little bit further where I was standing on the steps, and somebody come back and said somebody had shot President Kennedy.

Mr. Ball - Do you know who it was who told you that?

Mr. Frazier - Sir?

Mr. Ball - Do you know who the girl was who told you that?

Mr. Frazier - She didn't tell me right directly but she just came back and more or less in a low kind of hollering she just told several people.

Mr. Ball - Then you went back into the building, did you?

Mr. Frazier - Right.

Mr. Ball - And police officers came in there?

Mr. Frazier - Yes, sir; I would say by the time, you know some of us went back in, and it wasn't just a few minutes, I say there were several.

Mr. Ball - Did you stay on the first floor?

Mr. Frazier - Well, stayed on the first floor there for a few minutes and I hadn't eaten my lunch so I had my lunch down there in the basement and I went down there to get my lunch and eat it and I walked back up on the first floor there.

Mr. Ball - When you came back into the building, you came in the front door, didn't you?

Mr. Frazier – Right

Mr. Ball - Did you go down to the basement immediately or did you stand around on the first floor?

Mr. Frazier - No, sir; I stood around for several minutes there, you know, and then, you know, eventually the ones who hadn't eaten their lunch, some of them had taken their lunch outside.

Mr. Ball - Did other people go downstairs with you?

Mr. Frazier - No, sir; they didn't.

Mr. Ball - You went down alone, did you?

Mr. Frazier - Yes, sir.

Mr. Ball - Did you go at any time in the back end of the building back near the door to the loading dock?

Mr. Frazier - No, sir; I never did.

Mr. Ball - Perhaps I had better ask you to point out on the map here where you were. Come over here, please.

Mr. Frazier - O.K.

Mr. Ball - You came in back into the building?

Mr. Frazier - Right.

Mr. Ball - Tell us where you went and what you did?

Mr. Frazier - Well, you know like I said I come back through here. [indicating Commission Exhibit No. 362, diagram of first floor]

Mr. Ball - By "coming back through here," you mean you came down the hallway and into the entrance into the first-floor warehouse?

Mr. Frazier - Right, and you come by Mr. Shelley's office, that is his counter right here, after you get in, you get off here, that is his office, anyway, right out, I come out around here, you know where several of the people walked around here.

Mr. Ball - That is in the bin area?

Mr. Frazier - No, sir; the bins don't start automatically right up in here. I say, there is a little bit more or less, like more or less a hall through here, but anyway, you know, I say, you have two or three bins.

Mr. Ball - Through here you mean there is sort of a hall after you enter into the warehouse?

Mr. Frazier - Right.

Mr. Ball - Right.

Mr. Frazier - From it, after you come past this counter you have several rows of bins coming this way, but, I say, right after you get past, say, this last bin right here running that way, right out this general area right here you have a telephone and everything out in here.

Mr. Ball - Well, you indicated that everything that would be beyond this line, the bin lines, would be clear on the first floor.

Mr. Frazier - Right, beyond here.

Mr. Ball - Did you ever go into that area where it was clear before you went downstairs? From the time you came back into the room, did you go down into this area which was clear before you went downstairs?

Mr. Frazier - No, sir; I didn't go in here. I was right over right close to Mr. Shelley's office right around here and sit around and talked with some guys around there.

Mr. Ball - You are indicating around Mr. Shelley's office?

Mr. Frazier - Yes, sir; pretty close right there, like I say more or less right out over in here we have a—

Mr. Ball - Put a mark there.

Mr. Frazier - Let's see—

Mr. Ball - Put a circle to show the general area where you and the rest of them stood around and talked.

Mr. Frazier - Right in there is right around near the telephone and we were just right around in there.

Mr. Ball - Where did you go?

Mr. Frazier - We left, you know, after we stood and talked with some guys there, some of them had eaten and some of them didn't, some of them had sandwiches in their hands, so naturally I felt like eating and I walked around the bin and walked down the steps there.

Mr. Ball - Got your lunch?

Mr. Frazier - Right.

Mr. Ball - Come back up?

Mr. Frazier - No, sir; I didn't come back up. I was sitting eating my lunch. I looked at my watch and didn't have but 10 minutes, so I naturally ate faster than normal, so I was eating a couple of sandwiches, and ate an apple or something and come right back up and the guys, the people who worked there, standing around on the first floor, some of them eating their lunches and others merely talking.

Mr. Ball - You never went back to work?

Mr. Frazier - No, sir; we didn't. I didn't work anymore that day.

Mr. Ball - You stayed there on the job until you were told to go home?

Mr. Frazier - Yes, sir.

Mr. Ball - What time did they tell you to go home?

Mr. Frazier - It was between 1 and 2 there sometime, roughly, I don't know what time it was.

Mr. Ball - Had the police officers come in there and talked to you?

Mr. Frazier - Yes, sir; they come in and talked to all of us. They asked us to show our proper identification, and then they had us to write our name down and who to get in touch with if they wanted to see us.

Mr. Ball - Did they ask you where you had been at the time the President passed?

45

Mr. Frazier - Yes, sir; they had. I told them I was out on the steps there.

Mr. Ball - Asked you who you were with?

Mr. Frazier - Yes, sir; I told them and naturally Mr. Shelley and Billy vouched for me and so they didn't think anything about it.

Mr. Ball - Did you hear anybody around there asking for Lee Oswald?

Mr. Frazier - No, sir; I didn't.

Mr. Ball - At any time before you went home, did you hear anybody ask for Lee?

Mr. Frazier - No, sir; I don't believe they did, because they, you know, like one man showed us, we had to give proper identification and after we passed him he told us to walk on then to the next man, and we, you know, put down proper information where he could be found if they wanted to see you and talk to you anymore, and then we went on up to a little bit more to the front entrance more toward Mr. Shelley's office there with another man and stood there for a little while and told us all that was there could go ahead and go home.

Mr. Ball - Then you went on home?

Mr. Frazier - Right.

In November 2013 at the JFK Lancer conference Albert Rossi managed to approach Buell Wesley Frazier and show Darnell stills from Robin Unger's website on his laptop to him. On the ROKC Forum (1162) he made mention of this particular moment. He asked Frazier two questions: one was pointing to the man in the middle on top of the steps and ask him if that was him. And two, by pointing to *Prayer Man* and asking him who that was. Frazier answered *"very probably ... look at the hairline."* He also said that the image was not clear enough for certain identification, but it probably wasn't Lovelady because by that time he had taken off with Shelley for the railroad yard, which by itself is another confirmation that in Couch & Darnell, Billy Lovelady and Bill Shelley had taken off.

In 2015 Frazier has a speaker slot at The Lancer Conference in Dallas, according to Larry Hancock at his website (1163). Frazier said that, *"he went out on the steps and was intent on looking out and down, he can identify folks in front of him such as Lovelady but he does not recall ever turning around and looking to his side or behind him so he has no direct recollection of anyone at all standing where PM appears to be located. He can't make any identification from the photo...which is no big surprise. He also has no idea of whether that person had been there for a time or might have come out when everyone else was on the steps. I did get the impression that the steps filled up with people from the building and that it was unlikely any outsider had pushed through to the top of the steps so whoever it was somebody from inside the building."*

Hancock further states that, *"I need to make the qualification that my quoted comment is only my impression of what Frazier was saying – beyond the point that he definitely could not identify the person designated as Prayer Man. He stated that personally and separately to a specific question. As to the rest, that's a composite of remarks he made and responses to various questions from the audience. He spoke at some length as to why he had decided to stay at the top of the steps and let everybody else go out and down...so he would have the best view of the street. He also said he was focused on the street and motorcade and not generally looking around himself at the time, much less behind him. That's the best I can give on the subject at this point; we certainly hope and anticipate comments on other questions that Deb* [Conway, president of JFK Lancer] *has submitted to him to be forthcoming."*

In recent years, in Facebook posts and also in his own book, Frazier has mentioned *Prayer Man* and has fully denied it being Lee Harvey Oswald.

Phil Hopley asked him in 2021, through Gayle Nix Jackson, *"who was the person on the TSBD landing standing to his right? Buell said he didn't notice as he was too busy keeping an eye on Jackie Kennedy and didn't notice who was beside him."* Yet he stated in earlier interviews that he saw and spoke with Sarah Stanton who was standing to his left!

And finally, in early 2021 Frazier comments on his Facebook page: "To answer the question about *Prayer Man*: I have been looking at this all day, and I can tell you this: I 100% have no idea who that person is. I can also tell you 100% that is not Lee Harvey Oswald. First, Lee was not out there. I know that to be true. Second, for anyone who thinks *Prayer Man* is Lee, the individual has a much larger frame than Lee."

The quality of the images is so bad that the man's size is impossible to determine.

Carl Edward Jones

Carl Edward Jones (1164) is easily seen in Altgens 6, Wiegman and subsequently seen in the Couch (1165) and Darnell films walking towards a traffic sign and stepping up to get a better view down Elm (1166), he raises himself up while Marrion Baker passes him by. Check the GIF (1167) of Jones walking towards the traffic sign.

In the USSS report from December 7th (1168) Jones does his best to stay out of trouble not giving away much and keeping his distance from Oswald.

Jones' recollection of who was standing with him differs from the others. In CE 1381 (1169) he makes mention of Truly, Campbell and Mrs Robert Reid who all stood further in front of the steps, but have said in some of their statements
that they stood on the steps just before the motorcade passed by and then moved 30 ft forward. Good thing is he acknowledges Reid's presence who hasn't been identified in any of the footage as of yet.

He is later captured by Dallas morning news photographer William Allen (1170), standing around the entrance of the TSBD during the aftermath.

Roy Edward Lewis

Roy Edward Lewis (1171) stood in the door opening of the TSBD entrance. He can just about be seen behind Buell Frazier in the Darnell film at the end of the sequence that shows the front of the building.

In his interview with the USSS on December 7th 1963 (1172) he states that he stood out in front of the building. Lewis was later standing on the steps next to Carl Edward Jones (1173) in a photo by Phil Willis. A little after that he is recorded in the Cooper film (1174) and is being ushered away from the front of the TSBD as the DPD is locking that area down and cordoning it off. This is happening just before 1 PM.

In the Mary Ferrell Chronologies (1175), Roy Edward Lewis is placed just inside the vestibule and marked as "T 15". He was 17 years old and left at 1:15 PM. In the Secret Service report from December 7th 1963 (1176), Lewis mentioned that Oswald was a quiet person who kept to himself. He saw Oswald last at 10:30 AM. He also states that he was standing out in front of the building.
In his FBI report from December 9th 1963 (1177) Lewis is not stating where he was when it happened. He does repeat that he saw Oswald last at 10:30 AM. He also states again that Oswald kept quiet and kept to himself.

On February 18th the DPD Criminal Intelligence Section of the Special Service Bureau (1178) took a statement off Lewis, in which he stated that he knew Oswald but did not associate with him. He also mentioned standing in the front entrance when JFK was assassinated. Nor did he see anyone leave the building shortly after. He only saw Oswald at 10:00 that day. In CE 1381 (1179) Lewis states again that he stood just inside the entrance and that he got there at 12:25 PM. JFK was shot at about 12:30.

In Larry Sneed's *No More Silence (1180)*, he is quoted: *"Due to my lack of excitement, I was one of the last ones out of the building before the motorcade arrived. That's why I wasn't outside near the street like most everybody else. Instead, when I came out, I was standing with some ladies from up in the offices right in the middle of the steps in front of the building that led to the sidewalk beyond the glass door. They probably knew that I was on the steps and couldn't give them as much information as the guys who were on the upper floors that heard the bangs."*

As stated above, Roy Edward Lewis' position was marked as inside the vestibule which he confirmed in his March 1964 FBI statement (1181). He has been recognised as being behind Buell Wesley Frazier in the Darnell film (1182), meaning right in front of the door opening, yet made no mention of Baker nor Truly rushing past.

In 2018 I asked Ed Ledoux to get in touch with him since Lewis had been 'found' and interviewed shortly before, but the quality of that interview wasn't great. I myself had quite a few questions to ask. So, Ed spoke with Roy Lewis twice in August and October 2018 and again in May 2022. I copy the text relating to his observations while being on the TSBD steps. These transcripts have not previously been publicly available.

In the August 16th 2018 conversation Lewis shares a few interesting tidbits:

Ed Ledoux: Um, yeah, now he (Joe Molina-BK) would have been standing in front of you if you were in the entrance or just came out.
Roy E Lewis: Yeah, I was in the entrance but I stepped back.
Ed Ledoux: Yeah, so, he would have been right in front of you.
Roy E Lewis: He would have been right in front of me, okay.
Ed Ledoux: Yeah, him and do you remember Sarah Stanton, Pauline Sanders?
Roy E Lewis: Now those women was...we were never in contact with. They was up on the second floor, what they call the office.
Ed Ledoux: Yeah, they would have been next to Joe Molina in front of you.
Roy E Lewis: Yeah, they probably would because Joe Molina knew all them.
Ed Ledoux: So, all of those office people were kind of standing on those steps right there. Right in front of you where you would have been watching, um...Buell or Wesley would have been out there. He would have been on the steps. Ah, also, there were a couple...Hey I've got a question...um, now this was '63 was it, um...was it segregated? Was

there like, was there black and white bathrooms? Or did you guys all use the bathrooms?

Roy E Lewis: Nah, we all used the bathrooms the same.

Ed Ledoux: How about the, um…what about the water cooler?

Roy E Lewis: Nah, everything was the same.

Ed Ledoux: Everything was the same. There was a water cooler, right?

Roy E Lewis: Now, I don't remember that now.

Ed Ledoux: Did you use the …

Roy E Lewis: Now wait a minute. I don't even know if we had a water cooler.

Ed Ledoux: Yeah, wasn't there a water cooler on the second floor between the boys and the girls' bathrooms?

Roy E Lewis: That was on the second floor. See we wasn't allowed up there. It was segregated to that point. We was not allowed to go up there.

Ed Ledoux: Was that segregated for all of the warehouse employees?

Roy E Lewis: It was segregated for all of the employees…not just black. It was…nobody was allowed up there.

Ed Ledoux: Sure, like in any business they try to keep them separated.

Roy E Lewis: That was for office people and we was not allowed to mix with them.

Roy E Lewis: Right, right.

Ed Ledoux: Okay that's pretty good. That's pretty progressive. That was pretty nice to work there for you. Was it a good working environment…there wasn't any trouble?

Roy E Lewis: (Pause) Well…well we was okay, me being black. They had two brothers there, Frank Kaiser and Fred Kaiser, you remember them. They were kinda' a little bit on the prejudiced side. They weren't overbearing, but they was kind of on the prejudiced side.

Ed Ledoux: Sure, I understand

Roy E Lewis: But, anyway, me and him had some words and so Hank Norman stood up for me. Stepped in and so him and Freddie, not Freddie – Frank got into a fight. Oh, you don't have access to that so Frank and him got into a fight because Frank was pushing me out of the, see…I was the youngest. Frank was trying to bully me and Hank didn't like that. Hank said why don't you leave the young man alone. Hank bit into Frank and Hank pulled a tooth out (laughter).

Ed Ledoux: Oh! My God! (laughter)

Roy E Lewis: He bit him…I never will forget that because, see, 'cause Hank was a snaggletooth right there…(laughter). Guess what, if they let each other alone…. Old man Truly didn't like any of that fightin' goin' on. He and Billy Shelley didn't like that. You know, Billy Shelley, he was a supervisor.

Ed Ledoux: Yeah, we've got pictures of Bill. We found him. Yeah, we've got all his stuff. That's a great story!

Roy E Lewis: Yeah, I just remembered that.

Ed Ledoux: That's amazing.

Roy E Lewis: But you know...Here's what I don't understand, still...Why did the FBI miss me? How did they not...How did they not come to the same apartment I lived in and not be able to find me? I don't understand. The FBI or Secret Service, whoever it was...see, what I'm sayin,' why would you come to South Dallas, well Southeast Dallas? You've come to the same building, the same apartment I live in, but you can't find me? I mean, if you're the FBI you knock on every door 'cause you'd find me if you're interested.

Ed Ledoux; Yeah...they found everybody else.

Roy E Lewis: Didn't they though. That been puzzling me down through the years. Why...did they say the neighbour, didn't know nothing' about me? You don't take the neighbours word for it. You keep knocking on doors. You'd find me. You know, that's where I live.

Ed Ledoux: That's the apartments.

Roy E Lewis: Yeah 3306 Johnson Street

Ed Ledoux: Johnson...yeah when you lived on Johnson. Like I say, they don't have that address for you anywhere in their paperwork.

Roy E Lewis: Oh, they don't?

Ed Ledoux: That's weird. And they don't have any report of them like going to Johnson Street. Ah, that's really interesting. I appreciate that.

Roy E Lewis: Very interesting. Like I say, that bugged me on down through the years that they didn't come to the apartment and find me. And I lived upstairs...I can't remember 206 or something. I lived upstairs.

Ed Ledoux: The only reason they didn't contact people was when they thought that people might say something that they didn't want to hear, basically.

Roy E Lewis: I think so too.

Ed Ledoux: They think you saw something, maybe Lee being somewhere or something at a different time that didn't fit their storyline.

Roy E Lewis: Now let me say this now, I'm gonna have to start getting paid for this...for all this information I'm giving you. Now, I've got some more information...(laughing). Right before this I went up on the sixth floor where Lee Harvey Oswald was supposed to have shot him from. All I can say is, there was a stack of books over in the corner blocking anybody's view from coming over to see what was over there in the window.

Ed Ledoux: Right.

Roy E Lewis: Now, I'm sure you've probably got that in your report.

Ed Ledoux: Sure, yeah, and you know...we tried to figure out who moved those books. Was it Bonnie...was it you?

Roy E Lewis: What you mean who moved them?

Ed Ledoux: Well, see, you know they're putting down the flooring, the plywood, and they are fixing the floor on the sixth floor. And so, they

51

are moving the books. They are moving the stacks of books with a handcart and picking them up and running them down the aisle. Now they're running...

Roy E Lewis: That's not what I'm talkin' about... I'm talking about that stack over in the window. Stacking up. Nah, that's not what I seen...that's not what I seen. Like stacking books hiding...hiding over in that corner.

[And a little later...]

Ed Ledoux: Okay, so, Lee was 5'9." Would you be about the same height as Lee?

Roy E Lewis: Yes, I was about the same height as he was.

Ed Ledoux: That's good. Okay, um, now do you remember who was...do you remember standing there after you came out through the doorway? Out the door, do you remember who was standing there? Joe Molina – do you remember?

Roy E Lewis: I don't remember who was standing in front of me but I think Wes Frazier was standing on the side of me and I believe Billy Lovelace...What was his name Lovelace?

Ed Ledoux: Yeah, Billy Lovelady.

Roy E Lewis: Yeah, Lovelady. I think he was standing on one side of me and Wes was on one side. One of them was standing beside or behind me. I can't remember which one.

Ed Ledoux: Okay...very good. Very good. And let's see...do you remember, did you hear the shots themselves?

Roy E Lewis: Uh, yeah.

Ed Ledoux: Do you remember anything about them? Were they close together or far apart?

Roy E Lewis: Yeah, they were pretty close together. They was like, bam-bam (pause) bam.

Ed Ledoux: Okay, wow.

Roy E Lewis: There was like a little bit of pause in between. There was 3 shots, was there?

Ed Ledoux: Yeah, there were three shots, they say.

Roy E Lewis: Yeah, there was a pause between the two and the last one. Or there was a pause between the first and the last one. Yeah, it had a pause in there, but not that much.

Ed Ledoux: Okay, so after the last one, what happened? Did anybody say anything? Did you hear people talk? Did somebody say that sounds like shots?

Roy E Lewis: No. Let me tell you what happened. We all ran towards the grassy knoll.

Ed Ledoux: You and all the people on the steps?

Roy E Lewis: That's right. First of all, the women in front, from upstairs came up and started running that way too.

Ed Ledoux: That's weird.

Roy E Lewis: We start runnin' to the corner part of the... Okay, we went to the grassy knoll – the officer came from around the side of that and told us to go back..."*STOP! Don't come no further...go back."* I don't remember the officer's name. I know it was an officer or somebody dressed like an officer. I don't know who it was.

Ed Ledoux: Did he have a white cap on?

Roy E Lewis: Nooo...now I don't remember what he had on.

Ed Ledoux: Did it look like one of the...now there's Joe Marshall Smith and a few of the officers standing at the corner of Elm and Houston have running traffic...now one of those?

Roy E Lewis: Nah.

Ed Ledoux: Was it one of those guys with a white cap?

Roy E Lewis: No, it wasn't one of those. Somebody came out the side over there. Ah, I think they would have kind of been in front of us ...directing traffic.

Ed Ledoux: Yeah, directing traffic at the corner. There was 3 of them there at the corner. Two names... I can't think of the guys' names, but they were all there. Joe Marshall Smith ran towards the pergola then down Elm Street extension...the parking lot down there towards that grassy knoll. He had his pistol drawn and towards the bushes all the way down.

Roy E Lewis: Oh, I see. Well, I don't remember they went around that...I don't remember that. They just told us to stop and then.

Ed Ledoux: You went back, okay.

Roy E Lewis: Yeah, we went back.

Ed Ledoux: Oh, interesting, um, also, um...

Roy E Lewis: That should have been in every story. That should have been in there.

Ed Ledoux: Right. Well see, Truly said he ran into the building with Baker.

Roy E Lewis: That was not. He said that but if he ran in the building, I would have known it because by the time we got back he was probably already in the building.

Ed Ledoux: Interesting, Roy. Because we have film...the Darnell film that shows Roy Truly in front of the building, turn as Officer Baker runs by him. You and everybody else are not there. There's only a few people still on the steps by Darnell. Buell Wesley Frazier is standing there, uh, Sarah Stanton is standing there, Pauline...

Roy E Lewis: What about Billy Lovelady?

Ed Ledoux: Billy Lovelady and Billy Shelley, you can see them in the film as they are walking down the Elm extension. Billy Lovelady and Bill Shelley are both walking down the Elm extension.

Roy E Lewis: Oh, they wasn't up in front when Truly went in? They weren't there?

Ed Ledoux: No. They had already left the steps. Like, well, you and everybody else...they started going. There was Carl Edward Jones was a guy standing at the bottom of the steps. He was black. Do you know Carl Edward Jones?

Roy E Lewis: Where did he come from? He didn't work there.

Ed Ledoux: Yeah, he worked there. Carl Jones worked there.

Roy E Lewis: Carl Jones?

Ed Ledoux: Carl Edward Jones, yeah. You'd be standing next to him in most of the pictures. After you came back from the knoll. You would have come back and stood on the steps. Before you get back in. Is that because the cops had already blocked people from going back in?

Roy E Lewis: Right. I think so.

Ed Ledoux: Okay, so there you are. I'll print out the picture and send it to your address. You'll see you and Carl Edward Jones are standing there on the steps, as like the cops are blocking people and asking questions and whatever.

Roy E Lewis: Yeah, they let Truly tell them to come in...sayin' so and so, okay he works here, let him come on in. They want to talk to us.

Ed Ledoux: Sure, so Truly would have been at the front and sayin' this was the guy he works here.

Roy E Lewis: Yeah, he would have been sayin.'

Ed Ledoux: Because like you're out there, Carl Edward Jones is out there, so is Bonnie Rae Williams. Bonnie Rae Williams comes and walks back and gets in. They let him in. You can see him. Who else is there? Um...anyway, Billy Lovelady, Billy Lovelady is out there, uh, kind of down from you guys at the bottom of the steps.

Roy E Lewis: Right, right.

Ed Ledoux: He's smoking cigarette. He's just out there smoking a cigarette.

Roy E Lewis: I don't know how he can be smoking a cigarette...that time, I guess so, you know.

Ed Ledoux: Yeah, they blocked the entrance you couldn't get back in there. You know he stepped out and was just smoking a cigarette and waiting at the bottom and a couple of the other ladies from the office were trying to get back in too. They didn't let them back in. Maybe Roy didn't know them as well or whatever. Um, so those people waiting and getting back in slowly, you can see Bonnie Rae Williams, they let him right back in, um, and I don't know...I think maybe Hank Norman is with him, so they are letting a couple of people back in.

Roy E Lewis: It might have been Hank Norman, yeah.

Ed Ledoux: You know they are letting a couple of people back in there and these clips maybe 30 seconds to a minute long.

Roy E Lewis: Ahh, okay.

54

Ed Ledoux: So, they show different time periods and, like, you're there with Carl Jones. Billy Lovelady is there and a couple of other people. Yeah, it's interesting too. How long were you down at the knoll thing? You had only been down there a minute or two, tops, and the cop told you to go back?

Roy E Lewis: A minute or less because the officer – a whole crowd of us ran over in there, yeah, so I don't know... I can't tell you how many. There was quite a few of them that ran over there...and you know everybody else ran over there. So, you see everybody running over there so you know you think, what's going on over there?

[On October 23rd 2018 Ledoux has another short phone call with Lewis, in this chat more is discussed about Lewis' position and his movements during and after the shooting]

Ed Ledoux: Okay, those ones are interesting because we couldn't much, uh...everybody could pretty much have labelled themselves...um, Buell Wesley Frasier could label themselves and other people have cause they're still alive except for one person standing in the corner, so the one person in the corner, um, now it's hard to tell. Had you already left the steps? You might have already left the steps by Darnell but Wiegman, he panned over pretty quick.

Roy E Lewis: Who?

Ed Ledoux: This is Wiegman. His name is Dave Wiegman. He's an NBC photographer.

Roy E Lewis: Ah okay.

Ed Ledoux: He's in Camera Car 3 so he's just coming to the corner as all of this happened...the shots ringing out and such. So, he turned on his camera and they started filming and they hopped out of the car, and when he started filming, as the car turned the corner, he captured the front entrance of the depository. The steps that everybody is standing on and stuff and the same thing with Darnell. He's a second or two later. He also hops out of the car and, um, he starts his camera and pans out and stuff. He catches the doorway and then, so we pretty much can see people standing there at that time. I'm just trying to figure out if he had left that quick or not?

Roy E Lewis: No, I never been out cause, like I said, I was one of the last ones out of the building. I might not have been out if he jumped out as soon as it happened. I think I mean I knew I was the last one out but...

Ed Ledoux: You were outside...now think about it, you were outside. Did you hear the shots? Did you step out when you heard something?

Roy E Lewis: Yeah, I stepped out, yeah right as I heard the first shot. I stepped out of the building. I was standing on the top step.

Ed Ledoux: Wiegman would be right about the 3rd shot...you know, because he heard the 1st shot...he saw something happen, so he started his camera. So, his camera would have started about the 3rd shot and then he would have hopped out and soon after, so if you're still there Wiegman might have caught you.

Roy E Lewis: He should have caught me 'cause I was out when the 3rd shot went off.

Ed Ledoux: And then you can see by the time Darnell just a second or so later people on the steps had moved.

Roy E Lewis: Yeah, after that 3rd shot, a few seconds after that 3rd shot, peoples had moved, yeah.

Ed Ledoux: Yeah, like even Carl Jones, he was right on the first step at the bottom and he ran over to the island and he grabbed a pole. He tried to get up on this pole to see down Elm Street.

Roy E Lewis: Yeah.

Ed Ledoux: That's within a second, people ran off of the steps. Like to the island or kind of...

Roy E Lewis: They ran down towards the grassy knoll.

Ed Ledoux: Towards the knoll...yeah, down Elm extension, you see Billy Lovelady.

Roy E Lewis: But the police was comin,' they stopped...when we were about to go down...

Ed Ledoux: Yeah, they stopped you. And did you think about that some more? Was it a uniformed officer but no cap?

Roy E Lewis: I think, I think it was a uniformed officer. I can't remember for sure, but I think it was a uniformed officer.

Ed Ledoux: And, uh, do you remember who was standing next to you when the cop...?

Roy E Lewis: No, no, no. I don't remember none of that.

Ed Ledoux: Don't remember who was around you? You just wanted...

Roy E Lewis: No, no I don't remember any of that because we went over there and the police turned everybody around. First of all, everybody kind of hit the ground. Then when they got up, the second they got up to go towards the grassy knoll, some of them – first some of them hit the ground, some of them.

Ed Ledoux: Right, so some of them dived behind stuff. Yeah, okay interesting. And uh, so you went over to the knoll and the police officer told you to go back?

Roy E Lewis: Yeah, before we could get around the corner the police came and told everybody to go back.

Ed Ledoux: Did you see, um, perhaps Bill Shelley and, uh, Billy Lovelady maybe?

Roy E Lewis: No, because I didn't see them because I was close back of the group. I wasn't up front.

Ed Ledoux: Yeah, you weren't up front so you ended up in the back.

Roy E Lewis: Yeah, I was towards the back, right.

Ed Ledoux: Gotcha. Do you remember seeing your boss, Shelley, back in the building when you got back in the building or do you remember the first time you saw him?

Roy E Lewis: Yeah, he was back, Shelley and Roy Truly, too.

Ed Ledoux: Where, back in the building?

Roy E Lewis: Right.

Ed Ledoux: And where were they at? Were they near the entrance or back by...?

Roy E Lewis: Yeah, uh-huh, they were close to the front. I wouldn't say they were at the entrance, but they were at the entrance, but they were at the front. Yeah, they were close to the will call.

Ed Ledoux: And what were they doing at that time?

Roy E Lewis: They were just standing around, I think. If I'm not mistaken. I think the police had come in there and was talking to them.

Ed Ledoux: Came in and talked to them, right? And whenever you saw them talking to the police was that a uniformed officer like with a uniform and a hard helmet or a light cap or do you think it was a detective?

Roy E Lewis: I don't know. I think it was probably a detective, but I don't know for sure. I don't remember.

[Then in 2019 Ledoux called Lewis a couple more times, but the recording equipment fails and not until May 20th 2022 does he manage to talk with him again and obtain a decent sounding recording]

Ed Ledoux: OK. And you said that you were one of the last ones out? You were real excited to go outside.

Roy E Lewis: Right.

Ed Ledoux: Do you remember walking towards the front door?

Roy E Lewis: Well yeah. I stepped out the front door and I was standing out on the front steps up there.

Ed Ledoux: Sure, I remember you said you were the last one out.

Roy E Lewis: Right. I was.

Ed Ledoux: Do you remember who was in front of you?

Roy E Lewis: .....No, because I was, eh....I don't remember. Because I wasn't paying much attention.

Ed Ledoux: You weren't talking to anybody about going outside or anything?

Roy E Lewis: No.

Ed Ledoux: Pretty much by yourself?

Roy E Lewis: Right.

Ed Ledoux: Do you remember when you got outside, how long it was before the limo came?

Roy E Lewis: No...oh. Only a minute or two or seconds, it wasn't long.

Ed Ledoux: It wasn't long at all. Ok, cool.

Roy E Lewis: No, it wasn't long at all.

Ed Ledoux: Do you remember who was out on the steps? Do you remember seeing Shelley, Buell Frazier or any of the ladies out there?

Roy E Lewis: Well, some of the ladies; I don't remember their names.

Ed Ledoux: Right. I remember you said that before. Did you ever go, after the limo went by, and Shelley and Lovelady went down to the Elm extension, I think you said that you started to go down there?

Roy E Lewis: Yes, all of us went down there. I was behind the ladies that when we got over to the side there by the grassy knoll. We had the police that stopped us and we could not get nowhere close.

Ed Ledoux: So, after that what did you do? Did you just, eh, there is the film [Hughes-BK] that shows you over by the Elm extension near a light pole and stuff standing there.

Roy E Lewis: Right.

Ed Ledoux: Then there is some film of you standing back on the steps, but did you go back inside?

Roy E Lewis: Yes, we went back inside.

Ed Ledoux: And this is where James Jarman saw you?

Roy E Lewis: Yes, all of us had to go back inside.

Ed Ledoux: Jarman, he came down and he saw you. Did you see him?

Roy E Lewis: Oh man, it's been so long.....

Ed Ledoux: Hard to remember huh?

Roy E Lewis: I can't remember.

Ed Ledoux: But you didn't talk to him?

Roy E Lewis: No, I did not talk to him.

Ed Ledoux: Did you talk to anyone else about what was going on, like when you guys went back inside, did you guys all start talking about it?

Roy E Lewis: No, no we didn't talk about it.

Ed Ledoux: It was pretty quiet?

Roy E Lewis: Very quiet, 'cause Truly (Roy Truly-BK) had, eh, you know. He just said, you know, you all do this and you do that and we all were doing what he was saying.

Ed Ledoux: Gotcha, so that was the mood.

Roy E Lewis: Yeah.

Ed Ledoux: That's interesting. I remember you told me about the roll call, Truly and the police officer get your name and information. Were you driving? Did you have a driver's license that you showed him or anything?

Roy E Lewis: Eh, yes. I had a driver's license. I don't think they asked.

Ed Ledoux: When you were out on the steps you did not speak with anybody?

Roy E Lewis: No.

Ed Ledoux: What did you exactly hear when the limo went past?

Roy E Lewis: I just heard the shots when they went by.

Ed Ledoux: How loud where they? Were they really loud like you'd be at a firing range or right to them or did they sound distant?

Roy E Lewis: Eh.......they sound like they were close, they did not sound like they were distant.

Ed Ledoux: What did you exactly see when the limo went past. Did you get a view of the President? Were you able to see him?

Roy E Lewis: Yeah, I got a view of his back and the side of his head. And then after the shots I remember seeing his head snap and I thought Jackie was trying to get out of the limo, but they were saying that she was trying to get part of his head that had come off, I don't know.

Ed Ledoux: Right, that's what they said that she was trying to get a piece or chunk of his head of the trunk.

Roy E Lewis: All I saw was him, the last thing I saw do was brush his hair to the side. That's when the shots rang.

Ed Ledoux: Was it quiet when you started hearing the shots?

Roy E Lewis: No, another two shots ran off and that's when everyone went off towards the grassy knoll.

Ed Ledoux: You would think that most people thought that's where the shots came from, that's why they ran that way?

Roy E Lewis: That's what I said too. That's the reason I went down there. I was one of the youngest ones there.

Ed Ledoux: How long was it before you left the steps and ran down that way?

Roy E Lewis: A few seconds.

Ed Ledoux: And Bill Shelley and Billy Lovelady they went further down, did you follow them that far or did everyone get called back?

Roy E Lewis: Uhm yeah, yeah.

Ed Ledoux: When was the first time you saw Roy Truly, was that when you came back to the building?

Roy E Lewis: Right.

Ed Ledoux: Was he with anybody? Or was he with the cops? Was Truly with cops?

Roy E Lewis: Yeah. He was with the cops when we got back in.

Ed Ledoux: And the cops were helmeted policemen or undercover like plainclothes guys?

Roy E Lewis: No, they were regular cops. Right.

Ed Ledoux: And Roy was inside when you saw him?

Roy E Lewis: Right.

Ed Ledoux: How long was it before you got back and see Truly inside?

Roy E Lewis: A minute or two.

Ed Ledoux: I asked you about Carl Jones and you said you did not really remember Carl Jones?

Roy E Lewis: Eh.....

Ed Ledoux: You are seen standing next to him on the steps afterwards and also over near the light pole.

Roy E Lewis: Yeah, I don't remember.

[The conversation is interrupted by another call and Roy is absent for 40 seconds-BK]

Roy E Lewis: Hello?
Ed Ledoux: Hey?
Roy E Lewis: I can remember the name, but I can't put a face to Carl Jones.
Ed Ledoux: He's not a looker (laughs).
Roy E Lewis: I understand, that that's probably why I can't put a face to it (laughs).
Ed Ledoux: He didn't dress as nice as you did. He wore more like a uniform.
Roy E Lewis: Yeah, yeah.
Ed Ledoux: You looked real nice that day.
Roy E Lewis: Oh? I was? OK.
Ed Ledoux: You wore a reddish sweater and slate grey pants and shiny black shoes. And when you were there and the roll call was being held, you said that Lee was already gone. Like he was one of the first ones out.
Roy E Lewis: He was already gone. He'd been gone.
Ed Ledoux: OK.
Roy E Lewis: He left….he, he left. You know what? That might have been lunch time. He might have left before everybody, but he was the first one we thought of…like, I thought of, like, *'where's Lee?'* you know. Lee and Charles Givens.
Ed Ledoux: Right. And people mentioned or did you mention this to Truly? Or was someone saying it like *'hey, where's Lee or where's Givens?'*
Roy E Lewis: Eh no, nobody mentioned.

[And shortly after…]

Roy E Lewis: Still, what puzzles me is when they came out, eh, the Secret Service to the place I lived. They couldn't find me and I lived right upstairs. The neighbours downstairs wouldn't tell them *'we don't know where he is, we don't know where he lives.'* Now, if you were police and were looking for me then you beat on every door, but they never come up and beat on my door. That's what sticks out in my mind when they did that. Even though when my neighbours downstairs said that they didn't know me. All they had to do is keep knocking on doors and find out where I was.
Ed Ledoux: Right exactly, that's very interesting.
Roy E Lewis: Very interesting, me too.

Ed Ledoux: Very interesting as you were the last one out that door.

Roy E Lewis: Right.

Ed Ledoux: And standing at the back. Where, you know, you can see everything.

Roy E Lewis: Right.

Ed Ledoux: And you knew who came in....so did anybody.... So, let me ask you this, did anyone run back in? While you were standing there outside?

Roy E Lewis: No.

Ed Ledoux: No one ran back up the steps and ran back inside?

Roy E Lewis: No.

Ed Ledoux: That's so....

Roy E Lewis: Not that I can remember.

Ed Ledoux: Right. Right. And you stayed there for a little bit and then you went down the street and then went back inside?

Roy E Lewis: Right.

Ed Ledoux: Yeah, and it seems like...yeah, they would want to talk with you.

Roy E Lewis: You would think I'd be the one that they would want to talk to.

Ed Ledoux: Exactly. And you would have a good memory (laughs).

Roy E Lewis: Agreed, well back then I'd have a good memory (chuckles).

Ed Ledoux: Perfect. You have been the perfect person to talk to. I am glad I have been able to talk to you and hear all your stories and all the information you got. Anything else you could think of that was weird? Anything odd?

Roy E Lewis: Eh.. Well, no, you know...

Ed Ledoux: How about afterwards, you know, were people trying to come and get into the Depository to come talk to you guys? Like reporters and stuff?

Roy E Lewis: Oh, no, no, no. The police would, not nobody in. No, no, no. Nobody could get in there. No, no.

Ed Ledoux: Right and then...

Roy E Lewis: Some might have no, no. Nobody could get in there.

Ed Ledoux: And they kept you guys away from everybody?

Roy E Lewis: Yes, kept us away from everybody. Then things settled down and everybody could go on.

Ed Ledoux: How did things work afterwards? Was it tough trying to work there? Did you feel weird working there after it happened?

Roy E Lewis: Yeah, it did. Weird and sad.

Billy Nolan Lovelady

Billy Nolan Lovelady (1183) is a pivotal person in this perplexity.

- At first, he is noticed in a clip by Robert Hughes (1184), on the TSBD steps in the far distance. The Presidential Limo is about to turn onto Elm. His distinctive patterned reddish shirt (1185) is open with his t-shirt underneath in view.
- Then he is captured in Altgens 6 (1186), the photograph that makes him famous. It has the FBI visiting him that very same evening with a table sized print of that photo and Lovelady picking himself out to great relief of the FBI agents. This is confirmed by Roy Truly (1187) and Bill Shelley (1188).
- Lovelady is seen stepping down the steps in the Wiegman film (1189) before the camera man gets out of the car and starts running and filming towards the knoll.
- He is also seen, together with Bill Shelley, ten seconds later making his way towards the railroad yard in the Malcolm Couch film (1190). Here is a close-up (1191).
- View a still shot (1192) from that footage. And a comparison shot (1193).
- His immediate departure is supported by his FBI statement of November 22nd (1194).
- He contradicts this during his WC testimony in March 1964 (1195).
- Lovelady also makes mention of a policeman, Joe Marshall Smith (1196), running towards the railroad yard in the Houston Post of November 23rd (1197).
- After Lee Oswald is arrested and brought to City Hall's third floor, he is seen being escorted and is passing Billy Lovelady in this video (1198).
- He is economical about some things such as about going back inside through the side entrance of the TSBD which is in his original statement and escorting some cops through the building. The Martin (1199) and Hughes (1200) films show him outside at least 20 minutes after the assassination. They are waiting on the TSBD steps, but two policemen prevent people from entering as the building was locked down at that time.
- Lovelady's name being absent in the typed version of the Revill list (1201). He managed to leave without leaving his name at the door.
- In a Secret Service report from December 8th 1963 (1202) Lovelady states that: he never got to know Oswald, and that he was unfriendly, a wise guy and a loner. Saw Oswald last at 10:00. Lovelady was part of the floor laying crew.

- Billy Lovelady had a weapons charge hanging over him (1203). In the Washington Post of September 28th 1960 it was reported that 8 airmen at Andrews Air Force base had been arrested by the FBI for theft of government property. Billy Lovelady is one of them who is charged with the possession and resale of several 38-caliber revolvers. He had to pay a $200.00 fine, besides being discharged. He only managed to pay off part of the sum, thereafter he was re-arrested (1204) and had Ochus V Campbell [the Vice-President of the TSBD] help him pay off the remainder since Billy had a wife and 4 kids to feed and could not afford paying the remainder of the outstanding fine.
- Lovelady said during his HSCA interview (1205), at 29:20, that it was 25 minutes before he got back in. Which of course coincides exactly with the Martin & Hughes movies. But it contradicts his statement that he went back in with Bill Shelley through the side entrance and stayed inside and helped the DPD. If he did, it was after he was let back in.

During Lovelady's WC testimony (1206) it is becoming crystal clear that he is very economical with the truth; meeting Gloria Calvery, the timing of when Shelley and he are leaving and going back into the building. He also mentions an alleged encounter with Victoria Adams and is also "misspeaking" about the occupants of the TSBD steps in his close vicinity and is subsequently being "saved" by Joseph Ball:

Mr. Ball - What did you do after you went down and washed up; what did you do?
Mr. Lovelady - Well, I went over and got my lunch and went upstairs and got a coke and come on back down.
Mr. Ball - Upstairs on what floor?
Mr. Lovelady - That's on the second floor; so, I started going to the domino room where I generally went in to set down and eat and nobody was there and I happened to look on the outside and Mr. Shelley was standing outside with Miss Sarah Stanton, I believe her name is, and I said, *"Well, I'll go out there and talk with them, sit down and eat my lunch out there, set on the steps,"* so I went out there.
Mr. Ball - You ate your lunch on the steps?
Mr. Lovelady - Yes, sir.
Mr. Ball - Who was with you?
Mr. Lovelady - Bill Shelley and Sarah Stanton, and right behind me.
Mr. Ball - What was that last name?
Mr. Lovelady - Stanton.
Mr. Ball - What is the first name?
Mr. Lovelady - Bill Shelley.
Mr. Ball - And Stanton's first name?

Mr. Lovelady - Miss Sarah Stanton.

Mr. Ball - Did you stay on the steps?

Mr. Lovelady - Yes.

Mr. Ball - Were you there when the President's motorcade went by?

Mr. Lovelady - Right.

Mr. Ball - Did you hear anything?

Mr. Lovelady - Yes, sir; sure did.

Mr. Ball - What did you hear?

Mr. Lovelady - I thought it was firecrackers or somebody celebrating the arrival of the President. It didn't occur to me at first what had happened until this Gloria came running up to us and told us the President had been shot.

Mr. Ball - Who was this girl?

Mr. Lovelady - Gloria Calvary.

Mr. Ball - Gloria Calvary?

Mr. Lovelady - Yes.

Mr. Ball - Where does she work?

Mr. Lovelady - Southwestern Publishing Co.

[And a little later...]

Mr. Ball - Now, when Gloria came up you were standing near Mr. Shelley?

Mr. Lovelady - Yeah.

Mr. Ball - When Gloria came up and said the President had been shot, Gloria Calvary, what did you do?

Mr. Lovelady - Well, I asked who told her. She said he had been shot so we asked her was she for certain or just had she seen the shot hit him or--she said yes, she had been right close to it to see and she had saw the blood and knew he had been hit but didn't know how serious it was and so the crowd had started towards the railroad tracks back, you know, behind our building there and we run towards that little, old island and kind of down there in that little street. We went as far as the first tracks and everybody was hollering and crying and policemen started running out that way and we said we better get back into the building, so we went back into the west entrance on the back dock had that low ramp and went into the back dock back inside the building.

Mr. Ball - First of all, let's get you to tell us whom you left the steps with.

Mr. Lovelady - Mr. Shelley.

Mr. Ball - Shelley and you went down how far?

Mr. Lovelady - Well, I would say a good 75, between 75 to 100 yards to the first tracks. See how those tracks goes---

Mr. Ball - You went down the dead end on Elm?

Mr. Lovelady - Yes.

Mr. Ball - And down to the first tracks?

Mr. Lovelady - Yes.

Mr. Ball - Did you see anything there?

Mr. Lovelady - No, sir; well, just people running.

Mr. Ball - That's all?

Mr. Lovelady - And hollering.

Mr. Ball - How did you happen to go down there?

Mr. Lovelady - I don't know, because everybody was running from that way and naturally, I guess---

Mr. Ball - They were running from that way or toward that way?

Mr. Lovelady - Toward that way; everybody thought it was coming from that direction.

Mr. Ball - By the time you left the steps had Mr. Truly entered the building?

Mr. Lovelady - As we left the steps, I would say we were at least 15, maybe 25, steps away from the building. I looked back and I saw him and the policeman running into the building.

Mr. Ball - How many steps?

Mr. Lovelady - Twenty, 25.

Mr. Ball - Steps away and you looked back and saw him enter the building?

Mr. Lovelady - Yes.

Mr. Ball - Then you came back. How long did you stay around the railroad tracks?

Mr. Lovelady - Oh, just a minute, maybe minute and a half.

Mr. Ball - Then what did you do?

Mr. Lovelady - Came back right through that part where Mr. Campbell, Mr. Truly and Mr. Shelley park their cars and I came back inside the building.

Mr. Ball - And enter from the rear?

Mr. Lovelady - Yes, sir; sure did.

Mr. Ball - You heard the shots. And how long after that was it before Gloria Calvary came up?

Mr. Lovelady - Oh, approximately 3 minutes, I would say.

Mr. Ball - Three minutes is a long time.

Mr. Lovelady - Yes, it's---I say approximately; I can't say because I don't have a watch; it could.

Mr. Ball - Had people started to run?

Mr. Lovelady - Well, I couldn't say because she came up to us and we was talking to her, wasn't looking that direction at that time, but when we came off the steps--see, that entrance, you have a blind side when you go down the steps.

Mr. Ball - Right after you talked to Gloria, did you leave the steps and go toward the tracks?

Mr. Lovelady - Yes.

Mr. Ball - Did you run or walk?

Mr. Lovelady - Medium trotting or fast walk.

Mr. Ball - A fast walk?

Mr. Lovelady - Yes.

Mr. Ball - How did you happen to turn around and see Truly and the policeman go into the building?

Mr. Lovelady - Somebody hollered and I looked.

Mr. Ball - You turned around and looked?

Mr. Lovelady - Yes.

Mr. Ball - After you ran to the railroad tracks you came back and went in the back door of the building?

Mr. Lovelady - Right.

Mr. Ball - Did you go in through the docks, the wide-open door or did you go in the ordinary small door?

Mr. Lovelady - You know where we park our trucks--that door; we have a little door.

Mr. Ball - That is where you went in, that little door?

Mr. Lovelady - That's right.

Mr. Ball - That would be the north end of the building?

Mr. Lovelady - That would be the west end, wouldn't it?

Mr. Ball - Is it the one right off Houston Street?

Mr. Lovelady - No; you are thinking about another dock.

Mr. Ball - I am?

Mr. Lovelady - Yes; we have two.

Mr. Ball - Do you have a dock on the west side and one on the north side of the building?

Mr. Lovelady - East, and well, it would be east and west but you enter it from the south side.

Mr. Ball - Now, the south side---

Mr. Lovelady - Elm Street is that little dead-end street.

Mr. Ball - That's south.

Mr. Lovelady - I drive my truck here (indicating) but we came in from this direction; that would have to be west.

Mr. Ball - You came into the building from the west side?

Mr. Lovelady - Right.

Mr. Ball - Where did you go into the building?

Mr. Lovelady - Through that, those raised-up doors.

Mr. Ball - Through the raised-up doors?

Mr. Lovelady - Through that double door that we in the morning when we get there we raised. There's a fire door and they have two wooden doors between it.

Mr. Ball - You came in through the first floor?

Mr. Lovelady - Right.

Mr. Ball - Who did you see in the first floor?

Mr. Lovelady - I saw a girl but I wouldn't swear to it it's Vickie.

Mr. Ball - Who is Vickie?

Mr. Lovelady - The girl that works for Scott, Foresman.

Mr. Ball - What is her full name?

Mr. Lovelady - I wouldn't know.

Mr. Ball - Vickie Adams?

Mr. Lovelady - I believe so.

Mr. Ball - Would you say it was Vickie you saw?

Mr. Lovelady - I couldn't swear.

Mr. Ball - Where was the girl?

Mr. Lovelady - I don't remember what place she was but I remember seeing a girl as she was talking to Bill or saw Bill or something, then I went over and asked one of the guys what time it was and to see if we should continue working or what.

Mr. Ball - Did you see any other people on the first floor?

Mr. Lovelady - Oh, yes; by that time there were more; a few of the guys had come in.

Mr. Ball - And you stayed on the first floor then?

Mr. Lovelady - I would say 30 minutes. And one of the policemen asked me would I take them up on the sixth floor.

Mr. Ball - Did you take them up there?

Mr. Lovelady - Yes, sir; I sure did.

Joe Rodriguez Molina

Joe Rodriquez Molina (1207) was employed at the Texas School Book Depository (1208) for sixteen years as its Credit Manager.

At the time of the assassination Molina stood on the landing on the eastern side, next to his right was Bill Shelley and just in front of him, one or two steps lower, is his colleague Otis Williams.

- As previously stated, Molina did not see Marrion Baker enter. He does see Roy Truly enter while still standing there, as per his statement to BL Senkel (1209).
- He does not see the running white helmeted policeman go in as said during his WC testimony (1210).
- This is reiterated by him in an article for George and Patricia Nash (1211) with the emphasis on Truly entering alone.
- After the shooting has finished, he briefly remains on the first-floor landing in front of the glass entrance and subsequently makes his way to the railroad yard only to see that the police are closing down the gate to the parking area west of the TSBD
- He then goes back inside the building on the west side and is noticed as standing on the first-floor where he has an interaction with Gloria Calvery (1212) in the vestibule and also talks with OV Campbell (1213).

- He also notices Forest Sorrels (1214) of the US Secret Service arriving from Parkland Hospital and demanding that the building be sealed.
- Returning to the second-floor offices about 25 minutes after the shooting, he is recognised by Geneva Hine (1215) as part of a group entering the offices.

The strange thing is that not one of his fellow co-workers mentions Molina as a person that they have seen standing on those TSBD front steps, not even his co-worker Otis Williams. This has most certainly to do with the fact that Molina became tainted as a subversive character on the next day by Jesse Curry while talking to the press (1216) in the corridor of the third floor in City Hall. The fact that he was Hispanic must have been another factor. Victoria Adams ran down the back stairs and had left the building through the back entrance. She was turned back by a police man and is noted as the only one that did speak with him briefly after she had made her way back towards the building.

Molina's house is tossed on the early morning of the 23rd by none other than a pack of Dallas' heavyweight law enforcement officers such as assistant DA Bill Alexander, Jack Revill and Pat Gannaway from the Criminal Intelligence Division of the Special Service Bureau. The next day he is ordered to report at the DPD at 10:00 and was held there for most of the day.

The Dallas police thought him to be a subversive because he held membership in the Dallas Chapter of the American GI Forum (1217). The GI Forum was an organisation for Hispanic veterans who fought in the Spanish Civil War, this organisation was infiltrated by Communist Party members, but Molina wanted nothing to do with them. He actually was not a member of the GI Forum at all any more at the time of the assassination. He had left more than a year prior. In the Dallas Morning News of November 20th 1988 (1218) Joe Molina is interviewed and this is where some of his rough treatment he endured the early morning of November 23rd 1963 comes to light.

In this statement by Bill Senkel for the DPD, Joe Molina relays what happened on November 23rd 1963 (1219). But this report is not typed up until February 18th 1964, at which point he states that he went to the embankment towards Commerce St and that Roy Truly went back into the building (no mention of Baker) and says he (Truly) stayed(!) on the first floor. Staying on the first floor is of course a deathblow to any second-floor altercation. Molina did not see Oswald. Was on the steps with Shelley, Stanton, Reed, Sanders and Eddie Piper. Piper said he was inside on the first floor. On page 2 (1220), Senkel's report makes mention

68

of the presence of James Hosty of the FBI and also states that this report was not typed up back in November 1963 as Molina would not sign it. This is highly questionable, because Molina's second DPD statement on the 23rd (1221) to William Biggio who only records GI Forum related matters *is* signed by Molina! The FBI also takes a statement of Molina on the 23rd (1222) in which he states that he has not seen Oswald all day and that he left the office at 12:15 to go downstairs and take a position on the landing of the front entrance steps. He states that he met with Eddie Piper in the lobby after the shooting and that Piper stated that all people had been accounted for except Lee.

Molina's WC testimony (1223) is relatively short:

Mr. Ball. Now, November 22, 1963, the place you worked was in the second floor of this School Book Depository Building.
Mr. MOLINA. Yes, sir.
Mr. Ball. Did you go out on the street to see the motorcade?
Mr. MOLINA. Yes. I was standing on the front steps.
Mr. Ball. With whom?
Mr. MOLINA. Right next left of me was Mr. Williams and close to there was Mrs. Sanders.
Mr. Ball. Pauline Sanders.
Mr. MOLINA. Yes.
Mr. Ball. Did you see Roy Truly?
Mr. MOLINA. Yes; he was standing with Mr. Campbell; they were going out to lunch.
Mr. Ball. They were in front of you, were they?
Mr. MOLINA. Yes.
Mr. Ball. You saw the President's car pass?
Mr. MOLINA. Yes.
Mr. Ball. Did you see anything after that?
Mr. MOLINA. Well, I heard the shots.
Mr. Ball. Where--what was the source of the sound?
Mr. MOLINA. Sort of like it reverberated, sort of kind of came from the west side; that was the first impression I got. Of course, the first shot was fired then there was an interval between the first and second longer than the second and third.
Mr. Ball. What did you do after that?
Mr. MOLINA. Well, I just stood there, everybody was running and I didn't know what to do actually, because what could I do? I was just shocked.
Mr. Ball. Did anybody say anything?
Mr. MOLINA. Yes, this fellow come to me---Mr. Williams said, somebody said, somebody was shooting at the President, somebody, I don't know who it was. There was some shooting, you know, and this fellow said *"What can anybody gain by that?"* He just shook his head and I just stood

69

there and shook my head. I didn't want to think what was happening, you know, but I wanted to find out so I went down to where the grassy slope is, you know, and I was trying to gather pieces of conversation of the people that had been close by there and somebody said *"Well, the President has been shot and I think they shot somebody else,"* something like that.

Mr. Ball. Did you see Mr. Truly go into the building?

Mr. MOLINA. Yes.

Mr. Ball. Where were you when you saw him go into the building?

Mr. MOLINA. I was right in the entrance.

Mr. Ball. Did you see a police officer with him?

Mr. MOLINA. I didn't see a police officer. I don't recall seeing a police officer but I did see him go inside.

Mr. Ball. Did you see a white-helmeted police officer any time there in the entrance?

Mr. MOLINA. Well, of course, there might have been one after they secured the building, you know.

Mr. Ball. No, I mean when Truly went in; did you see Truly actually go into the building?

Mr. MOLINA. I saw him go in.

Mr. Ball. Where were you standing?

Mr. MOLINA. Right at the front door; right at the front door.

Mr. Ball. Outside the front door?

Mr. MOLINA. Yes, outside the front door I was standing; the door was right behind me.

Mr. Ball. Were you standing on the steps?

Mr. MOLINA. Yes, on the uppermost step.

Mr. Ball. You actually saw Truly go

Mr. MOLINA. Yeah.

Mr. Ball. You were still standing there?

Mr. MOLINA. Yes.

Mr. Ball. How long was it after you heard the shots?

Mr. MOLINA. Oh, I would venture to say maybe 20 or 30 seconds afterwards.

Mr. Ball. Had somebody come up and said the President was shot before you saw Truly go in?

Mr. MOLINA. No.

Mr. Ball. Do you know a girl named Gloria Calvary?

Mr. MOLINA. Yes.

Mr. Ball. Did Gloria come up?

Mr. MOLINA. Yes, she came. I was in the lobby standing there and she came in with this other girl.

Mr. Ball. What did she say?

Mr. MOLINA. She said "Oh, my God, Joe, he's been shot." They were both horrified. I said *"Are you sure he was shot?"* She said *"Oh, Joe, I'm sure. I saw his hair fly up and I'm sure he was shot,"* something to that extent.

Mr. Ball. You left the building that day about what time and went home?

Mr. MOLINA. Oh, it must have been around, I would say, I would say it was about 2, maybe a little before that, I don't know.

Mr. Ball. Had you ever seen Lee Oswald?

Mr. MOLINA. I had seen him in the building, yes, sir.

Mr. Ball. Did you ever speak to him?

Mr. MOLINA. No; I never spoke to him.

Mr. Ball. Did you see him at all on November 22nd.

Mr. MOLINA. I never did see him.

Mr. Ball. Did you see any strangers in the building on that day November 22nd?

Mr. MOLINA. No; like I stated before, I came in at--to work at 7 in the morning because I had a key and I was on the second floor all the time, never did leave except maybe to go to the restroom, something like that. Then I ate my lunch, took my lunch and ate it and went downstairs about 12:15.

Molina's HSCA testimony (1224) goes into depth about the moments just before, during and just after the assassination.

- Molina states he stood on the top of the TSBD front steps. He does not recall seeing Lee Harvey Oswald that day (page 10).
- He stood there for a while after the shots had been fired. After which he left the steps to go to the grassy knoll area (page 11).
- He re-enters the building through some red gates on the side of the building. He remains on the work floor for a while and acknowledges that Ochus Campbell was present. He also sees Forrest Sorrels entering the building and demanding the building be sealed off (page 12).
- He does not see anyone come out of the building while standing on the top of the steps. He does recall seeing Roy Truly going in. He also recalls seeing Bill Shelley and Billy Lovelady being present while standing on the steps (page 13).
- On pages 14 & 15 Molina is asked whether he would have recalled if Lee Harvey Oswald had been standing there. Which he answered that he did not.
- Billy Lovelady's resemblance to Lee Harvey Oswald is discussed (pages 16 & 17).
- Molina thinks that Lovelady and Oswald bore no resemblance (page 18).

Madeleine Reese

Madeleine Reese (1225), employed by the MacMillan Company which was housed on the third floor of the TSBD is captured in Altgens 6 (1226) as the lady who just about sticks out above the roof of the Secret Service follow-up car. She looks like a nurse wearing a white cap. Yet this is, once again, a mistaken situation of a 3D setting being flattened in a 2D photograph. It is in fact Otis Williams' belly. Reese stood with Ruth Dean in the middle of the lower steps. While the shooting is going on she is also being captured in Wiegman (1227) and Darnell (1228). Like in the Altgens 6 photo she holds her hand up in the Wiegman film. In Darnell she has resumed a somewhat normal posture about 10-15 seconds after the shooting.

Reese, in her November 24th FBI statement (1229), states that she could not remember ever seeing Oswald inside room 302 of the TSBD. She also says that she stood on the second step of the TSBD entrance steps. And at first, she thought that the shots had come from the alcove near the benches and then saw people looking up and presumed then the shots had come from the building.

In a statement taken by the Criminal Intelligence Division on February 18th 1964 (1230) Reese again states that she did not know Oswald and she had never seen him.

In CE 1381 (1231) she confirms that Ruth Dean (1232) was standing next to her. After the shooting she stayed on the steps for about five minutes and then went to go to a bank to take care of some personal business. She then gets back into the TSBD and is escorted alongside others to the third floor after which they stay for a while and were later told to leave their details at the front door before exiting the building (1233).

Reese is identified by Linda Giovanna Zambanini (1234) due to the brooch she is seen wearing in a now defunct forum post of ROKC. Check it out, while Reese is just about to exit the front door in a William Allen photograph (1235), when she and three other ladies (Lucy Whittaker, Patricia Ann Donaldson and Sandra Sue Ellerson) who are in front of her, were making their way down the front steps after they have been given permission by the DPD to leave the building.

Shortly before that she is captured in a William Murray photograph where Reese and Dean are talking (1236) to fellow members of the public standing in front of the Dal-Tex building. The brooch is even clearer in that image.

Pauline Sanders

Pauline Sanders (1237) is hard to find in the Wiegman and Darnell films. But she can be seen in a brief moment in the Wiegman (1238) and the Darnell (1239) films. Some more stills showing that Sarah Stanton stood next to Pauline Sanders (1240) in the Wiegman film.

Pauline Sanders' November 24th typed up FBI statement (1241) contains some very interesting info. She is recorded as saying she left at 11:25 (more than an hour before the motorcade arrived, and is more than likely a typo and should be 12:25). She also claims standing in the last line of spectators nearest the door of the TSBD, but studying the Wiegman and Darnell films shows that she stood first on a lower step next to Sarah Stanton and then moved upwards on the landing after the shooting had just finished.

Pauline Sanders also describes in that same statement seeing Marrion Baker running into the building, followed by Ochus Campbell. She herself entered the building five minutes after and said she did not see Oswald in the lobby. Is it not odd that she did not see Oswald in the lobby? Why mention this? To me it is as significant as Sean Murphy's find of Roy Truly's November 22nd FBI statement (1242) *"They saw no one there"* after allegedly arriving with Baker in the front lobby, the vestibule of the building. At the same time we can see in Darnell several people going up those steps and Otis Williams has gone inside already. Roy Edward Lewis stood in the door opening and Eddie Piper was just inside the main hall.

Take Carolyn Arnold's first FBI statement (1243) into consideration: Standing in front of the TSBD on Elm St she thought she had caught a fleeting glimpse of Lee Harvey Oswald standing in the hallway in-between the front door and the double doors located on the first floor. She could not be sure that this was Oswald, and believed the time to be a few minutes before 12:15.

And then, let's not forget Ochus Campbell's remark from the NYHT on November 23rd (1244) *"We had been outside watching the parade. We saw him (Oswald) in a small storage room on the ground floor."*

Could it be possible that Truly's secretaries, Sanders and Reid, have the same conversation with the TSBD's Vice-President just after the shooting?
Pauline Sanders who stood on top of the steps of the Texas School Book Depository, and Mrs Robert Reid who stood with Truly and Campbell

near Elm St both discussed the trajectory of where the shots came from just after the shooting, but with a few neat little twists.

Reid makes mention of it in her handwritten statement of November 23rd 1963 (1245), but there is one important fact that seems to be overlooked by many.
In it she says *"I remarked to Mr. Campbell who was standing nearby that I thought that the shots had come from our building. But I heard someone else say no, I think it was further down the street."*

In Reid's FBI affidavit of November 26th 1963 (1246) there is no mention of this conversation at all. Nor is there any mention of this in the Secret Service Report of December 4th (1247). And when it was time for her testimony in front of the WC; that *'someone else'* who replied to her on November 22nd had become OV Campbell instead!

Pauline Sanders makes mention of the OV Campbell conversation on November 24th in her FBI statement (1248), and she does not repeat it anywhere else nor does she get called up to testify so that's that. In her CE 1381 (1249) statement she again states that she stood at the top of the steps and that she noticed Sarah Stanton stand beside her.

Bill Shelley

Bill Shelley (1250) is also an important person in this whole scenario. He was the foreman and Oswald's boss. Shelley answered to Roy Truly and he stood on the landing (1251) while the motorcade passed by. Like Lovelady, they left immediately after the final shot from the steps and made their way towards the railroad yard as that is where they believed the shots had come from. I go into great detail about Shelley's departure on my website (1252).

- Shelley is seen in Altgens 6 (1253) and in the Wiegman (1254) film. In a close-up (1255) it shows he has moved more to the middle and seems to be following Lovelady going down the steps.
- Seconds later he is witnessed in the Couch film making his way towards the grassy knoll walking alongside Lovelady.
- Bill Shelly produces two hand written affidavits on November 22nd. The first one (1256) makes no mention of Oswald at all, the second one (1257) mentions only him.
- He confirmed his position on the top of the front steps just outside the glass doors.
- In the first statement (1258) he writes: "I ran across the street to the corner of the park and ran into a girl crying and she said the

74

President had been shot. This girl's name is Gloria Calvery and is an employee of this same building."

- He more or less repeats this in his March 18th 1964 statement to the FBI (1259)
- He saw Oswald last around 11:45-11:50 on the first floor near the telephone.
- Shelley said he was sent outside in an attempt to locate Charles Givens (1260). At 13:46 there is an APB sent out for Givens when the DPD is about to enter the Texas Theatre. This APB is very detailed compared to the one sent out for Oswald.
- At about 13:30 he is seen escorting Danny Garcia and Bonnie Ray Williams to a police car that takes them to the DPD (1261).
- In CE 1381 (1262) he states that he and Billy Lovelady escorted police officers to the railroad yard. And returned back into the TSBD about ten minutes later.
- Shelley claims in his WC testimony that he saw Truly walking towards the front steps along with Marrion Baker after they had left the steps.
- George W Bailey, in 2009 (1263), questions how Oswald could have known that Shelly was on the steps of the TSBD (as per the Fritz interrogation notes) when Shelly clearly stated in his WC testimony that he had not seen Lee Harvey Oswald at the time.
- Bill Shelley is filmed inside the vestibule of the Texas School Book Depository (1264). The man next to him wearing the glasses is leaning on the banister of the front steps.

From Shelley's first WC testimony (1265):

Mr. Ball - What time did you go down and eat lunch?
Mr. Shelley - It was around 10 'til.
Mr. Ball - Did you eat your lunch?
Mr. Shelley - No, I started eating.
Mr. Ball - Where did you start eating it?
Mr. Shelley - In my office next to Mr. Truly's and 1 ate part of it which I do usually and finish up later on in the day but I went outside then to the front.
Mr. Ball - Why did you go to the front?
Mr. Shelley - Oh, several people were out there waiting to watch the motorcade and I went out to join them.
Mr. Ball - And who was out there?
Mr. Shelley - Well, there was Lloyd Viles of McGraw-Hill, Sarah Stanton, she's with Texas School Book, and Wesley Frazier and Billy Lovelady joined us shortly afterwards.
Mr. Ball - You were standing where?
Mr. Shelley - Just outside the glass doors there.

Mr. Ball - That would be on the top landing of the entrance?

Mr. Shelley - yes.

Mr. Ball - Did you see the motorcade pass?

Mr. Shelley - Yes.

Mr. Ball - What did you hear?

Mr. Shelley - Well, I heard something sounded like it was a firecracker and a slight pause and then two more a little bit closer together.

Mr. Ball - And then?

Mr. Shelley - I didn't think anything about it.

Mr. Ball - What did it sound like to you?

Mr. Shelley - Sounded like a miniature cannon or baby giant firecracker, wasn't real loud.

Mr. Ball - What happened; what did you do then?

Mr. Shelley - I didn't do anything for a minute.

Mr. Ball - What seemed to be the direction or source of the sound?

Mr. Shelley - Sounded like it came from the west.

Mr. Ball - It sounded like it came from the west?

Mr. Shelley - Yes.

Mr. Ball - Then what happened?

Mr. Shelley - Gloria Calvary from South-Western Publishing Co. ran back up there crying and said *"The President has been shot"* and Billy Lovelady and myself took off across the street to that little, old island and we stopped there for a minute.

Mr. Ball - Across the street, you mean directly south?

Mr. Shelley - Yes, slightly to the right, you know where the light is there?

Mr. Ball - Yes.

Mr. Shelley - That little, old side street runs in front of our building and Elm Street.

Mr. Ball - It dead ends?

Mr. Shelley - There's concrete between the two streets.

Mr. Ball - Elm Street dead ends there just beyond the building, doesn't it?

Mr. Shelley - Well, that's also Elm that goes under the triple underpass.

Mr. Ball - That is Elm that goes under the triple underpass?

Mr. Shelley - Yes.

Mr. Ball - You went to the concrete between the two Elm Streets?

Mr. Shelley - Yes, where they split.

Mr. Ball - You went out there and then what did you do?

Mr. Shelley - Well, officers started running down to the railroad yards and Billy and I walked down that way.

Mr. Ball - How did you get down that way; what course did you take?

Mr. Shelley - We walked down the middle of the little street.

Mr. Ball - The dead-end street?

Mr. Shelley - Yes.

Mr. Ball - Did you see Truly, Mr. Truly and an officer go into the building?

Mr. Shelley - Yeah, we saw them right at the front of the building while we were on the island.

Mr. Ball - While you were out there before you walked to the railroad yards?

Mr. Shelley - Yes.

Mr. Ball - Do you have any idea how long it was from the time you heard those three sounds or three noises until you saw Truly and Baker going into the building?

Mr. Shelley - It would have to be 3 or 4 minutes I would say because this girl that ran back up there was down near where the car was when the President was hit.

Mr. Ball - She ran back up to the door and you had still remained standing there?

Mr. Shelley - Yes.

Mr. Ball - Going to watch the rest of the parade, were you?

Mr. Shelley - Yes.

Mr. Ball - The Vice President hadn't gone by, had he, by your place?

Mr. Shelley - I don't know. I didn't recognize him. I did recognize Mr. Kennedy and his suntan I had been hearing about.

Mr. Ball - How did you happen to see Truly?

Mr. Shelley - We ran out on the island while some of the people that were out watching it from our building were walking back and we turned around and we saw an officer and Truly.

Mr. Ball - And Truly?

Mr. Shelley - Yes.

Mr. Ball - Did you see them go into the building?

Mr. Shelley - No; we didn't watch that long but they were at the first step like they were fixin' to go in.

Mr. Ball - Were they moving at the time, walking or running?

Mr. Shelley - Well, they were moving, yes.

Mr. Ball - Were they running?

Mr. Shelley - That, I couldn't swear to; there were so many people around.

Mr. Ball - What did you and Billy Lovelady do?

Mr. Shelley - We walked on down to the first railroad track there on the dead-end street and stood there and watched them searching cars down there in the parking lots for a little while and then we came in through our parking lot at the west end.

Mr. Ball - At the west end?

Mr. Shelley - Yes; and then in the side door into the shipping room.

Mr. Ball - When you came into the shipping room did you see anybody?

Mr. Shelley - I saw Eddie Piper.

Mr. Ball - What was he doing?

Mr. Shelley - He was coming back from where he was watching the motorcade in the southwest corner of the shipping room.

Mr. Ball - Of the first floor of the building?

Mr. Shelley - Yes.

Mr. Ball - Who else did you see?

Mr. Shelley - That's all we saw immediately.

Mr. Ball - Did you ever see Vickie Adams?

Mr. Shelley - I saw her that day but I don't remember where I saw her.

Mr. Ball - You don't remember whether you saw her when you came back?

Mr. Shelley - It was after we entered the building.

Mr. Ball - You think you did see her after you entered the building?

Mr. Shelley - Yes, sir; I thought it was on the fourth floor awhile after that.

Mr. Ball - Now, did the police come into the building?

Mr. Shelley - Yes, sir; they started coming in pretty fast.

Mr. Ball - Did you go with them any place?

Mr. Shelley - Yes; Mr. Truly left me guarding the elevator, not to let anybody up and down the elevator or stairway and some plainclothesmen came in; I don't know whether they were Secret Service or FBI or what but they wanted me to take them upstairs, so we went up and started searching the various floors.

[And a little later...]

Mr. Ball - After you heard these noises you said sounded like firecrackers this girl came up and said the President was shot?

Mr. Shelley - Yeah.

Mr. Ball - You were still standing there?

Mr. Shelley - Yes, sir.

Mr. Ball - There was still some time lapse from the time you heard the noise like a firecracker and she came up?

Mr. Shelley - Yes.

Mr. Ball - Then you went out across Elm?

Mr. Shelley - Yes, to the divider.

Mr. Ball - Between the two Elm Streets?

Mr. Shelley - Yes.

Mr. Ball - The one street dead ends and the other street that goes on down under the viaduct?

Mr. Shelley - Yes.

Mr. Ball - Did you run out to the point or walk out?

Mr. Shelley - I believe we trotted out there.

Mr. Ball - Did you stay very long?

Mr. Shelley - Oh, it wasn't very long.

Mr. Ball - How long?

Mr. Shelley - Maybe a minute or two.

Mr. Ball - And that's the place you saw Truly and Baker, you say, going into the building?

Mr. Shelley - Yes, uh-huh.

Mr. Ball - Then you went down the Elm Street that dead ends to the first railroad track?

Mr. Shelley - Yes.

Mr. Ball - That's about what distance?

Mr. Shelley - Approximately 100 yards.

Mr. Ball - Did you trot, run or walk?

Mr. Shelley - We were walking but it was a pretty fast walk.

Mr. Ball - Did you stay there any length of time?

Mr. Shelley - Not very long.

Mr. Ball - How long would you say?

Mr. Shelley - I wouldn't say over a minute or minute and a half.

Mr. Ball - Then you went back to the building?

Mr. Shelley - Yes.

Mr. Ball - Did you trot or run back to the building?

Mr. Shelley - We just walked back; took our good, old easy time more or less.

Mr. Ball - Then you went into the west end?

Mr. Shelley - Yes.

Mr. Ball - Did you see Vickie Adams after you came into the building and did you see her on the first floor?

Mr. Shelley - I sure don't remember.

Mr. Ball - You don't?

Mr. Shelley - No.

[In Shelley's second WC testimony (1266) he goes into more detail about the sighting of Oswald]

Mr. Ball. On November 22, 1963, the day the President was shot, when is the last time you saw Oswald?

Mr. Shelley. It was 10 or 15 minutes before 12.

Mr. Ball. Where?

Mr. Shelley. On the first floor over near the telephone.

Mr. Ball. Did you ever see him again?

Mr. Shelley. At the police station when they brought him in.

Mr. Ball. Did you see him in the building at any time after 12?

Mr. Shelley. No.

Mr. Ball. Did you at any time after the President was shot see Oswald in the building?

Mr. Shelley. No, sir.

Mr. Ball. Did you at any time after the President was shot tell Oswald to go home?

Mr. Shelley. No, sir.

79

Mr. Ball. Did you tell anybody to go home?
Mr. Shelley. No.
Mr. Ball. You didn't tell anybody to leave the building at all?
Mr. Shelley. No, sir.

Sarah Stanton

Sarah Stanton (1267) was described by Buell Wesley Frazier as short and heavy set. Others have said she was blond and weighing 300 lbs. In her November 23rd FBI statement, taken by Nat Pinkston (1268), she places herself on the steps of the TSBD. After the shots have been fired, she "immediately" goes into the building and takes the elevator in the lobby to go one floor up to the second-floor office. If she had done this then she would have encountered Oswald with Mrs Reid together. She is still visible in the Darnell film which is shortly after the shots were fired.

And she would have seen Geneva Hine upon entry in the office, but she makes no mention of her. On the other hand, Stanton is noticed coming in by Geneva Hine, who was by herself in the second floor TSBD office at 12:25–12:35. Stanton was entering the office as part of a large group which included Ochus Campbell, Martha Reid, Otis Williams, Mrs Robert Reid and Joe Molina. This was twenty-five minutes after the event.

Buell Wesley Frazier also confirms in some videos that Sarah Stanton was standing to his left, as per her own statement on the east side of the steps along with Pauline Sanders. At 18:25 in this video (1269), and at 53:14 in this video (1270), Gary Mack specifically asks him, to his right or left? He then points and says, left! At 06:02, in a Sixth Floor Museum interview (1271), Buell Frazier, who uses both his hands, indicates only with his left hand, outwards. Stanton and Frazier are standing close to each other on the TSBD steps, it is only Joe Molina who is in-between them.

Then there is of course Sarah Stanton's statement for CE 1381 (1272). She mentions the people that were standing close to her. Billy Lovelady who stood on the west side of the steps but moved more east towards the railing to gain a higher vantage point. She also mentions Bill Shelley and Otis Williams.

Sarah Stanton as seen in Dave Wiegman (1273) and James Darnell (1274) stills. With the find of a better copy of the Wiegman film, it becomes clear that Stanton and Sanders stood next to each other (1275) on the east side of the steps.

Otis Williams

Otis Williams (1276), like Joe Molina (1277), worked in the accounting department of the TSBD on the second-floor office. He is recognised as one of the men who keeps shielding his eyes from the incoming sun. This is seen in the Weaver Polaroid (1278), Altgens 6 (1279), and also in stills from the Wiegman film. He is seen standing in front of Bill Shelley and slightly above Ruth Dean. And, of course, close to his co-worker Joe Molina.

Williams is not seen in Darnell, which confirms his rapid entry back inside the building.

- In his November 24th 1963 FBI statement (1280), Williams says the shots came from the Courthouse. And that he went up to the second floor. And later on, led a detective around that very same floor.
- From his DPD statement taken by WE Pots on February 18th, 1964 (1281) he thought the shots came from the west side of the TSBD. He went up to the second floor and left for the fourth after hearing the President has been assassinated. He also states not seeing Oswald on the day of the shooting.
- And from CE 1381 (1282), he thought the shots came from the viaduct which crosses Elm St and states that Pauline Sanders was standing close to him. He also shows a DPD officer around the second floor.
- Williams makes no mention of his colleague Joe Molina in any of the statements

In the aftermath photos taken by William Allen he is seen on the top left of the steps looking down (1283). In another Allen photo taken after the police have cordoned off the entrance, he is seen in the background in the centre of the photograph (1284). In these two photos it becomes apparent that it was custom to take your jacket off and wear it once outside, Bill Shelley is captured like this as well. These days' people do not bother as much but back then certain etiquettes were kept.

In Larry Sneed's "*No More Silence*" (1285), Otis Williams stated: "*I remember the day he came in because I was talking with Roy Truly. Truly said: 'I believe I've got an extra good help. I've got a good one, I think'. That's the first thing he said. He seemed to know more than an ordinary person they sent up to him. That was the first thing I ever heard of Oswald....*" *I didn't see Oswald on the day of the assassination. He apparently walked back through the office, but I didn't see him.*

Mrs. Reid said she spoke to him and told him that the President had been shot, and he didn't respond. He just kept walking out. I'm told that Oswald was seen after Truly and the officer came in the lunchroom. He and the officer thought the shots had come from the roof, and as they were going up steps, the officer saw Oswald with a Coke and said, "Who's that?' Truly responded, "Oh, he works here," and they went on.

I didn't see smoke or smell gunpowder. Fact is, as soon as the third shot happened, and everybody commenced milling around, I thought it came from the underpass. I entered the building immediately, climbed up the stairs back where the warehouse elevator was which led to the sixth floor and went up to the fourth floor, which was the first one I could see from to see the underpass.

After I got up there and saw that nothing was going on the underpass, I turned around and came back down to the office and called my wife. Soon, while we were talking, people came in, officers rushed in, and I had to get off the phone. I could have gone down the steps while Oswald came down, but he came down on the elevator [there was no way of getting off on the second floor from either goods elevators-BK]. Anyway, I walked down the steps and didn't see him or anything. The first impression I had that it came from our building was that the policemen and reporters commenced rushing into our office and were getting the telephone and things like that.

After the shots, the women on the fourth floor gathered at the windows on the west side of the building, which gave them a perfect view of the railroad yard and the area behind the picket fence. The fact that Williams states that he went up to the fourth floor first, before going down to the second, disputes his FBI statement from the 24th.

Then, also consider Victoria Adams' (1286) and Sandra Styles' (1287) descent at about the same time from that fourth floor.

Lee Harvey Oswald is Prayer Man

Against:

- No one present on those TSBD steps, at the time the shots were fired, said they saw him standing there. Especially the people standing closest to *Prayer Man;* Billy Lovelady, Bill Shelley, Buell Frazier, Joe Molina and Roy Edward Lewis have all stated that they *did not* see Lee Oswald. Not one person can account, according to the WR, for a sighting of Oswald after 12 noon.
- From all the statements gathered, nobody on those steps knows or admits who that male Caucasian is. Based on the statements and interviews we can see who mentioned seeing whom (1288) on those steps. Oswald was not seen, but there were others who were also not seen.
  1. Roy Edward Lewis who stood in the door opening was not seen by anyone. He stood behind Buell Frazier.
  2. Buell Wesley Frazier was not mentioned by anyone either. He got the wrong end of the stick with the DPD and got treated quite harshly and some intimidation was involved. Frazier's confrontation with a pre-made confession presented by Will Fritz to him is a fine example.
  3. Carl Edward Jones did not get a mention by any other TSBD employee either, yet he stood on the bottom step on the lower left in front of all the others.
  4. Joe Molina, who stood on the landing next to Bill Shelley also was not noticed by anyone else, not even by Otis Williams, his co-worker. It was only Victoria Adams who had gone round the building and mentioned him being there. Molina was branded a 'subversive' that same weekend. And the TSBD let him go just one month afterwards.

For:

- *Prayer Man* in the Wiegman and Darnell films looks like Lee Oswald.
- *Prayer Man* also looks like a late arrival due to his position on the steps so some of the people standing in front of him could not have noticed him.
- *Prayer Man* is no stranger to the people on the steps. All of them wrote in their March 1964 statements in CE 1381 (1289) that they saw no strangers. The only person who did see a stranger was Danny Arce Garcia who pointed to an elderly man to the restroom inside the TSBD 45 minutes prior the motorcade came

past. This man subsequently left in his car accompanied by three elderly ladies and made its way under the triple underpass.

- Oswald's first interrogation inside DPD with Will Fritz, Elmer Boyd, and Richard Sims was from approximately 14:45 – 16:00, and from 15:15 with FBI agents James Hosty and James Bookhout present as well. Of these five people who are present only James Hosty took notes (1290) during the interrogation and straight after. The first set makes mention of *"1st floor entrance office"*, but its true context cannot be fully understood until the second handwritten report of the Oswald interrogation appears. This second set of notes (1291) contains more specifics as to Oswald's alibi and where he was when the President's motorcade went past the TSBD: *"O. stated he was present for work at the TSBD on the morning of the 22nd and at noon went to lunch. He went to 2nd floor to get a coca cola to eat with lunch and returned to 1st floor to eat lunch. Then he went outside to watch P. Parade."* These notes had been gifted to the ARRB in early 1997 by Hosty, which was only about 6-7 months before the Will Fritz interrogation notes (1292) were anonymously donated. Not many had bothered to plough through these Hosty notes and realise its importance and its connection. Comparing the first set of Hosty notes with the second set (1293), it is evident that Oswald told them that he was outside near the entrance of the TSBD.

- The Will Fritz notes (1294) were kept away from the public until late 1997 when they were gifted to the ARRB. Although not contemporary, they have value where Fritz had noted down *"Out with Bill Shelley, in front"*. How did Oswald know that Shelley was there? Shelley denied, during his WC testimony, seeing Oswald on those steps.

- Ochus Campbell, the Vice-President of the TSBD, stated in the NYHT on November 22nd (1295): *"Shortly after the shooting we raced back into the building. We had been outside watching the parade. We saw him (Oswald) in a small storage room on the ground floor. Then we noticed he was gone."* This is not repeated by Campbell at any later given time.

- The statements of Roy Truly (1296) and Pauline Sanders (1297) which specifically state that no one was in the lobby/vestibule are cause for concern in combination with Oswald sightings by Ochus Campbell in the NYHT and Carolyn Arnold in her FBI affidavit (1298).

- When Oswald is arrested and brought to City Hall on the third floor, he is paraded past a handful of TSBD employees whose statements are taken there and then. Oswald, thought of as someone who keeps to himself at his place of work and who had not really been making friends inside the TSBD, is accused and arrested for being a cop killer. Shortly after, he is branded a commie defector as well. That by itself would leave quite an impression on these TSBD employees. They would want to distance themselves and not associate themselves with the accused in any way.

- Ed Ledoux phoned Marina Oswald after Stan Dane had sent enlargements of *Prayer Man* and a copy of his book in 2018. She volunteered *"It's Lee" (1299) and she* was not prompted at all. "*In the end*, she said, *it was between Lee and the other guy*" (Billy Lovelady-BK).

There are some other elements that appear to scratch some sort of surface that could point to Oswald being outside on the steps.

- Eddie Piper during his WC testimony (1300) said that Oswald said to him he was going *"up or out"*, he couldn't remember. Piper said only *"up"* in two previous statements.
- Billy Lovelady during his WC testimony (1301) is saved by Joseph Ball when he asks for Stanton's name again even when Lovelady mentioned her name twice only seconds prior.

Mr. Lovelady - That's on the second floor; so, I started going to the domino room where I generally went in to set down and eat and nobody was there and I happened to look on the outside and Mr. Shelley was standing outside with Miss Sarah Stanton, I believe her name is, and I said, *"Well, I'll go out there and talk with them, sit down and eat my lunch out there, set on the steps,"* so I went out there.
Mr. Ball - You ate your lunch on the steps?
Mr. Lovelady - Yes, sir.
Mr. Ball - Who was with you?
Mr. Lovelady - Bill Shelley and Sarah Stanton, and right behind me
Mr. Ball - What was that last name?
Mr. Lovelady - Stanton.
Mr. Ball - What is the first name?
Mr. Lovelady - Bill Shelley.
Mr. Ball - And Stanton's first name?
Mr. Lovelady - Miss Sarah Stanton.
Mr. Ball - Did you stay on the steps
Mr. Lovelady - Yes.

- Lovelady admits during his HSCA interview (1302) at 25:25, that Oswald could have stood on the steps without him knowing it.
- The films. They could be the icing on the cake. Can a better image be obtained? Hard to say. For starters, a better digital copy of

both films, Darnell and Wiegman, must be obtained and only then with a best possible high-end resolution scan. The only suitable approach, at this time, is to use AI to try and sharpen the *Prayer Man* image(s) of both films. The blurring is the biggest hurdle. In the Wiegman film there may be one or two half decent images to investigate further with. The Darnell film has more images available to test. The answer lies with NBC to facilitate this test. Unfortunately, from the very beginning and all along the way, NBC have been uncooperative with any JFK assassination related research requests. We can consider ourselves a little lucky that some copies have surfaced, but the quality just isn't great.

- Kent Biffle, of the Dallas Morning News, in his Sixth Floor Museum Oral History interview (1303) at 17:00: *"I have wondered often if I ran past LHO, in fact, going in with the cops"* And at 23:28 one fellow journalist is heard mentioning *"Just a little point. You wouldn't have recognised Lee Oswald if you had seen him"*. To which Biffle replies *"No I wouldn't have. I had seen photographs of him, but I am sure that was 3-4 years before and I just blindsided him. So, I wouldn't have made him out. I have wondered about that since, whether he may have been out front at the time we went in, but I wouldn't have known it"*.

- This spreadsheet displays TSBD employees ranked by their gender and colour and their whereabouts (1304) when the assassination happened. Plus, did they see any strangers inside the building?
Look at the group of people who stood on the steps (1305), which narrows it down even more. And subsequently enables us to disregard those that are female and also all non-Caucasians.

- Prayer Man's clothing is not that of an office worker, more of a labourer. Management and office staff wore suits and shirts.
This allows us to narrow it down even more.

Male Caucasian labourers working inside the TSBD that day were:
1. Jack Dougherty (who was inside the building on the fifth floor).
2. Buell Wesley Frazier (who identified himself in the Darnel film).
3. Billy Nolan Lovelady (who identified himself in the Altgens 6 photograph and had left the steps in Couch & Darnell).
4. Lee Harvey Oswald......

Chapter II

Inside the Texas School Book Depository

The majority of TSBD employees stood outside alongside Elm St while the motorcade passed. Several saw the President get shot up close. Then there were some on the front steps and the landing of the building's entrance, on the corner of Elm and Houston and further down Elm. A few left their workplace to run errands during their lunch break.

Some of the TSBD workers have been positively identified as to where they stood when the shots rang out, but there are still quite a few that have not been recognised. I will write about the people that were inside the building while the shots were fired.

Are their statements holding up? Is there a bigger picture emerging of what went down inside the building?

First Floor

These first-floor drawings made by the FBI (2001) are an excellent source and much more detailed as compared to the WC versions (2002).

After going up the front steps one would be on the first floor already. The building itself, technically, did not have a ground floor. This first floor was used for offices of Bill Shelley and Roy Truly. The main space was used for packaging and shipping the books. In the rear was the lunchroom for the labourers called the Domino Room. There are lots of photographs taken by the FBI inside the building and then used as WC exhibits at The Portal to Texas History (2003).

Eddie Piper

Eddie Piper had a DUI from 1951. Whether that was used as leverage by the DPD is anybody's guess. But what is a fact beyond a reasonable doubt is that Piper messed his primary WC testimony up so badly that he had to be dragged back in for a second time, and it still did not look good for Roy Truly's assertions as to how fast he came in and with whom.

Piper stated that he looked out of the window on the first floor. This would be a window that was behind the graphic brick work on the front of the building and give him an extreme limited view of the parade.

The first person who mentions Eddie Piper is Jack Dougherty in his November 22nd DPD statement (2004). When Dougherty has taken the trip from the fifth floor down to the warehouse on the first, he strikes up a conversation with Piper about the shots.

Piper's first statement is to the Sheriff's Department on November 23rd (2005) and Oswald told him he was going up to eat at 12:00. He states that he went to the front and looked through a window. He times the shooting at 12:25 and thinks that the shots came from within the building.

On December 7th 1963, the Secret Service (2006) filed a short report on him where Piper states that he saw Oswald at around 12:00 and that he would "go up for lunch." Again, states that his clock said 12:25 when he heard the shots being fired.

On February 17th 1964 (2007), the DPD Special Service Bureau took an affidavit from Piper in which he claimed to have seen Oswald going about his usual way when he arrived at 10:00. At 12:00, he heard Oswald say he was going up to eat.

Piper had his photo taken inside the TSBD as per this FBI statement from March 23rd 1964 (2008). He also states that he was in the southwest corner trying to look through a window.

Piper was called in twice before the WC. In his first WC testimony (2009) he says:

Mr. Ball. What time was it that you spoke to Oswald and said you thought you would have your lunch?
Mr. PIPER. Just about 12 o'clock.
Mr. Ball. And do you remember exactly what he said?
Mr. PIPER. No, sir; I don't remember exactly. All I remember him was muttering out something-I didn't know whether he said he was going up or going out.
Mr. Ball. He said something like that?
Mr. PIPER. Yes-something like that.
Mr. Ball. Did you see what he did?
Mr. PIPER. No, sir; I didn't.
Mr. Ball. Did you see where he went?

Mr. PIPER. No, sir; I didn't.

Piper made no mention of Oswald saying he was going 'out' option during his written statements. Then he said Oswald was going 'up'. It could be seen as indirect circumstantial evidence that brings Oswald closer to being *Prayer Man*.

[And a little later, during the same testimony]

Mr. Ball. You mentioned you saw Truly?
Mr. PIPER. I don't know whether it was a policeman or FBI or who it was, but another fellow was with him.
[That by itself is another sure sign that Baker, a white helmeted police officer, was *not* with Truly when he arrived inside the building-BK]

Mr. Ball. And where were you?
Mr. PIPER. Standing right there where they make coffee.
Mr. Ball. What did they do?
Mr. PIPER. He ran in and yelled, *"Where is the elevator?"* And I said, *"I don't know, sir, Mr. Truly."* They taken off and went on up the stairway and that's all I know about that.

In Piper's second WC testimony (2010) one could construe this as Piper being dragged back in again just to clarify a few matters. One of which is that the police officer that was with Roy Truly did *not* wear a helmet. During this same testimony he is also 'used' to contradict the timing of Victoria Adams' descent from the first floor. Piper also indicates that Charles Douglas Givens was absent for the line-up as well:

Mr. Ball. You told us that after the shooting you came out onto the floor?
Mr. PIPER. That's right.
Mr. Ball. And the first people that you saw on the floor after the shooting was who?
Mr. PIPER. Mr. Truly and some fellow---I really don't know who it was; like I say, it was some fellow that was with Mr. Truly.
Mr. Ball. Some fellow; how was he dressed?
Mr. PIPER. Oh, I don't know.
Mr. Ball. Was he an officer?
Mr. PIPER. Yes; I believe he was an officer.
Mr. Ball. A police officer?
Mr. PIPER. Yes; a police officer.
Mr. Ball. Did he have a white helmet on?

89

Mr. PIPER. No; I don't think so. I didn't pay any attention to it. I was already excited over the shooting or something when he came running into the building.

Mr. Ball. And what did Truly and this--some fellow do?

Mr. PIPER. Well, Mr. Truly and this fellow run up the steps. He just hollered for the elevator and I said, "I don't know where it is at," and I'm still standing over there by that table and he ran up on up the steps with this police officer--him and another fellow and I was standing there and the people began swarming out and around--different ones coming in, but it was where nobody could come out.

Mr. Ball. They were the first ones to go up the steps?

Mr. PIPER. That's right.

Mr. Ball. Had anybody come down the steps before they went up the steps?

Mr. PIPER. No, sir.

Mr. Ball. They weren't the first ones to come down?

Mr. PIPER. Yes; and when the elevators come down---I really don't know who brought the elevators down, but I know nobody ever come down the steps.

Mr. Ball. Did you ever see Vicki Adams come down the steps?

Mr. PIPER. No, sir; I don't know about that, if she said she did, it was after I got over here and walked over to the back door.

Mr. Ball. Did Vicki Adams come down before Truly and the man went up the steps?

Mr. PIPER. No, sir, no, sir; she didn't do it.

Mr. Ball. Did you at any time after the shooting miss Lee Oswald---did you notice he wasn't around?

Mr. PIPER. No, sir; I didn't notice it until the line-up. You know, I just figured all the people was there.

Mr. Ball. You did notice it at the line-up, did you?

Mr. PIPER. Yes.

Mr. Ball. Tell us about that.

Mr. PIPER. I did notice it in the line-up.

Mr. Ball. What do you mean by the line-up?

Mr. PIPER. I mean, when they lined us all up and told us to give our name and address and just to go home.

Mr. Ball. You say "they"; who do you mean?

Mr. PIPER. The detective---whoever it was.

Mr. Ball. The police?

Mr. PIPER. Yes; they had the building all surrounded. They went to locking the doors back and front and told us to all come up and then go home, and I told him, I says, "I've got to go down in the basement and get my clothes," and he said, "You can go down and get your clothes and come on back up here, but give me your identification and your name and tell us where you are staying," and everybody heard me say that, I guess, and he let us out of the building, one by one, and I went on out the front door.

Mr. Ball. Did you say something to anybody about not seeing Oswald there?

Mr. PIPER. No, sir; I didn't say it, but I just saw he wasn't in the line-up-- I didn't tell anyone because I didn't see him.

Mr. Ball. Just tell us what did you notice?

Mr. PIPER. I noticed he was not in the line-up.

Mr. Ball. You noticed that he was not in the line-up?

Mr. PIPER. Yes.

Mr. Ball. But you didn't mention it to anybody?

Mr. PIPER. No, sir; I didn't mention it but I knows he wasn't in the line-up, and Charles---I don't know whether he was, but he went out for lunch.

Mr. Ball. Was Charles Givens there?

Mr. PIPER. I couldn't remember seeing him. He went out for lunch and I don't remember whether he come out from the building again or not because I was getting dressed to get out of there myself.

Troy Eugene West

Troy Eugene West (2011) was the mail wrapper on the first floor. He packaged the books ready for shipment. His station (2012) was on the first floor in the shipping area (2013).

West's statements state that he did not see Oswald that day at all, which is mind boggling to say the least. Especially when Eddie Piper acknowledged his presence on the first floor. West has his FBI statement taken on November 25th (2014) and does not divulge much at all, a pattern that seems to repeat itself in later statements. Here he states that he did not see Oswald at all whereas on previous days he has seen him at work. Oswald was a quiet person who keeps to himself and does not socialize. He is unresponsive to friendly approaches, which is quite a thing to say. West tried to distance himself from Oswald as far away as humanely possible. It gets better with his December 7th Secret Service report (2015) like all the other employees and claims that he spoke with Oswald every day, but did not know his name until after the assassination. He also does not recall even seeing him that day and that is hard to swallow. Piper sees him all the time and West, the wrapper, does not in a space roughly 30 feet long & wide.

On December 23rd in an FBI report Troy West (2016) is quizzed about whether Oswald was associated somehow with Jack Ruby.

In CE 1381 (2017) West states that he was alone at the time and did not hear the shots, how is that possible when Piper makes it abundantly clear that the three shots came from within the building? Nor did he see Oswald that day.

Troy West's WC testimony (2018) is a great exercise of someone who doesn't want to get involved about anything at all and rather pleads ignorance. He has trouble hearing the shots, even though he said he heard them in his Secret Service statement from December 7th 1963. He doesn't see anyone on the first floor which is hard to swallow when you have Eddie Piper there on that floor standing near the coffee making area which is right next to West's packing area. There is no talk of Victoria Adams and Sandra Styles coming down, or of Otis Williams coming in and taking the backstairs going up to the fourth floor. Nor any mention of Roy Truly. All these people were on the first floor up to a minute after the shooting. The first one he sees are the police, who arrived 7-10 minutes after the deed.

David Belin swallows all this and does not bother to question him any further:

Mr. Belin - Now going back to November 22, you said you quit for lunch around noon on that day on Friday, November 22?
Mr. WEST - Yes. About 12 o'clock we always quit for lunch.
Mr. Belin - Do you remember any of the men coming down the elevator that day? Bonnie Ray Williams or James Jarman Jr., or Danny Arce, or anyone else coming down that morning? Charlie Givens? Do you remember them coming down the elevator, or don't you remember.
Mr. WEST - I don't remember.
Mr. Belin - Now, after you quit for lunch, you made the coffee then?
Mr. WEST - Yes, sir.
Mr. Belin - Where did you make the coffee?
Mr. WEST - I made the coffee right there close to the wrapping mail table where I wrap mail.
Mr. Belin - Then what did you do?
Mr. WEST - Well, I sit down to eat my lunch.
Mr. Belin - Then what did you do?
Mr. WEST - Well, I had just, after I made coffee, I just had started to eat my lunch because I was a little hungry - I didn't anything that morning before I went to work - and I had started to eat my lunch. But before I got through, well, all of this was, I mean, the police and things was coming in, and I was just spellbound. I just didn't know what was the matter. So, I didn't get through eating. I had to eat about half my lunch, and that is all.
Mr. Belin - Did you hear any shots fired?

Mr. WEST - I didn't hear a one. Didn't hear a one.

Mr. Belin - Did you see anyone else on the first floor while you were eating your lunch? Anyone else at all did you see on the first floor?

Mr. WEST - It wasn't anybody. I didn't see anybody around at that time.

Mr. Belin - At any time while you were making coffee or eating your lunch, did you see anyone else on the first floor?

Mr. WEST - No, sir; I didn't see.

Mr. Belin - Who was the first person you saw on the first floor after you - while you were eating your lunch? Someone came in the building?

Mr. WEST - Yes; before I got through. The officers and things were coming in the front door.

Mr. Belin - Who was the first person or persons that you saw coming through there while you were eating your lunch?

Mr. WEST - Well, that was the police.

Mr. Belin - A police officer?

Mr. WEST - Yes, sir.

Mr. Belin - Anyone else?

Mr. WEST - I guess it was a bunch of them, I guess, FBI men, and just a crowd of them coming in there.

Mr. Belin - Did you see Roy Truly coming in at all that time? Do you know Mr. Truly?

Mr. WEST - Yes, sir; that is the boss, the superintendent.

Mr. Belin - Did you see him, do you remember, while you were eating your lunch, come in the building?

Mr. WEST - Yes, sir; I think he came in with the police.

Mr. Belin - Was he one of the first people in, or did other people come in ahead of him, if you remember?

Mr. WEST - Really, I just don't know.

Mr. Belin - That is okay if you don't remember. That is all I want you to say if you don't remember. Did you hear anyone yelling to let the elevator loose or anything like that?

Mr. WEST - I can't remember.

Mr. Belin - Were you working when you were eating your lunch? Were you facing the elevator or not when you were eating your lunch? Were you facing any on the elevators back there?

Mr. WEST - No, sir; I was always - I mean I would always be with my back kind of, you know, towards the elevators and facing the front side over on the side.

Mr. Belin - The Elm Street side?

Mr. WEST - Toward Elm Street side.

Mr. Belin - So you don't know whether anyone was using the elevators?

Mr. WEST - No, sir; I don't.

Mr. Belin - Do you know whether anyone was going up and down the stairs?

Mr. WEST - No, sir; I don't.

93

Mr. Belin - Do you know anything else about what happened on November 22, that might be helpful or relevant here?

Mr. WEST - No, sir; I don't really.

Mr. Belin - Were you ever on the second floor on November 22?

Mr. WEST - No, sir; I never did hardly ever leave the first floor. That is, I just stayed there where all my work was, and I just stayed there.

Mr. Belin - On November 22, did you ever leave the first floor?

Mr. WEST - No, sir; I never did leave the first floor.

Mr. Belin - Anything else that you can think of, whether I asked it or not?

Mr. WEST - Well, I don't know anything else. I know of nothing else.

Mr. Belin - We want to thank you very much for coming down here, Mr. West. If you want, you can come back down again and read your deposition and sign it, or else you can just waive coming down here. You don't have to come down. You can tell the court reporter to send it directly to us, if you want to.

Mr. WEST - You mean when I get ready to sign it.

Mr. Belin - Now you do not have to sign it if you don't want to. You can just tell the court reporter to type it up and send it directly to us, or you can tell the court reporter you would like to read it and sign it before she sends it to us in Washington. You don't have to sign it. Or if you want to sign it, you can come back and sign it whichever you want to do.

Mr. WEST - Well I think - I don't know.

Mr. Belin - Do you want to come down here again and read it and sign it, or do you want to waive? You can waive and tell the court reporter that she can just sent it after she types it up, directly to us in Washington without your reading it and signing it.

Mr. WEST - Well, I think that is what I will do, just have it waived and send it on.

Mr. Belin - All right, that is fine. Thank you very much, sir.

The Stairs & the Elevators

There are three elevators in the building: in the front of the building inside the vestibule there are stairs and one elevator, which would only go up to the fourth floor. And there are two freight elevators (East and West) in the back and stairs in the North-West corner of the TSBD.

Roy Truly's statement to the FBI on November 22nd (2019) makes no mention of any elevators at all. His DPD statement on November 23rd (2020) doesn't mention a lot about this either. Besides: *"The officer and I went through the shipping department to the freight elevator. We then started up the stairway."* No mention of any lifts being stuck on the fifth floor at all.

His statement to the FBI on November 23rd 1963 (2021): *"They stopped at the freight elevators and, observing that these elevators were not on the first floor they ran up the stairway after he showed the officer where the stairway was."*

His Secret Service statement from December 4th 1964 (2022) *"We paused momentarily by the freight elevator but since neither were on this floor we ran up the back stairway up to the second floor."*

Roy Truly's WC testimony (2023):

Mr. Belin. Now, you got to the elevator, and what did you do then?
Mr. Truly. I looked up. This is two elevators in the same well. This elevator over here.
Mr. Belin. You are pointing to the west one?
Mr. Truly. I am pointing to the west one. This elevator was on the fifth floor. Also, the east elevator, as far as I can tell, both of them were on the fifth floor at that time. This elevator will come down if the gates are down, and you push a button.
Representative Ford. Which elevator is that?
Mr. Truly. The west one. But the east one will not come down unless you get on it and bring it down. You cannot call it if the gates are down.
Representative Ford. That is the east elevator?
Mr. Truly. The east elevator? There is a button and a little bell here. I pressed.
Mr. Belin. You might put a "B" on Exhibit 362 by the elevator for "button."
Mr. Truly. That is right on this surface. There is a little button. I pressed the button and the elevator didn't move. I called upstairs, "Turn loose the elevator."
Mr. Belin. When you say call up, in what kind of a voice did you call?
Mr. Truly. Real loud. I suppose in an excited voice. But loud enough that anyone could have heard me if they had not been over stacking or making a little noise. But I rang the bell and pushed this button.
Mr. Belin. What did you call?
Mr. Truly. I said, *"Turn loose the elevator."* Those boys understand that language.
Mr. Belin. What does that mean?
Mr. Truly. That means if they have the gates up, they go pull the gates down, and when you press the button, you can pull it down.
Mr. Belin. And how many times did you yell that?
Mr. Truly. Two times.
Mr. Belin. After you had first pushed the button?
Mr. Truly. That is right. I had pressed the button twice I believe, and called up for the elevator twice.

Mr. Belin. Then what did you do? First of all, did the elevator come down?
Mr. Truly. It did not.
Mr. Belin. All right. Then what did you do?
Mr. Truly. I went up on a run up the stairway.

In his FBI statement from September 23rd 1964 CE 3035 (2024) it becomes mega generic; one wonders whether Truly is showing fatigue rehashing the same old story over and over again as he states the following: *"The officer and I proceeded to the stairway located in the northwest corner of the Texas School Book Depository building in order to proceed to the upper part of the building to see if we could see who had fired the shots."* This is without a doubt the shortest description of this event. The steps, vestibule and the elevator elements are absent.

Leo Sauvage interviewed Truly (2025): *"I told them, as I just told you, that it was a very short time."*

In the Dallas Morning News of November 27th, 1978 (2026) Roy Truly is quoted by Earl Golz: *"Truly now contends that no one couldn't have ridden down from the sixth floor after the assassination in one of two freight elevators because "they were both up on the fifth floor with the gates up when we (Truly and Baker) passed them up there."* This contradicts Truly's own testimony but also Jack Dougherty's movements after the shooting. Dougherty was described by Truly as retarded. Just like Piper.

Marrion Baker's DPD statement from November 22nd 1963 (2027): *"I followed the man to the rear of the building and he said let's take the elevator. The elevator was hung several floors up so we used the stairs instead."*
Marrion Baker's WC testimony (2028):

Mr. Baker. I would say, the southeast corner of the building there where we entered it, and we went across it to the northwest corner which is in the rear, back there.
Mr. Belin. All right.
Mr. Baker. And he was trying to get that service elevator down there.
Mr. Belin. All right. What did you see Mr. Truly do?
Mr. Baker. He ran over there and pushed the button to get it down.
Mr. Belin. Did the elevator come down after he pushed the button?
Mr. Baker. No, sir; it didn't.
Mr. Belin. Then what did he do?
Mr. Baker. He hollered for it, said, "Bring that elevator down here."

Mr. Belin. How many times did he holler, to the best of your recollection?
Mr. Baker. It seemed like he did it twice.
Mr. Belin. All right. Then what did he do?
Mr. Baker. I said let's take the stairs...

[Discussion off the record.]

This obviously contradicts his November 22nd affidavit where he stated that Truly said that.

Mr. Belin. On the record. Officer Baker, when you related your story earlier you said that as you ran back on the first floor you first ran to the elevator shaft, is that correct?
Mr. Baker. That is right, sir.
Mr. Belin. And you stopped at the east or the west elevator door?
Mr. Baker. That would be the west.
Mr. Belin. All right. This was on the first floor, and did you look up the elevator shaft at that time?
Mr. Baker. Yes, sir; at that time, I did.
Mr. Belin. This was while Mr. Truly was calling for the elevator?
Mr. Baker. Yes, sir.
Mr. Belin. Was there any kind of a gate between you and the elevator shaft?
Mr. Baker. Yes, sir; there was.
Mr. Belin. Wood or metal, do you remember?
Mr. Baker. It is wood.
Mr. Belin. What did you see when you looked up the elevator shaft?
Mr. Baker. At that time, I thought there was just one elevator there, you know, one big freight elevator, and to me they looked like they were up there, I didn't know how many floors in that building but you could see them up there, it looked like just at that time, I thought it was just one, when I looked up there, and it looked to me anywhere from three to four floors up.
Mr. Belin. Was either elevator moving at the time or–pardon me, was there any elevator moving at the time you saw and looked up the shaft?
Mr. Baker No, sir.
Mr. Belin. Did you hear any elevator moving?
Mr. Baker. No, sir.
Mr. Belin. Mr. Truly pushed the button, I believe you said.
Mr. Baker. That is right, sir.
Mr. Belin. When he pushed the button did any elevator start moving?
Mr. Baker No, sir.

Mr. Belin. When you looked up the elevator shaft did it appear as if there was one elevator covering the complete shaft or did it appear there was one elevator that you saw covering half of the shaft?

Mr. Baker. Like I say, I thought it was one elevator there and it was covering the whole deal up there so to me it appeared to be one.

Mr. Belin. It didn't appear to be two elevators on different floors?

Mr. Baker. No, sir.

Mr. Belin. All right. Now, you got up to floor number two at the time and you did that with the stairs.

Mr. Baker. Yes, sir.

Mr. Belin. At the time you got up there was there any elevator on floor number two that you can remember, if you can remember? Maybe you cannot remember, I don't know.

Mr. Baker. Evidently now, I didn't look, evidently it wasn't because it seemed to me like the next floor up Mr. Truly said let's take the elevator.

Mr. Belin. At some higher floor after that?

Mr. Baker. Yes, sir.

Here Baker goes in the wrong, as Truly stated they got the elevator on the fifth floor. Baker states they get the lift the next floor up. If that is the fifth floor, then Baker's recollection, as per his original statement on the 22nd of his encounter on the third or fourth floor is bolstered with this admission.

In Larry Sneed's *No More Silence (2029)*, on page 124) Baker states: *"So he led us into the back, and we tried to get the elevators, the freight elevators. For some reason he couldn't get them down so he said, 'Come on, we'll take the stairway.' So, we started up the stairwell at the back."* In his WC testimony Baker stated *he* had said, *"Let's take the stairs."*

In the direct aftermath, the stairs and the elevators are being used by a few TSBD employees. If Truly and Baker went up as fast as they claimed they did, then they should have encountered other employees while going up. Or someone should have heard someone on those creaky and noisy stairs.

Jack Edwin Dougherty (2030), hears a loud bang while being on the fifth-floor and takes the West elevator down to the first floor. He then sees Eddie Piper, and asks him what has happened. His description of this 'event' during his WC testimony (2031) goes as follows:

Mr. Ball. Tell me this – when you heard that explosion of whatever it was that loud noise, where were you on the fifth floor-tell me exactly where you were?

Mr. DOUGHERTY. Well, I was about 10 feet from the west elevator-the west side of the elevator.

Mr. Ball. That's the elevator that uses the push button; is that right?

Mr. DOUGHERTY. Yes.

Mr. Ball. And what were you doing?

Mr. DOUGHERTY. I was getting some stock.

Mr. Ball. And what did you do then?

Mr. DOUGHERTY. Well, I came on back downstairs.

Mr. Ball. How did you come downstairs?

Mr. DOUGHERTY. I used that push button elevator on the west side.

Mr. Ball. Did you hear Mr. Truly yell anything up the elevator shaft?

Mr. DOUGHERTY. I didn't hear anybody yell.

It has to be said that Dougherty appeared to be very confused during his testimony and that he was wrong a few times when it came to his timings. Whether this was deliberate remains to be seen, and he was described as someone who wasn't very bright, yet had the responsibility to appear early in the morning to look after various equipment before all the other office workers started their work.

Troy West, who could have been an excellent witness, again did not divulge anything of value in his WC testimony (2032):

Mr. Belin – That is okay if you don't remember. That is all I want you to say if you don't remember. Did you hear anyone yelling to let the elevator loose or anything like that?

Mr. WEST – I can't remember.

Mr. Belin – Were you working when you were eating your lunch? Were you facing the elevator or not when you were eating your lunch? Were you facing any on the elevators back there?

Mr. WEST – No, sir; I was always – I mean I would always be with my back kind of, you know, towards the elevators and facing the front side over on the side.

Mr. Belin – The Elm Street side?

Mr. WEST – Toward Elm Street side.

Mr. Belin – So you don't know whether anyone was using the elevators?

Mr. WEST – No, sir; I don't.

Marvin Johnson's (2033) statement of Marrion Baker made no mention of elevators.

Otis Williams (2034) made his way back into the building almost immediately after the shots had been fired. He is seen in Altgens 6 and in the Wiegman film, but in the Darnell film he is absent from being on the steps. As per his statements, he used the back stairs to make his way up to the fourth floor to get a better view from which he then descended to the second floor and was noticed by Geneva Hine entering the office on the second floor as part of a group of people. He must have ascended the stairs after Adams and Styles came down and left the building via the back, and he saw no sign of Baker and Truly either!

Dorothy Ann Garner (2035): not until 1999 did she come into 'play' with the Martha J Stroud document (2036), which was found by Barry Ernest at NARA. It states: *Miss Garner, Miss Adams' supervisor, stated this morning, that after Miss Adams went downstairs, she (Miss Garner) saw Truly and the policeman come up.* Dorothy Garner's interview is nowhere to be found, there simply is no record of it.

It is overall shocking that Sandra Styles, Elsie Dorman and Dorothy Garner were not called up to testify and corroborate Victoria Adams' story. But that would make Oswald's descent from the sixth-floor a near impossibility in relation to their statements.

The whole elevator quagmire is also discussed internally by the WC in this March 25th 1964 memo from Norman Redlich (2037), after Roy Truly has given his testimony. It is overall interesting that the Commissioners are not 100% satisfied with the testimonies and explanations being given, and are even considering a second person being part of a plot to assassinate the President.

Here is a good document that shows a schematic of statements that are related to the elevators (2038).

Second Floor

The second floor consisted of offices. The landing near the backstairs (2039) was used for some boxes of stationary. The FBI has made some detailed drawings of the offices on this floor (2040).

Occupants of the offices:

- The TSBD office staff and management resided in room 200. Vice-President Ochus Campbell and the owner Jack Cason had their offices in the far corner. There was also a conference room (2041). No one could access the goods elevators on this floor.
- Lyons & Carnahan resided in room 201.
- The room designated for 202 is marked as "private."
- South-Western publishing was in room 203.

There are also photographs of the lunchroom and its nearby landing and corridor in an FBI booklet titled the "Texas School Book Depository" (2042). These photographs show the second-floor landing and the lunchroom. The reader should be aware that these photographs were taken with a wide-angle lens and distances appear to be larger and the setting appears to be more spacious than they actually are in reality.

Recently, the Sixth Floor Museum managed to acquire some photographs from Spaulden Jones (2043), who was a regional manager of Macmillan and Company. He took these shortly after the assassination. I share two which show the conference room and the front office entrance (very similar angle as the WR version) in colour.

It was on this floor that an alleged encounter took place shortly after JFK's assassination between patrolman Marrion Baker and Lee Harvey Oswald near the entrance to the lunchroom. Roy Truly supposedly witnessed this after arriving a moment later.

The door entry to the lunchroom (2044) is at roughly a 45-degree angle and is fitted with a closing mechanism. This angle prevents anyone from looking inside the lunchroom unless they move further away from the spot where one would arrive, just on top of the stairs and on the landing. They would need to go to where the boxes with stationary are located, to obtain a view inside the lunchroom. The only possible movement through that window would be to spot someone going from right to left, meaning he would have come from the corridor that would lead to the front stairs and elevator. The door was closed when Baker caught the glimpse, and was also closed when Roy Truly arrived, after he "realised" Baker was not following him.

Baker's testimony has only the briefest mention of this part in his WC testimony: "Mr. Truly had come up to my side here," while he confronted Oswald. Other than that, there is nothing about this in any of his statements.

Roy Truly on the other hand has plenty to tell, but not at first: In his first handwritten statement (2045) there is no mention of him being ahead at all. Nor is there anything in his typed-up version from November 23rd (2046). Neither is there anything about this in his FBI statement from November 22nd 1963 (2047). His FBI statement from November 23rd 1963 (2048) does not make any mention of this either!

In his Secret Service statement of December 4th 1963 (2049) he states: "*I had started to go up the stairway to the third floor when I noticed that the officer was not following, and I heard him say something. I then went back and found that he was standing near the entrance of the lunchroom."* This claim was made sixteen days after the assassination! He was standing near the entrance of the lunchroom! This report is the first mention that Truly was making his way up to the third floor already. The Secret Service agents (Arthur Blake, William Carter and Elmer Moore) interviewed various TSBD employees and this is where various statements were falsified with insertions of scenarios that contradicted initial statements.

In Roy Truly's WC testimony (2050), it becomes rather colourful:

Mr. Belin. All right. Then what did you do?
Mr. Truly. I went up on a run up the stairway.
Mr. Belin. Okay. And where was this officer at that time?
Mr. Truly. This officer was right behind me and coming up the stairway. By the time I reached the second floor, the officer was a little further behind me than he was on the first floor, I assume–I know.
Mr. Belin. Was he a few feet behind you then?
Mr. Truly. He was a few feet. It is hard for me to tell. I ran right on around to my left, started to continue on up the stairway to the third floor, and on up.
Mr. Belin. All right. Number 23, the arrow points to the door that has the glass in it. Now, as you raced around, how far did you start up the stairs towards the third floor there?
Mr. Truly. I suppose I was up two or three steps before I realized the officer wasn't following me.
Mr. Belin. Then what did you do?
Mr. Truly. I came back to the second-floor landing.

Defying common sense, with Truly going ahead of the armed Baker facing a possible assassin on his way, Truly makes an interesting admission during the same WC testimony:

Mr. Belin. Did you have any conversation with the officer that you can remember? About where you thought the shots came from?
Mr. Truly. Yes. When sometime in the course, I believe, after we reached the roof, the officer looked down over the boxcars and the railroad tracks and the crowd below. Then he looked around the edge of the roof for any evidence of anybody being there. And then looked up at the runways and the big sign on the-roof. He saw nothing. He came over. And some time about then I said, *"Officer, I think..."* let's back up. I believe the officer told me as we walked down into the seventh floor, *"Be careful, this man will blow your head off."*

102

In his interview with Truly, Barry Ernest states in *The Girl on the Stairs* (2051): *Truly told me he was ahead of the policeman by "several feet" when on his way up to the third floor, he noticed Baker was no longer behind him. Returning to the second-floor landing, Truly found Baker in the lunchroom (page 67).*

However, Roy Truly cannot keep up with this version of events. He participated in some interviews after the assassination, even one during the very same week when his Secret Service statement was taken. In the December 7th 1963 issue of the Detroit Free Press (2052) Truly is quoted by Gene Roberts as saying: *"The policeman ran up the stairs ahead of me and when I arrived on the second floor, he had his pistol out and was confronting Lee Oswald in the doorway of a little lunchroom."* This quote is a few days after his Secret Service report which has *him* walking ahead of Baker.

This from an interview with Leo Sauvage, a NY correspondent for French newspaper Le Figaro who wrote *The Oswald Affair (2053)*:

"We ran to the freight elevators in the back of the building because the front elevators do not go beyond the fourth floor, but the two freight cars had both been left somewhere up in the top floors and we took the stairs, the officer ahead of me. When I reached the second-floor landing, the officer was already at the open door of the lunchroom, some twenty or twenty-five feet away."

This quote was later re-published in the National Guardian of March 24th 1964 (2054). And Joachim Joesten uses this very same paragraph in his book *"Oswald Assassin or Fall Guy?"* (2055) in 1967, on page 35.

In the New York Journal American of May 24th, 1964 (2056), Truly is quoted:

"The policeman was a few steps ahead of me and when I got inside the lunchroom the officer was covering Oswald with a gun."

Three newspaper stories, interviews and quotes from early December 1963 until May 1964 which begs the question, if Baker went ahead of Truly why change the story around?

Marrion Baker and Roy Truly wanted to get to the roof as fast as possible and would not have strayed far from the stairwells. They would have turned left almost immediately when they arrived on the landing of each floor, something Truly allegedly did, and continued to do so (2057).

There are a few issues with the records that have been created that day and shortly after. In Baker's first affidavit on November 22nd (2058), he mentions an encounter on the 'third or fourth floor'. He makes no mention of a lunchroom, instead describing the encounter in an open area. He states 'a man walking away from the stairway.' It is hard to believe Baker lost his sense of direction and mixed up the third or fourth floor with the second floor lunchroom area.

Baker's statement is typed up (2059) and is a copy of the handwritten report and signed by him. He had plenty of time to think it over when signing the typed statement and thereby confirming his first handwritten report.

Baker's WC testimony (2060):

Mr. Belin – When you started up the stairs what was your intention at that?
Mr. Baker – My intention was to go all the way to the top where I thought the shots had come from, to see if I could find something there, you know, to indicate that.
Mr. Belin – And did you go all the way up to the top of the stairs right away?
Mr. Baker – No, sir; we didn't.
Mr. Baker – What happened?
Mr. Baker – As I came out to the second floor there, Mr. Truly was ahead of me, and as I come out, I was kind of scanning, you know, the rooms, and I caught a glimpse of this man walking away from this–I happened to see him through this window in this door. I don't know how come I saw him, but I had a glimpse of him coming down there.
Mr. Dulles – Where was he coming from, do you know?
Mr. Baker – No, sir. All I seen of him was a glimpse of him go away from me.
Mr. Belin – What did you do then?
Mr. Baker – I ran on over there
Representative BOGGS -You mean where he was?
Mr. Baker – Yes, sir. There is a door there with a glass, it seemed to me like about a 2 by 2, something like that, and then there is another door which is 6 foot on over there, and there is a hallway over there and a hallway entering into a lunchroom, and when I got to where I could see him, he was walking away from me about 20 feet away from me in the lunchroom.
Mr. Belin – What did you do?
Mr. Baker – I hollered at him at that time and said, "Come here." He turned and walked right straight back to me.

Representative BOGGS. And he came up to you, did he say anything to you?

Mr. Baker. Let me start over. I assumed that I was suspicious of everybody because I had my pistol out.

Representative BOGGS. Right.

Mr. Baker. And as soon as I saw him, I caught a glimpse of him and I ran over there and opened that door and hollered at him.

Representative BOGGS. Right.

Mr. Dulles. He had not seen you up to that point probably?

Mr. Baker. I don't know whether he had or not.

Representative BOGGS. He came up to you?

Mr. Baker. Yes, sir; and when I hollered at him, he turned around and walked back to me.

Representative BOGGS. Right close to you?

Mr. Baker. And we were right here at this position 24, right here in this doorway.

Mr. Belin. And you saw something move through a door which is marked as what number on Exhibit 497?

Mr. Dulles. Where was he when you first saw him?

Mr. Baker. At this doorway right here, this 23.

Mr. Belin. At 23.

As mentioned previously, the door is at a rough 45-degree angle, which prevents anyone seeing much inside the space between the lunchroom and the landing. What is troublesome is that the door was closed before Baker went in, and when Roy Truly came back down from the third-floor stairs it was still closed.

Baker said he glimpsed someone behind the window moving and then caught up with that person, allegedly Oswald. This glimpse was never mentioned before. According to Roy Truly, only just before Baker was about to give his testimony to the WC in Washington. That was mid-March 1964, 3 ½ months after the Big Event, the glimpse begins to appear in this scenario:

Mr. Dulles. May I ask you a question? Do you know why it was that the officer didn't follow you up the stairs, but instead was distracted, as it were, and went with Lee Harvey Oswald into the lunchroom?

Mr. Truly. I never knew until a day or two ago that he said he saw a movement, saw a man going away from him.

Mr. Dulles. As he was going up the stairs?

Mr. Truly. As he got to the second-floor landing. While I was going around, he saw a movement.

Mr. Dulles. And he followed that?

Mr. Truly. That is right.

Representative Ford. He saw a movement in the lunchroom or a man go into the lunchroom?
Mr. Truly. He saw the back of a man inside the door – I suppose door No. 23. But that isn't my statement. I didn't learn about that, you see, until the other day.

Here is Roy Truly being interviewed by CBS (2061), continuing his fairy tale. Oswald himself never said he was in the second-floor lunchroom during or after the shooting, he was there before!

WC Attorney Belin not once asked Baker during his WC testimony, if the person he caught a *"glimpse"* of through the window of the door on the second-floor landing was the same person (Oswald) he stopped and questioned in the lunchroom seconds later. Nor did he ever ask about the discrepancies in floors and the lack of a lunchroom description between his first affidavit and the ones after that!

Truly had walked past already and was making his way up the steps towards the third floor and the door was shut. The door had a self-closing mechanism and was not a pneumatic door as stated during the WC hearings (just as it was not a vestibule between the landing and the lunchroom either).

In 1968 Barry Ernest did a rough timing of how long the door would take before it was firmly shut, and it took 3 seconds to do so *The Girl on the Stairs (2062)* page 70. The door was the very same door as per the conversation Ernest had with Roy Truly. If you look at the Secret Service re-enactment video (2063), it takes up to 5 seconds for someone to open the door and pass through it and have it close behind them. So, where was Oswald coming from? If the door was closed and Baker saw a glimpse, which he only mentioned to Roy Truly, just before his WC testimony. Then Oswald must have come from the first floor! This scenario appeals to a lot of researchers offering a possibility that Oswald was on the second floor for a coke after the shooting.

On September 23rd 1964 the day before the WR is handed to LBJ (Lyndon Baines Johnson), meaning the WR has been printed up already, Baker gives an affidavit to the FBI (2064). Richard Burnett writes down this statement. There appear to be two corrections in it with Baker's initials scribbled above them. *"Third floor"* and *"drinking a coke"* have been stricken through. These two corrections are made because Baker was dictating and, after a review, they were stricken through and initialled by Baker.

This affidavit, and Roy Truly's, are being rushed back to Washington (2065) to make sure they are part of the WR! The typed version of this report (2066) does not show these corrections, of course! But the real question is, why would the FBI need additional statements from Baker and Truly, after their WC testimony and require these to be sent with great speed to Washington the day before the WR is released and handed to LBJ?

In Larry Sneed's *No More Silence (2067)*, pages 124 & 125, Baker states: *"Mr. Truly was ahead of me. As he had turned the corner and started on around toward the third-floor stairwell, I happened to look over in front of me, and about twenty feet away there was a doorway with a small glass. I caught a movement behind the glass, so I went over, opened up the door, and saw this man standing approximately twenty feet in this next room. At that time, I didn't know if it was a coffee room or what. By this time, I had drawn my pistol on the first flight of stairs. I called to him, 'Hey, you!' And he started to turn around toward me. He didn't have time to respond, it was momentary. He didn't have time to say anything and I didn't have time to observe him. About that time, Mr. Truly was beside me, I asked him if this man worked for him or if he knew him, and he said yes, he works for me."*

In his HSCA testimony (2068), Baker is quoted as: *"I hollered to him. He turned and faced me. Then Mr. Truly came back. I said does this man work here? He said yes."*

Marvin Johnson (2069), who took Baker's statement, wrote in his report, *"On about the 4th floor Officer Baker apprehended a man that was walking away from the stairway on that floor. Officer Baker then started to search the man"*. Actual physical contact not reported in any other affidavit or testimony by anyone else. In addition Johnson states in that very same affidavit (2070): *"When patrolman ML Baker identified Lee Harvey Oswald as the man that stopped in the Texas School Book Depository building, Patrolman Baker was in the Homicide Bureau and giving an affidavit and Oswald was brought into the room to talk to some Secret Service men. When Baker saw Oswald, he stated: That is the man I stopped on the fourth floor of the Depository."* There is no evidence of any of this happening. It is absent from Baker's handwritten and typed DPD statement.

That hugely important finding would have been reflected in Fritz's interrogation notes on November 22nd. And the FBI and USSS statements would make mention of this as well.

Johnson also asserts that Baker recognised Oswald from a line-up. Baker contradicted this when Allen Dulles of the WC asked him if he saw Lee Oswald in the DPD police line-up, Baker answered: *"I never did have a chance to see him in the line-up. I saw him when I went to give the affidavit."* Baker does *not* mention that he actually pointed him out.

Stavis Ellis (2071), Baker's commander, said during an interview for the Garrison investigation; (2072) *"The second part of the conversation was about one of Major Ellis' fellow motorcycle officers. This officer (as told by Ellis) stated he was directly under the building when the shots were fired. They locked the main entrance and after the supervisor arrived, he started up the stairs. The building was the Book Depository. Upon going up the stairs he and the supervisor encountered someone on either the third or fourth floor. This person was drinking water from the water cooler – he did not stop because the supervisor advised the officer that the man was an employee. MAJOR Ellis stated this officer later identified the man by the water cooler as LEE HARVEY Oswald! This is a summation of the conversation."* However, this is not the only time Stavis Ellis comments on Baker's actions on that day. Again, from Larry Sneed's *No More Silence (2073)*, he says that on the second floor they encountered Oswald having a coke.

In a telephone interview with Denis Morissette in 1992 (2074), he says:

1. Baker found Oswald on the floor below from where the shooting started. Which would be the fifth floor.
2. Oswald was drinking a coca cola and eating a bar of candy when Baker found him.
3. Marrion Baker should have sealed the building instead.

Major Stavis Ellis cannot be relied upon when it comes to his statements about the encounter with Oswald; he gives a different location/scenario on all three occasions. The first account for the Garrison investigation (2075) is telling, as he recounts that it happened on the third or fourth floor which is what Baker originally stated in his first affidavit.

From Truly's November 22nd FBI statement (2076): *"…and he accompanied the officer immediately up the stairs to the second floor of the building, where the officer noticed a door and stepped through the door, gun in hand, and observed Oswald in a snack bar there, apparently alone. This snack bar has no windows or doors, facing the outside of the building, but is located almost in the centre of the building. The officer pointed to Oswald and asked if Oswald was an employee of the company, and he, Truly, assured the officer that Oswald was an employee."*

Roy Truly's Statement to the DPD dated November 23rd 1963 (2077): *"We hit the second floor landing the officer stuck his head into the lunchroom area where there are coke and candy machines. Lee Oswald was in there. The officer had his gun on Oswald, and asked me if he was an employee. I answered yes."*

Truly's FBI statement from November 23rd 1963 (2078) says: *"As they reached the second floor landing, the officer opened a door to a small lunchroom next to the business office on that floor, and stuck his gun in the door.' LEE Oswald was in the lunchroom. The officer asked him if he was an employee,* to which Oswald replied that he was. *Truly and the officer gave this no further consideration, inasmuch as Oswald was an employee, and they ran up to the fifth floor."* Oswald replied! That's a new one.

Jesse Curry was quoted in The New York Times of November 24th 1963 (2079): *"The first officer to reach the six-story building,"* Lieutenant Curry said, *"found Oswald among other persons in a lunchroom."* Curry stated this on the 23rd when it became 'official' and was shared with the press around lunch time that day.

Truly's Secret Service statement from December 4th 1963 (2080) states, *"I had started to go up the stairway to the third floor when I noticed that the officer was not following and I heard him say something, I then went back and found that he was standing near the entrance to the lunchroom and he had drawn his weapon. Just inside the lunchroom door Lee Oswald was standing and the officer was facing him. At that time the officer asked me if this man worked here to which I replied, 'yes.'"*

Roy Truly's WC testimony (2081):

Mr. Belin. What did you see?
Mr. Truly. I saw the officer almost directly in the doorway of the lunchroom facing Lee Harvey Oswald.
Mr. Belin. And where was Lee Harvey Oswald at the time you saw him?
Mr. Truly. He was at the front of the lunchroom, not very far inside; he was just inside the lunchroom door.
Mr. Belin. All right.
Mr. Truly. 2 or 3 feet, possibly.
Mr. Belin. Could you put an *"O"* where you saw Lee Harvey Oswald?
All right. You have put an *"O"* on Exhibit 497. [CE 497 has a small 'O' near the lunchroom door entrance which contradicts Oswald's position in CE 1110-BK] What did you see or hear the officer say or do?

Mr. Truly. When I reached there, the officer had his gun pointing at Oswald. The officer turned this way and said, *"This man work here?"* And I said, *"Yes."*

Mr. Belin. And then what happened?

Mr. Truly. Then we left Lee Harvey Oswald immediately and continued to run up the stairways until we reached the fifth floor.

Mr. Belin. All right. Let me ask you this now. How far was the officer's gun from Lee Harvey Oswald when he asked the question?

Mr. Truly. It would be hard for me to say, but it seemed to me like it was almost touching him.

Mr. Belin. What portion of his body?

Mr. Truly. Towards the middle portion of his body.

Mr. Belin. Could you see Lee Harvey Oswald's hands?

Mr. Truly. Yes.

Mr. Belin. Could you see?

Mr. Truly. I am sure I could, yes. I could see most of him, because I was looking in the room on an angle, and they were this way.

Mr. Belin. When you say you were looking in the room on an angle…

Mr. Truly. What I mean–this door offsets the lunchroom door.

Mr. Belin. By this door, you mean door No. 23 is at an angle to door No. 24?

Mr. Truly. Yes. One this way and the other one is this way.

Mr. Belin. All right. Could you see whether or not Lee Harvey Oswald had anything in either hand?

Mr. Truly. I noticed nothing in either hand.

Mr. Belin. Did you see both of his hands?

Mr. Truly. I am sure I did. I could be wrong, but I am almost sure. I did.

Mr. Belin. About how long did Officer Baker stand there with Lee Harvey Oswald after you saw them?

Mr. Truly. He left him immediately after I told him, after he asked me, does this man work here. I said, yes. The officer left him immediately.

Mr. Belin. Did you hear Lee Harvey Oswald say anything?

Mr. Truly. Not a thing.

Mr. Belin. Did you see any expression on his face? Or weren't you paying attention?

Mr. Truly. He didn't seem to be excited or overly afraid or anything. He might have been a bit startled, like I might have been if somebody confronted me. But I cannot recall any change in expression of any kind on his face.

Victoria Adams was asked by Barry Ernest (2082) whether she happened to notice any activity in or around that lunchroom when she passed by on November 22nd? *"I don't recall noticing anything or anyone on the second floor,"* she said. *"But, remember, I wasn't looking for anything in the building. My intent was to get outside as quickly as possible. I*

110

can't answer whether anyone could have been in the lunchroom. If they were, they should have been the ones doing the noticing. I mean, here were people running out of the building. For all anyone else knew, we could have been the ones who did it. Do you know what I mean?" (page 252).

Mrs Robert Reid

There is an additional happening on that very same floor and it is in the form of another alleged encounter in the office next to the lunchroom, room 200, the office of the TSBD management and accounting. One of the employees working in that office was Mrs Robert Reid, her maiden name being Jeraldeane Bray. Reid was Roy Truly's secretary, and after the shooting she apparently rushed back up and encountered Oswald shortly after the alleged lunchroom encounter.

Her name pops up at first in Roy Truly's handwritten DPD affidavit from November 23rd (2083). Reid's name in his handwritten statement is at the bottom of the second page. Reid stated in her handwritten statement here (2084) and here (2085), that she encountered Lee Oswald just after the so-called lunchroom encounter. Truly and Reid had their statements taken by Jim Leavelle btw.

There are some issues:

- Oswald wore a white T-shirt (2086), whereas Baker stated he wore a long-sleeved brownish shirt. In an interview of Roy Truly by Arch Kimbrough (2087) just before he gives his WC testimony he says that he saw Lee Oswald wearing just a white T-shirt, of course matching Mrs. Reid's statement, but contradicting Marrion Baker's.
- *Oswald had a coke in his hands* (which was inserted at the top in her handwritten statement on November 24th (2088) and appears as well in the November 26th FBI affidavit (2089). It was Oswald who mentioned to Fritz he had gotten a coke *for* his lunch from the second-floor lunchroom during his first interrogation. Reid's DPD affidavit is the very first mention of a coke in Oswald's hands. She also tells the same story in her Secret Service report from December 4th 1964 (2090). And also, in the Secret Service report from December 7th 1964 (2091).
- If she was so certain the shots came from above her, why on earth did she go back inside as fast as she said she had? The gunman was still in the building!

111

Reid's alleged encounter is also repeated in Pauline Sanders' FBI statement from November 24th (2092) on page 2, as Sanders mentions she had an alleged telephone conversation with Reid and this hearsay is declared as gospel.

Her WC testimony (2093):

Mr. Belin. You went into the building in the main lobby?
Mrs. Reid. Yes; I did.
Mr. Belin. Did you take the elevator or the stairs?
Mrs. Reid. No; I went up the stairs.
Mr. Belin. Was this the front stairs or the back stairs?
Mrs. Reid. No; the front stairs.
Mr. Belin. All right. You went up through the stairs and then what did you do?
Mrs. Reid. I went into the office.
Mr. Belin. You went into your office?
Mrs. Reid. Yes.
Mr. Belin. And then what did you do?
Mrs. Reid. Well, I kept walking and I looked up and Oswald was coming in the back door of the office. I met him by the time I passed my desk several feet and I told him, I said, *"Oh, the President has been shot, but maybe they didn't hit him."*

He mumbled something to me, I kept walking, he did, too. I didn't pay any attention to what he said because I had no thoughts of anything of him having any connection with it at all because he was very calm. He had gotten a coke and was holding it in his hands and I guess the reason it impressed me seeing him in there, I thought it was a little strange that one of the warehouse boys would be up in the office at the time, not that he had done anything wrong. The only time I had seen him in the office was to come and get change and he already had his coke in his hand so he didn't come for change and I dismissed him. I didn't think anything else.
Mr. Belin. When you saw him, I believe you said you first saw him when he was coming through the door?
Mrs. Reid. Yes, sir.

[And...]

Mr. Belin. What about the other men in the warehouse, did they have occasion to come into that office space?
Mrs. Reid. Occasionally they come up to get change.
Mr. Belin. Apart from getting change or getting paid?

Mrs. Reid. No; very seldom unless they are sent up there to get something. I mean they just don't come in there and wander around. It is some business for them.

Now, I did see him in the lunchroom a few times prior to this eating his lunch but I didn't even know his name.

Mr. Belin. Did you know his name on the day you saw him?

Mrs. Reid. No; I did not. When I saw his picture, I still didn't know his name until they told us who it was.

Mr. Belin. How did you know the person you saw was Lee Harvey Oswald on the second floor?

Mrs. Reid. Because it looked just like him.

Mr. Belin. You mean the picture with the name Lee Harvey Oswald?

Mrs. Reid. Oh, yes.

Mr. Belin. But you had seen him in the building?

Mrs. Reid. Other than that day, sure.

Mr. Belin. Do you remember what clothes he had on when you saw him?

Mrs. Reid. What he was wearing, he had on a white T-shirt and some kind of wash trousers. What colour I couldn't tell you.

Mr. Belin. I am going to hand you what has been marked Commission Exhibits (2094), first 157 and then 158, and I will ask you if either or both look like they might have been the trousers that you saw him wear or can you tell?

Mrs. Reid. I just couldn't be positive about that. I would rather not say, because I just cannot.

Mr. Belin. Do you remember whether he had any shirt or jacket on over his T-shirt?

Mrs. Reid. He did not. He did not have any jacket on.

Mr. Belin. Have you ever seen anyone working at the book depository wearing any kind of a shirt or jacket similar to Commission Exhibit 150 or do you know?

Mrs. Reid. No; I do not. I have never, so far as I know ever seen that shirt. I have been asked about that shirt before, I have seen it once before but not since all this happened.

But what is most damning, is that in that same office Mrs. Reid claimed she saw Oswald walk through, was occupied by someone else at that time. Someone who stayed behind in the office by herself, while everyone else had left to watch the motorcade. Her name was Geneva Hine (2095). Hine destroys Reid's testimony about a possible encounter with Oswald in the second-floor office.

Geneva Hine

Geneva Hine (2096) becomes pivotal in the follow up to the second-floor lunchroom encounter. She destroyed Mrs Robert Reid credibility be it unwittingly.

She stayed behind in the second-floor office and noticed that the phone lines and the power was shut down while the motorcade passed the building. After the shooting, she went into the corridor to knock on a few doors of neighbouring offices and got no reply from anyone (even though she heard someone on the other side of the door speaking on the phone). She then went back into the office and said as per her WC testimony that she saw Reid come back into the office as part of a group!

Hine's FBI statement from November 23rd (2097) states:

1. She was alone in the office between 12:25 and 12:35 (Oswald was supposed to have left one minute after the encounter which allegedly happened two minutes after the shooting! So, he would have gone in three minutes!
2. She was aware of who Oswald was, not knowing his name though, but that he would come to the 2nd floor to get change for the Coke machine from one of the other employees.
3. She did NOT see him on November 22nd!
4. The first person to arrive in the offices was a policeman, who told her not to leave.

All by herself between 12:25 – 12:35. No Oswald, no Mrs R Reid. In CE 1381 (2098) Geneva Hine does not share much valuable info besides her leaving the building at 14:30.

Hine says a few remarkable things during her WC testimony (2099):

- She knew Oswald, as he would come into the office and ask for change for the coke machine.
- Otis Williams leaves at the very last minute to go down and have a quick look.
- She looked through the window and saw the motorcade turn on Elm St and heard the shots shortly after.
- The shots came from within the building.
- She does *not* see Mrs Reid come back in on her own, only as part of a group and it is several minutes after the event.

Mr. Ball. Now, in November, November 22, 1963, where was your desk; in what part of the building?

Miss Hine. My desk was on the second floor, the inside wall just along by the corridor.

Mr. Ball. Did you spend most of your time at your desk?

Miss Hine. At that time?

Mr. Ball. Yes; at that time.

Miss Hine. No, sir; the girls were gone and they wanted to go out and see.

Mr. Ball. I mean did you spend most of your time in your work--it was a desk job?

Miss Hine. Yes; that's right.

Mr. Ball. Did you go in the other floors of the building any?

Miss Hine. Yes; sir; as my duties necessitated, I did.

Mr. Ball. Did you ever know a fellow named Lee Harvey Oswald?

Miss Hine. Yes, sir.

Mr. Ball. When did you first meet him?

Miss Hine. I never met him to know his name but I saw him every day.

Mr. Ball. Where did you see him?

Miss Hine. Downstairs in the warehouse or stockroom whichever you want to call it.

Mr. Ball. The first floor?

Miss Hine. Yes.

Mr. Ball. Did you see him on any other floors?

Miss Hine. Yes, sir; I saw him on the second floor about noontime almost every day. He would come in and ask for change, for a dime or quarter.

Mr. Ball. Did you see him use any part of the second floor?

Miss Hine. No.

Mr. Ball. Did you ever see him spend the dime to buy anything with it?

Miss Hine. No, sir; the coke machine isn't in our room and I wouldn't have seen it.

Mr. Ball. Where is the coke machine?

Miss Hine. Out in the little lunchroom back of our office.

Mr. Ball. Did you ever speak to Oswald?

Miss Hine. Yes, sir.

Mr. Ball. Did he ever speak to you?

Miss Hine. No, sir.

Mr. Ball. He never replied to you?

Miss Hine. No, sir.

Mr. Ball. Would you say he was unfriendly?

Miss Hine. Yes, sir; I would.

Mr. Ball. Did you ever see him smile or laugh?

Miss Hine. No, sir.

Mr. Ball. What kind of an expression did he have on his face most of the time?

115

Miss Hine. I describe it as being stoic.

Mr. Ball. That's a pretty good description if he doesn't smile.

Miss Hine. It was just----

Mr. Ball. Did you ever mention this to any of the people around there about Oswald?

Miss Hine. Yes, sir; I mentioned it to Mr. Shelley.

Mr. Ball. What did you tell him?

Miss Hine. One day I said to Mr. Shelley, *"Who is that queer duck you have working down here,"* and I said that just as a matter of slang because I've known Mr. Shelley for a long time and I was just talking to him, you see, and usually, all the boys that work down there speak to me because I have to go down here to pick up the little *"comp"* or gift slips on my desk. Every time I went by him, I would speak to him, say *"Good morning"* and he would never catch or meet my gaze, so I just made that remark to Mr. Shelley because I had spoken to him so many times and he never answered.

Mr. Ball. What did Shelley say?

Miss Hine. He said that was just his way.

Mr. Ball. On the 22nd of November 1963, did you know that there was to be a motorcade or parade come by your building?

Miss Hine. Oh, yes, sir.

Mr. Ball How did 'you find that out?

Miss Hine. Sir, I don't remember. I probably heard over the news but I cannot remember.

Mr. Ball. You were just aware of the fact?

Miss Hine. Yes; I knew it and the girls were discussing it in the office that morning. Many of them, probably six, had not seen the President close. You see, I had seen him on two different occasions and I had been very close to him and so they were lamenting that they couldn't go out so I spoke up and said, *"I will be glad to answer the telephone so you girls may go out and see the motorcade,"* and I had previously answered the telephone when we were in the other building before we moved in this building, so they were delighted and I thought nothing about it.

Mr. Ball. Did they all go out?

Miss Hine. Yes, sir; everyone went out.

Mr. Ball. Was there anyone left in the office part of the building on that second-floor office?

Miss Hine. Only Mr. Williams and myself and he stayed with me because he was working on his desk until he thought that the motorcade was about there.

Mr. Ball. Then he went out?

Miss Hine. When he thought it was about there, he said *"I think I will go out for 5 minutes."*

Mr. Ball. What is his name?

Miss Hine. Otis N. Williams.

Mr. Ball. He works in the office, too?

Miss Hine. Yes.

Mr. Ball. Did you have to change your desk over to another desk?

Miss Hine. Yes, sir; to the middle desk on the front row.

Mr. Ball. Was there a switchboard?

Miss Hine. No, sir; we have a telephone with three incoming lines, then we have the warehouse line and we have an intercom system.

Mr. Ball. You don't have a switchboard?

Miss Hine. Not now; we did in the other building.

Mr. Ball. Were you alone then at this time?

Miss Hine. Yes.

Mr. Ball. Did you stay at your desk?

Miss Hine. Yes, sir: I was alone until the lights all went out and the phones became dead because the motorcade was coming near us and no one was calling so I got up and thought I could see it from the east window in our office.

Mr. Ball. Did you go to the window?

Miss Hine. Yes, sir.

Mr. Ball. Did you look out?

Miss Hine. Yes, sir.

Mr. Ball. What did you see?

Miss Hine. I saw the escort car come first up the middle of Houston Street.

Mr. Ball. Going north on Houston Street?

Miss Hine. Yes, sir; going north on Houston Street. I saw it turn left and I saw the President's car coming and I saw the President and saw him waving his hand in greeting up in the air and I saw his wife and I saw him turn the corner and after he turned the corner I looked and I saw the next car coming Just at the instant I saw the next car coming up was when I heard the shots.

Mr. Ball. How many did you hear?

Miss Hine. Three.

Mr. Ball Could you tell where the shots were coming from?

Miss Hine. Yes, sir; they came from inside the building.

Mr. Ball. How do you know that?

Miss Hine. Because the building vibrated from the result of the explosion coming in.

Mr. Ball. It appeared to you that the shots came from the building?

Miss Hine. Yes, sir.

Mr. Ball. Did you know they were shots at the time?

Miss Hine. Yes, sir; they sounded almost like cannon shots they were so terrific.

Mr. Ball. That is when you were at the window, is that right?

Miss Hine. Yes, sir; that is when I was at the window, because the next car, you see, was coming up and turning and I looked. Of course, I looked when I heard the shots. I just stood there and saw people running to the east up Elm Street. I saw people running; I saw people falling down, you know, lying down on the sidewalk.

Mr. Ball. That was on Houston Street?

Miss Hine. No, sir; Elm.

Mr. Ball. You could see could you see any part of Elm?

Miss Hine. East, yes, sir.

Mr. Ball. You could see east on Elm?

Miss Hine. Yes, sir; I could see east on Elm. I saw them run across east on Elm away from where his car had gone and my first thought was if I could only see what happened, so I went out our front door into the foyer.

Mr. Ball. You mean the front door to the office?

Miss Hine. Yes, sir.

Mr. Ball. That opens on---

Miss Hine. The foyer, little hall, and---

Mr. Ball. Steps lead down?

Miss Hine. Yes, sir; but there is a door before the steps and the elevator is to my left and I went past the hall that goes to my right and I knocked on the door of Lyons and Carnahan; that's a publishing company.

Mr. Ball. What did you do then?

Miss Hine. I tried the door, sir, and it was locked and I couldn't get in and I called, *"Me, please let me in,"* because she's the girl that had that office, Mrs. Lee Watley, and she didn't answer. I don't know if she was there or not, then I left her door. I retraced my steps back to where the hall turns to my left and went down it to Southwestern Publishing Co.'s door and I tried their door and the reason for this was because those windows face out.

Mr. Ball. On to Elm?

Miss Hine. Yes; and on to the triple underpass.

Mr. Ball. I See.

Miss Hine. And there was a girl in there talking on the telephone and I could hear her but she didn't answer the door.

Mr. Ball. Was the door locked?

Miss Hine. Yes, sir.

Mr. Ball. That was which company?

Miss Hine. Southwestern Publishing Co.

Mr. Ball. Did you call to her?

Miss Hine. I called and called and shook the door and she didn't answer me because she was talking on the telephone; I could hear her. They have a little curtain up and I could see her form through the curtains. I could see her talking and I knew that's what she was doing and then I turned and went through the back hall and came through the back door.

Mr. Ball. Of your office, the second-floor office?

Miss Hine. Yes; and I went straight up to the desk because the telephones were beginning to wink; outside calls were beginning to come in.

Mr. Ball. Did they come in rapidly?

Miss Hine. They did come in rapidly.

Mr. Ball. When you came back in did you see Mrs. Reid?

Miss Hine. No, sir; I don't believe there was a soul in the office when I came back in right then.

Mr. Ball. Did you see anybody else go in through there?

Miss Hine. No, sir; after I answered the telephone then there was about four or five people that came in.

Mr. Ball. Was there anybody in that room when you came back in and went to the telephone?

Miss Hine. No, sir; not to my knowledge.

Mr. Ball. Did you see Mrs. Reid come back in?

Miss Hine. Yes, sir; I think I felt sure that I did. I thought that there were five or six that came in together. I thought she was one of those.

Mr. Ball. Mrs. Reid told us she came in alone and when she came in, she didn't see anybody there.

Miss Hine. Well, it could be that she did, sir. I was talking on the phones and then came the policemen and then came the press. Everybody was wanting an outside line and then our vice president came in and he said, *"The next one that was clear, I have to have it,"* and so I was busy with the phone.

Mr. Ball. From the time you walked into the room you became immediately busy with the phone?

Miss Hine. Yes, sir; sure was.

Mr. Ball. Did you see Oswald come in?

Miss Hine. My back would have been to the door he was supposed to have come in at.

Mr. Ball. Were you facing the door he is supposed to have left by?

Miss Hine. Yes, sir.

Mr. Ball. Do you recall seeing him?

Miss Hine. No, sir.

Mr. Ball. Do you have any definite recollection of Mrs. Reid coming in?

Miss Hine. No, sir; I only saw four or five people that came by and they all came and were all talking about how terrible it was.

Mr. Ball. Do you remember their names?

Miss Hine. Yes, sir.

Mr. Ball. Who were they?

Miss Hine. Mr. Williams, Mr. Molina (spelling), Miss Martha Reid, Mrs. Reid, Mrs. Sarah Stanton, and Mr. Campbell; that's all I recall, sir.

There is enough to doubt Mrs. R. Reid's story. How could Geneva Hine have missed both Reid and Oswald when she was at that front desk

119

where she was occupying the phones? The` same space where Reid is supposed to have come in and Oswald to have gone out, have an exchange and not be noticed by Geneva Hine? Note: Hine was able to name every one of the group of people that came in much later.

One might ask whether, under questioning, would you trip up your supervisor? Would you be willing to sit quite close in the office to someone you had basically called a liar in front of the WC? Would your job still be safe?

Carol Hughes

Carol Hughes stayed by herself in the office of the South-Western Publishing during the assassination. Her fellow co-workers went outside and stood alongside Elm St. When Geneva Hine knocked on the South-Western office door Carol Hughes did not answer it as she was on the phone at that time.

In her statement in CE 1381 (2100), page 23, Hughes mentions that she stood behind a South facing window which overlooks Elm and saw the President get shot. She must have had quite a good view of it. It is odd that there is nothing added about that view she had and what she exactly saw. She was alone in the office.

Carolyn Arnold

Carolyn Arnold (2101) is another person of interest. Although she was outside when JFK was murdered, she mentions a first-floor observation of Oswald in her FBI statement from November 26th (2102). She worked on the second floor as Vice-President Ochus Campbell's secretary and was pregnant at that time. Arnold is first seen in the Dave Wiegman film (2103) standing in front of the TSBD while the motorcade is passing by. She is looking towards the Dal-Tex building, during the shooting, strange as that may seem. This is before the headshot.

It is possible that she went back to the steps after the shots were fired and is captured in the Darnell film (2104), but due to its blurring it is impossible to confirm this for a full 100%. She is also captured in one of Gordon Willis' photographs (2105) and the Cooper film (2106) in the aftermath while the TSBD employees are made to stay outside until roughly 30 minutes after the assassination.

Carolyn Arnold's statement to the FBI on November 26th (2107) is interesting because she stated she had left between 12:00 and 12:15 and thought she saw a fleeting glimpse of Lee Oswald standing in the

120

hallway between the front door and the double doors leading to the warehouse, while standing in front of the TSBD. Carolyn Arnold is not called up as a witness for the WC (2108). The November 26th statement is suppressed, but was dug out by Harold Weisberg and is widely written about inside his book *Photographic Whitewash* (2109).

During the tenure of the HSCA Carolyn Arnold gave a handful of interviews. The first was with the National Enquirer for a very small article. The photo I saw of it was too low res to discern what was being said. Next one was with Earl Golz for the Dallas Morning News in 1978 (2110), page 18. In that interview she disowns the FBI statement from November 26th 1963. She also claims having seen Oswald sitting in the lunchroom that day.

Then there is another interview in Anthony Summers' *Not In Your Lifetime* (2111). From this book, (page 92) I quote the following: "*When the author contacted Arnold in 1978 to get a first-hand account, she was surprised to hear how she had been reported by the FBI. Her spontaneous reaction, that the* FBI had misquoted her, came before the author explained to her the importance of Oswald's whereabouts at given moments. Arnold's recollection of what she observed was clear— having spotted Oswald had been her one personal contribution to the record of that memorable day. As secretary to the company vice president, she knew Oswald; he had been in the habit of coming to her for change. What she claimed she told the FBI is very different from the Bureau report of her comments: *"About a quarter of an hour before the assassination,"* she said in 1978, *"I went into the lunchroom on the second floor for a moment... Oswald was sitting in one of the booth seats on the right-hand side of the room as you go in. He was alone as usual and appeared to be having lunch. I did not speak to him, but I recognized him clearly."*

Arnold had some reason to remember having gone into the lunchroom. She was pregnant at the time and had a craving for a glass of water. She also recalled, in 1978, that this was, *"about 12:15. It may have been slightly later."*

There are, however, five issues with this:
1-According to Virgie Rackley's FBI statement (2112), she left with Carolyn Arnold, Betty Dragoo, Bonnie Richey and Judy Johnson together at about 12:15. Bonnie Richey confirms this time stamp as well in her FBI statement (2113).

2-And there is also Pauline Sanders' FBI statement from March 19th 1964 (2114) which states that she left the lunchroom at approximately 12:20.

Surely she would have seen Oswald? Yet her November 24th statement (2115), which also contains her hearsay phone call conversation with Mrs. Robert Reid, states she left at 11:25, an hour before the motorcade was expected to pass by the TSBD! This can also be a typo. If it is, and it is 12:25 then that makes it even more strange, she could have made mention of Oswald's presence.

And then there is Joe Molina's statement to BL Senkel on November 23rd (2116) in which he states that he did not see Oswald and that he left the lunchroom at 12:15.

3-And then there is Mrs. Robert Reid during her WC testimony (2117):

Mr. Belin. All right. Do you know about what time it was that you left the lunchroom, was it 12, 12:15?
Mrs. Reid. I think around 12:30 somewhere along in there
Mr. Belin. Were you the last person in the lunchroom?
Mrs. Reid. No; I could not say that because I don't remember that part of it because I was going out of the building by myself, I wasn't even, you know, connected with anyone at all.
Mr. Belin. Were there any men in the lunchroom when you left there?
Mrs. Reid. I can't, I don't, remember that.
Mr. Belin. All right.
Mrs. Reid. I can't remember the time they left.

4-The observation brought forward of Oswald sitting down and eating lunch in that particular lunchroom. The second-floor lunchroom was for office staff and management only. The labourers only had access to this lunchroom to grab a drink out of the machine and to get out and eat their lunch outside or downstairs on the first floor in their place; the Domino Room.

Roy Edward Lewis confirmed this in Larry Sneed's *No More Silence (2118)* and again in his interviews with Ed Ledoux in August 2018, and he stated categorically, "*We weren't allowed up there, not just blacks, it was for all warehouse employees.*" There was a class divide at that time, and even these days, in some companies, manual workers sit at a different place away from office and senior employees.

5- "*Getting a glass of water.*" Study the photograph of the second-floor lunchroom (2119) and see that one cannot just walk in to a kitchen sink with tap and get themselves a glass of water. Nor is there a water fountain or a water cooler visible inside that lunchroom. The only option (which has not been confirmed by anyone) would be jugs or bottles of water in the fridge. BUT! You can get a glass of water at the water cooler down the hall (2120) about 15 feet away from the lunchroom entrance. You will be able to see this water cooler marked in green in the FBI schematic (2121) made by FBI Agent Roy Rose on March 8th 1964.

No water supply is near the door of the lunchroom. The JFK Oliver Stone film makes the mistake of positioning the fountain there. Nothing present as you can see in the same schematic (marked in red).

As a matter of fact, they are way down in the corridor leading to the stairs going to the first floor. Had she left the office and gone back to get some water it would not have been physically possible to see Oswald sitting inside the second floor lunchroom.

If Oswald had been sitting there, other office employees who had lunch before they went downstairs would have noticed and mentioned this. Yet not one did.

Think also about the timing perspective she mentions. Carolyn Arnold claimed, in 1978, that she saw Oswald in the lunchroom around 12:15. Compare that with the statement of Marrion Baker, who claimed, in 1964, he saw Oswald walking into the lunchroom around 12:31. How does one put these two happenings together?

So, if you believe her defence of the 12:15 sighting of Oswald in the lunchroom, it creates an issue for Oswald being the shooter as well, as Arnold Rowland (2122) saw two persons on the sixth floor in the 'sniper's nest' at that very same time. The 'combination' of these two witnesses' time stamped statements would exonerate Oswald. Funny thing is that no one picked up on that particular fact until years later.

News Reports

There are news reports and statements by big names in this case which seem not to get repeated. They indicate that Oswald was encountered on the *first floor*, while trying to leave the building.

Roy Truly was overheard by Kent Biffle who reported in the November 23rd edition of the Dallas Morning News (2123): *"In a storage room on the first floor, the officer, gun drawn, spotted Oswald. Does this man work here? The officer reportedly asked Truly. Truly, who said he had interviewed and had hired Oswald a couple of months earlier reportedly told the policeman that Oswald was a worker."* Biffle makes a mention of this again in a DMN article from November 21st 2000: *"Hours dragged by. The building superintendent showed up with some papers in his* hand. I listened as he told detectives about Lee Oswald failing to show up at a roll call. My impression is there was an earlier roll call but it was inconclusive inasmuch as several employees were missing. This time, however, all were accounted for but Oswald. I jotted down all the Oswald information. The description and address came from company records already examined by the superintendent. The superintendent would recall later that he and a policeman met Oswald as they charged into the building after the shots were fired."

Biffle repeats this in his Oral History talk with the Sixth Floor Museum (2124), at 07:30: *"I had been in the Depository all day. I got here early, I say we're here in the school depository building. And I arrived and there was a fella from Channel 8 TV, who managed to get in before they closed the door. I went in with what I thought was the first wave of policemen when the depository became a suspect building. Well, I went in and almost immediately they locked the doors and kept the rest of the press out, but since we were already in, we were wandering around the building. Anyhow, I spent most of the day in the building* (2125) *and it was much later in the afternoon in fact when Roy Truly the manager of the building, the school book depository building, came and said ehm... and told Captain Fritz we have an employee who didn't report back after lunch. And my impression was that they had had a roll call earlier in the day and several were still absent, but this one was later in the afternoon and he was the only one not accounted for. And Fritz asked him for the name of the employee and he called him Lee Oswald. It didn't register with me, because I associated Lee Oswald with Fort Worth and any way he was in Russia and I never would have thought of him until later. I was heading back towards the building when it dawned on me Lee... Oswald.... Lee Harvey Oswald and I connected him with Fort Worth and this was the defector you know that I had written about in Fort Worth 3-4 years earlier and it was sort of a revelation. And by the time I got back to the News (Dallas Morning News-BK) Oswald had already been arrested and so it was no big revelation to anybody else, but it was to me. I didn't know he had been arrested when I was heading back that way.*

Ochus Campbell, the vice president of the TSBD stated in the NYHT on November 22nd (2126): *"Shortly after the shooting we raced back into the building. We had been outside watching the parade. We saw him (Oswald) in a small storage room on the ground floor. Then we noticed he was gone."* Mr. Campbell added: *"Of course he and the others were on their lunch hour but he did not have permission to leave the building and we haven't seen him since."*

There were other (TSBD) employees missing after the assassination.

Detective Ed Hicks is quoted in the London Free Press on November 23rd (2127) and in various other newspapers stating: *"As the Presidential limousine sped to the hospital the police dragnet went into action. Hicks said at just about that time, Oswald came out of the front door of the red bricked warehouse. A policeman asked him where he was going. He said he wanted to see what all the excitement was all about."*

In the Washington Post of November 23rd (2128) Dallas Police Chief Jesse Curry is quoted: *"As an officer rushed into the building Oswald rushed out. The policeman permitted him to pass after the building manager told the policeman that Oswald was an employee."*

Henry Wade during a press conference, which by the looks of it is published unedited in the New York Times on November 26th (2129), states: *"A police officer, immediately after the assassination, ran in the building and saw this man in a corner and tried to arrest him; but the manager of the building said he was an employee and it was all right. "*

J Edgar Hoover in a November 29th telephone conversation (2130) with LBJ states: *"at the entrance of the building he was stopped by police officers, well he is alright, he works here, you needn't hold him. They let him go."*

Third Floor

A third-floor schematic (2131). A considerable amount of floor space was used for book storage.
- Room 301 Allyn & Bacon Inc.
- Room 305 McGraw Hill.

Doris Burns

Doris Burns worked on the third floor at MacMillan & Company. The FBI first interview her on November 25th 1963 (2132) and she stated that she knew Oswald from riding the elevator with him a week prior the assassination, yet she had not seen him on November 22nd. While the President passed by the building she had walked from her office to Allyn & Bacon to get a better look of the motorcade. As she walked to the office Steven Wilson stated that there has been a shooting. Something she had been completely oblivious about, as she did not even hear the shots. She returned to her office and then used the ladies room which is positioned near the back stairs and heard someone running down, but was unable to tell who that was.

Burns was interviewed by Billy Senkel (2133), on February 18th 1964. She stated that she was in Steven Wilson's office when she heard the last shot through the open window, but this is hard to believe as per Steven Wilson's testimony and the Dillard photo (2134), the window was screwed shut due to the air conditioning present on that floor! This contradicts her FBI statement.

She did know who Oswald was, as she rode on the goods elevator once with him. But she had not seen him on November 22nd. In CE 1381 (2135), page 6, she mentions very little else of real value. In both statements she stated she heard only one shot, just like Jack Dougherty did on the fifth floor.

Her WC testimony (2136) on April 7th 1964:

Mr. Ball. On November 22nd, what were you doing that day?
Miss BURNS. I was listening to the radio as I worked.
Mr. Ball. About noon, did you go to lunch?
Miss BURNS. Well, I had lunch at the office and then I didn't intend to go see the President, didn't have any desire to but I left about--I don't remember the exact time but, anyway, when I left, they said on the radio that he that the motorcade was coming up, I believe it was Cedar Springs; anyway, he hadn't been away from the airport long and that he was going about 5 miles an hour so everybody could see him. Well, thinking he was going that slowly, I thought I had plenty of time, so I walked up to Sanger's.
Mr. Ball To where?
Miss BURNS. Sanger's.
Mr. Ball. Where is that?
Miss BURNS. It's about four blocks up Elm Street.
Mr. Ball. Which way on Elm---east?
Miss BURNS. East; you see, we are down at the extreme west end of the street; nothing else down there.
Mr. Ball. Then what happened?
Mr. BURNS. I bought some Kleenex and came back, and everybody was out on the steps to look, but I didn't stop. I went on back to the office.
Mr. Ball. That is the third floor?
Miss BURNS. Yes.
Mr. Ball. Was anybody in the office?
Miss BURNS. Yes; Mrs. Case hadn't ever gone out. She was there. I believe she was the only one.
Mr. Ball. What did you do?
Miss BURNS. I listened to the radio, and by that time they said that he was on Main and turning at Houston or Main by the Courthouse, so since

he was that close, I thought, well, I guess I will go look out the window. I didn't care-- enough to go downstairs, but I thought I will go look out the window. So, I thought I would have plenty of time, if he was just coming around Main Street that I could still get around there, so I went around to American Book Co., which is the office closest to us that had a window looking out on Elm. There was nobody in there, so then I started down the hail to Allyn and Bacon. As I went down this hall towards the windows that looked out on Houston Street, I heard a shot, but I didn't think much about it. I didn't, of course, know it was a shot because when you hear tires backfire and all, they all sound alike to me, so I didn't think a thing about that.

I went around to Allyn and Bacon, and Mr. Wilson, the manager, was at the window looking out. He was the only one in there, so I asked him if I could look out the window with him. About that time, he said, *"Oh, my God, there's been a shooting."* I still didn't think anybody, of course, had been killed, just thought somebody had shot in the air or something, so I said, *"Has the President already passed?"* And he said *"Yes,"* so I looked out and that big bus that had the press in it, had the word *"Press"* or whatever it was on the bus, was passing. So, I said *"Well, I guess I have missed the President then,"* and I started on back out of the office and I just said as I left, *"Well, I hope nobody got hurt."*

Mr. Ball. You heard how many shots?

Miss BURNS. One.

Mr. Ball. Just one?

Miss BURNS. It must have been the last one because I didn't hear any more.

Mr Ball. Did you have any idea where it was coming from?

Miss BURNS. Well, it just sounded as though it was back of me. You see, I was going towards Houston Street. I was facing east and it sounded to me as it came toward my back.

Mr. Ball. You were in the building?

Miss BURNS. Yes; I was in the building.

Mr. Ball. Walking down the hall?

Miss BURNS. Walking down the hall going towards Allyn and Bacon.

Mr. Ball. Now, what happened after that?

Miss BURNS. I came on back and listened to the radio some more and in a few minutes, why, they told it.

Mr. Ball. Did you ever know Lee Harvey Oswald?

Miss BURNS. I rode on the elevator with him one time.

Mr. Ball. That's all?

Miss BURNS. But I didn't know who he was--about a week before.

Mr. Ball. You never talked to him?

Miss BURNS. I never talked to him.

Mr. Ball. Who were you with at the time this happened?

Miss BURNS. The Macmillan Co.

Mr. Ball. Who was in the office with you?

Miss BURNS. Mrs. Case, but I couldn't see her.

Mr. Ball. She was in the same office?

Miss BURNS. I have a private office. She was around the corner where her office is.

Mr. Ball. Mrs. Case?

Miss BURNS. Yes.

Mr. Ball. Did you hear anybody running down the stairs at any time?

Miss BURNS. Yes, but I didn't know

Mr. Ball. When?

Miss BURNS. It was after that; I went to the restroom.

Mr. Ball. How long after?

Miss BURNS. I imagine maybe it was 25 minutes. I imagine it was the policeman or somebody; of course, I don't know who it was.

Edna Case

In her first statement to the FBI on November 24th (2137) she states that she did not know Oswald and that she did not hear the shots while looking out of the window

The Special Service Bureau interviewed her as well on February 18th 1964 (2138), during which she stated that it was only after the shooting had occurred, she was made aware of the shooting of the President. What on earth was she looking at then? She had a perfect view of the parking lot and the activity down there! See for yourself on page 7!

In CE 1381 (2139) Edna Case states that she was looking outside of the Western window while sitting at her desk. The only other person present in the office was Sandra Sue Ellerson. She did not hear any shots being fired.

Sandra Sue Elerson

Sandra Sue Elerson (2140), Patricia-Ann Lawrence, Lucy Whittaker and Madeleine Reese are pictured coming down the TSBD steps in this photograph by William Allen (2141) of the Dallas Morning News taken at about 14:00.

Elerson is interviewed by the FBI on November 25th (2142) and she said that she was looking out of the window on the third-floor office, she saw the limo turn on to Elm, but did not hear any shots. Did not know or recognised Lee Oswald.

128

In CE 1381 (2143) on page 15 she states again she did not hear the shots while looking out of the window and seeing the car turn on to Elm. She never met Oswald.

Hard to believe 'not hearing the shots. There is much more to this than led to believe. Did they notice something that did not fit the picture and were told to keep quiet?

Steven Wilson

Steven Wilson (2144) is visible behind the third foor window in the Tom Dillard photo (2145). This image is the one mostly used to show Bonnie Ray Williams, James Jarman and Harold Norman .

In CE 1381 (2146) Wilson takes five pages to explain himself. He tells in great detail what his movements were when it happened. He was alone in the main office of Allyne & Bacon. Shortly after the limo's turn on to Elm St. his view is obscured by the trees. He only hears three shots. This is with the window screwed closed. Following this he stands around in front of the window for a while and also acknowledges the Dillard photo above. The women return to the office and are crying and telling him the President has been shot. It is only at that time Wilson knows what really happened. He descends to the restroom on the 2nd floor, then goes back up and lies down on the couch. Then the officers appear and question everyone before they leave at 14:30.

He does not know Lee Oswald but remembers a few sightings of him.

During the Garrison investigation another statement is taken from Wilson (2147). It seems that Wilson is more than willing to testify and is also a believer of a conspiracy. The shots appeared to come from his right, which means west of the TSBD.

Fourth Floor

Fourth floor FBI drawings (2148).

- Room 401: Scott Foresman.

There is something strange going on in some of the statements of the employees of this floor. What at first looked like nothing special became a major issue. And law enforcement agencies did their best to hide and alter possible supporting evidence that would hinder the reliability of their findings.

Victoria Adams came into view of the WC with her statement that she and Sandra Styles left from the fourth floor window facing Elm St almost immediately after the shots had been fired and then becoming a problem by being on the back stairs at the same time as Oswald was supposedly descending those same stairs on his way to the second floor lunchroom. It became clear that her departure from the TSBD threw a huge spanner into the works of the so-called official story. They did not see Oswald. Nor did they see Roy Truly and Marrion Baker coming up as they allegedly raced into the building and ran up those same stairs. Nor did they encounter Otis Williams who made his way back up those stairs as well.

Law enforcement agencies and the WC did their best to keep quiet about what really happened on that floor as much as they possibly could. Several people could attest to the departure of Adams and Styles. But according to the statements no one was asked until a letter from Martha Joe Stroud (2149) appeared in 1999, thanks to Barry Ernest.

From the documents of the employees inside the building on this floor and the additional info gathered, I can state that Judyth McCully (2150) was on the fourth floor and not on the front steps as she had initially stated in her first affidavit. Since Avery Davis (2151) stated she was with McCully it is quite possible she was on the fourth floor at the time of the shooting. Neither woman is identified in any of the film and photo material that are available. Nor has any other employee on those steps identified or mentioned them as being there.

If they were on the fourth floor then why did the FBI tell McCully to change her location? Would it be that too many occupants would draw attention to Victoria Adams and would then tend to confirm her story?

There were ten women on this floor while the limo passed by on Elm St So, what did these law enforcement agencies do? They covered this up. Close inspection of the fourth-floor drawings show that there wasn't much compartmentalisation with offices going on. The Scott Foresman (2152) office covered five windows; the other room was a supply room. Reading the statements of these women shows that they were standing close together and they could have corroborated Victoria Adams' and Sandra Styles' timing of their descent easily. But these law enforcement officers didn't do this as this could cause a huge problem for Oswald's so-called 'escape'.

Furthermore, there are strong indications that there was a gathering near the back stairs on the fourth floor of the building by these employees after the shooting. What is also interesting to know is that the fifth-floor crew of Bonnie Ray Williams, Harold Norman and James Jarman, upon their descent from the fifth floor stopped on the fourth and interacted with these ladies. How long they stopped is of dispute, but something happened and again, there are traces of making things go away as you will see in the fifth-floor chapter.

Betty Alice Foster

In CE 1310 (2153) she states that she was in the stockroom with Marie Hollies. Betty Alice Foster heard some 'firecrackers', but had no idea what had happened. She did not know Oswald, nor had ever seen him before. She was later spotted outside near the east side of the TSBD entrance in the Roy Cooper film (2154), and shortly before that in front of the TSBD steps in one of Jay Skaggs' photographs (2155).

Mary Hollies

Mary Hollies (2156), stood also in the stock room along with Betty Alice Foster. Shortly after the shooting she heard footsteps above her, which must have been the three African Americans, Harold Norman, Bonnie Ray Williams and James Jarman. She and Foster made their way outside where they were spotted by Jay Skaggs in one of his photographs (2157) and in the Cooper film (2158).

In Hollies' statement to WE Potts February 18th 1964 (2159), she says that she was standing with Alice Foster on the fourth floor. She heard three shots and thought they sounded like they came from within the building. She did not know Oswald, but had seen him in the lunchroom on numerous occasions. And in CE 1381 (2160), page 21, she pretty much recites the same.

Judyth McCully

Judyth McCully's (2161) story of her whereabouts during the shooting is very interesting to say the least. First, in her November 24th FBI affidavit (2162) she states she was on the fourth floor. Then, in the next affidavit for the DPD, taken by detective Walter E Potts on February 18th 1964 (2163), she states she was on the front steps with Avery Davis. Every person on the steps is accounted for in the Wiegman film. In CE 1381 (2164) McCully states that she knew Oswald from having seen him in the second-floor lunchroom.

At the end of November, 2018, I managed to get in touch with her daughter who was very gracious in talking to me and helping to clarify this matter. According to her, her mom did not really speak about it, and definitely not to outsiders. Any enquiry would have to go through her grandmother. She was fenced off from outsiders by her. McCully was on the fourth floor of the TSBD as the shooting occurred. She acknowledged that she looked out of the window, but further details of that moment were not discussed. The reason why the statement changed from the fourth floor to the front steps was because the FBI 'advised' her to.

Avery Davis

Avery Davis (2165), working at Scott-Foresman, at first sounds like a solid witness.

Even though she states she was on the front steps of the TSBD she cannot be visually accounted for in any of the available footage and stills. Not in Altgens 6, Wiegman, nor in Darnell. Nor has anyone else noticed her or mentioned seeing Davis in their statement(s); that is, not until McCully's second FBI statement.

You can take Davis' later recorded admission that she was with Judyth McCully, who first stated that she was on the fourth floor, and then see that after a chat with the FBI, the fourth floor location has now changed to the front steps.

That change is needed because the front steps were chosen already on the 23rd as can be seen in the Nat Pinkston report. It looked like McCully's and Davis' stories did not rhyme

On February 18th 1964 Bill Senkel of the DPD (2167) interviewed Davis. This is the same day while Judyth McCully is interviewed by Walter E Potts. In each of their statements they acknowledge the other's presence on the TSBD steps.

In that February 18th 1964 statement she claimed to have left the TSBD at 12:00 or a little later, and then positioned herself on the steps. She thought the shots came from the railroad yard and she stood with Judy McCully on the TSBD steps. Not one other person is mentioned as being there. After the shots have been fired she then went back inside and takes the elevator to the fourth floor. This makes the *"traffic"* of employees going straight back in and up to the second and fourth floors a very busy affair. After getting back to the fourth floor she was interviewed by the police. She had never seen Oswald in the building and her 'excuse' for that is the fact that she would take the elevator in the vestibule and would not be in contact with the TSBD employees.

In CE 1381 (2168), page 11, she makes a strange observation of a policeman running towards the President's car. There is no policeman that did that, but USSS agent Clint Hill did. She thought the shots had come from the viaduct. She did not know Oswald, and did not ever see him in the TSBD.

Yola Hopson

Yola Hopson (2169) stated in her December 4th FBI statement (2170) that she was looking outside through the fourth window (which could not be opened) on the fourth floor. When the shots were fired, she thought they had been fire-crackers. She could not see the car as it was obscured by a tree. Afterwards, she and other employees milled around the office. From where she was standing, she did not see anyone coming down the stairs.

In CE 1381 (2171), page 22. Hopson says that she stood near the middle double window on the fourth floor. She was there with Ruth Nelson. She could not see the limo due to the trees. She had never seen Oswald before.

Ruth Nelson

Ruth Nelson (2172) was a part-time employee of Scott Foresman. On February 18th 1964 Billy Senkel interviewed Ruth Nelson (2173). She stated she was looking through the fourth window on the fourth floor. She thought the three loud reports were part of the celebration then she saw policemen run. She moved more west to look out from that side and then went back to work. Police questioned her and then she was let out between 14:00 and 14:30. She did not know Oswald. She took the front elevator to the fourth floor.

In CE 1381 (2174), page 34, she again stated her position on the fourth floor and that she stood there with Yola Hopson.

Victoria Adams

A lot of people were first introduced to Victoria Adams (2175) and Sandra Styles in the Oliver Stone film JFK (2176). They were depicted during a sequence after the shots have been fired as they descend the back stairs of the TSBD and do not encounter Oswald going down those very same stairs.

This particular happening had ramifications not only for Oswald's descent that never was, but also for the second-floor lunchroom encounter that never was, and finally, the Lovelady and Shelley encounter that, you guessed it, never was. These three non-events created by the DPD, the FBI and the WC were needed to demonstrate Oswald's guilt and discredit these two ladies. The truth of their experience showed that Oswald could not and did not come down those stairs after the shots had been fired.

On November 24th the FBI (2177) took Adams' statement in which she said that her view was partially obscured, but she did observe the limo speeding up and rushing away. She heard three shots and at first thought they were firecrackers. She thought the sounds came from the right of the building, with her facing out, meaning from a westerly direction. She and Sandra Styles immediately made their way downstairs via the backstairs. They did not see anyone else. Once downstairs they exited from the back and make their way through the railroad yard and saw lots of people milling about before encountering a police officer who commanded them to go back inside which they did by going back thru the TSBD front door. They returned, be it separately, through the front door. Adams is the only one who saw Joe Molina and made mention of his presence.

On December 19th (2178) she was contacted again about anything connecting Ruby with Oswald. Since she barely knew of Oswald, she could not add anything.

In CE 1381 (2179), page 1, she repeats what she said in her November 24th statement.

Victoria Adams' WC testimony (2180) stated that she and Sandra Styles left the fourth-floor window shortly after the shots were fired and descended the back stairs to the first floor. Then left through the back door and made their way to the rail road yard. Once there they were told by a police officer to go back where they came from which they did by going back thru the front door. They returned, be it separately, through the front door. Adams is the only one who saw Joe Molina and made mention of his presence.

The timing of their movement is pivotal. According to the WC's conclusions the pair would have been on those stairs at the same time Lee Oswald supposedly was, as he (allegedly) raced down from the sixth floor. Clearly, that was unacceptable for them.

Victoria Adams was interviewed by Barry Ernest for his book *The Girl on the Stairs (2181)*, page 244, who recorded her saying "*As I watched the motorcade proceed toward the Depository, the President and Mrs*

134

Kennedy were clearly visible. I thought Mrs Kennedy looked stunning with roses on her lap. As they rounded the corner, they turned toward our building, waving and smiling. The car continued moving slowly and a tree obstructed my view. That is when I heard what I thought was a firecracker go off. As the car came back into view, I saw that something was wrong and watched as Mrs Kennedy appeared to be trying to climb out of the car. I saw a Secret Service man jump in and the car began speeding up toward the triple underpass. Before it reached that I turned to Sandra and I said, 'I want to see what is going on.' "We ran to the back of the office and down the stairs." "We ran down the stairs," Ms Adams continued. "We were both in high heels. No one was there. We would have heard other steps. The noise on those steps is very obvious. And remember, the elevator cables were not moving. It was quiet. "We ran outside and noticed a lot of people running toward the railroad tracks. The railroad yard behind the grassy knoll was quite a distance away. I could not see anything other than people running toward the railroad cars and I tried to run that way, too. But a policeman stopped us. I didn't get very far—maybe 10 or 20 feet from the Depository building. So, we turned back to Houston and to the front of the building."

Neither Miss Adams nor her colleague, Sandra Styles, had seen or heard anyone as they descended the stairs. This anomaly was ignored by the WC for it never bothered to refer to Miss Adams or Miss Styles in any of the time tests conducted regarding Lee Harvey Oswald's supposed escape. These alleged time tests were done with Marrion Baker, Roy Truly and Mrs Robert Reid. Not one journalist was able to observe these time tests.

In the end the WC, especially David Belin, did not believe her. She was summoned to meet him in Dallas. "He was another of those patronising types." "He told me that all my answers and his questions were 'off the record' and that he would invite a court reporter in to take my actual deposition and I was to exactly answer exactly what I had said to him – no variations. During the informal part he leaned back in his chair, crossed his arms and looked at me straight.... 'Now Miss Adams don't you think you could be wrong? Memory is a funny thing and tricks some people.' I looked him straight in the eye and said 'I could be, but I am not wrong. I know what I saw, what I did and what I heard.' He told me at the end of his questioning he would ask me if I had anything to add that I hadn't mentioned. I was supposed to say 'No', as I had in the initial session. But I didn't. As I started speaking, he looked startled, especially when I talked about seeing Jack Ruby on the corner across the street from the Depository building (page 248)."

Once the WR was issued it simply concluded that Oswald was on the stairs at that time and if Victoria Adams did not see or hear Oswald, then she was wrong. She must have come down the stairs later than she thought, the WR concluded, after Oswald had passed the fourth floor going down, after the lunchroom encounter had occurred, and after Marrion Baker and Roy Truly had advanced beyond the fourth floor going up to the roof.

Dorothy Ann Garner refutes this in the Martha Joe Stroud letter as you can see in her chapter.

Then something strange happened; it is when Jim Leavelle takes another statement from Miss Adams on February 17th 1964 (2182). Adams had only moved into this apartment the day before Leavelle knocked on her door, and she had not yet notified anyone with a change of address.

From Barry Ernest's book *The Girl on the Stairs* (2183), pages 246-247: "*One time, a detective from the Dallas police came to my apartment, showed his badge and asked to talk to me. I asked him why he needed to talk with me since I had already given my testimony to the Dallas police. 'Oh', he responded, 'the records were all burned in a fire we had and we have to interview everyone again'.*

That 'fire' is not true, since there is no evidence of it at the DPD at that time.

In an interview decades later, he was asked by Ernest about this episode and Leavelle told him that it was during the Ruby investigation. We know from the statements that a few TSBD people were questioned on Febuary 17th /18th 1964.

In this statement the names Billy Lovelady and William Shelley appear. This alleged encounter on the first floor of the TSBD with these two men appears to contradict the actual timing of Adams' and Styles' descent. Shelley and Lovelady claimed in their WC testimonies that they kept standing on the steps for a few minutes, but they were seen leaving the steps in the Malcolm Couch and Jimmy Darnell films just after the shots rang out. They were seen walking towards the railroad yard and, subsequently, according to Shelley's first affidavit, he met with Gloria Calvery. They hung about in the area for a while and allegedly made their way back into the TSBD. Read more about Shelley's and Lovelady's departure (2184).

Lovelady and Shelley lie during their WC testimonies claiming they kept standing on the steps of the front entrance much longer, for a few minutes, before leaving. In fact, so much longer that this exaggerated claim completely contradicts their statements to the DPD and the FBI. Moreover, they would have seen Oswald leave the building after the alleged second floor lunchroom encounter!

Could those two ladies be *that* wrong about the timing of their departure? I doubt it. Were Shelley and Lovelady used to counter Victoria Adams' claims?

Lovelady's WC testimony (2185) mentions Adams' first name, although he would not swear to it as the person he encountered on the first floor, nor can he describe where it actually happened:

Mr. Ball – Who did you see in the first floor?
Mr. Lovelady – I saw a girl but I wouldn't swear to it it's Vickie.
Mr. Ball – Who is Vickie?
Mr. Lovelady – The girl that works for Scott, Foresman.
Mr. Ball – What is her full name?
Mr. Lovelady – I wouldn't know.
Mr. Ball – Vickie Adams?
Mr. Lovelady – I believe so.
Mr. Ball – Would you say it was Vickie you saw?
Mr. Lovelady – I couldn't swear.
Mr. Ball – Where was the girl?
Mr. Lovelady – I don't remember what place she was, but I remember seeing a girl as she was talking to Bill or saw Bill or something, then I went over and asked one of the guys what time it was and to see if we should continue working or what.
Mr. Ball – Did you see any other people on the first floor?
Mr. Lovelady – Oh, yes; by that time there were more; a few of the guys had come in.

Bill Shelley's WC testimony (2186) sounds a bit more honest in this particular instance:

Mr. Ball – When you came into the shipping room did you see anybody?
Mr. Shelley – I saw Eddie Piper.
Mr. Ball – What was he doing?
Mr. Shelley – He was coming back from where he was watching the motorcade in the southwest corner of the shipping room.
Mr. Ball – Of the first floor of the building?
Mr. Shelley – Yes.

137

Mr. Ball – Who else did you see?

Mr. Shelley – That's all we saw immediately.

Mr. Ball – Did you ever see Vickie Adams?

Mr. Shelley – I saw her that day but I don't remember where I saw her.

Mr. Ball – You don't remember whether you saw her when you came back?

Mr. Shelley – It was after we entered the building.

Mr. Ball – You think you did see her after you entered the building?

Mr. Shelley – Yes, sir; I thought it was on the fourth floor awhile after that.

In Victoria Adams' WC testimony (2187) the following is being said about this encounter:

Miss ADAMS - And after the third shot, following that, the third shot, I went to the back of the building down the back stairs, and encountered Bill Shelley and Bill Lovelady on the first floor on the way out to the Houston Street dock.

Mr. Belin - When you say on the way out to the Houston Street dock, you mean now you were on the way out?

Miss ADAMS - While I was on the way out.

Mr. Belin - Was anyone going along with you?

Miss ADAMS - Yes, sir; Sandra Styles.

Mr. Belin - Sometime after the third shot, and I don't want to get into the actual period of time yet, you went back into the stockroom which would be to the north of where your offices are located on the fourth floor, is that correct?

Miss ADAMS - Yes, sir; that's correct.

Mr. Belin - When you got into the stockroom, where did you go?

Miss ADAMS - I went to the back stairs.

Mr. Belin - Are there any other stairs that lead down from the fourth floor other than those back stairs in the rear of the stockroom?

Miss ADAMS - No, sir.

Mr. Belin - Those stairs would be in the northwest comer of the building, is that correct?

Miss ADAMS - That's correct.

Mr. Belin - You took those stairs. Were you walking or running as you went down the stairs?

Miss ADAMS - I was running. We were running.

Mr. Belin - What kind of shoes did you have on?

Miss ADAMS - Three-inch heels.

Mr. Belin - You had heels. Now, as you were running down the stairs, did you encounter anyone?

Miss ADAMS - Not during the actual running down the stairs; no, sir.

Mr. Belin - After you left the Scott Foresman office and went into the stock-room, did you see anyone until you got to the stairs on the fourth floor other than the person you were with?

Miss ADAMS - Outside of our office employees; no.

Mr. Belin - Would these office employees that you might have seen, all be women?

Miss ADAMS - Yes, sir.

Mr. Belin - Then you got to the stairs and you started going down the stairs. You went from the fourth floor to the third floor?

Miss ADAMS - That's correct?

Mr. Belin - Anyone on the stairs then?

Miss ADAMS - No, sir.

Mr. Belin - Let me ask you this. As you got to the stairs on the fourth floor, did you notice whether or not the elevator was running?

Miss ADAMS - The elevator was not moving.

Mr. Belin - How do you know it was not moving on some other floor?

Miss ADAMS - Because the cables move when the elevator is moved, and this is evidenced because of a wooden grate.

Mr. Belin - By that you mean a wooden door with slats in it that you have to lift up to get on the elevator?

Miss ADAMS - Yes.

Mr. Belin - Did you look to see if the elevator was moving?

Miss ADAMS - It was not; no, sir.

Mr. Belin - It was not moving?

Miss ADAMS - No.

Mr. Belin - Did you happen to see where the elevator might have been located?

Miss ADAMS - No, sir.

Mr. Belin - As you got to the third floor, did you take a look at the elevator again at all, or not, if you remember?

Miss ADAMS - I can't recall.

Mr. Belin - As you got off the stairs on the third floor, did you see anyone on the third floor?

Miss ADAMS - No, sir.

Mr. Belin - Then you immediately went to the stairs going down from the third to the second?

Miss ADAMS - That's correct.

Mr. Belin - As you ran down the stairs, did you see anyone on the stairs?

Miss ADAMS - No, sir.

Mr. Belin - All right. You got down to the second floor. Did you see anyone by the second floor?

Miss ADAMS - No, sir.

Mr. Belin - Did you immediately turn and run and keep on running down the stairs towards the first floor?

Miss ADAMS - Yes.

Mr. Belin - When you got to the bottom of the first floor, did you see anyone there as you entered the first floor from the stairway?

Miss ADAMS - Yes, sir.

Mr. Belin - Who did you see?

Miss ADAMS - Mr. Bill Shelley and Billy Lovelady.

Mr. Belin - Where did you see them on the first floor?

Miss ADAMS - Well, this is the stairs, and this is the Houston Street dock that I went out. They were approximately in this position here, so I don't know how you would describe that.

Mr. Belin - You are looking now at a first-floor plan or diagram of the Texas School Book Depository, and you have pointed to a position where you encountered Bill Lovelady and Mr. Bill Shelley?

Miss ADAMS - That's correct.

Mr. Belin - It would be slightly east of the front of the east elevator, and probably as far south as the length of the elevator, is that correct?

Miss ADAMS - Yes, sir.

Mr. Belin - I have a document here called Commission's Exhibit No. 496, which includes a diagram of the first floor, and there is a No. 7 and a circle on it, and I have pointed to a place marked No. 7 on the diagram. Is that correct?

Miss ADAMS - That is approximate.

Mr. Belin - Between the time you got off the stairs and the time you got to this point when you say you encountered them, which was somewhat to the south and a little bit east of the front of the east elevator, did you see any other employees there?

Miss ADAMS - No, sir.

Mr. Belin - Any other people prior to the time you saw them?

Miss ADAMS - No, sir.

Mr. Belin - Now when you were running down the stairs on your trip down the stairs, did you hear anyone using the stairs?

Miss ADAMS - No, sir.

Mr. Belin - Did you hear anyone calling for an elevator?

Miss ADAMS - No, sir.

Mr. Belin - Did you see the foreman, Roy Truly? Did you see the superintendent of the warehouse, Roy S. Truly?

Miss ADAMS - No, sir; I did not.

Mr. Belin - What about any motorcycle police officers?

Miss ADAMS - No, sir.

Mr. Belin - Now what did you do after you encountered Mr. Shelley and Mr. Lovelady?

Miss ADAMS - I said I believed the President was shot.

Mr. Belin - Do you remember what they said?

Miss ADAMS - Nothing.

Mr. Belin - Then what did you do?

Miss ADAMS - I proceeded out to the Houston Street dock.

Barry Ernest discusses this encounter with Adams in his book and even sent her a copy of the statement written up by Jim Leavelle. She had not kept a duplicate of her deposition and had read it only once, in California, some thirty-five years earlier. *"This makes me really wonder about that section in my testimony,"* she wrote after reviewing her words. *"It sounds like the way I did in the rest of the testimony, but I am beginning to wonder if that (her statements regarding Shelley and Lovelady) was inserted into my testimony later."*

Her testimony quoted her as saying she spoke in passing to both men, thinking that Kennedy may have been shot. She did recall making that comment to someone on the first floor, but not to Shelley or Lovelady *"I remember saying to a fairly big black man inside the building right near the loading dock right after I got down the stairs that I thought the President may have been shot. I don't know what his name is. I do know that he worked for the Depository and I think he was a warehouse worker."*

There were two black workers on the first floor at that time, Troy West (2188) and Eddie Piper (2189), of which Eddie Piper appears to be the taller man.

Later, she states: *"And how could I have seen them on the first floor anyway if they were outside the building for that long? When I came down, they wouldn't have returned yet. They weren't there!"* she emphasized (page 256). And when asked by Ernest about the passage in her WC testimony about this encounter she replied, *"I don't recall seeing that section at all, if it had been in there, and since I didn't see them, I would have edited it out."* This of course means that the WC inserted this falsehood or that Adams' was mistaken. Sandra Style's interview with Ernest confirms that the WC was economical with the truth. More about this in her chapter.

When it comes to the evidence, CE 496, is supposed to show the spot where she encountered Shelley and Lovelady. But CE 496 (2190) is Oswald's work application copy at the TSBD and not the floor plan.

In 1999 Ernest called Jim Leavelle and after asking him about a witness called Victoria Adams, Leavelle replied *"No, I don't recall that name."* After some prodding the temporary amnesia started to clear a bit. *"I vaguely recall interviewing a young woman who said that,"* he replied. *"But it wasn't germane to what we were looking for."* *"Wasn't* germane?" I echoed. "What were you looking for?" "We were preparing for trial," Leavelle explained, "and if the witness couldn't provide anything we could use against Oswald, it wasn't important." The trial Leavelle was referring to was Jack Ruby's, and Adams did mention she saw Ruby outside in front of the TSBD.

Then there is another issue with Victoria Adams' WC testimony and that is the fact that she went over her testimony and applied corrections. This is confirmed by the Martha Joe Stroud document from June 2nd 1964 (2191). There are two copies of her WC testimony, one of them was declared *Top Secret (2192)*. Both of them state that the signature was waivered, yet the one that was classified *Top Secret* does bear 'her' signature and has corrections in ballpoint pen applied. The signature version was declassified first on November 21st 1967 and then again on February 9th 2011. It is rather peculiar that this document needed to be declassified twice.

When all is said and done, the signed version does include the passage about the Lovelady and Shelley encounter, so how is it possible she overlooked this? On the very same page mentioning them there is one of her corrections. Adams told Barry Ernest that she did not see their names in the WC testimony transcript copy she corrected. And why did the Commission not use this copy as it would be more legitimate since she signed it or, did they have to hide the fact that she corrected this copy and did *not* waive her signature as she had corrected it as shown in the copy from NARA and the Stroud letter?

Sandra Styles

The WR gives the impression that Sandra Styles (2193) did not descend the stairs along with Victoria Adams. Styles could have easily corroborated Adams' story of the descent and the timing of it, but they did not call her to give her testimony. Nor did they call the other two women who were standing near her at the window; Dorothy Garner and Elsie Dorman.

Overall, the documentation on Styles is minimal. She is only recorded in CE 1381 (2194), which was taken in March of 1964. In this document she said that she never knew Oswald let alone actually seeing him in the building. She thought the shots were fireworks and she was unaware where they came from. She and Victoria Adams left to go downstairs via the back stairs and exited the building through a back door. From there on they went through the railroad yard and she was told by a policeman to go back to the front of the building and make her way in. She obliged and made her way through the front entrance and took the front elevator to the fourth floor.

In Barry Ernest's book, *The Girl on the Stairs (2195)*, Victoria Adams asked the people that interviewed her to interview Styles as well. "*In fact, during the initial briefing before my testimony was taken by the attorney (Belin), I asked him why didn't they call Sandra Styles? He said they didn't need her. They had me. That was enough. Looking backwards I think they didn't want to corroborate any evidence. I repeatedly asked all of the agencies that interviewed me to interview and question Sandra Styles. They kept saying they didn't need to. I always thought that very strange, since what I did and when I did it was so important to them, and Sandra was with me until we got outside. She returned to the building before I did, but her descent was at the same time as mine. What I kept saying over and over was that Sandra could affirm what we did immediately after the gunshots.*"

In Ernest's phone interview with Styles the departure to go downstairs after the shots had been fired was discussed: "*Well, I watched the motorcade as it approached and turned the corner,*" she said. "*I saw Jackie's pink suit, and then it went behind a big tree in the front of the building. I heard the shots and thought they were firecrackers. The car was moving slowly and I saw Jackie get onto the trunk there was lots of movement by Jackie. I saw the Secret Service agent get on the car and push her back in. I can't remember anymore.*" "*Mrs. Butler,*" I said, "*think hard. Do you remember whether you actually saw Kennedy's car go into the underpass?*" She paused. "*No, I don't remember seeing that at all,*" she answered. "*That was when we left.*"

In 2013 Sean Murphy had an email exchange with Sandra Styles (2196). Some of the answers were surprising to hear.

"*In my first email I asked Sandra to respond to the following words from Barry (as posted on a research forum), who was himself responding to what Sandra had told me a couple of years back.*"

'*When I interviewed Sandra Styles in 2002, she said absolutely nothing of the kind to me. What she did say was, she couldn't be sure exactly how quickly she left the window and went down the stairs, but she recalled she did so "rather quickly," in her words, and "when Vicki did," again in her words. Why she would say otherwise now, especially when she said what she did then and added, "Vicki was the more observant one," is beyond me.*'

Here was Sandra's response: *'First of all, I do not recall that Barry put much emphasis on the timing or that we spent time discussing that aspect. I stand by what I said to you. At the time, I first thought we went downstairs quickly; but in thinking about it further, I came to the conclusion that it was not immediately. I told an interviewer (FBI? not sure) that when we got downstairs, the police were there so I assumed we went down quickly; however, the interviewer told me that it took the police 15-20 minutes to get to the Depository, so I accepted that we must have taken longer to get downstairs than I first thought. I went with what Victoria said because she spoke with such certainty; since I couldn't say for sure, I didn't argue with her. She also told office workers that on the way down, she noticed the freight elevator cables were moving. I'm not sure what that would prove; but since I did not notice that, that is what I meant when I said she was more observant. Barry was working closely with her, and I didn't want to get into it with her when I couldn't prove it either way.*

Barry's main discussion with me concerned the outlay of the office: the exact location of the back stairs in relation to the other elevator, which direction the building faced, etc. Since I didn't have scanning capabilities, I had to describe all that verbally in several emails. We were all interviewed several times by different entities over the next year. I always said the same thing to each one: that I had nothing of importance to help their investigation. Their concern was whether I knew Oswald, had ever seen him, etc. As to the timing of the whole thing, I wasn't sure then and can't say for certain now. I only go by what seems reasonable. I can only report my personal recollections the best I can. I was easily led back then, lol. If she said we went down immediately, I thought that must be true. If the interviewer said that was not possible due to the amount of time it took the police to get over there, I re-thought it and accepted HIS assessment. The truth may lie somewhere in between.

What is logical is that, in all the pandemonium, it is unlikely that we would hear shots and head for the back stairs!'

In my reply, I put two points to Sandra:

1) The authorities' claim that it took 15-20 minutes for police to get to the Depository was way off.

2) Barry had come across the so-called Stroud document, in which Dorothy Ann Garner is reported to have told authorities she saw Baker and Truly come up onto the fourth floor AFTER Adams and Styles had left it.

144

Sandra's response: *'Hmmmmmmm, points to ponder. At this point, I'm wondering whether I was even there! Hahaha. My initial sense was that we went down soon after, and the 15-20 minute delay given by the investigator DID seem a bit long, but I took his word for it. We did linger at the window a bit trying to sort it out, and I'm sure it was Vicki's idea to go find out what was going on; therefore, we wouldn't have waited a long time to make the decision to go downstairs. I am certain that we went to the public elevator first, but may not have waited long there either. My hesitancy on the timing in all the interviews probably accounts for why they did not pursue further information from me. As I told everyone who ever asked, I had no real sense of that aspect of the investigation. Still, logic tells me it had to take a couple of minutes at least for things to sink in and to make the decision to go. Therefore, I'll give up a few of those minutes but still don't remember it's being a matter of a few seconds. However, I yield to wiser heads if the evidence is there.*

I know nothing of Dorothy Garner's part. I don't know where she was at the time. Her office was near the front elevator, but she could have been in the lunch area on the other side near the back stairs. It seems odd to me that if the two men ran up the back stairs a minute or so after the shooting, we did not encounter them on our way down even if we had left immediately and even more strange that Mrs. Garner would have been in a position to see them coming up. It all goes back to the fact that I could be totally off on my calculations, and anything is possible. I cannot swear in any venue that what I thought was actually true. I still see it all in my mind's eye and have not changed my opinion about what we did and when, but I could be mistaken about the number of minutes. I suppose I could blame the fact that I am 71 and let it go at that!! No, that would be too easy.'

In my reply, I asked Sandra a number of follow-up questions:

Could she recall what her initial time estimate for their going to the stairs was - i.e. before she was told that the police didn't get to the Depository for 15-20 minutes?

Her answer: *'Not less than a minute, I thought more like a couple. I do realize that time takes on feet of its own in a situation like a shooting or other catastrophe, and witnesses have different takes on it. I am glad to have the 15-minute thing put to rest; even then it didn't make sense that it would take the DPD that long to cross the street.'*

Could she describe the layout of the fourth floor?

Her answer: *'Here is the layout of the office: Mr. Bergen's office was in the SE corner and opened into the reception area, as did the public elevator and Dorothy's office. Directly across from Dorothy's office was a small conference room. Behind the reception area were the desks of the Customer Service Reps (I was one of those) and Records (Elsie's job). Then there were the stacks where free teacher aids and supplies were kept. On the other side of the stacks was the break/lunch area (not a separate enclosed room), which had a table, coffeepot and a refrigerator (no drink machine). It was all open; the only doors were in the bosses' offices, the conference room, and the back. The elevator opened directly into the reception area. The door in the NW corner of the break room led to the stairs/freight elevator/ storage area.'*

Could she give any more detail on Victoria's observation about the elevator cables moving?

Her answer: *'I don't remember any of that. She didn't mention it to me on the way down or up. As I recall, she only mentioned it later offhandedly, but I don't recall the circumstances as to how or exactly when it came up in conversation.'*

When it comes to the so called Shelley and Lovelady encounter Sandra Styles said the following in Barry Ernest's book, *The Girl on the Stairs (2197)*, page 260. *"A few people were milling around on the first floor,"* she said. *"One was a black man."* That was apparently the same man Ms Adams had mentioned. I casually asked her if William Shelley or Billy Lovelady were there. *"No,"* she said, emphasizing she would have recognized them, since she knew both men well.

At a later date when Ernest asked her again whether she saw Shelley and Lovelady on the first floor she answered *"No, I didn't. I believe they were at the front entrance, and we went out the back door and around to the front of the building. I believe most of the Depository employees were watching from the front entrance. I have seen at least one picture in which Billy is with that group."* When Ernest tells her that Victoria Adams' testimony refers to Shelley and Lovelady being there when both women arrived there, she said *"I can't imagine why Vicki would have said that-if she did. They definitely weren't there."* And when asked for her opinion about a possible insertion of said incident into Adams' WC testimony she replied *"All I can say, is that Shelley and Lovelady definitely were not on the first floor when we got there."* (page 261).

This independent corroboration destroys the so-called Lovelady and Shelley encounter created in February 1964 in the report made up by

Jim Leavelle and also its insertion into the WC testimony of Victoria Adams.

In this rare interview Styles states she did not see Oswald come down the stairs (2198).

Elsie Dorman

Elsie Dorman (2198) was a supervisor of book distribution for Scott Foresman Educational Publishers. She stood close by to Victoria Adams, Sandra Styles and Dorothy Garner in the open window on the fourth floor. Dorman had borrowed the camera, a Kodak Brownie 2, from her husband. View the Elsie Dorman film here (2199).

She had never used the camera before and it shows. The limo is facing the TSBD and turning on to Elm. From a camera POV this is not the best footage. You can see the Towners on the corner and also Rosemary Willis (the girl that ran along the limo) who was also captured by Zapruder.

Dorman is first interviewed by the FBI on November 24th (2200). She does not know Oswald and failed to recognise him from photographs. She was filming when the limo turned and when the shots began, she stopped filming. She thought the shots came from the County Records building.

In CE 1381 (2201), page 13 she describes that she was filming with her husband's camera which she did not know that well. While filming she hears the noise of gunshots. She did not know Oswald or recognise him.

In 1978 Dorman is interviewed by the HSCA (2202). When *"trouble"* started, she stopped filming and moved away from the window. The window was the sixth from the Houston St side. She then left the office to look out the window from the west side of the building and then returned back to her office. She also relays that she was fingerprinted and so were her colleagues. They had to leave their details before they could leave the building. First time I heard that employees were fingerprinted *before* they could leave. This is a mix up. Their fingerprints were taken in the week(s) shortly after until Roy Truly put a stop to it. The document continues with, *"Hazy as to the type of persons officiating."* The FBI and the USSS did get in touch with her, but she cannot exactly recall when this was. The FBI did *not* take possession of her film, which was not developed for quite some after the assassination. She saw the stills first when they were published in LIFE magazine.

147

Dorothy Garner

Dorothy Garner (2203) was the supervisor of Victoria Adams and Sandra Styles, and like Styles her testimony was completely ignored. Victoria Adams described her as an efficient, no-nonsense kind of lady, demanded punctuality and a great job. She basically ran the branch by herself. *"Quite frankly she intimidated me and I followed her orders and instructions to a 'tee', because I was both scared of her and respected her. She demanded the best, watched the clock like a hawk and tolerated no nonsense no talking when she ruled her kingdom."*

"If you can picture and old-fashioned prim librarian telling everyone to 'shush', you have an idea of the power and demeanour of Dorothy Garner. To my recollection nothing ever slipped by Dorothy Garner, except us that day. She was extremely detail oriented and was very proud of what she did. She was both feared and respected by the staff" (page 253).

In CE 1381 (2204), she states that she was looking through the fifth window from the east on the fourth floor. Elsie Dorman was sitting next to her. And next to them Adams and Styles in the sixth window. At the time of the gunshots, she could not see the limo as it was obscured by a tree. She thought they were coming from the west of the building. She did not recall ever seeing Lee Oswald in the building. She left the TSBD at 14:30.

When Garner was interviewed by Barry Ernest and was asked how fast Victoria Adams and Sandra Styles left from the window*? "The girls did,"* she responded. *"I remember them being there and the next thing I knew, they were gone."* They had left *"very quickly . . . within a matter of moments,"* she added (page 267).

She leaves the window shortly after Adams and Styles have left and makes it towards the North Western corner of the TSBD near the stairs. This area is where several TSBD employees gathered due to the excellent view of the railroad yard and the picket fence area. The three African Americans, (Williams, Jarman and Norman) descending from the fifth floor saw them looking out from the North Western windows.

From Ernest's book, Mrs. Garner said she immediately went to this area, following *"shortly after . . . right behind"* Miss Adams and Miss Styles. She couldn't remember exactly why she went there, other than *"probably to get something."* Mrs. Garner said she did not actually see *'the girls'* enter the stairway, though, arriving on the fourth-floor

148

landing seconds later. When I asked how she knew they had gone down right away, Mrs Garner replied, "I remember hearing them, after they started down. I remember the stairs were very noisy" (page 267).

But then in 1999 Barry Ernest finds a whopper of a document at the National Archives (2205). -- *one that slipped through the cracks*. This particular document first shows that Victoria Adams had corrections applied to her testimony, but then shifts to Garner's statement. What statement? Where is it? Then it also shows that she saw Baker and Truly had ascended the stairs *after* Adams and Styles had descended them.

Fifth Floor

The fifth floor was solely for storage; there were no offices present. Here is the fifth floor FBI diagram (2206).

This floor got a lot of attention due to the Dillard photo (2207) of the three African Americans, Bonnie Ray Williams (2208), Harold Dean Norman (2209) and James 'junior' Jarman (2210) looking through the windows in the South Eastern corner of the building just after the shots had been fired. They were noticed by a few spectators down below including Howard Brennan. Some of the photographers also noticed them. Tom Dillard (2211) took a very sharp photo of the whole building with them in it, and so did Military Intelligence officer, James Powell 2212).

These three men are, to my mind, the most inconsistent witnesses during and just after the assassination of JFK. By putting the statements that they have made alongside with their WC and HSCA testimonies, cracks start to appear in their story. These three witnesses, like the two on the first floor, must have been under tremendous pressure from the authorities during that time.

And while they are upstairs on the fifth floor and descend to the fourth, they stay there for a short while to talk to the women who have gathered to look out of the window on the West side near the stairwell. This indicates that they are not bothered at all about a possible gunman two floors higher up, neither do they convey any of this to the women; if they had, then those women would be marching downstairs rapidly.

Once arriving on the first floor they are prevented from leaving through the front door. They happen to see Howard Brennan talking to Herbert Sawyer, yet they still make no mention whatsoever of their experience.

If they had relayed what they ultimately testified to, the cops would have run up to the sixth floor directly!

It is only Williams who is sent to the DPD to give a statement; Jarman does this on the 23rd and Norman (who claimed to hear the bolt movement and shells drop) does this on the 26th.

Then there are photographs (2213) of the three men to re-enact where they were in the fifth-floor windows (2214). These three guys along with Eddie Piper and Troy West are the only employees photographed and profiled in this manner.

Bonnie Ray Williams

- Williams managed to get outside and hook up with Danny Garcia. They were recorded in the Robert Hughes (2215) and John Martin (2216) films trying to get back in the building. This is at about 12:50-13:00.
- At about 13:30, Williams is seen walking alongside Bill Shelley and Danny Arce Garcia (2217) towards a Dallas Police patrol car which takes them to City Hall. In this Jack Beers photograph (2218), you can clearly see the dust marks across his shirt from leaning out of the window.
- The first handwitten DPD statement Williams (2219) gave, was taken shortly after Oswald was brought straight in after his arrest at the Texas Theatre.
  The statement says that he travelled back up to the fifth floor with Norman and Jarman after grabbing their lunches from the first floor.
- After the shooting, in that same statement Williams states after some officers had come up, they took the elevator down to the fourth floor and stayed there a while.
- The handwritten statement has also been typed on November 22nd (2220).
- In his handwritten DPD (November 22nd), his FBI November 23rd (2221) and Secret Service December 7th (2222) statements, he hears two shots coming from above.
- His FBI statement from November 23rd (2223) states that Williams worked until 11:30 and took an elevator from the sixth floor down to the first. He saw that Charles Douglas Givens was in the other elevator. He saw Oswald on the fifth floor while going down. He saw him before at 08:00. At noon he went back up to the sixth floor with an elevator, he stayed on that floor for about

150

three minutes. He then descended to the fifth floor using the stairs and then joined Hank Norman and James Junior Jarman. He leaned out and looked up after the two shots, but saw nothing. They then ran to the west to look out of the window from that side not realising the President had been shot. A policeman came up to the fifth floor and looked all around and then left. Would this be Marrion Baker? None of the three saw anyone coming down from the sixth floor via the stairs. They then make their way down to the fourth floor where many women (!) had gathered around the West side of that floor.

- In his USSS statement from December 7th (2224) Williams states that Oswald asks, just before lunch, from either the fifth or sixth floor to have the elevator sent back up. This is not done. Why not?

- It is Williams' bag that is found soon afterwards by the DPD on the sixth floor. The lunch bag is filled with chicken bones and there is also an empty bottle of Dr. Pepper. He consumed his lunch there before he moves down to the fifth floor. He says that he hooks up with Jarman and Norman at or just before 12:15. During the shooting he does *not* hear the shells fall nor hears the bolt action of the rifle. After the shots have been fired, they move to the West side of the building and look out of the windows there. Saw a policeman near the stairwell, who did not see him. Did not know whether he was going up or down. About five minutes had passed when they decide to go downstairs to the first floor.

- In CE 1381 (2225), page 50, he mentions three shots from above.

- In that same CE 1381 document he states that little pieces of cement hit him on top of his head. He repeats this during his WC testimony. Williams is not directly below the so-called sniper's window.

- In both FBI reports he states that after going west to look out he sees a policeman coming out of the elevator before the three men make their way down via the stairs to the fourth floor.

- Disputes going from the sixth floor to the fifth via the stairs, he used the east elevator instead.

- During an HSCA interview Williams disputes going to the fifth floor with Norman and Jarman. Yet he is the one who wrote the DPD affidavit. The sixth-floor omission may be due to fear of being implicated with the assassination.

151

Williams is recorded by the networks a few times, here filmed for CBS (2226) in 1964. Then by the same network for The WR (2227) documentary.

Bonnie Ray Williams' WC testimony (2228).

- Williams never spoke with Oswald; he would see him in the lunchroom (that is the Domino room on the first floor) and he would eat a sandwich or read the paper.
- Williams saw Oswald a little after 08:00 with a clipboard in his hand. He saw him again at 11:30 and ten minutes before 12:00. Williams works on the sixth floor all morning with Bill Shelley, Charles Givens and Danny Arce.
- He is not sure whether he saw Oswald on the sixth floor. He thinks he saw him messing around with some boxes on the Eastern side of the elevator.
- Williams states that Oswald shouts out for an elevator to be sent back up. He is not sure whether it was from the fifth or sixth floor.
- He returns later with his lunch to the sixth floor and is by himself eating his lunch in the third or fourth set of windows from the Southeast corner. He stays there for 5-10, 12 minutes. But a little later he will not stick to the 5 minutes, he has no idea how much time he spent on the sixth floor.
- He then moves to the fifth floor by taking the East elevator down. He sees Harold Norman and James Jarman there.
- The November 23rd FBI affidavit is brought up in which Williams stated he took the stairs instead of the elevator, but he denies having said that.
- In the January 14th FBI affidavit Williams is recorded as having taken the West elevator. He denies this as well.
- When the shots were fired, he heard the second and third shots closer together.
- Does not remember sticking his head out.
- Does not pay attention to the first shot, but says that the second and third shots sounded like it was right in the building.
- Cement/gravel/dirt fell on his head; Harold Norman made him aware of that. Norman also says that the shots came from over their heads and he can even hear the shell being ejected and dropping on the floor. Yet Williams cannot as he isn't paying attention.

- James Jarman moved towards Williams and Norman and says that someone is shooting the President. Jarman does not mention from overhead. They then run to the West side of the building. They look out and see policemen running in the railroad yard.
- Has no real explanation for not going to the sixth floor. Did not think about it. It was Jarman who said, *"maybe we better get the hell out of here."* So, they run down to the fourth and then went further down.
- He knows he stated in his FBI affidavit that he heard two shots, but he was excited and couldn't remember too well (he had stated in his DPD, FBI and USSS statements that he heard 2 shots over a two-week period.
- While having lunch on the sixth floor he did not hear the elevators going.
- While standing at the West end of the building he saw a motorcycle police officer coming round the East elevator wearing his white helmet, which is the only thing he manages to see. Did not hear anyone go up or down the stairs, nor did he hear foot steps up above.
- Upon departure from the fifth floor and going down to the fourth they paused for a minute as they see 2-3 women looking out of the Westerly windows.
- Upon arrival on the first floor, they see policemen had rushed in and firemen were coming in as well.
- Law enforcement officers took their names, addresses and searched them. Once knowing they and others have been working on the sixth floor they are summoned to the Courthouse where they fill in affidavits.
- No one was allowed to leave the building. Jarman and Norman were not with him even though all three came down on the first floor at the same time. They also stayed behind inside the building when Williams left with Shelley and Arce to have their affidavits taken.
- Williams had difficulty timing the descent after the shots were fired, but ultimately said it was about 15 minutes.
- An officer asked Truly whether *"everyone was here?"* He then heard Roy Truly saying, *"where is Lee?"* and also knows of Charles Douglas Givens who was also missing.

At about 13:30 Bill Shelley, Danny Arce Garcia and Bonnie Ray Williams make their way to a police car which drives them to the DPD as seen in this video (2229) and this still photograph (2230).

153

Harold Dean Norman

- Norman doesn't bring Williams' sixth floor descent up until the WC is in session. Three reports from before his WC testimony state that they all went to the fifth floor together.
- His November 23rd FBI (2231) report makes mention of him stating he stuck his head out and looked up. He disputes this during his WC testimony.
- He heard three shots and also caught the sound of the shells dropping on the floor above him along with the bolt action.
- During that same WC testimony, he says that he could not hear anyone moving above him.
- Did not see any dust falling, but noticed some in Williams' hair.
- Disputes statements made in USSS report from December 7th (2232) In this report he says that he was casually acquainted with Oswald. He saw him last at 10:00 that day. At 12:15 he, Bonnie Ray Williams and James Jarman went to the fifth floor. Heard three shots of which the last two were spaced closely together. He knew immediately that the shots came from above. He heard the bolt action of the rifle and the shells dropping on the floor. He also claimed that dust fell down from the ceiling. He looked out and saw many people go to the Western side of the TSBD. They followed suit by moving West and looked out of the windows on that side. They then decided to move downstairs to the first floor. The time elapsed until their descent was about five minutes. There is no mention of a stop on the fourth floor.
- In CE 1381 (2233) Norman states that he was on the fifth floor with Jarman and Williams between 12:10-12:20. He heard three shots, believed from the floor above him. He leaves the building at about 14:00.
- During his WC testimony (2234) he disowns the fourth floor stop even after asked about it by John J McCloy during his WC testimony by saying *"I believe we went all the way."*
- Does not remember making a statement that he said that he knew the shots came from directly above them.
- Nor does he remember saying that he heard shots several seconds later.
- By the time he gets outside he sees Brennan being interviewed who confirms Norman as one of the people he saw in the window.

154

- He times the period from the first shot to their descent to the first floor at between 10-15 minutes.
- Norman makes it to outside on the steps and is told to get back inside.
- During his HSCA interview on October 20th 1977 (2235) he disputes giving a statement to the FBI on November 26th (2236)
- He also did not see Jack Dougherty while being on the fifth floor.
- In the Indiana Gazette of November 8th 1983 (2237) Norman states: *"I didn't see the gun barrel, but I did see the debris that fell in one of my friend's hair. I could hear a gun going off above us and the debris fell each time there was a shot. "The debris was dust and tiny pieces of concrete broken loose by the concussion of the rifle"*.
- In this video (2238) for The Men Who Killed Kennedy documentary, Norman remembers seeing Oswald earlier in the morning and not after that.

Harold Norman's WC testimony (2239):

Mr. Ball. The document that I have here shows the date 4th of December 1963. Do you remember having made a statement to Mr. Carter, Special Agent of the Secret Service, on that day?
Mr. NORMAN. I can't remember the exact date but I believe I remember Mr. Carter.
Mr. Ball. I want to call your attention to one part of the statement and I will ask you if you told him that:

"Just after the President passed by, I heard a shot and several seconds later I heard two more shots. I knew that the shots had come from directly above me, and I could hear the expended cartridges fall to the floor. I could also hear the bolt action of the rifle. I also saw some dust fall from the ceiling of the fifth floor and I felt sure that whoever had fired the shots was directly above me."

Did you make that statement to the Secret Service man?

Mr. NORMAN. I don't remember making a statement that I knew the shots came from directly above us. I didn't make that statement. And I don't remember saying I heard several seconds later. I merely told him that I heard three shots because I didn't have any idea what time it was.
Mr. Ball. I see. Did you tell them that you heard the bolt action of the rifle?
Mr. NORMAN. Yes.
Mr. Ball. And that you heard the expended cartridges fall to the floor?

155

Mr. NORMAN. Yes; I heard them making a sound.
Mr. Ball. I would like to offer this into evidence.
Mr. McCloy. It may be admitted.

(The document referred to, heretofore identified as Commission Exhibit No. 493 for identification, was received in evidence.)

Norman is also quoted in the Lubbock Avalanche Journal of September 28th 1964 (2240), which rhymes nicely with the release of the WR.

Norman is also part of The Trial of Lee Harvey Oswald (2241), held in London. That he is in prosecutor Vincent Bugliosi's pocket is more than evident. As soon as defence attorney Gerry Spence is questioning him Norman throws looks towards Bugliosi's direction.

During Norman's HSCA interview (2242) he states the following:

- All three of them went up together in the freight elevator.
- Williams got his lunch off the food truck outside, Norman and Jarman brought theirs.
- They sat by the windows on the fifth floor on boxes.
- He does not notice Jack Dougherty on the fifth floor.
- Jarman tells Norman of the debris in his hair.
- After telling Oswald that The President would be coming past, Oswald apparently draws two imaginary pistols from his non-existent holster and goes 'pfew' like a cowboy would and he makes his way somewhere else.
- Even though he has heard the shells dropping, debris fell on his hair and is of the opinion that the shots were fired from above, Norman has not heard any footsteps at all.
- After having a look from the opposite end to see what is happening down in the railroad yard, they depart for the fourth floor and see several ladies standing and looking out of the windows in the North Western corner.
- They then leave for the first floor and as soon they arrive policemen arrive inside the building.
- Norman says he saw Roy Truly on the first floor but is not sure whether that was when they arrived downstairs. Later on, he states that Truly tells him that they cannot leave as one of the officers had told him so.
- Norman does not recall Billy Lovelady being on the first floor when they arrived down there. This is because Lovelady is still outside the TSBD and does not gain entry until 12:50 – 13:00.
- When Norman and others are let go there is no idea that they were looking for Oswald as being the shooter of The President.

Later, during his testimony, he does not recall that anyone was missing after a head count. He repeats this during the interview.

- Neither the police nor anyone else talked to him about what happened that day or during the weekend.
- In March/April 1964 he is fingerprinted.
- The DPD took no affidavit from him; Norman disputes giving one to the FBI on November 26th.
- He disputes that he stuck his head out and looked upwards.
- He sees Truly standing close by the front door and his office who then vouches for him, Jarman and Williams.

In this documentary for PBS Frontline (2243) he says: *"We were looking out towards Elm Street, so he walked up and asked us, said, 'What is everybody looking for? What's everybody waiting on?' So, we told him we was waiting on the President to come by. He put his hands in his pocket and laughed and walked away, so I don't know where he went, or if he went upstairs or downstairs or where."* And later, *"The shots came from above and there was a gun and the shots were sounding, 'Boom! Click, click. Boom! Click, click. Boom! Click, click,' So there was three shots fired right up over us when we were sitting on the fifth floor."*

James 'Junior' Jarman

- In the Tom Dillard photo (2244) James Jarman can be seen in the far left window on the fifth floor.
- His DPD affidavit from the 23rd (2245) mentions only Oswald and the morning of the 22nd up to the moment of the shooting and stops there.
- In his November 24th affidavit from the FBI (2246) and the Secret Service report from Dec 4th 1963 he states that he went up to the fifth floor with Williams and Norman.
- In that same FBI affidavit, he states that after going West they discussed and decided the shots had come from above.
- Harold Norman made a remark about something falling on his head and piece of debris hitting him in the face.
- In the Secret Service Report from December 7th (2247) he states that he did not hear the shells drop nor the bolt action.
- His estimate is that they stayed upstairs for about 5 minutes before making their way down.
- Saw woman leaning out of a window on fourth floor on their way down! Did not see police officer come up.

- In an affidavit for the FBI on January 14th 1964 (2248) on page 15 Jarman says that the three of them had lunch at 12:00 on the first floor and went to the fifth floor at 12:25 using the West elevator. There is a peculiar sentence in this document: *"He said that Ray and Norman were with him all the time he was on the first floor and they did not see Lee Harvey Oswald at any time between 12 noon and until they returned to the first floor after the shooting"*.
- During his WC testimony (2249) Jarman stated that they went back around the building and Norman and he went with an elevator to the fifth floor. The East one was stuck on the sixth floor. Their arrival on the fifth floor is timed by Jarman at 12:25-12:28.
- Bonnie Ray Williams arrived a few minutes later while on the fifth floor.
- Three shots (second and third in quick succession), thought the first one came from below. After the third shot he gets up and moves towards Harold Norman and tells them that someone is shooting at The President.
- Notices debris in Williams' hair. Norman was sure the shot came from inside the building.
- Confirms Norman stating the sound of the shells and the bolt action *after* they had moved West. He did not hear it at all when it happened.
- While on the West side of the fifth he could not see the elevators, nor Roy Truly, a motorcycle policeman or hear the elevators go up.
- When they ran for the West elevator, it had gone down. They took the stairs instead and pause a few minutes on the fourth floor.
- Once arriving on the first floor he sees Eddie Piper and Roy Edward Lewis first.
- Norman and Jarman make their way out of the front door.
- He sees Howard Brennan run and talk to a police officer (must be Herbert Sawyer who is captured interviewing him) and overhears him speaking about the rifle barrel sticking out of the window. And that the shots came from inside the building. Jarman confirmed this to Sawyer and is then rushed back inside.
- Confirmed his November 23rd statement for the DPD
- Says that Givens and Oswald were missing after a line-up showing their IDs.

- Did not hear any noises from above him just before and just after the shooting.
- He timed the departure for going West from the original position at about one minute.
- On Friday the 22nd he had heard Bill Shelley talk about The President passing by. After that, Lee Oswald approached Jarman and asked him what it was about and he explained, to which Oswald replied with, *"Oh; I see."*
- In CBS' *The Warren Report* (2250) Jarman says that Oswald had asked him what the people gathered outside for. And Jarman had told him that The President was to come by that morning. After which Oswald asked him at what time and which direction he would be coming by. Then turned around and left.
- During his HSCA testimony (2251) Jarman says at first, he thought the shots came from below. Norman stated they came from above.
- He pointed out the debris on Williams' head.
- Hank Norman wanted to take the elevator down after which Jarman said, *"damn the elevator."*
- Jarman had heard from Billy Lovelady that Oswald was allowed out after Roy Truly said he was alright. The police told them to go back inside when they got to the door.
- In an HSCA checking over his DPD/FBI/USSS statements on April 17th 1978 (2252) he states that the Secret Service statement is wrong with attributing him as being part of the floor laying crew.

Jack Edwin Dougherty

At this point in time Jack Dougherty's (2253) photo is not available. Several people have tried to find and recognise him in photographs from High School or military classes and so far, none have been confirmed as being him. His family members have been recognised and I know about his face a bit. But so far, no cigar.

Jack Edwin Dougherty suffered from what we now call PTSD He had fought during the Second World War and that had quite an effect on him in subsequent years. He routinely arrived for work early in the morning; Joe Molina would open up the building while Dougherty went about with his checks of the equipment inside the TSBD.

Roy Truly described Jack Dougherty in his WC testimony (2254):

Mr. Belin. Did you see anyone on the fifth floor?

Mr. Truly. Yes. When coming down I am sure I saw Jack Dougherty getting some books off the fifth floor. Now, this is so dim in my mind that I could be making a mistake. But I believe that he was getting some stock, that he had already gone back to work, and that he was getting some stock off the fifth floor.

Mr. Belin. You really don't know who was operating the elevator, then, is that correct?

Mr. Truly. That is correct.

Mr. Belin. What is your best guess?

Mr. Truly. My best guess is that Jack Dougherty was.

[And later...]

Mr. Belin. Mr. Truly, you mentioned the fact that you thought Jack Dougherty was the one operating that west elevator. Is that correct?

Mr. Truly. Yes, sir.

Mr. Belin. Could you tell us a little bit about Jack Dougherty?

Mr. Truly. Jack Dougherty has been working for us 12 or 14 years. Until we moved into this building, he has been mostly in our State Department, the building at 1917 North Houston. He would fill orders for--that called for many cartons of books on a three-textbook-order basis to the various schools in Texas. And he seemed to be intelligent and smart and a hard worker. The main thing is he just worked all the time. I have never had any occasion to have any hard words for Jack. A few times he would get a little bit---maybe do a little something wrong, and I would mention it to him, and he would just go to pieces--not anything--but anything the rest of the day or the next day would not be right. [Deletion] He is a great big husky fellow. I think he is 39 years old. He has never been married. He has no interest in women. He gets flustered, has a small word for it, at times. He has never had any trouble. He is a good, loyal, hard-working employee. He always has been.

Mr. Belin. Would you _consider him of average intelligence?

Mr. Truly. Yes, sir. I think what is wrong with him mostly is his emotional makeup. I would say that for the work he is doing, he is of average intelligence.

Mr. Belin. When you got to the fifth floor, as I understand it, the west elevator was not there, but when you started up from the first floor, you thought it was on the fifth floor.

Mr. Truly. No. When I came down from the second floor---from the seventh floor with the officer, I thought I saw Jack Dougherty on the fifth floor, which he would have had plenty of time to move the elevator down and up and get some stock and come back.

160

- In his handwritten DPD statement (2255) from November 22nd Dougherty is already way off. By stating that he went back up after lunch at 12:45 and then hears a shot. The time of the shooting is at or just after 12:30. It is Walter Eugene Potts who takes his statement who notes in his HSCA interview (2256) that Dougherty recognised Oswald when he was brought in just after 14:00.
- He goes down to the fifth floor to get some stock and hears a shot that came from inside the building, but couldn't tell where from.
- He goes down to the first floor and meets Eddie Piper who tells him he heard three shots.
- He saw Oswald on the sixth floor shortly before noon and did not see him in the building after lunch.
- His DPD typed statement from November 22nd (2257) does not differ from the handwritten one.
- Dougherty states in this handwritten FBI report on November 22nd (2258) he did not see Lee Oswald after 11:00.
- While being on the fifth floor Dougherty hears a shot that came from above.
- His typed FBI November 22nd statement (2259) does not differ from the handwritten one.
- In his USSS report from December 7th (2260) Dougherty states that he has been with the firm for 11 years.
- He was part of the floor laying crew.
- Dougherty is described as confused about times & places. Roy Truly describes him as mentally retarded, but a good and hard worker. He has trouble remembering dates, times, places and facts. And has been especially confused since the assassination. And therefore, the interview was discontinued.
- In an FBI affidavit from December 14th (2261) he goes back to not knowing where the shot had come from! And this time he saw Oswald shortly before noon on the sixth floor. Dougherty's dad is with him explaining his son's issues.
- In his December 19th FBI affidavit (2262) he states that he did not see Oswald after 11:00. He again states that he quits for lunch at 12 noon and then goes back to the sixth floor at 12:45 and then goes down to the fifth floor. He then heard the shot, assuming it is from within the building, but not knowing where. He then goes down to the first floor and meets Eddie Piper and asked him whether he heard the loud noise and he says that he heard three of them and that someone had shot The President. Then he takes the elevator back up to the sixth floor. It is again

mentioned that Dougherty has difficulty correlating his speech. Dougherty's father is present while this affidavit is taken.

- The WC is not too impressed with Dougherty. In a memo from March 12th 1964 (2263) Melvin A Eisenberg writes that he wants a thorough investigation of Jack Dougherty as he is suspicious of him for various reasons.
- In CE 1381 (2264) Dougherty states he was ten feet away from the fifth-floor elevator when he heard the shot. He left the TSBD at 13:30 to give an affidavit at the DPD and returns at 16:30 to collect his coat.

Dougherty's WC testimony (2265):

- Lunch is at 12 noon. Work starts at 08:00, but Dougherty gets there an hour earlier.
- Saw Oswald come through the door at 08:00 while he was sitting on the wrapping table (Troy West's domain), Oswald was not carrying anything. He is asked 3x about this by Joseph Ball.
- Saw Oswald on the sixth floor at about 11:00. And he did not see him after that.
- Confusion reigns during Dougherty's testimony around the noon period.
- He makes his way down to the first floor by elevator and he eats his lunch in the Domino Room.
- Dougherty did not go outside on the steps as they were too crowded.
- After lunch he goes back to the sixth floor and from there down to the fifth to grab some stock when he hears one shot which to him sounded from overhead somewhere.
- He made his way down to the first floor and spoke to Eddie Piper who tells him that he heard three shots and that The President has been shot.
- Dougherty was confronted with his previous statements to show the inconsistencies.
- He was confronted strongly by Joseph Ball about his impression of where the gunfire came from. At the time of the statement, he did not tell them where it came from, yet at the time, he did think that the shot came from above.
- He was ten feet away to the West from the West elevator when it happened. His took that elevator down to the first floor.
- Did not hear Roy Truly shouting up the shaft.

162

- Nor did he see Truly when he was on the first floor. He was subsequently asked to find him by an FBI agent. He does not manage to find him, but he finds out later that he (Truly) was on the fourth floor. Why can Dougherty not find Truly who is in a relatively small and open building?
- Bill Shelley told him after the assassination that Oswald had carried in a package.
- While Dougherty was on the fifth floor when the shot rang out, he did not see anyone else there. Same for the sixth floor.
- Then confusion is back when Dougherty states he heard the shot before lunch not after.

I managed to track down a taped interview of him with Fred Newcomb in the early 70's. Dougherty mentions that he:

- Had worked at the TSBD for 18 years. Still working for them after the move at the time of his interview.
- Doesn't blame law enforcement agencies for the treatment they gave him, *"they had a job to do."*
- When asked when somebody took his statement on the 22nd he first states that it was a newspaper reporter from Ohio who called him at 03:00 the night after the assassination (there is proof he spoke to the FBI and the DPD that day and he wrote down his statements).
  When asked again he responds, *"Oh, same day."* FBI agents taking statements of employees inside the TSBD.
- He sees four FBI agents on the second floor and two on the first questioning employees.
- Later, when asked about his WC testimony appearance he said that he was on holiday at that time and was half asleep when he gave his testimony.
- When the subject of his co-workers on the fifth floor is brought up, he becomes very careful with his answers and said he could not see them due to the boxes and that he was on the other side of the floor.
- He claims to have seen Oswald eating his lunch in the second-floor lunchroom and to have had lunch in the Domino Room. The reality is that Oswald come lunch time would sit in the Domino room and drink his 'coke' with his lunch! And in statements for the DPD and the FBI, he did not see him (Oswald) after 11:00 or just before noon, whichever statement you wish to choose.

163

- He says he saw Roy Truly when he came down to the first floor, which strains Truly's speed of ascent up to the second floor and above. Dougherty did not relay what had happened to Truly since he was not asked by him.
- Did not see a helmeted police officer while being down on the first floor.
- Truly had gone to a different floor when he was asked to find him by an FBI agent.

It is obvious that Dougherty is a very inconsistent as a witness.

Sixth Floor

There are quite a few photographs (2266) taken of the sixth floor. You can see that the floor is covered with boxes containing books. The area where the rifle was found and the 'sniper's nest' are mapped out as well.

Spaulden Jones (2267) took a very interesting photograph of two agents inside the 'sniper's nest' with a phone line at their disposal on November 23rd.
There is no evidence of Oswald being there during the shooting.

Seventh Floor

The seventh floor was only used as a storage area. It had a ladder going to the roof of which the door to it was locked with a latch.
There are two FBI drawings: HERE (2268) and HERE (2269).
Deputy Sheriff John Wiseman (2270), found access to the roof to be locked on the inside by a gate type lock latch. There is no one else who can attest to Truly & Baker being up there and looking over the rooftop edge and spending that much time on that roof.

Chapter III

The Interrogations

The reports on Oswald's interrogations inside the WR can be read at Mary Ferrell's website (3001). The WR addresses the interrogations, Oswald's legal rights, the press and subsequent death in Chapter Five entitled *"Detention and Death of Oswald." (3002)*

The WC Report: An early critique by Sylvia Meagher (3003), released in November 1964 produced, only two months after the WR release can be regarded as one of the first in-depth looks into Oswald's interrogations (pages 23-27).

Oswald at Youth House in New York 1953

One aspect of this case I wanted to include in this segment was Oswald's Youth House psychiatry tests in 1953 (3004). He stayed at Youth House due to his increased absence from school late 1952 to the beginning of 1953, in New York. Youth House was a remand centre for delinquent boys who had gotten into trouble with the court and were remanded to Youth House for a brief period of diagnostic study.

These psychiatry tests may give us some insight into who Lee Harvey Oswald was at this stage of his life. And do these tests have any relation to his behaviour while being incarcerated November 22nd - 24th 1963?

Oswald was admitted on April 16th 1953, and his first psychiatry test was taken and reported upon April 21st by John Carro (3005). Some of the pages of the above linked document are very hard to read due to the terrible reproduction quality. The first 4/5 pages of the 33 is the report that has been made up by Carro. Pages 1 & 2 start with Oswald's background and then on the second page it states that *Lee is a boy of average height and weight and the boy impressed the PO* (probation officer-BK) *of a boy of normal mental and physical development. Lee was pleasant and friendly though withdrawn to himself. During the interview the boy's expression was one of indifference. He more or less of' a blank expression, registered little enthusiasm nor emotions. When questioned, he generally answers affirmatively by saying "I guess so." He tried to evade an impression of unconcern as to what had taken place. The PO observed that the boy is somewhat shallow and seems to be immature to have little capacity for comprehension.*

On page 4 it is stated that, *the boy, the PO observed, is a friendly, likeable boy who portrays very little emotions. Rendition to the present situation is one of indifference. The PO feels that we are dealing with a boy who feels a great deal of insecurity and the need for acceptance. As it does not seem that this can be done with the boy remaining at home, but it was felt that perhaps placement in an institution where these needs can be met would be beneficial at this time. However, recommendation is being held in acceptance pending the receipt of the psychiatric examination.*

John Carro is called by the WC and in his testimony (3006) he does not relay much valuable info as to Oswald's personality but there is an exchange as to what was in the planning for Oswald:

Mr. Liebeler - You mentioned that the boy was going to go to your own psychiatric clinic. That is a different proposition from the Youth House, is it not?
Mr. CARRO - Yes. This is the psychiatric court clinic, that is on 22nd St, which in some instances, where we are not able to effect the kind of placing we need or so, we will utilize that as a last resort, and the boy would go there periodically and be seen by the psychiatrist.
Mr. Liebeler - It would be an outpatient-type situation?
Mr. CARRO - An outpatient-type of situation, yes.

[And a little later...]

Mr. Liebeler - Would you say that Oswald was more mentally disturbed than most of the boys that you had under your supervision at that time?
Mr. CARRO - Not at all, actually. I have handled cases of boys who committed murders, burglaries, and I have had some extremely disturbed boys, and this was one of the problems, this was just initially a truancy situation, not one of real disruptive or acting out delinquent behaviour.

Back to the psychiatric reports document and on that same page four Dr Renatus Hartogs (3007) continues with his summary on May 1st 1953:
This 13-year-old well-built boy has superior mental resources and functions only slightly below his capacity level in spite of chronic truancy from school which brought him into Youth House. No finding of neurological impairment or psychotic mental changes could be made. Lee had to be diagnosed as a personality pattern disturbance with schizoid features and passive aggressive tendencies. Lee has to be seen as an emotionally, quite disturbed youngster who suffers the impact of really existing emotional isolation and deprivation, lack of affection, absence of family life and rejection by a self-involved and

conflicted mother. Although she denies that he is in need of any other form help other than "remedial" one, we gained the definite impression that Lee can be reached through contact with an understanding and very patient psychotherapist and if he could be drawn at the same time into group psychotherapy. We arrive therefore at the recommendation that he should be placed on probation under the condition that he seek help and guidance through contact with a child guidance clinic, where he should be treated preferably by a male psychiatrist who could substitute, to a certain degree at least for the lack of a father figure. At the same time, his mother should be urged to seek psychotherapeutic guidance through contact with a family agency. If this plan does not work out favourably and Lee cannot cooperate in his treatment plan on an out-patient basis, removal from the home and placement could be resorted to at a later date, but it is our definite impression that treatment on probation should be tried out before the stricter and therefore more harmful placement approach is applied to the case of this boy.

On May 7th (page nine) Hartogs writes another report:

He is a tense, withdrawn and evasive boy who dislikes intensely talking about himself and his feelings. He likes to give the impression that he doesn't care about others and rather likes to keep to himself so that he is not bothered and does not have to make the effort of communicating. It was difficult to penetrate the emotional wall behind which this boy hides and he provided us with sufficient clues, permitting us to see increased anxiety, shyness, feelings of awkwardness and insecurity as the main reasons for the withdrawal tendencies and solitary habits. Lee told us: "I don't want a friend and I don't like to talk to people." He describes himself as stubborn and according to his own saying likes to say "no." Strongly resistive and negativistic features were also noticed but psychotic mental content was denied and no indication of psychotic mental changes was arrived at.

He is a youngster with superior mental endowment functioning presently on the bright range of mental efficiency. His abstract thinking capacity and his vocabulary are well developed. No retardation in school subjects could be found in spite of his truancy from school.

An excerpt of Hartog's WC testimony (3008):

Mr. Liebeler. In your capacity as chief psychiatrist for the Youth House did you have occasion at any time to interview Lee Harvey Oswald?
Dr. Hartogs. Yes.

167

Mr. Liebeler. Would you tell us when that was and all that you can remember about that interview in your own words?

Dr. Hartogs. That is tough. I remember that--actually I reconstructed this from what I remembered from the seminar. We gave a seminar on this boy in which we discussed him, because he came to us on a charge of truancy from school, and yet when I examined him, I found him to have definite traits of dangerousness. In other words, this child had a potential for explosive, aggressive, assaultive acting out which was rather unusual to find in a child who was sent to Youth House on such a mild charge as truancy from school. This is the reason why I remember this particular child, and that is the reason why we discussed him in the seminar. I found him to be a medium-sized, slender, curly haired youngster, pale-faced, who was not very talkative, he was not spontaneous. He had to be prompted. He was polite. He answered in a somewhat monotonous fashion. His sentences were well structured. He was in full contact with reality.

Mr. Liebeler. He was?

Dr. Hartogs. He was in full contact with reality. I found his reasoning to be intensely self-centered, his judgment also centering around his own needs, and the way he looked at life and his relationships with people. This was mostly in the foreground. So, this is what I remember actually.

Hartog's recollection is not based on the documentation made in 1953/54 but on a seminar in which he and colleagues discussed the case in an informal non-documented manner. What is not explained is why he did not use his original report?

During the same testimony, Hartogs claims Oswald was recommended to be sent to an institution. But the paperwork signed by Hartogs in 1953 does not support this at all, it was all on a probationary basis!

Mr. Liebeler. Do you recall what recommendation you made to the court in respect of Oswald?

Dr. Hartogs. If I can recall correctly, I recommended that this youngster should be committed to an institution.

Mr. Liebeler. What type of institution, do you recall?

Dr. Hartogs. No; that I don't recall.

Mr. Liebeler. But you are quite clear in your recollection that you recommended that he be institutionalized immediately because of the personality pattern disturbance; is that correct?

Dr. Hartogs. Yes; that is right. That I remember; yes.

[And a little later...]

Mr. Liebeler. Can you recall what kind of institution you recommended that Oswald be committed to?

Dr. Hartogs. I never make a recommendation as to the name, the specific institution. This is a prerogative of the court.

Mr. Liebeler. Do you make a recommendation as to the type of institution which you recommend for a child?

Dr. Hartogs. Yes; I do that, either a mental hospital or training school or residential treatment center, but I do not recall in this case what I recommended.

Mr. Liebeler. But you do recall quite clearly that you did recommend, because of this boy's personality pattern, disturbance?

Dr. HARTOGS. Yes; that he should not be placed in the community.

Mr. Liebeler. Or placed on probation?

Dr. Hartogs. Yes; that is right.

Mr. Liebeler. Do you recall being interviewed on this question by the FBI?

Dr. Hartogs. Yes.

Mr. Liebeler. Do you remember approximately when they interviewed you?

Dr. Hartogs. No; I don't know the date.

Mr. Liebeler. Do you remember that you told them the same thing, that is, that you recommended institutionalizing Oswald as a result of his psychiatric examination which indicated that he was potentially dangerous?

Dr. Hartogs. Yes.

Dr Renatus Hartogs is exposed and criticised for his contradictory remarks in the New York Post (3009) in November 1964.

Evelyn Strickman, a social worker, also questioned Lee and wrote a report on May 7th (3010) on pages 19-24 (3010).

Lee Oswald is a seriously detached, withdrawn youngster of thirteen years.

Laconic and taciturn, Lee answered questions, but volunteered almost nothing about himself spontaneously. Despite the fact that he is very hard to reach, Lee seems to have some ability to relate which in view of the solitary existence he has been leading, is somewhat surprising. There is a rather pleasant, appealing quality about this emotionally starved, affectionless youngster which grows as one speaks to him, and it seems fairly clear that he has detached himself from the world around him because no one in it ever met any of his needs for love.

Lee was able to respond to expressions of understanding for his lonely situation, but he denied that he really felt lonely. Questioning elicited the information that he feels almost as if there is a veil between him and other people through which they cannot reach him, but he prefers this veil to remain intact. He admitted, however, the tearing aside of the veil in talking to a social worker was not as painful as he would have anticipated. He was not comfortable in talking but he was not as disturbed in talking about his feelings as he thought he might be. When this was used as an opportunity to inquire into his fantasy life, he responded with a reminder that "This is my own business." He agreed to answer questions if he wanted to, rejecting those which upset him and acknowledged fantasies about being powerful, and sometimes hurting or killing people, but refused to elaborate on this. None of these fantasies involved his mother, incidentally. He also acknowledged dreaming but refused to talk about the dreams other than to admit that they sometimes contained violence, but he insisted that they were pleasant.

Observation of Lee's relationship with other boys during his stay at Youth House showed that he detached himself completely, and repulsed any efforts at friendship by others. Although he reacted favourably to supervision and did whatever was asked of him without comment when on his floor, he sat by himself and read. At 8:15 every evening he asked to be excused so that he could go to bed. The other boys appeared to respect his seclusion and didn't force themselves on him. He did not encourage conversation with anyone, and when asked questions was very terse in his replies. He was very neat and clean and always finished his work before going out to the floor.

In the recreation area he was usually quiet and withdrawn sitting by himself. If he did become involved in any minor altercation, he was very hostile and belligerent and somewhat defiant of supervision. He seemed to be respected by group members who left him alone.

This pattern was some very minimal movement in his relationship with his social worker, although it was so small as to be almost not noticeable. Ordinarily when approached he remained polite but uncommunicative, but when he was shown some special attention and concern when he had an earache, he responded somewhat. He never sought his caseworker out, and asked for nothing, nor did he volunteer anything further about himself.
Lee Oswald is a seriously withdrawn, detached and emotionally isolated boy of 13, who is at Youth House for the first time on a charge of truancy.

Lee became a reclusive child who was thrown upon himself and his own resources and he never made friends with other children. His mother who worked and who, when he was an infant, demonstrated her need to shift responsibility for him by leaving him with her sister and then *placing him for a while in a home, appears to be a rigid, self-involved woman with strong ideas and she has little understanding of this boy's behaviour nor of the protective shell he has drawn around himself in his effort to avoid contact with people which may result in hurt for him. It is possible that her own negative attitude about casework help and probation officers may communicate itself to Lee, interfering with his chances for help. On the other hand, there would be little accomplished by placing him in the impersonal setting afforded by an institution without seeing, first, if he can be reached in therapy. Despite his withdrawal, he gives the impression that he is not so difficult to reach as he appears and patient, prolonged effort in a sustained relationship with one therapist might bring results. There are indications that he has suffered serious personality damage but if he can receive help quickly this might be repaired to some extent.*

Strickman also appears in front of the WC, but she does not elaborate anything further during that short session on Oswald's personality.

The FBI requested the test become part of the evidence and New York judge Florence Kelley (3011) grants the FBI (3012) their request due to extraordinary circumstances.
The psychiatric report from April 17th 1953 (3013) by Irving Sokolow states: *"All his scores are above the average for his age group, appreciably so in the verbalization of abstract concepts and in the assembly of commonly recognizable objects. His method of approach was generally an easy, facile and a highly perceptive one. Although presumably disinterested in school subjects he operates on a much higher than average level."*

This FBI report quotes from Evelyn Strickman on April 30 (3014) pages 2 & 3:

"This is a seriously detached withdrawn youngster who has preserved some ability to relate, but is very hard to reach, He is laconic and taciturn and while he answered questions, he volunteered almost nothing about himself. Toward the end of the interview, he occasionally would say something gratuitously without my asking him but on the whole, everything had to be pulled from him. What is really surprising is that this boy has not lost entirely his ability to communicate with other people because he has been leading such a detached, solitary existence for most of his life." The full assessment can be read on pages 11-14 of the Youth House report (3015).

Edgar A. Buttle of the law firm Finch & Schaefler writes to Melvin Roman of the Domestic Relations Court on December 14th 1953 (page 25): *It is*

171

my thought that some serious consideration should be given to having the boy receive private clinical treatment if it is really necessary. It has been my impression that the boy has the feeling he is being kept under surveillance so extensively that he is beginning to feel abnormal. While I am highly in favour of psychiatric treatment and its accomplishments, I feel in this case it is being overdone.

Three days later Bessie Ford (page 26), a chief psychiatric social worker of the Domestic Relations Court states that the family has moved to New Jersey in December 1953. Lee is apparently doing much better at his new school which he attends regularly, as per Marguerite's correspondence to them. From thereon they leave NY jurisdiction by having left for New Orleans. They cannot be traced any more so not much else can be done.

On December 30th 1963 the FBI (3016) writes a report about Buttle and his then contact with the Domestic Relations Court about the handling of Oswald and states that *"it was conceivable that the problem of the boy in question could be the result of too close supervision of the boy by the court or school officers, resulting in a psychiatric condition being forced upon the youth."*

Justice in the Sixties: Conviction at All Costs

Henry Wade (a former FBI agent) was elected to become the Dallas District Attorney in 1952 and stayed in that position until 1988. He was one of the most recognised and known DAs in the US. He held a conviction ratio that no other DA in the US could match. The motto, *"conviction at all cost...."* has been used to describe his tenure as a District Attorney. The promotion system under Wade rewarded prosecutors for high conviction rates.

What goes hand in hand with Wade's high rate of success in solving cases is DPD Captain of Homicide & Robbery, Will Fritz's clearance rate, which was documented in a recent article in the Dallas Observer (3017), and stated that Fritz had a 98% clearance rate (compared to about 50% these days). *"Over the past quarter century, he and his aides have solved roughly 98 per cent of the 54 to 98 homicides committed each year."* (Dallas Morning News, March 1st, 1959.) This 98% clearance rate is hard to swallow, but 10 years prior he already had an excellent rating (3018). That by itself is food for thought on how law upkeep was done in those days. You can look at the crime rate figures presented through Dallas City Hall (3019) during that time period. Why are its methods to achieve such amazing results not copied by every police force in the USA? Or worldwide even?

The Texas Monthly (3020) stated that Dallas PD Captain of Homicide & Robbery Will Fritz was one of three (the other two being Bill Decker (3021) and Bill Richburg (3021) who could put a 'hold' on a prisoner- meaning any district judge would grant their request not to release them on a bond or a writ.

Back to Wade: from an article in Texas Monthly in September 2007 (3023): A 1963 treatise advised, "Do not take Jews, Negroes, Dagos, Mexicans or a member of any minority race on a jury." In 1969 Jon Sparling (3024), one of Wade's top assistants, wrote a training manual warning against picking, among others, "free-thinkers" and "extremely overweight people," and said, "You are not looking for a fair juror but rather a strong, biased and sometimes hypocritical individual who believes that defendants are different from them." In a NYT article from 2002 (3025) Sparling states: "It's not something I'd want the world to see", referring to his memo, which he said he was asked to write informally for other prosecutors. "I wrote it very quickly. I wasn't careful with my words. I'm not making any excuses for it." "Everything has changed since then," he added. In 2005, when the U.S. Supreme Court overturned the 1986 capital murder conviction of Thomas Miller-El because Dallas County prosecutors had thrown ten of eleven eligible blacks out of the jury pool, it referred to the Sparling manual (3026).

In an article from D Magazine in 1977 entitled The Law and Henry Wade (3027), it becomes more than evident that Wade liked to win. Wade ended his first year of tenure with a stunning record: 1002 convictions, including 132 trials, only seven of which resulted in acquittals. He had produced 13 death sentences, seven life imprisonment sentences, and convicted 746 hot check writers, more than half of whom went to prison.

When Wade's career was winding down in the 1980's troubling cases started to surface. A study by the Center for Public Integrity (3028) looked at cases in Texas from 1970 to 2002 and revealed that there were 215 in which appellate courts found prosecutorial misconduct at trial, and Dallas County had more than a third of them. The conduct mostly included things like failing to turn over exculpatory evidence favourable to the defendant also known as a Brady violation (3029) which the DA is required to do.

Nineteen convictions, three for murder, and the rest involving rape or burglary won by Wade and two successors who trained under him have been overturned after DNA evidence exonerated the defendants. A few hundred more cases are under review.

No other county in America, and almost no state, for that matter, has freed more innocent people from prison in recent years than Dallas County. Evidence was ignored and defence lawyers were kept in the dark.

Craig Watkins, who in 2006 became the first African-American DA for Dallas Country, had a small team to look into the DNA of the evidence that Henry Wade ordered to be preserved in the 1980's (something many other District Attorneys in the U.S.A. have not done). He also got a crew of The Innocence Project (3030) involved, which to date, nationwide, has exonerated 362 cases based on DNA evidence. Watkins described Wade's tenure (3031) stating, *"there was a cowboy kind of mentality and the reality is that kind of approach is archaic, racist, elitist and arrogant."*

The police officers from his own jurisdiction were not happy with what Watkins was doing either, in a 2010 interview in The Guardian (3032) Watkins stated *"Obviously police officers were taken aback because we were calling in to question the work they had done for all these years. It was the same among some folks in this office. They were afraid of the consequences of this Pandora's box being opened"*.

In Edward Gray's book *"Henry Wade's Tough Justice"* (3033) I was a bit surprised to hear a younger attorney recall a talk Wade made to his law class at SMU. He said that Wade addressed the probable cause issue saying *"If my officers don't have probable cause when they make an arrest, they will have it when they get to the courthouse."* One could put the argument forward that Henry Wade was not endorsing this practice, but just acknowledged the inevitability of it. Yet he took no action to inhibit or prevent it, which, to me, makes him complicit.

Even though Wade and his assistants can be held accountable for some grave injustices, the reader should also be aware that Henry Wade was one of the most respected prosecutors in the USA, had the support of the public, and stayed on his job for 36 years without any scandals. Not many other DA's can claim such accomplishments.
And then also ponder the fact that many of these wrongful convictions are the result of various law enforcement officers who would lie under oath or exaggerate 'facts.'

The JFK assassination happened almost 20 years before it was decided that the DNA evidence that was stored away on Wade's orders could be examined by Watkins, which then lead to the reopening and vacating of felony convictions. Watkins also focused his attention on a stash of documents pertaining to the assassination of President Kennedy. He made public the existence of 15,000 pages (3034) that the DA's office had been keeping away from the public eye for over forty years. The Sixth Floor Museum now has these archived.

Recording the Interrogations

Dallas police work in the 60's was a lot less procedural than it is these days. Handwritten notes and typed reports were made, but they were mere summarisations of sessions or day reports which might entail several hours of questioning. Will Fritz had DPD detectives present during his interrogations so that cases brought to Court would have supporting back up regarding what was said during those sessions between Fritz and the suspect.

There are some handwritten notes of Lee Oswald's interrogations available, but these did not appear until many years later after the fact.

Ronnie Duggar, the editor of the Texas Observer, spoke with Fritz fifteen or so years after the assassination. He asked him where the notes, records and recordings were, and Fritz confirmed to him that there weren't any. Such anomalies persist was Duggar's comment (3035) at 10:17. And we know now that Fritz was economical with the truth as Will Fritz's notes were released in late 1996 (3036), roughly 33 years after the assassination, thanks to an anonymous donor. Recently I asked Robbie Robertson to ask Tom Samoluk of the ARRB during an interview (3037) about how they got these notes.

It is highly doubtful that the Fritz notes represent contemporary notes taken during the interrogations. The notes mention *"the deceased"* meaning Oswald was already in the morgue.

Jim Hosty mentions in his Church Committee testimony (3038) that he was the only person taking notes during the very first interrogation. We also know that Harry Dean Holmes, the U.S. Postal Inspector took notes during Oswald's seventh interrogation on November 24th thanks to Charles Dhority's WC testimony (3039). These handwritten notes have never appeared in public.

Part of James Hosty's handwritten notes were released in his book Assignment Oswald (3040).

In February 2019, in Malcolm Blunt's archives, I found a set of handwritten notes that the ARRB had released publicly on March 10th 1997 (3041), about eight months before the release of the Will Fritz notes. These contain a pre-report made after the first interrogation (3042) of Oswald on DPD affidavit paper.

Then there is only one-half page of Forrest Sorrels' handwritten notes (3043) inside the WR and mixed with Jack Ruby interrogation notes as discovered by Larry Haapanen.

Will Fritz did not audio record any of the interrogation sessions. It was not normal custom with police forces to do this across the country until the early 1980's. Fritz claimed that they tried on two separate occasions, before the assassination, to obtain a tape recorder, but the requests were not approved as becomes evident during Fritz's WC testimony (3044):

Mr. Ball. Did you have any tape recorder?
Mr. Fritz. No, sir; I don't have a tape recorder. We need one, if we had one at this time, we could have handled these conversations far better.
Mr. Ball. The Dallas Police Department doesn't have one?
Mr. Fritz. No, sir; I have requested one several times but so far, they haven't gotten me one.

Nor did Fritz bother asking for any sound recording equipment from any of the many reporters out in the hallway less than 20 feet away! Inside the offices of the DPD were a group of secretaries who were typists and answered the phones for the Homicide & Robbery Bureau. They were not asked to type up anything during these interrogations. Due to the magnitude of this case, he should have recorded every interrogation, then again, he ran his 'shop' as his own fiefdom and no one messed with it, not even the Chief of Police.

Others came up with their view on this particular aspect.

Bill Alexander (3045) in Larry Sneed's *No More Silence (3046): Captain Fritz and I worked closely on numerous cases for years as well as on this particular case. The Dallas police and Fritz in particular were chastised by many for not recording the interrogations of Oswald. What most people don't realize is that we had Miranda in Texas before the Miranda decision. Nothing that he said to us would have been admissible. Under Texas law at that time, the only [admissible] statements of a man made under arrest would be in writing after he'd been warned that he did not have to make any statement which could be used in evidence against him. He therefore voluntarily made his statement reduced to writing and signed it in the presence of a witness. In that first interrogation that I attended, Captain Fritz wanted information and Oswald wouldn't give him a statement.*

Elmo T Cunningham (3047), Lt at the Forgery Bureau, in Larry Sneed's *No More Silence*, gives a few good insights into Fritz's MO: "*There was always a problem between Will Fritz, captain of the Homicide and Robbery Bureau, and the Chief of Police ever since I was in the department.*

"*As a general rule, the chiefs left Fritz alone. In fact, I suspect that he liked Curry and got along better with him than any other chief that he served under because Curry left him alone. Before Hansson was made chief, there was a lot of support to make Will Fritz chief because a lot of people liked him. He had a lot of publicity because he had cleared some difficult cases and some big cases which had gotten nationwide publicity which no one thought would be cleared. But Fritz wasn't an administrator. He was an outstanding investigator and a super interrogator, but he was not an administrator in any sense of the word. He told me that he didn't particularly want to be chief, but he said, 'Now these people that's passed the word around that I turned it down are wrong. I wasn't offered the job. If I'd been offered the job, I'd have probably taken it.' To my way of thinking, Fritz was absolutely, beyond any question of doubt, the greatest interrogator I've ever heard talk to a person. He was a thorough, good investigator, and a good man. He was also a hard man and an unforgiving man. There was a saying that, once you got on his list, you stayed there. But if he liked you, there wasn't anything he wouldn't do for you. If he liked an officer that was working for him, and he thought that that officer was doing the best that he could, there was no way that he would ever fail to stand behind him. Now if he thought the officer was not doing his best, he got rid of them, and he did it himself. He wouldn't put the man down in front of or to anyone else, but he would handle it personally. I think a lot of the techniques he used in interrogation just came naturally, and some of them he developed himself. For instance, when he was talking to a man or woman, he never let his eyes stray away from their faces. He looked them right in the eye and right in the face the whole time he talked to them so that he noticed the least little quiver of a lip and raising or lowering of the eyelid and so on.*"

Fritz himself offered another explanation in this HSCA document from October 24th 1977 (3048):

Captain Fritz was asked again if he had taken any notes or used any tapes. He said that he had seen too many cases where a suspect of witness refused to say anything when a tape recorder was being used or notes being taken. He stated that his normal procedure was to have one of his men sit in a corner of the room and be present for corroboration and also to take notes. He couldn't remember if he had one of his men doing this or who it may have been.

Secret Service Inspector Thomas Kelley's WC testimony (3049) who attended Oswald's interrogations from Saturday morning the 23rd goes into the subject of recording the interrogations he attended as well during his WC testimony:

Mr. EDGAR. Thank you, Mr. Chairman. Mr. Kelley, I notice from some briefing materials that we have in our booklets that you were present during several interviews by Captain Will Fritz of Lee Harvey Oswald; is that correct?

Inspector KELLEY. Yes, sir.

Mr. EDGAR. Can you indicate for us why none of those interviews were taped?

Inspector KELLEY. The Dallas police didn't have a tape recorder and I didn't have one with me, and apparently no one else had one. They didn't have a tape recorder for Captain Fritz anyway.

Mr. EDGAR. Wouldn't it have been a logical thing in 1963 for—

Inspector KELLEY. Yes.

Mr. EDGAR. [continuing] For an investigative person like yourself from the Secret Service to demand or request or require a tape recorder be present when interrogating such a sensitive witness?

Inspector KELLEY. Well, I didn't feel when I was allowed to come into the interrogation room that I had the right to insist on a recordation of it. I was there as a guest of the Dallas Police Department and Captain Fritz was handling it. On hindsight, I should have wired myself before I went in there. But it was just my own position that I did not think I should insist on a recording of it.

Mr. EDGAR. You used the phrase *"you didn't think you were allowed,"* or you were given permission to go in and listen in on the interview. Was there a breakdown in lines and chains of command that made you feel as though you didn't have full or equal opportunity with the captain of the Dallas Police Department to interrogate this witness?

Inspector KELLEY. No, there was certainly no lack of cooperation between the Dallas Police Department and ourselves and Captain Fritz and me. As a matter of fact, when we first went in to do the interviews, I didn't know whether they had a recording or not. I guess I just assumed they had, but I did find out later that the interview was not being recorded.

Mr. EDGAR. In your conversation with Lee Harvey Oswald, what did he say to you?

Inspector KELLEY. He indicated to me that he was a Communist but not a Marxist. The only other things he talked to me about, or I talked to him about, was the fact that he had been accused by the police department as being the assassin and we were concerned about whether he was or whether there was somebody else that assassinated President Kennedy and I would like to talk to him about it, and he indicated, I will talk to you later.

Mr. EDGAR. Did he indicate to you at that time that you were the first Secret Service agent to talk with him?

Inspector KELLEY. No; I don't recall that conversation with him.

Mr. EDGAR. Had he encountered any other Secret Service agents prior to your conversation with him?

Inspector KELLEY. No; he hadn't. [Yes, he did; it was with Forrest Sorrels at around 16:00 on the 22nd-BK]

Harry Dean Holmes (3050), wrote in his report from December 17th (3051) that Fritz asked Oswald about the Hidell I.D. card, and Oswald 'flared up' and stated, *"I've told you all I'm going to about that card. You took notes, just read them for yourself, if you want to refresh your memory"* (3052). Oswald could have been referring to anyone in that room.

Dallas DA Henry Wade summarises it best when it comes to Will Fritz and his 'methods' during his WC testimony (3053):

"But Fritz runs a kind of a one-man operation there where nobody else knows what he is doing. For instance, he is reluctant to tell me, either. But I don't mean that disparagingly. I will say Captain Fritz is about as good a man at solving a crime as I ever saw, to find out who did it but he is poorest in the getting evidence that I know, and I am more interested in getting evidence and there is where our major conflict comes in." This is also repeated in 1967 to Bob Considine for the WJT in New York (3054). Wade also states this again in an interview he does for the Dallas Morning News from November 21st 1993 (3055): *"I worked with (police Capt. Will) Fritz and he was probably the best person I ever worked with in finding out who done it, and the poorest person I ever worked with for taking notes. I don't think the police had recorders back then. Of course, what he said wasn't admissible anyway".*

In his Oral History interview for the Sixth Floor Museum (3056) Wade repeats this: *Well, I worked with Fritz and he was probably the best person I ever worked with in finding out who's done it. And the poorest person I ever worked with on taking notes. And I don't think any of the police had recorders back then. I'm sure they made them, but I never heard of anyone using them. And of course, what they say under arrest is not admissible anyway. It's not admissible if you're under arrest and haven't seen a lawyer.*

The Settings on the Third Floor of City Hall

Lee Oswald was captive for almost forty-five hours until he was murdered by Jack Ruby. He was interrogated for about twelve hours inside Captain Fritz's office (which measured 14 x 9.5 ft.) in the Homicide and Robbery Bureau on the third floor of the DPD station (3057) without any legal representation present.

There were quite a few people from the DPD, FBI, Secret Service, US Marshall Office, State Troopers and ATF agents that were present inside Room 317. There is a list of FBI and Secret Service agents (3058) who were present inside the DPD while Oswald was in custody.

There are some people missing:

From the DPD: John Adamcik, Gus Rose, Richard Stovall, and LG Montgomery. From the FBI: Vince Drain (although not present during the interrogations, but very close to Wade and Curry on the 22nd). Ex assistant-DA James K Allen, which is not a surprise as he was there as a private citizen at that time. But he was a good friend of Will Fritz so he had all the access to room 317.

The photo by Daryl Heikes (3059) is a good example of what the media presence in front of the Homicide & Robbery Bureau, Room 317 on the third-floor corridor, looked like. There were not hundreds of people down there as some have claimed. See Jesse Curry facing the press just outside Homicide & Robbery room 317 (3060).

November 22nd

13:50 Lee Harvey Oswald is Arrested at the Texas Theatre

When Oswald is arrested inside the Texas Theatre the reports vary about what Oswald said. Sergeant Gerald Hill said that Oswald had requested counsel at the time of his arrest inside the Texas Theatre.
During Hill's WC testimony (3061):

Mr. HILL .....Now, if we can back up a little bit to where we made the, got him handcuffed in the theatre, before we started moving out with him, he started, Oswald, or the suspect at this point, we didn't know who he was, so we will keep on calling him the suspect, started making statements about *"I want a lawyer. I know my rights. Typical police brutality. Why are you doing this to me?"*

Later, during the same testimony:

Mr. HILL ....he had previously in the theatre said he wanted his attorney.
Mr. Belin. He had said this in the theatre?
Mr. HILL. Yes; when we arrested him, he wanted his lawyer. He knew his rights.

The group of five DPD personnel manhandle Oswald into an unmarked patrol car while the crowd screams for blood. During the ride to City Hall, Oswald is in the back of the car seated in the middle between two detectives. His wallet is taken from his back pocket and his name is radioed in to the DPD.

Paul Bentley, in his Oral History Interview from 2008 (3062) for the Sixth Floor Museum: *At 18:30, "I asked him, inside the car on their way to City Hall, 'Did you kill our President?' to which Oswald replied: 'I haven't shot a damn person.'"*

14:00 Oswald is Brought in to the Third Floor Inside City Hall

Frank Underwood filmed Oswald in the elevator of the DPD station (3063) in the first scene. From Richard Trask's *Pictures of The Pain (3064)*: *"I reached City Hall in time to film Oswald being brought in, and I rode up in the elevator with him. A police sergeant said, "we got witnesses that saw him shoot Tippit." The police tell us whether or not a suspect is good for the charges, and we know how to play the story. But Oswald leaned around and looked straight at me, saying defensively, "I didn't kill anybody"* page 421.

In this video (3065) you can see Oswald arriving at the DPD with his shirt hanging off his shoulder and being led past Billy Lovelady seated on the right, inside the Homicide & Robbery Bureau. The clock in the background of the video shows the time at about 14:03.

Charles Truman Walker, wearing his white cap, was part of the crew that arrested and transported Oswald from the Texas Theatre to the DPD. In his HSCA statement (3066) he states, *"Being alone in there with him made me think. He could still have a weapon, so I searched him good, but found nothing."*

On February 3rd 1964 Paul Bentley (3067) speaks to the FBI who has stated to them that he completely searched Oswald and *nothing* was left in his pockets.

Bentley is interviewed in the hallway (3068) while on crutches, due to twisting his ankle inside the Texas Theatre while trying to arrest Oswald. Bentley and Walker together followed standard procedure when someone is arrested and taken into custody. They would have made sure Oswald did not have anything left in his pockets once handed over. Keep this in mind for later on when Oswald is brought down for his first line-up just after 16:00 with Helen Markham and is being frisked again by Elmer Boyd and Richard Sims.

Initial Questioning of Oswald Inside the DPD

Jim Leavelle, who is probably one of the most famous Dallas cops to come out of this tragedy, is claiming that he interrogated Oswald regarding the Tippit murder. The strange thing, is that there is no mention whatsoever of this in his statement nor in his WC testimony! No evidence exists at all that he interrogated Oswald, besides Leavelle's own say so, in later years after the assassination. When Leavelle testified before the WC, he claimed that the first time he had ever sat in on an interrogation with Oswald was on Sunday morning, November 24th, 1963. When Joseph Ball asked Leavelle if he had ever spoken to Oswald before this interrogation (page 269), he stated; *"No, I had never talked to him before."* Leavelle then stated during his testimony that, *"the only time I had connections with Oswald was this Sunday morning (November 24th, 1963). I never had (the) occasion to talk with him at any time..."*

Compare the above with a part of a transcript from an interview with *Joe Nick Patoski* published in Texas Monthly at least thirty years later:

TM: Where were you on November 22nd?
Jim: Since my partner was on vacation, I was assigned to cover anything that came in the office. And all my other cohorts in homicide were given different assignments, some of them on the street, a lot of them out at the trade mart, and two of them [were] in the motorcade.
TM: You had work to do on the 22nd. At what point did you come in contact with Lee Harvey Oswald?
Jim: After he was arrested, they brought him in and set him in the interrogation room and I talked to him strictly about the shooting of Officer Tippit. I didn't have any idea he was going to be a suspect in the Presidential assassination.
TM: As the reports of the crime came in, did it seem clear that this guy did the crime?
Jim: We didn't know at the time. 'Course, another thing that we didn't know was whether he was acting alone or had somebody with him and it took a lot of legwork and time for us to determine he actually was alone.
TM: So, you had an opportunity to interrogate him?
Jim: I talked to him, yeah, about 10, maybe 15 minutes one-on-one before Captain Fritz and the other officers came back from the book depository, preparatory to going [to] look for him, and found out he was already there. When the Captain [came] in and asked me what his name was, and I told him, he asked me where he worked, and he said the book depository, he said, 'You're the one I want to talk to.' So, in essence, they took my prisoner away. I lost my prisoner.
TM: When did you see him again?
Jim: Oh, I saw him off and on for the next day or so, but I didn't talk to him because the powers that be were talking to him. But I spent my time making a case on it for the shooting of the officer.

In Jim Leavelle's Oral History video from the Sixth Floor Museum, the conversation turns very interesting at 14:55.

Leavelle walked into the office on the third floor and Oswald was already sitting there. He claims that he interviewed Oswald for 15 minutes before Will Fritz took him away from him. Leavelle said he interviewed Oswald only about the Tippit shooting and when he relayed this info he stated that Oswald was telling lies and so on.

Leavelle himself during his WC testimony, used "*I do not recall*" 30 times in two testimony sessions and "*I don't remember*" nine times. Quite a few instances of failed memory when it comes to his actions during that big important day only about four months earlier. But in later years he was able to give precise details surrounding all his interactions with Oswald without any trouble.

Leavelle is quoted by Joseph McBride's *Into The Nightmare* on page 319: "*When I walked in (to Captain Fritz's office to help interrogate Oswald) and I started talking to him about the shooting of officer Tippit, I had no idea whatsoever that he was going to be a suspect in the presidential shooting. Not one bit.*"

In the Oral History video from 2008 (at 10:45) Leavelle also states that Oswald stated "*I did not shoot anybody.*"

It is pretty clear that Jim Leavelle has been economical with the truth regarding his so-called interrogation of Lee Oswald on November 22nd.

Joe R Cody, Detective, Burglary and Theft, says the following in Larry Sneed's *No More Silence*: *At that time, we already had a tremendous amount of people in City Hall. Hill, Bentley, and McDonald asked, "What are we going to do with him?" And I said, "Bring him over and we'll put him in Burglary and Theft." So, I talked to him and said, "Now, what is your name?" He said, "My name is Lee Harvey Oswald." "Where do you work?" He said, "Texas School Book Depository." Then it began to dawn on me what had happened when he told me where he worked. Initially, I was alone in the little interrogation room with Oswald. When he told me his name, it kind of rang a bell. The only things that he told me were his name, which he had been in the Marine Corps, his serial number, and where he lived and worked. He wasn't arrogant. In fact, he reminded me of a captured war prisoner: Just give your name, rank, and serial number. I was sure that he had shot the officer and was pretty sure that he was the one who had shot the President, and still am. I figured that we finally had closed the case. It was relatively simple then, but in the years since, it's gotten rather complicated.*

Compare the above statement in Larry Sneed's *No More Silence* with an article published in Today Cedar Hill (Duncanville, Tex.), Vol. 36, No. 6, Ed. 1 Thursday, April 26th 2001 (3080).

In a 1989 interview (3081) by Bob Milner, Cody, who is in a hotel room alongside with Jim Leavelle relays the following:

"Mr. Cody, did you have any involvement in the interrogation of Oswald and did you happen to have an opportunity to observe his actions and moods?"

"Well, yes, I did. Jerry Hill, Nick McDonald, and Paul Bentley brought him up to the Office. At that time, we didn't know that Oswald was involved in killing the President, but we did know that he was involved in killing an Officer out there. And they brought him up to Burglary & Theft and I talked to him a little while. I ask him his name and he told me and I ask where he worked and he said, the Texas School Book Depository, and that's when the light dawned. I went across and told Captain Fritz that we had him in there, in the interrogation room over there. I think Jim Leavelle talked to him later. (Leavelle sitting on the bed shakes his head, yes). That's how we knew that Oswald was involved in the shooting of the President." So now Cody did the talking at first, then Leavelle and then Fritz? And what about Rose and Stovall?

Cody in Barry Ernest's *The Girl on the Stairs* says: *"They tried to get him (Oswald) into Homicide and they couldn't so they took him over to Burglary and Theft. They put him into an interrogating room and I'm talking to him and I said, 'What's your name?' He said, 'Lee Harvey Oswald.' 'Where do you work?' 'Texas School Book Depository.' I said, 'Did you work today?' He said, 'Yes.' So, I called an officer in and said, 'Kill him if he moves."* This scenario is hard to reconcile with what actually happened.

Lieutenant TL Baker confirms on page 4 of his report (3083) that Rose and Stovall spoke to Oswald first and there is no mention of Cody and Leavelle.

14:15 Oswald is Questioned by Gus F Rose and Richard S Stovall

Bob Carroll, a detective who was part of the group of men filmed bringing in Oswald after his arrest at the Texas Theatre states in his WC testimony (3084) that Gus Rose was one of the first officers talking to Oswald.

Richard Stovall (3085) described this initial encounter with Oswald in the joint report made up with Gus Rose and John Adamcik (3086). At 14:15 Oswald was brought in to Robbery & Homicide after which Rose and Stovall talked to him briefly. That is 10-12 minutes after his arrival in the holding cell. At about 14:30 Fritz, Sims and Boyd entered and sent Rose and Stovall to Irving.

Richard Stovall's WC testimony (3086) mentions the following about this interrogation:

185

Mr. Ball. Were you given an assignment as soon as you got down there?

Mr. Stovall. No, sir; I wasn't--as soon as I got there. I got there and one of my partners, GF. Rose, got there about the same time. We were talking to a witness that had seen all the people standing out there--he didn't actually see anything, so we didn't even take an affidavit from him because he didn't see anything. While talking to him, the officers brought Lee Harvey Oswald into the Homicide Bureau and put him into an interrogation room we have there at the bureau. After we finished talking to this witness, we went back there and talked to him briefly.

Mr. Ball. Do you remember what was said to him and what he said to you?

Mr. Stovall. I don't recall exactly--I went in and asked him for his identification, asked him who he was and he said his name was Lee Oswald, as well as I remember. Rose and I were both in there at the time. He had his billfold and in it he had the identification of *"A. Hidell,"* which was on a Selective Service card, as well as I remember.

Mr. Ball. That's [spelling] H-i-d-e-l-l, isn't it?

Mr. Stovall. I'm not positive on that--I believe it was [spelling] H-i-d-e-l-l, I'm not sure. And he also had identification of Lee Harvey Oswald, and I believe that was on a Social Security card and at that time Captain Fritz opened the door to the office there and sent Rose and I to go out to this address in Irving at 2515 West Fifth Street in Irving. That was--I don't know where the captain got the address, but it was an address where he was supposed to be staying part of the time.

Gus Rose's WC testimony (3087) states:

Mr. Rose. There were some people in the office from the Book Depository and we talked to a few of them and then in just a few minutes they brought in Lee Oswald and I talked to him for a few minutes.

Mr. Ball. What did you say to him or did he say to you?

Mr. Rose. Well, the first thing I asked him was what his name was and he told me it was Hidell.

Mr. Ball. Did he tell you it was Hidell?

Mr. Rose. Yes; he did.

Mr. Ball. He didn't tell you it was Oswald?

Mr. Rose. No; he didn't, not right then--he did later. In a minute--I found two cards--I found a card that said "A. Hidell," and I found another card that said "Lee Oswald" on it, and I asked him which of the two was his correct name. He wouldn't tell me at the time, he just said, "You find out." And then in just a few minutes Captain Fritz came in and he told me to get two men and go to Irving and search his house.

Mr. Ball. Now, when he first came in there--you said that he said his name was *"Hidell"?*

Mr. Rose. Yes.

Mr. Ball. Was that before you saw the two cards?

Mr. Rose. Yes; it was.

Mr. Ball. Did he give you his first name?

Mr. Rose. He just said *"Hidell"*; I remember he just gave me the last name of *"Hidell."*

Mr. Ball. And then you found two or three cards on him?

Mr. Rose. Yes; we did.

Mr. Ball. Did you search him?

Mr. Rose. He had already been searched and someone had his billfold. I don't know whether it was the patrolman (referring to C.T. Walker-BK) who brought him in that had it or not.

Mr. Ball. And the contents of the billfold supposedly were before you?

Mr. Rose. Yes.

And from that short interview session they each had with Oswald something important becomes apparent: Rose and Stovall contradict each other in their WC testimonies with Rose claiming that Oswald ID-d himself as Hidell, whereas his partner Stovall said Oswald used his real name. After further deep investigation it is safe to say that Gus Rose spun fairy tales when it comes to the Hidell ID. The Hidell ID will be discussed in depth a little later.

Gus Rose (3088) took no notes during Oswald's chat, but in this article in 1998 for D Magazine (3089) he said the following about what Oswald said:

"The suspect had suffered a small red abrasion over his right eye while scuffling with officers at the Texas Theatre in Oak Cliff. But the young man didn't seem dazed or confused at all. He was angry and arrogant. "I don't know what I'm doing here," he said.

A homicide detective for only three years. Rose would later gain renown as a skilled interrogator. Blocking out the hubbub, he turned his attention to the hostile suspect.

"I don't own a gun," the man said. *"I didn't have that gun. They planted that on me when they arrested me."*

"Have you ever owned a gun of your own?" Rose asked evenly.

"No," he retorted. *"I never owned one."*

In the same article he also mentions that a knock at the door interrupted the detective's ruminations. He opened the door a crack, blocking the suspect's view. There stood his boss. Capt. Fritz.

"We've just come from the book depository." Fritz said. *"We've pretty well finished with the investigation at the site. We've accounted for all the employees who work there except one I want you to get some officers to go with you and find the guy who's missing. He's a suspect."*

Rose winced. *"Well, I would. Captain,"* Rose said, *"but I'm talking to the guy here that killed Tippit."* If another interrogator stepped in, the process would be set back.

"I'll have somebody else work that out," Fritz said. *"I want you to find this guy."*

"Well, okay," Rose said reluctantly. *"What's his name?"*

Fritz fished around in the breast pocket of his blue suit and brought out a piece of yellow paper.

"His name is Lee Oswald."

Rose went cold. He turned to look at the suspect, who stared back defiantly. On the table lay the two identification cards. Rose looked down at them. One read *"Alek Hidell."* The other: *"Lee Oswald."*

"Captain," Rose said, *"I think we've got him right here."*

Oswald was not the only employee missing at that time (Charles Douglas Givens of the TSBD crew and several publishing company employees were also missing). Nor was Oswald ever deemed a suspect, the description of the possible suspect radioed over the police channel was very generic.

The next person who can shed more light on this is reporter Kent Biffle from the Dallas Morning News. He joined the DPD as they went inside the TSBD building, and wrote in the DMN in 1982 the following on missing people:

. . . only two of us (reporters) had arrived at the ambush building (the Depository) by this point. . . . Getting in was no problem. I just hid my press badge . . . and went in with the first wave of cops. . . . Hours dragged by. The building superintendent showed up with some papers in his hand. I listened as he told detectives about Lee Oswald failing to show up at a roll call. My impression is that there was an earlier roll call that had been inconclusive because several employees were missing. This time, however all were accounted for except Oswald. I jotted down the Oswald information. . . . Neither the police in the building nor the superintendent (Roy Samson Truly-BK) *knew that Oswald already was under arrest.* Biffle left the TSBD after mid-afternoon. His best guess would be some time after 16:00.

Before Fritz got to talk to Oswald, he made a little detour from the TSBD via Bill Decker's office.

Richard Sims' WC testimony (3090):

Ball. Now, you left the building about what time?

Mr. Sims. Well, we arrived at the city hall around 2 o'clock--I'll have to look at the record---on this--about 2:15--we left there evidently about 2 o'clock.

Mr. Ball. You and who?

Mr. Sims. Captain Fritz and Boyd.

Mr. Ball. Then where did you go?

Mr. Sims. Captain Fritz went over and talked to Sheriff Decker. He sent word he wanted to talk to Captain Fritz, so we talked to the sheriff and then we went to the city hall.

Mr. Ball. Where was Decker when he said he wanted to talk to Fritz?

Mr. Sims. Well, I didn't go inside the sheriff's office--I stayed out in the corridor there.

Elmer Boyd confirms this in his WC testimony (3091), but goes no further than that:

Mr. Ball. Did you go to Decker's office with Fritz?

Mr. Boyd. Yes sir.

Mr. Ball. And then you went with Fritz up to your office?

Mr. Boyd. Yes, sir.

I would have liked to have been a fly on the wall during that particular conversation. What was so important that Fritz had to pop over and speak to Decker in person instead of over the phone?

Some initial reports on Oswald's ID are in this NBC timeline (3092).

14:30 First Interrogation by Will Fritz

Present:
DPD: Will Fritz, Elmer Boyd and Richard Sims.
FBI: James Bookhout and James Hosty join at 15:15.

Captain John Will Fritz (3093) of Homicide & Robbery is our main man. Fritz was regarded as a legend who could squeeze a confession out of almost anyone. Almost! Fritz did not record the interviews nor used a stenographer, many fellow law enforcement officers attested to this. There is no record of what was said during the first 45 minutes before the FBI agents had arrived and joined in the interrogation. He himself confirmed that he had not taken any notes at that time during his WC testimony (3094):

Mr. Fritz. I can remember the thing that I said to him and what he said to me, but I will have trouble telling you which period of questioning those questions were in because I kept no notes at the time, and these

189

notes and things that I have made I would have to make several days later, and the questions may be in the wrong place.

During that same WC testimony, it shows that he has these notes with him as he manages to state who was present at the interrogation of the 23rd.

The interrogation notes are fascinating by itself, they differ in parts with Fritz's report which he submitted later, and which will be reviewed later. In some areas, this runs parallel with other law enforcement officer's notes and in some key moments it does not. He also used this undated report in conjunction with his WC testimony. The handwritten notes (3095) did not become public until they were handed to the ARRB in 1997 (3096).

This first page is key to Oswald's whereabouts during and just after the shooting. At the top it states the co-presence of Bookhout and Hosty and then underneath in the right column it says:

"Claims 2nd floor coke when officer came in."

Although this may seem clear cut, it isn't. It doesn't place Oswald on the second floor at all after the shooting, it says that he had a coke from the second floor when a police officer came in.

"To first floor had lunch," strengthens the claim that Oswald had the coke from the 2nd floor and had made his way down to the first floor and then had his lunch.

In the same column Fritz writes, *"out with Bill Shelley in front,"* which can only be Oswald's answer as to where he was during the shooting or when the motorcade passed by.

Again, how did Oswald know that Bill Shelley was standing outside in front? It has been well documented, with Shelley's statements and seen in the Malcolm Couch film that he left those steps immediately after the shooting and went back inside through the side entrance minutes later and was not seen outside again until being filmed escorting Danny Garcia and Bonnie Ray Williams to a squad car outside the TSBD at about 13:30. Oswald, supposedly, spoke to Shelley about no work being done this afternoon and left shortly after. If he did speak to Shelley then it would have been inside the TSBD and not outside.

190

The Hidell ID doesn't get a mention during these interrogations at all, which is rather strange if you believe what Gus Rose said. The ID is only mentioned during the end of the interrogations on the morning of the 23rd at about 11:30 according to Fritz's notes from that interrogation and also from the USSS and FBI reports of that very same interrogation session. The 'find' of the rifle order happens to be shortly just before that interrogation. An amazing coincidence.

Fritz surmises the first interview in his WC testimony (3097) as follows:

Mr. Ball. Who was present when you talked with him?

Mr. Fritz. At that time, when I first brought him in there, there would be Sims and Boyd and probably one or two officers from the office, I am not sure, just who else might have been there. I know those two, I am sure, I believe those two were there. Just about the time I started talking to him, I had just started to question him, I got a phone call from Mr. Shanklin, Gordon Shanklin, agent in charge of the FBI calling for Mr. Bookhout, and I asked Mr. Bookhout to go to pick up the extension.

Mr. Ball. Was Mr. Bookhout there?

Mr. Fritz. He had just come into the lieutenant's office and Mr. Shanklin asked that Mr. Hosty be in on that questioning, he said he wanted him in there because of Mr. Hosty knowing these people and he had been talking to them and he wanted him in there right then. So, I got up from my desk and walked over to the lieutenant's office and asked Mr. Bookhout to come in, the reason I asked both of them to come in and Mr. Bookhout is in my office most of every day and works with us in a lot of cases and asked him to come in with Mr. Hosty.

Mr. Ball. So, Bookhout and Hosty came into your office?

Mr. Fritz. Yes, sir.

Mr. Ball. Was anyone else present?

Mr. Fritz. I don't remember whether there was anyone else right at that time or not.

Mr. Ball. Do you remember what you said to Oswald and what he said to you?

Mr. Fritz. I can remember the thing that I said to him and what he said to me, but I will have trouble telling you which period of questioning those questions were in because I kept no notes at the time, and these notes and things that I have made I would have to make several days later, and the questions may be in the wrong place.

Mr. Ball. What is your best memory of what you said to him when he first came in?

Mr. Fritz. I first asked him as I do of most people something about where he was from, and where he was raised and his education, and I asked him where he went to school and he told me he went to school in New York for a while, he had gone to school in Fort Worth some, that he

191

didn't finish high school, that he went to the Marines, and the Marines, and finished high school training in the Marines.

And I don't remember just what else. I asked him just the general questions for getting acquainted with him, and so I would see about how to talk to him, and Mr. Hosty spoke up and asked him something about Russia, and asked him if he had been to Russia, and he asked him if he had been to Mexico City, and this irritated Oswald a great deal and he beat on the desk and went into a kind of a tantrum.

Mr. Ball. What did he say when he was asked if he had been to Mexico City?

Mr. Fritz. He said he had not been. He did say he had been to Russia; he was in Russia; I believe he said for some time.

Mr. Ball. He said he had not been in Mexico City?

Mr. Fritz. At that time, he told me he had not been in Mexico City.

Mr. Ball. Who asked the question whether or not he had been to Mexico City?

Mr. Fritz. Mr. Hosty. I wouldn't have known anything about Mexico City.

Mr. Ball. Was there anything said about Oswald's wife?

Mr. Fritz. Yes, sir. He said, he told Hosty, he said, *"I know you."* He said, *"You accosted my wife on two occasions,"* and he was getting pretty irritable and so I wanted to quiet him down a little bit because I noticed if I talked to him in a calm, easy manner it wasn't very hard to get him to settle down, and I asked him what he meant by accosting, I thought maybe he meant some physical abuse or something and he said, *"Well, he threatened her."* And he said, *"He practically told her she would have to go back to Russia."* And he said, *"He accosted her on two different occasions."*

Mr. Ball. How long a time did you sit with Oswald and question him this first time?

Mr. Fritz. The first time, not but a few minutes.

Mr. Ball. That was the time Hosty and Bookhout were there?

Mr. Fritz. That is right. But sometimes when I would leave the office to do something else, it is hard to imagine how many things we had happening at the one time or how many different officers we had doing different things without seeing it but we were terribly busy.

I had called all my officers back on duty and had every one of them assigned to something, so going back and forth kept me pretty busy running back and forth at the time of questioning. I don't know when I would leave, I suppose Mr. Bookhout and Mr. Hosty asked him a few questions, but I don't believe they questioned him a great deal while I was gone.

Mr. Ball. You said just a few minutes, what did you mean by that, 15, 20, 25?

Mr. Fritz. It would be pretty hard to guess at a time like that because we weren't even quitting for lunch so I don't even know, time didn't mean much right at that time. For a few minutes, you would think 30 or 40 minutes the first time.

Mr. Ball. Thirty or forty minutes?

Mr. Fritz. I am guessing at that time.

Mr. Ball. Did you ask him what happened that day; where he had been?

Mr. Fritz. Yes, sir.

Mr. Ball. What did he say?

Mr. Fritz. Well, he told me that he was eating lunch with some of the employees when this happened, and that he saw all the excitement and he didn't think--I also asked him why he left the building. He said there was so much excitement there then that, *"I didn't think there would be any work done that afternoon and we don't punch a clock and they don't keep very close time on our work and I just left."*

Below is a segment of Fritz's testimony where he stutters and startles when it comes to the alleged second floor lunchroom encounter. From the mountain of evidence that is available it has become abundantly clear that the encounter never happened inside the second-floor lunchroom and that Will Fritz, Roy Truly and Nat Pinkston made things up to look like it did happen:

Mr. Ball. At that time didn't you know that one of your officers, Baker, had seen Oswald on the second floor?

Mr. Fritz. They told me about that down at the bookstore; I believe Mr. Truly or someone told me about it, told me they had met him--I think he told me, person who told me about, I believe told me that they met him on the stairway, but our investigation shows that he actually saw him in a lunchroom, a little lunchroom where they were eating, and he held his gun on this man and Mr. Truly told him that he worked there, and the officer let him go.

Mr. Ball. Did you question Oswald about that?

Mr. Fritz. Yes, sir; I asked him about that and he knew that the officer stopped him all right.

Mr. Ball. Did you ask him what he was doing in the lunchroom?

Mr. Fritz. He said he was having his lunch. He had a cheese sandwich and a Coca-Cola.

Mr. Ball. Did he tell you he was up there to get a Coca-Cola?

Mr. Fritz. He said he had a Coca-Cola.

Elmer Boyd (3098) who departed the TSBD alongside with Captain Fritz was present at the majority of Oswald's interrogations, yet seems unable to recall very much during his WC testimony (3099):

Mr. Boyd. Well, they participated in the interrogation-Mr. Hosty asked him some questions and he was pretty upset with Mr. Hosty.

193

Mr. Ball. What do you mean by that, what gave you that impression-what happened?

Mr. Boyd. Well, just by Oswald's actions, he said he had been to his house two or three times talking to his wife and he didn't appreciate him coming out there when he wasn't there.

Mr. Ball. Is that what he said to Hosty?

Mr. Boyd. Yes, sir.

Mr. Ball. Anything else?

Mr. Boyd. I don't recall-I know Mr. Hosty asked him several questions and finally he jumped up and hit the desk, Oswald did, and sat down, and like I say, he was pretty upset.

Mr. Ball. Was he handcuffed at that time?

Mr. Boyd. Yes; I believe he was handcuffed.

Mr. Ball. Was he handcuffed with his hands behind him?

Mr. Boyd. No, sir.

Mr. Ball. Had his hands been handcuffed behind him before he came into the room?

Mr. Boyd. I couldn't say if they had or not-they could have been.

Mr. Ball. Do you know whether the handcuffs were changed after he got in the room?

Mr. Boyd. They could have been changed after he got in the room-I'm not certain.

Mr. Ball. Who changed them?

Mr. Boyd. I don't recall.

Mr. Ball. Now, when Oswald jumped up and struck the desk, he struck the desk with what? With his hand?

Mr. Boyd. With his hands.

Mr. Ball. What did Hosty ask him before that?

Mr. Boyd. He had asked him about a trip to Mexico City?

Mr. Ball. Who did?

Mr. Boyd. Mr. Hosty.

Mr. Ball. What did Oswald say?

Mr. Boyd. He told him he hadn't been to Mexico City.

Mr. Ball. What else?

Mr. Boyd. I don't recall just exactly-I think that the words that he used when he was talking to Mr. Hosty was that he had been out there and accosted his wife, I believe that's the words that he used and like I said, after he talked to him, he said he didn't appreciate him coming out there to his house.

Mr. Ball. What was it that Hosty said before Oswald got up and struck the desk with his hand-what question did he ask?

Mr. Boyd. I don't remember what the question was. I know it had something to do with-let me see--I'm not sure if he was still talking to him about his wife or the trip to Mexico City.

Mr. Ball. You remember he did ask him if he took a trip to Mexico?

Mr. Boyd. Yes, sir.

Mr. Ball. Oswald said he had not?

Mr. Boyd. He said he had not been to Mexico.

Mr. Ball. And what did Hosty say to that?

Mr. Boyd. He asked him if he denied being to Mexico City-I've just forgotten-it wasn't too awful long before that-I don't recall just exactly what time that he said---I know it was something recent.

Mr. Ball. What did Oswald say?

Mr. Boyd. He said he had not been there.

Mr. Ball. Do you remember anything else that was said?

Mr. Boyd. No, sir not right offhand-I don't.

Mr. Stern. Did he ask him anything about Russia?

Mr. Boyd. Yes, sir; something was asked him-I don't recall who asked him about that, and he told us about going over to Russia, I believe he was there in 1959, or something like that-about 1959. I'll tell you, I didn't keep notes in there because of the fact I was sitting right beside Oswald-right in front of him more or less.

Mr. Ball. Did anybody keep notes?

Mr. Boyd. I saw the FBI man writing-they had a little book-across the table over there.

Mr. Ball. Did you have any microphones in there to record the conversation?

Mr. Boyd. No, sir.

Mr. Ball. Do you as a practice record the interrogations of your prisoners?

Mr. Boyd. No, sir; we don't.

Mr. Ball. How long did this take--how long was he questioned at this time?

Mr. Boyd. Let me see-we took him down to the first show up right after 4 o'clock, I think I have the exact time here 4:05 is when we left.

Mr. Ball. Was he in Captain Fritz' office from the time you took him in there-what time was that?

Mr. Boyd. At 2:15-2:20.

Mr. Ball. From 2:20 until 4 o'clock?

Mr. Boyd. Yes, sir.

That time frame makes it look that Hosty and Bookhout arrived about 55 minutes after Fritz had started the interrogation of Oswald. If this were the case then there are 50 minutes unaccounted for in any shape besides the memories of the DPD detectives and Captain Fritz.

During his HSCA testimony (3100) Elmer Boyd states that the notes he took during the interrogations (whereas during his WC testimony he claimed that he did not take any notes!) were transposed into his statement.

195

In the 2013 documentary "Capturing Oswald" (3101) Boyd says about Oswald's interrogations: *"He had an answer for everything. It may not be the right answer, but he'd give you an answer, you know."* After Hosty had joined the 'party' Boyd says: *"He just came down like this and hit the table. And eh, he just quit. He just quit talking to him, he won't talk to him anymore. I wish that Captain Fritz would have had time to talk to him by himself and one of us with him* (which would have usually been the case-BK) *I think we would have learned a lot more, I really believe that."*

In this video for the Sixth Floor Museum (3102) Elmer Boyd talks about the first interrogation. Once asked about Oswald's whereabouts during the shooting Boyd's mannerisms are odd combined with his reluctance to talk about it.

Richard Sims was with Dallas police since 1948 and homicide since 1957, was with Fritz and Boyd at the Trade Mart when things kicked off, and then accompanied them to the TSBD.

He probably is the most forgetful person of the whole bunch. Harold Weisberg (3103) noted this already decades ago: *"Sims is another case of a man who remembers nothing, is not asked searching questions to find out, if in fact he does remember anything, or why he doesn't remember anything. He is exceedingly careful to say nothing involving any superior. He remembers Oswald was questioned, he remembers he questioned Oswald, he remembers none of the questions he asked and none of the answers Oswald gave."* A succinct review; see for yourself below.

Richard Sims' WC testimony (3104):

Mr. Ball. What happened then?
Mr. Sims. Well, I don't know, let's see, we took Oswald at 2:20, Boyd and I, took Oswald from the interrogation room to Captain Fritz' office.
Mr. Ball. You and Boyd?
Mr. Sims. Yes.
Mr. Ball. At 2:20 took Oswald--that's the first time you saw Oswald?
Mr. Sims. Yes, sir; that's right, he was there in that interrogation room.
Mr. Ball. And who was in Fritz' office at that time?

Mr. Sims. Well, let's see, during the interrogation, there was Mr. Bookhout, that's Jim Bookhout, and Mr. Hosty, and Boyd and I and Captain Fritz.
Mr. Ball. Did you make notes of what was said at that time?
Mr. Sims. No, sir; I didn't.

Mr. Ball. Did your partner, Boyd, make notes, do you think?

Mr. Sims. I don't know if he did or not.

Mr. Ball. Do you have anything from which you can refresh your memory as to what was said in that interrogation?

Mr. Sims. No, sir.

Mr. Ball. You have some memory of what was said, don't you?

Mr. Sims. Well, not the exact wording or the exact questions.

Mr. Ball. Give us your memory of the substance of what was said there at that time.

Mr. Sims. Well, I couldn't say that. I know that it consisted of his name and where he lived and things of that nature, and where he worked.

Mr. Ball. Now, tell us all you can remember, even though it is not complete, just tell us as much as you can remember.

Mr. Sims. I don't remember--I know, like I say, he asked him his name and where he worked and things of that nature.

Mr. Ball. Did they ask him whether or not he had killed Tippit?

Mr. Sims. Yes, sir; I believe he did.

Mr. Ball. What did he say?

Mr. Sims. He said, *"No."*

Mr. Ball. Did they ask him if he had shot the President?

Mr. Sims. I don't remember now what--I wouldn't want to say for sure what questions he did ask him.

Mr. Ball. Who did the questioning?

Mr. Sims. Captain Fritz.

Mr. Ball. Did anyone else ask him questions?

Mr. Sims. Well, I don't know if they did or not.

Mr. Ball. Did you ask him any questions?

Mr. Sims. No, sir.

Mr. Ball. Well----

Mr. Sims. Not at this time here, I didn't but I talked to him later on that evening.

Mr. Ball. But you didn't ask him any questions at the time you were there then?

Mr. Sims. No, sir; I never did actually do any interrogation myself then.

Mr. Ball. Was he handcuffed at that time?

Mr. Sims. I don't remember if he was or not.

Mr. Ball. Wasn't he handcuffed with his handcuffs behind his back, and didn't he ask to be more comfortable?

Mr. Sims. I don't remember.

Mr. Ball. Do you remember any incident where Oswald said he would be more comfortable if he could get his hands from behind his back, or something of that sort?

Mr. Sims. No, sir; I don't.

Mr. Ball. Do you remember changing his handcuffs at any time so that he could put his hands in front of him.

197

Mr. Sims. Of course, when he took the paraffin cast of his hands, he wasn't handcuffed.

Mr. Ball. But that was late that evening?

Mr. Sims. Yes; it was around--it was after dark, I believe.

Mr. Ball. Now, I'm talking about--only about the interrogation that commenced about 2:20 in the afternoon of November 22.

Mr. Sims. I just don't remember.

Mr. Ball. You don't remember changing the handcuffs?

Mr. Sims. No, sir; I don't.

Mr. Ball. How long was he in Captain Fritz' office?

Mr. Sims. Well, let's see, we first went in there at 2 and we stayed in there evidently--this says here that the Secret Service and the FBI took part in the interrogation of Oswald with Captain Fritz, and we took him down to the first show up at 4:05.

Mr. Ball. Then, would you say he was in Captain Fritz' office from about 2:20 until 4 o'clock?

Mr. Sims. Well, he had to be either in Captain Fritz' office or the interrogation room--that's the only two places that he was kept.

Mr. Ball. All right, do you have any memory of how long he was in Captain Fritz' office the first time for the interrogation?

Mr. Sims. No, sir; I don't recall if he stayed in there from 2:20 until showup time at 4:05 or not. He may have stayed in there all that time or he may have been put back in the interrogation room, which is right next door.

Mr. Ball. Where is the interrogation room from Captain Fritz' office?

Mr. Sims. It's in the same office, but just a different room--there's just a hall separating them.

Mr. Ball. And in the interrogation room, were you with Oswald?

Mr. Sims. Yes, sir.

Mr. Ball. You and Boyd?

Mr. Sims. Yes, sir.

Mr. Ball. When he was in the interrogation room for the first show up, did you ask him any questions?

Mr. Sims. Yes; we talked to him.

Mr. Ball. Do you remember what you said to him?

Mr. Sims. No, sir; I don't remember--it was just--I know I asked him his-- later on I asked him about his life in Russia and about him being in the service and things of that nature.

Mr. Ball Did you ask him that at this time? Before the first show-up at 4:05?

Mr. Sims. I don't remember what time it was.

Mr. Ball. There was sometime then that you asked him about his life in Russia?

Mr. Sims. Yes, sir.

Mr. Ball. Are you able to tell us about what time that was?

Mr. Sims. No, sir; I sure don't know what time it was.

Mr. Ball. Could it have been after he had been in Captain Fritz' office and before the first show up?

Mr. Sims. It was after he had been in Captain Fritz' office; yes, sir.

Mr. Ball. And it was in the interrogation room?

Mr. Sims. I--well, I don't know--I have talked to him both places, and I don't know--I know he wouldn't talk at all about the assassination of the President or of Officer Tippit, but he would talk about his life in Russia and some things over here and about his family and things.

Mr. Ball. Now, you say he wouldn't talk about the assassination of the President, what do you mean?

Mr. Sims. Well, he would just deny knowledge of it.

Mr. Ball. And you say he wouldn't talk about Officer Tippit's death, what do you mean by that; what would he say, if anything?

Mr. Sims. Well, he would make some remark and he just wouldn't talk about it.

Mr. Ball. Well, did he ever deny that he had anything to do with it?

Mr. Sims. Yes, sir.

Mr. Ball. He did?

Mr. Sims. Yes, sir.

Mr. Ball. Did he ever make any admission to you that he had any knowledge of Officer Tippit's death?

Mr. Sims. Not at all; no, sir.

Mr. Ball. Did he ever make any admission to you that he had any knowledge of the shooting of the President at all?

Mr. Sims. None at all.

14:55 Oswald's Photo Appears on the Wire

Fred Kaufman of Associated Press manages to photograph Oswald while he is brought into the DPD, after first missing the opportunity to do so at the Texas Theatre. He reckoned he took the photo inside the DPD at about 14:10. He then has it immediately processed and it is transmitted at 14:55 on the Associated Press Wire Photo System. Any TV station and newspaper that is subscribed to that feed has access to the photograph in question, which is captioned.

Taking the timing of the above into consideration, Oswald is declared guilty for the Tippit killing while Fritz is interrogating Oswald for the very first time.

Read more about this at Mary Ferrell here (3105).

I have tried to find out what photograph in question was put on the wire, but to this day I have not been able to ascertain that for sure. I contacted AP in mid-2021, but received no reply.

There is an interview by the Sixth Floor Museum with Fred Kaufman (3106) from 2013. At about 13:30 minutes Kaufman describes the event which led him to be able to photograph Oswald's arrival at the DPD. The picture shown at 14:40 however is from after the first interrogation (after 16:00), because his handcuffs are in front of him and not behind his back. Fritz had this changed during the first interrogation.

This photograph (3107) is definitely taken before the first interrogation, since Oswald has his hands cuffed behind his back. During the first interrogation session with Will Fritz, he has his hands cuffed in front and they remain that way during his incarceration that weekend. Furthermore, his shirt is unbuttoned; we also see Oswald on his arrival at City Hall in films with his shirt hanging off his right shoulder. After the first interrogation photos show his shirt buttoned up.

15:01 Hoover tells RFK He Thinks Oswald Killed the President

At 15:01 Dallas time J Edgar Hoover has a report made (3108) detailing his conversation with RFK. 15:01 means fourteen minutes before Hosty and Bookhout entered the room. No interrogation had happened yet and Hoover thinks the man dropped off an hour earlier at DPD is the main suspect!
I called the attorney general at his home and I told him I thought we had the man who killed the President down in Dallas, at the present time. I stated the man's name is Lee Harvey Oswald; that he was working in the building from which the shots had been fired that hit the President and the Governor…

15:15 Hosty and Bookhout Join Captain Fritz

Fritz's handwritten notes show Hosty and Bookhout being part of the whole interrogation. Even though Bookhout saw Oswald arrive at the DPD at 14:00 and Gordon Shanklin ordered Bookhout to wait for Hosty since he was the one that had his file. Bookhout describes in a report from November 29th (3109) that Oswald lost his cool and accused Hosty of accosting his wife. Also shown is Oswald's interrogation as timed by Bookhout from 15:15 to 16:00.

Hosty's WC testimony (3110) goes into depth about the interrogation and its settings, and the "*so you are Hosty*" remark:

Mr. Stern. I show you a two-page document marked Commission No. 832 for identification. Can you identify that?

Mr. HOSTY. Yes, sir. This is an interview form which I made for my interview with Lee Harvey Oswald on the 22d of November 1963. It was dictated as the form will indicate, on the 23d of November 1963.

Mr. Stern. Let me ask you there, Mr. Hosty, about your practice in reducing to formal form your notes of interviews. This happened the next day?

Mr. HOSTY. Right.

Mr. Stern. Is that faster than usual because of the circumstances?

Mr. HOSTY. Because of the circumstances. We have to reduce them to writing within 5 days.

Mr. Stern. In 5 days?

Mr. HOSTY. Five working days.

Mr. Stern. Did you retain the notes of this?

Mr. HOSTY. No. After the interview is reduced to writing, I get it back and proofread it. My notes are then destroyed because this is the record.

Mr. Stern. And in this particular instance did you destroy your notes of this?

Mr. HOSTY. Yes, sir.

Mr. Stern. Now you say that you are required to reduce your notes of an interview to writing within 5 working days.

Mr. HOSTY. Right.

Mr. Stern. Did that happen with respect to the interviews you conducted on October 29, November 1, and November 5?

Mr. HOSTY. To make this a little clearer, this would be an interview of a subject, not of a witness, unless this witness has something that was quite pertinent to the investigation. Routine-type matters do not have to be put on these interview forms, but pertinent interviews would be. Now everything in this case after the assassination was declared to be pertinent. All interviews, regardless of how insignificant, were to be put on these forms.

Mr. Stern. But the interviews you conducted at the beginning of November and the end of October were not within this rule?

Mr. HOSTY. No; because they were not an interview of the subject or anything that contained anything of major importance.

Mr. Stern. Do you yourself destroy the notes?

Mr. HOSTY. Yes.

Mr. Stern. Do you recall specifically destroying the notes of your interview?

Mr. HOSTY. Yes, sir; in the wastebasket.

Mr. Stern. Your interview of Oswald, on November 22, you put the notes in the wastebasket?

Mr. HOSTY. Right..

Mr. Stern. Do you recall specifically what you did with the notes of your interviews of October 29, November 1, and November 5?

Mr. HOSTY. After I reduced them to writing, such as I did here, and I got the form back, I proofread it, then I threw them away.

Mr. Stern. And you testified that the notes of your end of October early November interviews were transcribed after November 22, is that correct?

Mr. HOSTY. Right

Mr. Stern. Were the notes destroyed after you transcribed those interviews, also after November 22?

Mr. HOSTY. Yes.

Mr. Stern. Did you give any consideration to retaining the notes in view of the turn that the case had taken?

Mr. HOSTY. No.

Mr. Stern. The intervening assassination?

Mr. HOSTY. No; because this is the record and the notes would not be as good as this record, because the notes are not written out fully as this is. It would just be abbreviations and things of that type.

Mr. Stern. And you received no instructions about retaining notes?

Mr. HOSTY. No; we had no instructions. We were following the same rule we had always followed.

Mr. Stern. Why don't you tell us now, turning to your memorandum of the November 22 interview of Lee Harvey Oswald, what transpired from the time you first entered Captain Fritz' office.

Mr. HOSTY. As this interview form will show, the interview commenced at 3:15 p.m. I am certain of that time because I checked my wristwatch, and Agent Bookhout checked my wristwatch. We both agreed on the time, 3:15. We came in and identified ourselves as agents of the FBI. I told Oswald my name and he reacted violently.

Mr. Stern. How do you mean?

Mr. HOSTY. To both Agent Bookhout and myself. He adopted an extremely hostile attitude towards the FBI.

Mr. Stern. Was it the FBI or the name Hosty?

Mr. HOSTY. Both. He reacted to the fact that we were FBI, and he made the remark to me, *"Oh, so you are Hosty. I've heard about you."*

He then started to cuss at us, and so forth, and I tried to talk to him to calm him down. The more I talked to him the worse he got, so I just stopped talking to him, just sat back in the corner and pretty soon he stopped his ranting and raving.

Mr. Stern. What was he saying? Please be specific.

Mr. HOSTY. Well, he said, *"I am going to fix you FBI,"* and he made some derogatory remarks about the Director and about FBI agents in general. I don't specifically recall the exact wording he used.

Representative Ford. Had this been the attitude that existed prior to you and Bookhout coming into the----

Mr. HOSTY. Apparently not; apparently not. I couldn't say because I wasn't in the room. We walked into the room. I immediately identified myself, told him I was with the FBI, and was a law-enforcement officer, and anything he said to me could be used against him. He did not have to talk to us.

Senator Cooper. Can you describe the tone of his voice and his manner?

Mr. HOSTY. I beg your pardon, sir?

Senator Cooper. Can you describe the tone of his voice?

Mr. HOSTY. He was highly excited. He was very surly, I think would be about the best way to describe him, very surly; and he was curt in his answers to us, snarled at us. That would be his general attitude.

Representative Ford. Did he use profanity?

Mr. HOSTY. Yes, sir. I can't recall any specific statements he made, however.

Mr. McCloy. Did he complain that you had been abusing or harassing his wife in anyway?

Mr. HOSTY. He made the statement, *"If you want to talk to me don't bother my wife. Come and see me."* He didn't say that I had abused his wife in any manner, and I hadn't. He did criticize me for talking to her. He said, *"Come talk to me if you want to talk to me."*

Representative Ford. Is that why he knew your name, because of your conversations with her?

Mr. HOSTY. Yes; apparently.

Mr. Stern. Had you ever seen Oswald before?

Mr. HOSTY. Not until that time. That was the first time I had seen him.

Senator Cooper. Can you remember what he said about the FBI specifically?

Mr. HOSTY. He called us gestapo, secret police, we were harassing people. It was along that line. I don't recall the exact wording.

Mr. Stern. Was he handcuffed at this time?

Mr. HOSTY. He was handcuffed behind him. After he calmed down, he asked Captain Fritz if they could remove the handcuffs. Captain Fritz ordered one of his detectives to remove them from the rear, and they handcuffed him in front.

Mr. Stern. This happened right after you came into the room?

Mr. HOSTY. Shortly after we came in the room.

Mr. Stern. Before or after his outburst?

Mr. HOSTY. After his outburst; after he had calmed down.

Mr. Stern. Please continue.

Mr. HOSTY. Captain Fritz actually conducted the interview. Agent Bookhout and myself sat back in the corner and observed. Captain Fritz asked Oswald if he had ever owned the rifle. He denied he had ever owned a rifle. He said that he had seen the superintendent of the School Book Depository with a rifle in his office a couple of days before the assassination, but that he had never had a rifle in the building. He then told Captain Fritz that he had been to the Soviet Union and resided there for 3 years, and he had many friends in the Soviet Union. Captain Fritz then showed him a piece of paper which had *"Fair Play for Cuba"* on it, and Oswald admitted to Captain Fritz that he was secretary for the Fair Play for Cuba Committee in New Orleans a few months ago.

He told Captain Fritz that the Fair Play for Cuba Committee had its headquarters in New York City. Captain Fritz then showed Oswald a marksman's medal from the Marine Corps, and Oswald admitted that this was his medal, that he had received a sharpshooter's medal while in the Marine Corps.

Mr. McCloy. Was it a sharpshooter's or a marksman's? There are two different types, you know.

Mr. HOSTY. I believe it was a sharpshooter, sir. He then told Captain Fritz that he had been living at 1026 North Beckley, that is in Dallas, Tex., at 1026 North Beckley under the name O. H. Lee and not under his true name.

Oswald admitted that he was present in the Texas School Book Depository Building on the 22d of November 1963, where he had been employed since the 15th of October. Oswald told Captain Fritz that he was a labourer in this building and had access to the entire building. It had offices on the first and second floors with storage on third, fourth, fifth and sixth floors.

Oswald told Captain Fritz that he went to lunch at approximately noon on the 22nd of November, ate his lunch in the lunchroom, and had gone and gotten a Coca Cola from the Coca Cola machine to have with his lunch. He claimed that he was in the lunchroom at the time President Kennedy passed the building.

He was asked why he left the School Book Depository that day, and he stated that in all the confusion he was certain that there would be no more work for the rest of the day, that everybody was too upset, there was too much confusion, so he just decided that there would be no work for the rest of the day and so he went home. He got on a bus and went home. He went to his residence on North Beckley, changed his clothes, and then went to a movie.

Captain Fritz asked him if he always carried a pistol when he went to the movie, and he said he carried it because he felt like it. He admitted that he did have a pistol on him at the time of his arrest, in this theatre, in the Oak Cliff area of Dallas. He further admitted that he had resisted arrest and had received a bump and a cut as a result of his resisting of arrest. He then denied that he had killed Officer Tippit or President Kennedy.

Mr. Stern. The memorandum says, *"Oswald frantically denied shooting..."*

Mr. HOSTY. It should be emphatically, I believe, rather than frantically. I think this probably should be *"emphatically denied."*

Mr. Stern. Is this your memorandum?

Mr. HOSTY. Yes, sir.

Mr. Stern. It is signed or initialled both by you and by Mr. Bookhout.

Mr. HOSTY. Right. The procedure is that when there are two agents involved, they both must approve it, so there can be no discrepancies.

Mr. Stern. But you dictated it.

Mr. HOSTY. I dictated it and he read it and we both approved it.

Mr. Stern. Have you been over it recently in preparation for your testimony?

Mr. HOSTY. Yes, sir.

Mr. Stern. Is it accurate? Is there anything you would like to add to it?

Mr. HOSTY. I think it is correct as it stands.

Mr. McCloy. I didn't hear you repeating your testimony that he denied ever having been in Mexico.

Mr. HOSTY. Oh, yes; he was being questioned about his activities outside of the United States, where he had been outside of the United States. He told Captain Fritz that he had only been to Mexico to visit at Tijuana on the border, and then he did admit having been in Russia.

Mr. McCloy. He only admitted to having been at Tijuana in Mexico?

Mr. HOSTY. Right.

Mr. McCloy. Not to Mexico City.

Mr. HOSTY. Not to Mexico City; that is right.

Representative Ford. There was no recording made of this interrogation?

Mr. HOSTY. No, sir; it was notes I took. Agent Bookhout and I took notes, and we dictated from the notes the next day.

Mr. Stern. Did you ask him any questions?

Mr. HOSTY. No; like I say, he was acting in such a hostile condition towards us that we did not. This was Captain Fritz' interview anyway. We were just sitting in as observers.

Mr. Stern. Did you tell Captain Fritz at this time any of the information you had about Oswald, about his trip to Mexico, for example?

Mr. HOSTY. No.

Mr. Stern. About his being in touch with the Russian authorities seeking a visa?

Mr. HOSTY. No.

Mr. Stern. About his previous residence in the Soviet Union?

Mr. HOSTY. Oswald himself told Captain Fritz of this. I didn't have to. Oswald came right out and told him.

Mr. Stern. About the affair in New Orleans and his arrest there?

Mr. HOSTY. No.

Mr. Stern. Did you subsequently tell Captain Fritz?

Mr. HOSTY. No; I didn't tell Captain Fritz; no.

Mr. Stern. Was any of this information provided to the Dallas police as far as you know?

Mr. HOSTY. I provided it to Lieutenant Revill earlier, as I pointed out. He would have been the person I would have furnished this information to as the head of the intelligence section. He would be the logical and correct person to give this information to.

Mr. Stern. Was that the extent of your advice to the Dallas police?

Mr. HOSTY. Right.

Mr. McCloy. Did you tell Chief Curry that you had a file?

Mr. HOSTY. No, sir; I haven't talked to Chief Curry in several years. Of course, I don't deal with him too much on a chief level.

Mr. Stern. Wouldn't it be difficult for Lieutenant Revill to have gotten this information from you under the conditions that you described, running up the stairway and the rest of it? Do you think he heard enough of this?

Mr. HOSTY. Well, that is true, he might not have. But you see Oswald then proceeded to tell himself, he told the police all this information, so there was no point in me repeating it when he himself, Oswald, had furnished it directly to the police.

Mr. McCloy. But you did tell Revill that you had a file on Oswald?

Mr. HOSTY. No; I didn't tell him I had a file; no, sir.

Hosty, was the only person in that room who took notes during the first interrogation, but claimed he had torn them up after the joint Bookhout-Hosty report was typed up.

But two pages of the hand written notes (3111) 're-appeared' when Hosty published his book Assignment Oswald (3112).

"First floor outside office" would relate to where Oswald was when the motorcade passed by. And I tend to lean that way, mainly after comparing the notes above with the second set, and also, after comparing these with Fritz's notes.

Hosty has sectioned his notes, none of the phrases are related to each other inside these compartments, if you care to compare all contents.

"Chose to go home because of confusion," and this matter was also broached by Thomas J Kelley of the Secret Service in his report, which he wrote on the 24th and Kelley did not get to sit in on the interrogations until the morning of the 23rd. This is something Shelley denied. But it is

quite significant that Hosty brings this up and Kelley, one day later, does as well.

So, we can conclude that Oswald mentioned this during *two* interrogations.
Hosty did not attend any later interrogations, whereas James Bookhout did. But Hosty did hang around Will Fritz's office that day. He noted down on the third notebook page (3113) that Oswald went to a line-up at 16:15 and that he spoke with Forrest Sorrels of the USSS ten minutes after that.

Early February 2019 I came across a handwritten document (3114) from James Hosty that was written on the back of a blank DPD affidavit sheet of paper in Malcolm Blunt's archives. It is part of the James Hosty papers which were made public by the ARRB in 1997 (3115). It was that particular *"Affidavit in any Fact"* bit, in mirrored writing, that got my first attention and only then did I start to read what the actual document said. Hosty mentions the date and time, but also something so significant that since I have shown it online it has caused a few ripples. This document was part of a batch called *The* Hosty Papers (3116), which only surfaced through the ARRB. That other researchers, besides Harold Weisberg, did not take a closer look, especially after the release of the Fritz notes a few months prior, just boggles the mind.

I quote from the middle of the page: "*O. stated he was present for work at the TSBD on the morning of the 22ⁿᵈ and at noon went to lunch. He went to 2ⁿᵈ floor to get a coca cola to eat with lunch and returned to 1ˢᵗ floor to eat lunch. Then he went outside to watch P. Parade.*" It is safe to say that P. stands for Presidential.

The first important element of this paragraph is that he got his coke *for* his lunch which was *before* the shots were fired. This element is re-confirmed in the joint Hosty-Bookhout (3117) report and destroys the second-floor lunchroom encounter due to the timing of it.

And then there is the bomb-shell that states that Oswald was outside to watch the Presidential Parade *after* his lunch.

Hosty's book, *Assignment Oswald* (3118), describes how he kept on taking notes even after the interrogation:

I decided nonetheless, that I would remain at the police station. Just because I couldn't talk to the police didn't mean I couldn't learn things from them. I headed back to Fritz's office, where I knew the police were keeping Oswald's personal belongings. Nothing there, but in the second

207

inner office, which belonged to Lieutenant Walter Potts, I spotted Oswald's things, which had been removed from his person and from his apartment at the Oak Cliff rooming house. Among the items on Potts's desk was Oswald's black address book. I pulled out my pad of blank police affidavit forms and started transcribing the entries in his book, thinking I might find some interesting leads or even some possible co-conspirators.

Then if you compare the notebook pages and the handwritten partial draft statement, something else becomes apparent. The James Hosty Oswald interrogation notes (3119).

James Hosty used his notebook notes to compile this draft on DPD affidavit paper, and this also means that the phrase *"2ndr entrance office"* in Hosty's notebook notes directly relates to Oswald's whereabouts as described in the draft on the DPD affidavit paper (the green highlighted areas on both documents). Before the February 2019 find it was assumed that *"first-floor entrance office"* was related to Warren Caster's, Wednesday, November 20th visit, when he showed Roy Truly and a few others two rifles he had brought in to the TSBD. *"First floor entrance office"* means first floor entrance *of the* office.

Hosty had a bloc of blank DPD affidavit papers. He not only wrote this draft on them, but he also took notes of Oswald's address book which were in a separate office inside room 317 of Homicide & Robbery.

Not even a scribble about that Hidell ID. Read more about this HERE (3120).

He writes in his book *Assignment Oswald* (3121), about an exchange, from his memory how the questioning went on during that first interrogation:

Okay now, Lee, you work at the Texas School Book Depository, isn't that right?
Yeah, that's right.
When did you start working there?
About October fifteenth.
What did you do down there?

I was just a common labourer.
Now, did you have access to all floors of the building?
Of course.
Tell me what was on each of those floors.

The first and second floors have offices. The third and fourth floor are storage. So are the fifth and sixth.

And you were working there today, is that right?

Yep.

Were you there when the president's motorcade went by?

Yeah.

Where were you when the president went by the book depository?

I was eating my lunch in the first-floor lunchroom.

What time was that?

About noon.

Were you ever on the second floor around the time the president was shot?

Well, yeah. I went up there to get a bottle of Coca-Cola from the machine for my lunch.

But where were you when the president actually passed your building?

On the first floor in the lunchroom.

And you left the depository, isn't that right?

Yeah.

When did you leave?

Well, I figured with all the confusion there wouldn't be any more work to do that day.

Again, Oswald, according to Hosty's recollections, makes mention of the reason why he left work. But what is significant is that the second-floor lunchroom encounter simply does *not* exist at that time; at best Oswald got his coke *for* his lunch. Not *after!*

More important is that Oswald provided Fritz and Hosty an alibi, neither of which anyone checked out further. Hoover makes a half-hearted attempt weeks later (3122), but it ends with that.

Accor*ding to a summary of* Hosty's HSCA testimony (3123), Will Fritz led the interrogation, but was fed information by Hosty about Russia, Marina, Mexico City and the FPCC (Fair Play for Cuba Committee).

James Hosty speaks with the Church Committee over three dates in December 1975. These transcripts contain 550 pages of testimony in which many aspects of his involvement are discussed. They are a good read to get some valuable background info on what he was doing when all this was all going on.

During the December 5th 1975 testimony session (3124). Pages 30-47 deal with the interrogations:

- Mexico City is brought up (page 30).

- Hosty took notes during the interrogation, but subsequently destroyed them (pages 31 & 32).
- Oswald did not respond to the Mexico City question as Will Fritz went into another question. Later, Hosty states that the interrogation was suddenly halted as they were going to take Oswald downstairs for the Markham line-up (page 45).
- James Bookhout did not ask any questions, he just sat and observed (page 46).
- Fritz did all the questioning; Hosty fed info to Fritz who in turned asked Oswald the questions (page 47).
- Other than Mexico City, Hosty forwarded questions to Fritz about Russia, Marina, New Orleans and the FPCC (page 46). The session goes off the record straight after this and when reconvened the subject has been changed (page 47).

From December 12th 1975 (3125), this 164 page document does not discuss much when it comes to the interrogations:

- Hosty only knows of his own report and the ones made by James Bookhout (page 98).
- The inconsistencies of the reports of what was allegedly said by Oswald and what actually was said by him are brought up (page 100).
- Hosty and Warren DeBrueys who had come in from New Orleans went through the evidence together, *before* it was released by the DPD (page 151).

On December 13th 1975 (3126), his second day of his testimony, there is more:

- Hosty recounts the interrogations. The Mexico City question is broadly discussed, without any real effect and how quickly Will Fritz moved on to a different question.
- He describes his and James Bookhout's reports.
- Hosty took notes but there are no transcripts (page 31).
- Hosty pictures the setting of him feeding questions to Will Fritz who then asks Oswald (page 68).
- The Mexico City question was denied by Oswald and did not get a follow-up as the interrogation was interrupted for a line-up (page 70).
- Fritz asked all the questions. Started with background questions to get Oswald go along after being upset with Hosty's presence.

- Oswald had his hands cuffed behind him (3127) when Hosty and Bookhout had made their entry. It was Hosty who suggested to Fritz to remove the handcuffs with his hands behind him (page 136).
- Upon his arrival in the room Hosty heard them talk about the JFK and Tippit shootings and Oswald being questioned where he was inside the TSBD at that time. Then confirms that DPD and FBI do not take any transcripts; that many law enforcement officers don't do this is in preliminary investigation and that it is normal procedure (page 137).
- After Oswald has been removed from the room and is on his way to the first line-up Hosty makes his way to where Oswald's evidence has been laid out. Included is Oswald's address book which is the only item brought up in his answer (page 138). There is no mention of a Hidell ID.
- The encounter with Oswald is discussed again (pages 139-141).

A recent find of mine in the Malcolm Blunt Archives (3128) is an 82 page document, which is a HSCA staff review interview on August 25th 1978 (3129). This document had no online presence anywhere before; it does now! In this interview Hosty again discusses the interrogations:

- Oswald is only slightly upset when Hosty has introduced himself upon entry into the room (page 21 of the PDF!).
- Hosty feeds Fritz questions (page 21).
- He sat alongside Fritz (page 23).
- The questioning about Mexico City does not last long as shortly after the interrogations are ended, they are ready for the first line-up with Helen Markham (page 24).
- Hosty discusses with James Bookhout whether they could talk to Oswald alone. Bookhout did not seem to think that was feasible knowing Fritz's temperament and attitude (page 25).
- He sees Oswald talking to Forrest Sorrels of the Secret Service and also to Manning Clements of the FBI at a later time (pages 30 & 31).
- Hosty is told not to attend any further interrogations (page 30).

James Bookhout (3130), with more than 20 years of law enforcement experience under his belt and who was the liaison between the DPD and the FBI had arrived at the DPD station before Will Fritz. Actually, he witnessed Oswald being brought in from his arrest at the Texas Theatre. Bookhout is instructed to wait for Hosty to arrive and they ask Fritz if they can join the questioning, which happens at about 15:15.

Fritz mentions the goings on in his WC testimony (3131):

Mr. Ball. You mentioned that Hosty, the first day he was there, you said that he said he knows these people. Did he tell you that he knew Oswald?
Mr. Fritz. Well, I will tell you, he wasn't talking to me really.
Mr. Ball. What did he say to Oswald?
Mr. Fritz. That was the agent--what did Hosty say to Oswald?
Mr. Ball. Yes.
Mr. Fritz. Or what did----
Mr. Ball. Did Hosty say?
Mr. Fritz. I thought you meant what about Shanklin said to Hosty.
Mr. Ball. Did Hosty say to you that he knew Oswald?
Mr. Fritz. I heard Mr. Shanklin tell Mr. Hosty on the telephone. I had Mr. Bookhout pick up the telephone and I had an extension.
Mr. Ball. What did he hear?
Mr. Fritz. He said, *"Is Hosty in that investigation?"* Bookhout said, *"No."* He said, *"I want him in that investigation right now because he knows those people he has been talking to,"* and he said some other things that I don't want to repeat, about what to do if he didn't do it right quick. So, I didn't tell them that I even knew what Mr. Shanklin said. I walked out there and called them in.

Bookhout's WC testimony (3132) about that very first interrogation:

Mr. Bookhout - I was not in the office at that time. I called our office, advised them he had been brought in, and that the interview was starting and shortly thereafter Mr. Shanklin, our SAC called back and said the Bureau wanted the agents present in the interview and that Hosty, James P. Hosty, I believe, was to sit in on the interview, and I was to also be present with Hosty. So, at that time, we asked Captain Fritz to sit in on the interview, and that was approximately 3:15 p.m. [Hosty is recorded as arriving at 14:45 in the basement-BK]
Mr. Stern - How long had the interview gone on before you were present?
Mr. Bookhout - Very shortly. I would give a rough estimate of not more than 5 to 10 minutes at the most.

[Bookhout is covering his rear here; Fritz started the interrogation some time before 15:00, and the joint Hosty-Bookhout report says that the time was undetermined-BK]

Mr. Stern - How long did that first interview last?
Mr. Bookhout - A little under an hour.
Mr. Stern - Was it interrupted at any point, if you remember?

212

Mr. Bookhout - Well, what I am thinking, we have got several interviews here. I know from time to time I can't recall whether it was this interview, or subsequent interviews, Captain Fritz would have to leave the office for a second or two. By *"office,"* I mean the immediate office that the interview was being conducted in, but still within the homicide and robbery office.

Mr. Stern - Did the interviewing continue when he was out of the room, or did you wait for his return?

Mr. Bookhout - No; it would continue.

Mr. Stern - By whom was the interview conducted?

Mr. Bookhout - Primarily it was conducted by Captain Fritz and then before he would leave from one point to another he would ask if there was anything we wanted to ask him particularly on that point.

Mr. Stern - By *"we,"* you mean Agent Hosty and yourself?

Mr. Bookhout - Right.

Mr. Stern - What was Oswald's demeanour in the course of this interview? Did he seem in control of himself, excited, or calm? Can you describe his conduct?

Mr. Bookhout - He was very arrogant and argumentative. That is about the extent of the comment on that.

Mr. Stern - Is this as to you and Hosty, or also Captain Fritz? Did he differentiate in his conduct between Captain Fritz and the two of you?

Mr. Bookhout - Now--no; that would apply to everyone present.

Mr. Stern - Did he answer all questions put to him or did he refuse to answer the questions?

Mr. Bookhout - No; there would be certain questions that he refused to comment about.

Mr. Stern - When this happened was the question pressed, or another question asked?

Mr. Bookhout - Anyone asking another question would be asked.

Mr. Stern - What sort of question would he refuse to answer? Was there any pattern to his refusing?

Mr. Bookhout - Well, now, I am not certain whether this would apply then to this particular interview, the first interview or not, in answering this, but I recall specifically one of the interviews asking him about the Selective Service card which he had in the name of Hidell, and he admitted that he was carrying the card, but that he would not admit that he wrote the signature of Hidell on the card, and at that point stated that he refused to discuss the matter further. I think generally you might say anytime that you asked a question that would be pertinent to the investigation that would be the type of question he would refuse to discuss.

Mr. Stern - Would you say he had a pretty good idea of what might be incriminating and what not incriminating?

Mr. Bookhout - Well, I think that would call for an opinion, and I can only report the facts to you, and based on the example of the type of questions that I had commented on that he refused to answer, you will have to draw your own conclusion on that.

Mr. Stern - Fine. I am just trying to get at whether he seemed in command of himself and alert, and whether he handled himself responsibly from his own viewpoint, but if you don't want to venture an opinion, that's fine.

When you first joined the interview, did you advise him that you were an agent of the FBI, and did you say anything about warning him that evidence--that anything he said might be used?

Mr. Bookhout - Yes; that was done by Agent Hosty.

Mr. Stern - Did he, at that point, or later say anything specifically regarding the FBI?

Mr. Bookhout - Yes.

Mr. Stern - Tell us what that was.

Mr. Bookhout - He accused the FBI of, generally, unfair tactics in interviewing his wife on some previous occasion.

Mr. Stern - Was this directed specifically at either you or Hosty, or to the general----

Mr. Bookhout - It was directed against Hosty.

Mr. Stern - He did not, Oswald did not indicate that he knew Hosty himself, did he?

Mr. Bookhout - No.

Mr. Stern - But there was a complaint about an interview, or interrogation of Marina Oswald?

Mr Bookhout - Right.

Mr. Stern - Did he say anything about FBI interviews of him that had occurred in the past, any complaint about such interviews?

Mr. Bookhout - I don't know that that would be in this particular interview, but in one of the interviews which has been reported he stated that he had been interviewed at Fort Worth, Tex., by agents upon his return to the United States from Russia, and he felt that they had used unfair means of interviewing him, or something. Those are not his exact words, but that is the impression he conveyed.

Mr. Stern - Unfair in what respect?

Mr. Bookhout - I don't know.

Mr. Stern - Did he say?

Mr. Bookhout - No.

Mr. Stern - Tell us the nature of his complaint.

Mr. Bookhout - I think he probably used the expression, *"Unfair tactics,"* or something in their interviews.

Mr. Stern - Yes. Did he indicate that he felt that the interview that was then going on was unfair in any way? Did he complain about that?

Mr. Bookhout - No, he didn't complain about the interview. He made a complaint or two, as I recall, that one of the interviews that has been reported, in fact, I believe it was in this first interview he complained about his hands being handcuffed behind his back, and asked Captain Fritz to remove the handcuffs. Captain Fritz had one of his officers uncuff his hands from behind his back and re-cuff them in front and asked him if that was more satisfactory and he stated that it was.

[And a little later...]

Mr. Stern - During the first interview was he asked whether he had ever been in Mexico, and if so, by whom?

Mr. Bookhout - Yes; I recall Hosty asking him if He had ever been in Mexico.

Mr. Stern - What did he say?

Mr. Bookhout - He said he had not. I believe he mentioned he had been in Tijuana, Mexico, I believe, but I believe the question was whether he had ever been in Mexico City.

Mr. Stern - Was he asked about an organization called the Fair Play for Cuba Committee and if so, by whom?

Mr. Bookhout - Yes, he was asked if he belonged to that. I don't recall specifically who raised the question.

Mr. Stern - What did he say?

Mr. Bookhout - He said he was a member of it, and was secretary of the New Orleans branch. I believe he said the headquarters was in New York City.

Mr. Stern - Was there much discussion of this, or just the identification?

Mr. Bookhout - Well, now, that is another instance where he balked on answering a question. He was asked who the officers were, and at that point he said he refused to discuss the matter further.

Mr. Stern - Was he asked his residence address in Dallas and did he give it?

Mr. Bookhout - Yes; he furnished the address of 1026 North Beckley.

Mr. Stern - Did he say that he was living there under another name, or was another name and particularly the name O. H. Lee mentioned at all in this connection?

Mr. Bookhout - He was asked why he was using the name Lee at this address, and he attempted to pass it off by stating that the landlord was an old lady, and his first name was Lee and she just had gotten it in her head that he was Mr. Lee. He never did explain about the initials O. H.

Mr. Stern - Was he asked whether he had shot the President, or Officer Tippit?

Mr. Bookhout - Yes; he was asked that, and denied shooting either one of them, or knowing anything about it.

215

Mr. Stern - Was he asked whether he was carrying a pistol at the time he was in the Texas Theatre?

Mr. Bookhout - Yes; that was brought up. He admitted that he was carrying a pistol at the time he was arrested. He claimed that he had bought this some time ago in Fort Worth.

Mr. Stern - He said he had gotten it in Fort Worth?

Mr. Bookhout - That is my recollection, and there again, in trying to follow through on that line of thought, he refused to answer any further questions as to whereabouts in Fort Worth he had bought it.

Mr. Stern - Did he talk about his arrest and his resistance of arrest at the Texas Theatre?

Mr. Bookhout - He admitted fighting with the officer at the time of the arrest, but I don't recall any explanation as to why he was doing it.

Mr. Stern - Did he admit that he might have been wrong in doing that, or say anything to that effect?

Mr. Bookhout - Seemed to me like he made the comment that the only thing he was guilty of, or the only thing he could be charged with would be the carrying of a concealed weapon, and of resisting the arrest.

Mr. Stern - When he was asked about involvement in the assassination of President Kennedy, or the shooting of Officer Tippit, how would you describe his denials?

Mr. Bookhout - Well, I don't know exactly how to describe it, but as I recall, he spoke very loudly. In other words, he was--he gave an emphatic denial that is about all I can recall on it.

Mr. Stern - I believe that in the report you filed on this first interview, you or Agent Hosty, who joined in the report with you, used the adverb *"frantically"* to describe his denial of an involvement. Does that refresh your recollection as to that? Would you use that word now, or was that your word?

Mr. Bookhout - No; that was written by Hosty, and that would be his expression of describing it.

Mr. Stern - Do you think *"emphatically,"* is perhaps the more descriptive word now?

Mr. Bookhout - Well, that would be the way I would describe it. As I said, he spoke----

Mr. Stern - I am not trying to put words into your mouth.

Mr. Bookhout - He spoke loudly.

Mr. Stern - I am most interested in getting the tone of this interrogation and his state, the way he conducted himself, and that is why I ask this question, and there is something of a difference between saying a man is acting frantically as opposed to his acting emphatically.

Mr. Bookhout - Well, I suppose the word, *"frantically,"* would probably describe it. In other words, I said that he spoke loudly. There just wasn't a normal type of denial. He was--it was more than that. That is the reason I say that probably *"frantically,"* might be a descriptive word.

216

Mr. Stern - Did that occur only in connection with questions about whether he had shot the President, or was the general tone of this interrogation, as far as he was concerned, at that level?

Mr. Bookhout - No; he wouldn't use the same expression of speech in answering all questions. He would have certain kinds there, and certain types of questions that he would apparently have stronger feelings on.

Mr. Stern - Do you recall at any time his pounding on the desk, or making any other physical gestures of that kind?

Mr. Bookhout - I don't recall him pounding on the desk; no, sir.

Mr. Stern - Now, this interview, as I understand, took approximately an hour?

Mr. Bookhout - That's correct.

Mr. Stern - According to this report, you and Agent Hosty entered the interviewing around about 3:15 p.m., and it ended at 4:05.

Mr. Bookhout - That would be correct.

Mr. Stern - Were these times that you or Hosty would have recorded at that moment in the ordinary course of your participation?

Mr. Bookhout - That's correct. There was no log made of it, as such, but those were the times recorded for that particular interview.

Mr. Stern - Your normal practice is to get times down pretty accurately in matter of this.

Mr. Bookhout - Try to.

Mr. Stern - And did you make the record of these times, or did Agent Hosty?

Mr. Bookhout - I can say that I did. Whether he did or not, I don't know.

Mr. Stern - Incidentally, normally, do you preserve those notes or destroy them when you make a formal report?

Mr. Bookhout - They will be, normally, destroyed at the time you make your--what we refer to as an interview report.

Mr. Stern - And in this case, did you destroy your notes?

Mr. Bookhout - That's correct.

Mr. Stern - So, you have no notes respecting this whole matter?

Mr. Bookhout - No, other than the reported interviewing report.

James Hosty and James Bookhout state in their joint November 23rd report (3133) on the first Oswald interrogation that day: *"Oswald stated that he went to lunch at approximately noon and he claimed he ate his lunch on the first floor in the lunchroom; however, he went to the second floor where the Coca-Cola machine was located and obtained a bottle of Coca-Cola for his lunch. Oswald claimed to be on the first floor when President JOHN F. KENNEDY passed by his building."*

According to Bookhout's WC testimony (3134) the interview was in progress for about 5 or 10 minutes. Yet in this joint statement with James Hosty dated November 23rd he states that time as 15:15: *"Oswald frantically denied killing Dallas Police Officer JD Tippit or President John F Kennedy.*" Since Fritz took no notes at that time it is hard to determine how long Oswald was being interrogated before Bookhout and Hosty entered the interrogation room.

After Oswald has been murdered things get turned around from the Hosty joint report with Bookhout's solo report on November 25th (3135) about the very same interrogation. This report sinks Oswald's alibi. This is after the release of the report by Nat Pinkston of Roy Truly later on the 22nd (3136).

15:15 Robert E Jones Contacts the DOJ/FBI

In a DOJ report from 15:15 on November 22nd (3137) on page 9 it is mentioned that Lieutenant Colonel Robert E Jones, of the 112th INTC [US Army Intelligence 112th Intelligence Corps Group], has telephoned them and relays that Oswald has been arrested for killing JD Tippit. According to the document he found out due to the news broadcasts, but at a later date, Jones states that he was called by the DPD (no name of the officer is ever furnished) between 13:00-14:00. Bear in mind that Oswald is arrested at 13:50. Oswald is only just being interrogated by Will Fritz and FBI agents Hosty and Bookhout who have only just entered the room at the time Jones contacts the DOJ. Jones has quite a file ready; it holds several newspaper clippings related to Oswald, his defection to Russia and the FPCC shenanigans in New Orleans.

This document is the first official record mentioning the Hidell ID on November 22nd 1963, which is quite a feat since the five detectives who arrested and transported Oswald made no mention of this ID in documents or interviews that day or the next! "*When arrested today in Dallas, according to information Colonel Jones has, Oswald was carrying a Selective Service Card bearing the name of Alex Hidell. Jones stated that INTC records here reflect reference to an AJ Hidell who reportedly had been distributing leaflets 'Hands of Cuba' literature.*" It is not clear where this info came from.

There is another teletype of the FBI (3138) on page 7 mentioning the same which is released at 16:25.

In that statement from the FBI, it states that it was reported through news broadcasts that Oswald killed a police officer in a theatre and that he was a suspect in The President's death. Really? Two and a half hours after his arrest and he is already condemned. The Selective Service Card of Oswald is attributed to Alek James Hidell.

And again at 21:25 on November 22nd the Selective Service Card is mentioned in an FBI communique (3139), *"which was allegedly in possession of Oswald."* And the FBI in New Orleans have no trace of Hidell over there.

Not one officer of the 112th INTC was interviewed during the WC investigation. The FBI made no mention of them at that time; the WC never got these statements. But during the HSCA, interviews do take place with Jones and others. In these interviews, he goes into greater depth about the Hidell ID situation.

In the April 4th 1977 (3140) interview for the HSCA Jones mentions that:

- He suspected that Oswald was an intelligence agent.
- An Army Intelligence source rang him and he had learned that Lee Harvey Oswald had been accused of murdering The President.
- He telephoned the FBI and they did *not* request any of his files.
- Harold Leap of the HSCA is the first person to talk to him about the assassination.
- He wanted Oswald's stomach pumped to ascertain he had eaten chicken; this was not done.
- Hidell was an alias, not a different person.
- He did not believe Oswald was a lone gunman.
- The answers are not displayed in exact order in that document.

In the April 28th 1977 (3141) HSCA report Jones states:

- Early afternoon November 22nd 1963 he received a telephone call that an AJ Hidell had been arrested or came to their attention (page 1-18).
- Did not recall the Dallas people mentioning a draft card with the name AJ Hidell (page 1-18).
- Upon learning of the name Hidell, Jones went through his card index and that there also was the name *"Lee Harvey Oswald/"* mentioned as an aka (page 1-19).
- Rings San Antonio FBI office and forwards this information (page 1-19).
- Possible follow-up call(s) that same afternoon with the FBI (page 1-20).
- Expected to be contacted by someone from the WC as he had reported everything to the FBI and assumed it was of public records (pages 1-21 & 22).

- The Oswald and Hidell names were stored with two index cards but only lead to one file (page 1-23).
- The name Hidell was placed on literature he was distributing in New Orleans, but upon his arrest he was named as Lee Harvey Oswald. (page 1-23).
- Estimates the time of the phone call to him at 13:30 – 14:00 hrs (page 1-25). [Oswald was arrested at 13:50 and placed in holding at just after 14:00.-BK]
- After reading the DOJ document Jones corrects that it was a phone call from the DPD, he cannot recall who, and not news reports that advised him (page 1-27).
- Does not recall that he stated at that time Oswald was carrying a Selective Service Card unless told so by the source from the DPD (page 1-27).
- Again, he states that Oswald carrying a Selective Service Card would be from information gathered from Dallas (page 1-31).
- Jones called the FBI offices in San Antonio and then was in contact in Dallas (page 1-42).
- Jones never questioned Oswald and Hidell being the same person (pages 1-53 & 54).
- The 112th was not responsible for the secret cable of the 4th Army Command to the Strike Command on the evening of November 22nd 1963 (3142). It contains info on Oswald being a card carrying communist. This information in this cable comes from Don Stringfellow who works for the DPD; his name only comes forward with this document; Jones has not mentioned him at all in either HSCA interview. It appears the original DPD source for Jones is still unknown to this day. Stringfellow's HSCA interview on October 26th 1977 (3143) contains no info regarding the document sent late on November 22nd.
- Jones in a separate HSCA document on November 28th 1978 (3144) discusses the Stringfellow document again. He feels the term 'card carrying communist' who had defected to Cuba in 1959 (bad info from Stringfellow) was made in excitement and haste. He also explains the document's importance and says that it was sent to the Dallas group first before it was shared with others.

In an initial phone call from the ARRB to Stephen Weiss on February 28th 1997 (3145), he mentions two phone calls he has had with Don Stringfellow. There is no mention of a Hidell ID.

With all these statements it looks like the DOJ/FBI inserted the Hidell ID in its reports earlier on November 22nd 1963 making it look like Col Robert E Jones of the 112th INTC passed this information on to them;

whereas Jones says, that info would have come from the DPD source. These FBI documents and the 112th INTC documents were never passed on to the WC!

Jones denied mentioning the Hidell ID to the DOJ/FBI during his HSCA interview.

15:15 Nicholas Katzenbach Wants to Release a Statement of Oswald's Guilt

An FBI document from Clyde Tolson (3146) on page 2 states that Nicholas Katzenbach wants to release a statement saying *"We are now persuaded that Oswald killed the President; however, the investigation by the Department of Justice and FBI is continuing."*
In other words, Washington is one hour ahead of Dallas time and the Assistant Attorney General of the United States wants to release a statement of Oswald's guilt ASAP.
At that time there was no Hidell ID, not one line-up held at all, no backyard photo, no rifle and its fingerprints and revolver evidence developed and so on.
This sentiment is continued in documents from Hoover on November 24th (3147) on page 2. *"The thing I am concerned about, and so is Mr. Katzenbach, is having something issued so we can convince the public that Oswald is the real assassin."*
Nicholas Katzenbach on November 25th (3148) on page 27: *"The public must be satisfied that Oswald was the assassin; that he did not have confederates who are still at large; and that evidence was such that he would have been convicted at trial."*

16:00 Oswald Interrogated by Forrest Sorrels

Forrest Sorrels gets to talk to Oswald next, just after 16:00. He gets Oswald into the back room of Fritz's office and Sorrels and his fellow Secret Service agents manage to build a rapport with Oswald. What becomes rather evident is that Oswald shows his ignorance as to what he is being accused of.

Part 1 of Sorrels' WC testimony (3149):

Mr. Sorrels - At that time, I made a phone call to my office, because I had not been in contact with them since we had departed from Love Field. I was informed that an FBI agent had called the office and said that Captain Fritz of the Homicide Bureau had been trying to get in touch with me, that he had a suspect in custody.

Mr. Stern - About what time was that?

Mr. Sorrels - That would be fairly close to 2 o'clock, I imagine.

Mr. Stern - About an hour after you had returned----

Mr. Sorrels - Yes. I would say that it was at least that long--maybe a little bit longer. So, when I got that information, I told Mr. Zapruder that I would contact him later and get the pictures, because I wanted to get right down to Captain Fritz' office. So, I left then with the same police car and had them take me to Captain Fritz' office.

And upon arrival there, there were many officers around there, there were already cameras out in the hall, tripods, and so forth, and all of the City Hall down there. And there were a number of officers in the detective bureau office there, and Captain Fritz' office, which is an office within the large office, was closed, and the blinds were drawn in his office there. I did not knock on the door or anything, because I did not want to interfere with him if he was talking to someone. So, I just waited there until Captain Fritz opened the door, and he had a man who I later found out to be Oswald in custody at the time. *And I told Captain Fritz, I said, "Captain, I would like to talk to this man when I have an opportunity."* He said, *"You can talk to him right now."*

And he just took him on back around to the side of Captain Fritz' office, and there were a number of other officers there, might have been some FBI agents too, there, because there were numbers of FBI agents around in that vicinity almost all the time from that time on. And some of the detectives there. And I started talking to Oswald, started asking him some questions, and he was arrogant and a belligerent attitude about him.

And he said to me, *"I don't know who you fellows are, a bunch of cops."* And I said, *"Well, I will tell you who I am. My name is Sorrels and I am with the United States Secret Service, and here is my commission book."* I held it out in front of him and he said, *"I don't want to look at it."* And he held his head up and wouldn't look at it at all. And he said, *"What am I going to be charged with? Why am I being held here? Isn't someone supposed to tell me what my rights are?"*

I said, *"Yes, I will tell you what your rights are. Your rights are the same as that of any American citizen. You do not have to make a statement unless you want to. You have the right to get an attorney."*

"Aren't you supposed to get me an attorney?"

"No, I am not supposed to get you an attorney."

"Aren't you supposed go get me an attorney?"

I said, *"No, I am not supposed to get you an attorney, because if I got you an attorney, they would say I was probably getting a rake off on the fee,"* or words to that effect, and kind of smiled and tried to break the ice a little bit there.

I said, *"You can have the telephone book and you can call anybody you want to."*

I said, *"I just want to ask you some questions. I am in on this investigation. I just want to ask you some questions."*

Mr. Stern - Was there anything further said about an attorney?

Mr. Sorrels - Not that I recall at that time. I don't recall anything further said about an attorney. I asked him where he worked. He told me worked at this Book Depository. And as I recall it, I asked him what his address was and where he was living, and he explained to me that he was living apart from his wife, and that she was living over in Irving, Tex. I asked him, as I recall it, what his duties were at this Book Depository, and he said filling orders. I asked him if he had occasion to be on more than one floor, and he said, yes. I asked him if he had occasion to be on the sixth floor of the building. He said, yes, because they fill orders from all the floors. But he said most of his activity was down on the first floor. And I think I asked him whether or not he had ever been in a foreign country and he said that he had travelled in Europe, but more time had been spent in the Soviet Union, as I recall it.

And then he just said *"I don't care to answer any more questions."* And so, the conversation was terminated.

Mr. Stern - Did he give you his address?

Mr. Sorrels - As I recall it, he did give me an address. I don't remember what it was offhand.

Mr. Stern - Then were you finished with your questions, or did he refuse to answer any more?

Mr. Sorrels - He just said, *"I don't care to answer any more questions."*

Mr. Stern - You wanted to ask him other questions?

Mr. Sorrels - Oh, yes.

Mr. Stern - And what happened then?

Mr. Sorrels - He was taken by the officers, as I recall it, and was taken out of that area and I suppose put back in jail.

Mr. Stern - Did you then talk to Captain Fritz?

Mr. Sorrels - Yes. As I recall it, I asked Captain Fritz whether or not he had gotten anything out of him or not, and Captain Fritz said that he hadn't been able--that he had not made any admissions or anything like that at that time, and that he was going to talk to him again. That is all I recall that transpired at that time. Of course, I contacted the Chief's office, when I got that information as to who he was, and gave that information to them.

Mr. Stern - This is Chief Rowley?

Mr. Sorrels - I think I talked to Deputy Chief Paterni.

Mr. Stern - Of the Secret Service here in Washington?

Mr. Sorrels - Yes, sir.

Mr. Stern - Did anything else transpire between that time and the Friday night show up?

Mr. Sorrels - I did not talk to Oswald again, and I was around there. When I contacted Washington, I was informed that Inspector Kelley was being directed to be there, and he would be there later on that evening, that they had caught him out on the road, and he would come there to help out.

[Sorrels' WC testimony (3150) [continues]

Mr. Hubert. Well, now, for example, when Captain Fritz afforded you an opportunity to speak to Oswald and indicated that you could do so at a little office around the corner, did that mean that you had to pass Oswald out of Fritz' office, and through this third-floor corridor, where all the newsmen were gathered?
Mr. Sorrels. No, sir.
Mr. Hubert. That was still within Fritz' office?
Mr. Sorrels. Yes, sir; in other words, there was an office there, and Captain Fritz had an office built within that office just merely to take him out of the door and right around the corner of his inside office there.
Mr. Hubert. Then you did interview Oswald.
Mr. Sorrels. I talked to him, started asking him questions, and he was belligerent and arrogant in his attitude and he said to me, *"I don't know who you fellows are, a bunch of cops."*
Mr. Hubert. How long did you speak to him?
Mr. Sorrels. Not very long.
Mr. Hubert. In point of time.
Mr. Sorrels. Not over--I don't think over 10 minutes at the most.
Mr. Hubert. Do you know what happened to him after that?
Mr. Sorrels. As far as I know, he was taken back to the jail.

In a preliminary interview of Forrest J. Sorrels by Samuel A Stern for the WC April 10th 1964 (3151) pages 5&6. Sorrels stated that Oswald quizzed him about legal representation and even asking him what he was charged with. This directly contradicts Will Fritz and other DPD men that Oswald did not want a lawyer on the 22nd of November. It tends to suggest that Oswald was kept in the dark. And after only one interrogation Will Fritz was certain Oswald was the assassin (page 6), how's that for detective work!

William Patterson, of the Secret Service was also inside City Hall on the third floor. During his Schweiker Committee interview (3152) he mentioned Sorrell's brief interrogation of Oswald and that he answered no questions. He makes the mistake of it happening on the 23rd, whereas it just happened after 16:00 on the 22nd.

Winston Lawson of the Secret Service was in charge of planning the Dallas visit. And after the assassination and once AF1 had departed, he made his way alongside Jesse Curry and others towards City Hall and eventually saw Sorrels talk to Oswald as per his WC testimony (3153):

Mr. Stern. When did you first observe Lee Harvey Oswald, Mr. Lawson?
Mr. Lawson. It was early in the evening of November 22. He had been in police headquarters for a little while at least before I first saw him, and they had already interrogated him as I understand it, and various detectives, police officials, and Mr. Sorrels and a couple other agents and myself saw Lee Harvey Oswald when he was brought in for Mr. Sorrels to talk to at Mr. Sorrels' request.
Mr. Stern. Did you interrogate him?
Mr. Lawson. No, sir; I did not.
Mr. Stern. Did Mr. Sorrels handle the interrogation alone?
Mr. Lawson. Yes, sir; that particular one.
Mr. Stern. What were the questions and answers as best you can recall?
Mr. Lawson. He asked information as to name.
Mr. Dulles. Who is *"he"* How?
Mr. Lawson._Mr. Sorrels in asking the questions already had some background on Mr. Oswald before he started questioning Mr. Oswald. The detectives or other individuals had told them what they knew up to this point about Oswald, his name, that he had been out of the country previous to this time to Russia, and a few other things. It was known at the particular time, perhaps 6 or 7 o'clock.
Mr. Stern. I take it you had phoned his name to your headquarters in Washington as soon as you knew Oswald's name?
Mr. Lawson. I didn't. Perhaps Mr. Sorrels did.
Mr. Stern. Did your office advise you whether they knew anything about Oswald or had found out anything about Oswald?
Mr. Lawson. Not me personally.
Mr. Stern. That you know of?
Mr. Lawson. Not me personally.
Mr. Stern. Were any other questions asked?
Mr. Lawson. Yes; I recall Mr. Sorrels asking if he had been out--where he had been living, where he had been employed over the last years, and other information Mr. Sorrels already knew about.
Representative Ford. What was his attitude? What was the attitude of Oswald during this period?
Mr. Lawson. Oswald just answered the questions as asked to him. He didn't volunteer any information. He sat there quite stoically, not much of an expression on his face.
Mr. Dulles. Quite what?
Mr. Lawson. Stoically.
Mr. Dulles. Stoical?
Mr. Lawson. Yes, sir.
Representative Ford. Was he belligerent?

225

Mr. Lawson. No, sir; he didn't seem to be belligerent at all.

Representative Ford. Did he resent the interrogation?

Mr. Lawson. I didn't get the impression that it was a great resentment. He just answered the questions as they were asked of him.

Mr. Dulles. Did he answer all the questions?

Mr. Lawson. I believe he did.

Mr. Dulles. These were questions that Mr. Sorrels put to him?

Mr. Lawson. Yes; of course, Mr. Sorrels, I don't believe at that time, as I remember it, didn't ask him everything that we knew about him.

Representative Ford. Was there a transcript kept of this interrogation?

Mr. Lawson. I don't know.

Mr. Stern. Do you recall any other questions that were asked?

Mr. Lawson. I don't. At this time, they were just general-type questions.

Mr. Stern. What was his physical condition?

Mr. Dulles. Could I ask one question there? The question wasn't asked him at this time, at least while you were present, whether he was or was not guilty of the attack on the President?

Mr. Lawson. This I do not recall. During this I recall I was called out for a phone call a couple of times. We were given information from Mr. Max Phillips, who was in our PRS section, and I believe it was during this that someone, an agent, was wanted on the phone, and I went out and answered this, and they gave us some information on people that it might have been--a case that wasn't Oswald.

Mr. Stern. What was his physical condition?

Mr. Lawson. He was quite, well, unkempt looking, and I recall that he had a few bruises on his face.

Mr. Stern. A few bruises?

Mr. Lawson. I believe over an eye, a bruise or two. I can recall that he had a bruise over an eye or on a cheekbone, or someplace on his face, in looking back. And had a shirt and a pair of pants on. He wasn't very tidy looking, a little unkempt in his appearance.

Mr. Stern. Was he handcuffed, do you recall?

Mr. Lawson. I don't recall. I know I saw him handcuffed around police headquarters quite a bit, but during this interrogation I don't remember if he was handcuffed or not.

Representative Ford. How long did this interrogation go on?

Mr. Lawson. This was not long.

Representative Ford. Five minutes?

Mr. Lawson. Five to ten minutes at the most; yes, sir.

Mr. Stern. Then what happened? Did Mr. Sorrels finish?

Mr. Dulles. May I ask one other question there? Was there an interrogation just conducted by Mr. Sorrels, or were there others in on it, the police or the FBI?

Mr. Lawson. I don't know if there were FBI agents there. There were other plainclothesmen there, and a few uniformed officers.

Mr. Dulles. Mr. Sorrels conducted the investigation?
Mr. Lawson. Mr. Sorrels was asking these particular questions, general-type questions, and when he finished, the police took him back to another area.

16:15 Hoover Contacts Assistant DA Norbert Schlei

At 16:15 Dallas time J Edgar Hoover writes another report, this time about contacting Assistant DA Norbert Schlei (3154) pages 1-3. *"I told Mr Schlei I thought very probably we had in custody the man who killed the President in Dallas but this had not definitely been established."*
On page 2: *"I said Oswald, if he were the man, would be in the category of being an extreme radical of the left; that he was a member of the Fair Play for Cuba Committee; that several leaders of this group had been indicted; but that this man was never a leader."*
And on pages 2 & 3: *"I stated I would think Oswald would be the one. I stated our agents view him as a nut as he freezes up and withdraws into himself when he is being questioned as he did this afternoon."* This is a quick conclusion since the interrogation only finished ten minutes prior this report.
"I stated Oswald is the principle suspect in the case."

16:25 Hosty and Sorrels Meet Briefly

USSS Agent William Patterson in his November 25th report (3155) states that he has a chat with an FBI agent from the subversive desk: *"He stated that Oswald had contacted two known subversive agents about 15 days before the shooting but the entire information was top secret and he could not tell us any more, but he felt sure that the file would be turned over to our chief."*
William Patterson discusses this also during his Schweiker Committee interview (3156) on pages 15-17. He makes the mistake of attributing it to November 23rd. He then goes slightly more in depth about the settings and handlings of the above documented interaction with James P Hosty.
Hosty has a different interpretation of this meeting. During his WC testimony (3157), he states that he saw Secret Service agent Forest Sorrels take Oswald to the rear outside from Fritz's office where he was interrogated at 16:05:

Mr. HOSTY. Yes, sir; at approximately 4 p.m. on the 22nd of November 1963, Special Agent in Charge Forrest V. Sorrels of the United States Secret Service entered Captain Fritz' office with about five or six Secret Service agents. He then proceeded to interview Lee Harvey Oswald. I was not present during this interview. I did see him take Lee Oswald to the rear of Captain Fritz' outer office and interview Lee Oswald. It appeared to me that Forrest Sorrels of the Secret Service had appeared for the purpose of representing the United States Secret Service in this investigation. I was aware at this time that the FBI did not have jurisdiction over this matter, that is, the assassination of the President of the United States, and that if any Federal agency did have jurisdiction, it would be the United States Secret Service. As I later determined, no Federal agency had jurisdiction over this assassination. When Forrest Sorrels concluded his interview with Lee Oswald, I called him aside and advised him that there was some additional information on Lee Oswald which the FBI headquarters in Washington could furnish to the headquarters of the Secret Service in Washington, and that there were two items, and that I did not feel that I could give them to him directly since they were secret in nature.

Mr. Stern. Was anyone else present during this conversation?

Mr. HOSTY. As I said, this took place in the outer office of Capt. Will Fritz. There were about 30 or 40 people milling around out there. There were three or four Texas Rangers. There were perhaps a dozen Dallas police officers. There were, as I said, five or six Secret Service agents.

There were three other FBI agents besides myself, various clerical personnel from the police department who were assigned to the homicide division. I recognized two postal inspectors. I directed this conversation to Mr. Sorrels. I called him to one side and directed this to him directly.

16:30 Oswald is Being Frisked Again

Just before Oswald's first line-up for Helen Markham, Detective Elmer Boyd finds five rounds of live ammo in his left front pants pocket and detective Richard Sims finds a bus ticket (3158) in his shirt pocket. Oswald is allegedly being frisked for the third time by Elmer Boyd (3159) and Richard Sims (3160), each *"finding"* the items described above. How can these items appear all of the sudden when Charles Truman Walker and Paul L Bentley have frisked him two hours prior and on two separate occasions? Did they lie, or were they grossly incompetent. One could suspect Boyd and Sims of inserting evidence.

It is common sense and part of standard procedure to search a person for weapons and identification after an arrest *and not* before a line-up, especially after two hours of interrogating.

Marlin G Hall (3161) came into the office at 15:00 where he saw Fritz and Boyd interrogating Oswald. He took an affidavit off Lee Bowers and was then involved with escorting Oswald for his first line-up with Helen Markham. There was not one single word about Boyd and Sims finding anything in Oswald's pockets. This report by Hall typed on the 22nd (3162) is detailed and, like some of his other reports, very accurate. Compared with the earlier statements by Paul Bentley and Charles Truman Walker, there is a serious issue with the veracity of these so-called finds of the bullets and the bus ticket. That fact, in turn, raises concerns about the bus ride and Oswald's possession of the handgun, which Oswald said, responding to Gus Rose, had been tossed at him.

16:35 First Line-up with Helen Markham

James Leavelle's notes on the Helen Markham line-up (3163).

Picture this: Lee Oswald with cuts and bruises, lined up among three males who work inside the building and who match only in skin colour. Would anyone have any trouble picking out the guy with the cuts and bruises? Furthermore, the other 'fillers' made-up fictitious answers whereas Oswald would state where he worked at that time: the TSBD -- the building where allegedly The President was shot from which was broadcast within 30 minutes after the shots had been fired. Oswald's photo had by this time already been published on the news.

During this and the next line-up, Oswald's co-participants, or 'fillers,' are policemen from the Vice Bureau and a jail clerk.

- Detective WE Perry confirms during his WC testimony (3164) that it was Will Fritz who personally made the call to the Vice Bureau to get two detectives down and participate in that very first line-up. Something that was very rare, according to Perry. He is given clothing, a brown sports jacket to wear from the Homicide Bureau!
- Richard Clark, another detective, who had never been in a line-up before, confirmed Fritz's call in his WC testimony (3165). He is given a red vest from the Homicide Bureau to wear. He also states he is not handcuffed to Don Ables, after which the *'discussion goes off the record.'*
- Oswald, on the other hand, is wearing his roughed- up shirt with a hole at the right elbow.
- Will Fritz testified to the Commission that the police officers *"fixed themselves where they would look like prisoners."* Detective Clark testified that those items of clothing were taken from the Homicide Office.
- Elmer Boyd admits in his WC testimony (3166) that the other three were probably better dressed.

229

- Don Ables, the jail clerk who was present for all three line-ups on November 22nd, is asked by his jail supervisor to join in on very short notice (3167).
- Jim Leavelle said in his WC testimony (3168) that it was not normal procedure for police officers to join in on line-ups.
- Will Fritz, during his WC testimony (3169), was of the opinion that other prisoners would harm Oswald, hence him asking for 'fillers' who worked inside the building to stand in on the first two line-ups. Jim Leavelle thought the same thing during his WC testimony (3170). There were four official line-ups in total that day. That same evening, during the third line-up, Oswald was handcuffed to two fellow prisoners. So, those security concerns evaporated quite quickly.

Helen Markham (3171), a 47-year-old waitress who witnessed the Tippit murder, did not have an unobstructed view of what went down. She was regarded as a pivotal witness. All the other witnesses only managed to see a part of the murder; its immediate aftermath, a possible shooter moving away from the scene of the crime where Officer JD Tippit was slain.

- In many of the statements and interviews Markham gave after the Tippit murder, the killer was described in different ways.
- She covered her face during the event.
- She fainted shortly after at the scene of the crime and left her shoes on top of the car CE 1974 (3372).
- She stated she was with Tippit for 20 minutes before someone showed up, something other witnesses' dispute.
- Five other eye witnesses did not see her there.
- Detectives administered smelling salts for her to be able to attend the line-up.
- Wesley Liebeler stated (3173) on page 24 "*some questions might be raised when the public discovers there was only one person who saw Oswald kill him. All the rest saw subsequent events. Mrs Markham is nicely buried there, but I predict not for long*".
- Joseph Ball, who was senior counsel to the WC, referred on December 4th 1964 in a public debate with Mark Lane (3174), to her testimony as being *"full of mistakes"* and to her as an *"utter screwball."* And as *"utterly unreliable"*, which of course was the exact opposite of the WR's conclusion about her.
- Markham's son was paroled in the summer of 1963, after being imprisoned in 1962 for a 5-year term for burglary. The DPD had leverage on her, to say the least.
- The physical description of the killer's clothes are described in different colours in this video of Markham at 0:31 (3175).

Oswald was never confronted with this jacket at any time while incarcerated to determine ownership. Nor were there any of Oswald's fingerprints or fibres found on that jacket.

- In Into the Nightmare by Joe McBride (3176) on page 482 Helen Markham told researcher Greg Lowrey that the Dallas Police cheered when she identified Oswald. She also testified being under pressure pointing out the man she had seen.
- In late June 1964, Marguerite Oswald, Vincent Salandria, Harold Feldman and his wife Immie visited Markham at her home. On their first visit they are asked to leave as she does not have the time to talk as she is caring for her granddaughter. While leaving, Bill Markham who is her son, approaches them and confides to them that the Secret Service said that there would be trouble if his mom talked. Returning later, Mrs Oswald and the others see two DPD cars pull away and after arriving at the front door and again, Mrs Markham pleads for them to go away. Vincent Salandria: *"I have never seen that kind of terror, their teeth were actually chattering."* This whole episode is reported in The Realist from September 1964 (3177).
- Markham denies she ever spoke to Mark Lane when she is asked about this during her WC testimony (3178). Yet when the tape of this call is played in front of her, she has to admit that that is her voice, but she is not really forthcoming about it. In the interview she says that the assailant had bushy hair. Oswald had no bushy haircut. The WC mention this matter in a draft report (3179) page 14.

During her WC testimony she denied recognising Lee Harvey Oswald six times. And only with the "guidance" from Joseph Ball did she point him out:

Mr. Ball Mrs. Markham, you were taken to the Police Department, weren't you?
Mrs. Markham. Yes, sir.
Mr. Ball. Immediately.
Mrs. Markham. Yes, sir.
Mr. Ball. Later that day they had a showup you went to?
Mrs. Markham. A line-up?
Mr. Ball. A line-up.
Mrs. Markham. Yes.
Mr. Ball. How many men were in the line-up?
Mrs. Markham. I believe there were, now I am not positive, I believe there were three besides this man.
Mr. Ball. That would be four people altogether?

231

Mrs. Markham. I believe that is correct.

Mr. Ball. Were they of anywhere near similar build or size or colouring?

Mrs. Markham. Yes, they were all about the same height.

Mr. Ball. Who were you in the line-up room with?

Mrs. Markham. Who was I in the room where they had this man?

Mr. Ball. Yes.

Mrs. Markham. Policemen.

Mr. Ball. More than one?

Mrs. Markham. The room was full.

Mr. Ball. It was. In this line-up room, the room was full of policemen. Weren't there just one or two men with you?

Mrs. Markham. One or two with me, but I don't know who they were.

Mr. Ball. But there were other officers?

Mrs. Markham. There were all policemen sitting in the back of me, and aside of me.

Mr. Ball. In this room?

Mrs. Markham. Yes, sir. They were doing something.

Mr. Ball. Before you went into this room, were you shown a picture of anyone?

Mrs. Markham. I was not.

Mr. Ball. Did you see any television?

Mrs. Markham. I did not.

Mr. Ball. Did a police officer say anything to you before you went in there, to tell you—

Mrs. Markham. No, sir.

Mr. Ball. That he thought *"We had the right man,"* or something of that sort? Anything like that?

Mrs. Markham. No, sir.

Mr. Ball. No statement like that?

Mrs. Markham. No, sir.

Mr. Ball. Did anybody tell you that the man you were looking for would be in a certain position in the line-up, or anything like that?

Mrs. Markham. No, sir.

Mr. Ball. Now when you went into the room you looked these people over, these four men?

Mrs. Markham. Yes, sir.

Mr. Ball. Did you recognize anyone in the line-up?

Mrs. Markham. No, sir.

Mr. Ball. You did not? Did you see anybody--I have asked you that question before did you recognize anybody from their face?

Mrs. Markham. From their face, no.

Mr. Ball. Did you identify anybody in these four people?

Mrs. Markham. I didn't know nobody.

Mr. Ball. I know you didn't know anybody, but did anybody in that line-up look like anybody you had seen before?

Mrs. Markham. No. I had never seen none of them, none of these men.

Mr. Ball. No one of the four?

Mrs. Markham. No one of them.

Mr. Ball. No one of all four?

Mrs. Markham. No, sir.

Mr. Ball. Was there a number two man in there?

Mrs. Markham. Number two is the one I picked.

Mr. Ball. Well, I thought you just told me that you hadn't—

Mrs. Markham. I thought you wanted me to describe their clothing.

Mr. Ball. No. I wanted to know if that day when you were in there if you saw anyone in there—

Mrs. Markham. Number two.

Mr. Ball. What did you say when you saw number two?

Mrs. Markham. Well, let me tell you. I said the second man, and they kept asking me which one, which one. I said, number two. When I said number two, I just got weak.

Mr. Ball. What about number two, what did you mean when you said number two?

Mrs. Markham. Number two was the man I saw shoot the policeman.

Mr. Ball. You recognized him from his appearance?

Mrs. Markham. I asked--I looked at him. When I saw this man, I wasn't sure, but I had cold chills just run all over me.

Mr. Ball. When you saw him?

Mrs. Markham. When I saw the man. But I wasn't sure, so, you see, I told them I wanted to be sure, and looked, at his face is what I was looking at, mostly is what I looked at, on account of his eyes, the way he looked at me. So, I asked them if they would turn him sideways. They did, and then they turned him back around, and I said the second, and they said, which one, and I said number two. So, when I said that, well, I just kind of fell over. Everybody in there, you know, was beginning to talk, and I don't know, just—

Mr. Ball. Did you recognize him from his clothing?

Mrs. Markham. He had on a light short jacket, dark trousers. I looked at his clothing, but I looked at his face, too.

Mr. Ball. Did he have the same clothing on that the man had that you saw shoot the officer?

Mrs. Markham. He had, these dark trousers on.

Mr. Ball. Did he have a jacket or a shirt? The man that you saw shoot Officer Tippit and run away, did you notice if he had a jacket on?

Mrs. Markham. He had a jacket on when he done it.

Mr. Ball. What kind of a jacket, what general colour of jacket?

Mrs. Markham. It was a short jacket open in the front, kind of a greyish tan.

Mr. Ball. Did you tell the police that?

Mrs. Markham. Yes, I did.

Mr. Ball. Did any man in the line-up have a jacket on?

Mrs. Markham. I can't remember that.

Mr. Ball. Did this number two man that you mentioned to the police have any jacket on when he was in the line-up?

Mrs. Markham. No, sir.

Mr. Ball. What did he have on?

Mrs. Markham. He had on a light shirt and dark trousers.

[Representative Ford is now in the Commission hearing room.]

Mr. Ball. Did you recognize the man from his clothing or from his face?

Mrs. Markham. Mostly from his face.

Mr. Ball. Were you sure it was the same man you had seen before?

Mrs. Markham. I am sure.

Mr. Ball. Now, what time of day was it that you saw this man in the line-up?

Mrs. Markham. I would say it was four, a little after.

Mr. Ball. That was four in the afternoon?

Mrs. Markham. I was so upset I couldn't even tell you the time. In fact, I wasn't interested in the time.

Mr. Ball. Yes.

Mr. Dulles. Could I ask just one question?

Mr. Ball. Yes.

Mr. Dulles. You referred to his eyes; they were rather striking. Can you give any impression of how his eyes looked to you? I realize that is a very vague question.

Mrs. Markham. Yes. He looked wild. They were glassy looking, because I could see—

Mr. Dulles. He had no glasses on?

Mrs. Markham. No. When we looked at each other, he just stared, just like that. I just don't know. I just seen him--I would know the man anywhere, I know I would.

Mr. Dulles. Thank you.

Will Fritz (3180) had a few words to say about this line-up during his WC testimony (3181):

Mr. Ball. You had a showup that afternoon?

Mr. Fritz. That first showup was for a lady who was an eye witness and we were trying to get that show-up as soon as we could because she was beginning to faint and getting sick. In fact, I had to leave the office and carry some ammonia across the hall, they were about to send her

234

to the hospital or something and we needed that identification real quickly, and she got to feeling all right after using this ammonia.

Mr. Ball. Do you remember her name?

Mr. Fritz. I have her name here.

Mr. Ball. Was that Mrs. Markham?

Mr. Fritz. Yes, Helen Markham.

Mr. Ball. That was the first show-up, was it?

Mr. Fritz. Yes, sir.

Mr. Ball. Were you there?

Mr. Fritz. Yes, sir.

Mr. Ball. With her?

Mr. Fritz. Yes, sir.

Mr. Ball. Will you tell me what happened there?

Mr. Fritz. She looked at these people very carefully, and she picked him out and made the positive identification.

Mr. Ball. What did she say?

Mr. Fritz. She said that is the man that I saw shoot the officer.

Mr. Ball. Who did she point out?

Mr. Fritz. She pointed out Oswald; yes, sir.

Mr. Ball. In your showup room you have the prisoners separated from the visitors?

Mr. Fritz. There is a screen. They are on a stage with numbers over their heads for identification, and measurements to show their height, and this is lighted back there so the people can see them plainly, and the people who are looking at them usually sit at desks out some distance, probably as far as here from that window from the showup screen.

Mr. Ball. Near the window, you mean about 15, 20 feet.

Mr. Fritz. Yes; about that far.

Mr. Ball. And then, now in this show-up there were two officers of the vice squad and an officer and a clerk from the jail that were in the show-up with Oswald?

Mr. Fritz. That is true. I borrowed those officers, I was a little bit afraid some prisoner might hurt him, there was a lot of excitement and a lot of feeling fight about that time so we didn't have an officer in my office the right size to show with him so I asked two of the special service officers if they would help me and they said they would be glad to, so they took off their coats and neckties and fixed themselves where they would look like prisoners and they were good enough to stand on each side of him in the showup and we used a man who works in the jail office, a civilian employee as a third man.

Mr. Ball. Now, were they dressed a little better than Oswald, do you think, these three people?

Mr. Fritz. Well, I don't think there was a great deal of difference. They had on their regular working clothes and after they opened their shirts and took off their ties, why they looked very much like anyone else.

Mr. Ball. They were all handcuffed together, were they?

Mr. Fritz. I am not sure; I don't remember for sure if they were all handcuffed together or not. They probably did. I couldn't be positive about that.

LC Graves (3181) in his WC testimony (3182):

Mr. Graves. Well, I held a showup along with Leavelle and the Chief and Captain Fritz, and I don't remember who else, about a roomful.

Mr. Belin. Could you state what occurred in that show up? How many people were in this showup?

Mr. Graves. I don't remember exactly how many people.

Mr. Belin. You mean of the men that were actually lined up?

Mr. Graves. I don't know. I believe four or five, I think. He was identified as No. 2 man. Let me see. He was identified as No. 2 man in a four-man line-up, yes.

Mr. Belin. Do you know who the people were who were in this particular line-up?

Mr. Graves. I don't know. Nobody but Oswald.

Mr. Belin. Do you know that Lee Harvey Oswald was No. 2 man in that line-up?

Mr. Graves. Yes, I do.

[And a little later, during the same testimony...]

Mr. Belin. Now, could you tell us what Mrs. or Miss Markham did or said when this particular showup took place? Were you standing right next to her?

Mr. Graves. About as close as I am to you, which would be approximately 4 or 5 feet.

Mr. Belin. All right; the men walked in, I assume, is that correct?

Mr. Graves. That's right.

Mr. Belin. Where was Mrs. Markham at that particular time?

Mr. Graves. She was standing in the centre of the room, approximately in the first row of seats near the front.

Mr. Belin. She was seated?

Mr. Graves. No; she was standing.

Mr. Belin. She was standing?

Mr. Graves. Yes.

Mr. Belin. Did she look through an opening in the wall?

Mr. Graves. No; this is a screen, a nylon screen of some kind. I am sure you have seen them?

Mr. Belin. She can see through, as I understand, but the people in the showup room cannot see the people on the other side of the screen. Is that correct?

Mr. Graves. That's correct.

Mr. Belin. All right. Do you remember what she said or did after the men in the showup came in?

Mr. Graves. Well, she began to cry when he came in. He was next to the last man that come in in that order. No. 4, 3, 2, 1, and so forth that came in.

Mr. Belin. You mean No. 4 came first, then No. 3 and then No. 2 and then No.1.

Mr. Graves. That's right.

Mr. Belin. When did she start crying?

Mr. Graves. When he walked in, Oswald walked in.

Mr. Belin. You mean when the No. 2 man walked in?

Mr. Graves. Yes.

Mr. Belin. Were they still walking at the time she started crying?

Mr. Graves. Yes. As soon as she saw him; yes. He would have to walk as far as from here to that stand, approximately.

Mr. Belin. That would be about 6 or 8 feet?

Mr. Graves. Yes, sir; roughly.

Mr. Belin. All right. What did she do or say?

Mr. Graves. Well, of course she said that was the man that she saw, Oswald. I mean at this particular time.

Mr. Belin. Did she ask to have the men turn so that she would see their profiles?

Mr. Graves. Well, I don't recall if she asked that or not, but that is the normal procedure that we do that. We turn him profile, right, left and to the rear, and back to the front, in that order.

Mr. Belin. Do you remember anything specific that she said at the time that she made the identification?

Mr. Graves. Nothing other than he is the one, No. 2 is the one.

Mr. Belin. Was anything said by any of the men in the showup that would--did they speak any words or say anything at all?

Mr. Graves. If they did, I don't remember what was said. I am reasonably sure they asked some questions. That is the usual procedure. If they were at this point, I just don't remember what was said.

Mr. Belin. Do you remember the dress of the people in the showup?

Mr. Graves. No; positively not.

Mr. Belin. Does your police department ever take any photograph of an actual show-up, I mean, insofar as still shots, to have any written or pictorial record of the men in the showup, as to what they were wearing or what they looked like?

Mr. Graves. That was not a policy or an order at this time, but it has been done, however, in the past. But for various reasons, as I say, it is not the customary thing, because we have quite a number of showups that would necessitate a time element there, sometimes waiting on the proper people to take the picture, and so forth.

Mr. Belin. Anything else that you have, any recollection in connection with this show-up of Mrs. Markham or Miss Markham's identification?

Mr. Graves. I don't remember anything outstanding at this moment; no.

Mr. Belin. Do you remember about when this took place, this actual show-up?

Mr. Graves. Well, let's see if I have it written down here. We put Lee Oswald in a four-man line-up in the city hall on November 22, 1963, at 4:30 p.m., and had Helen Markham view this line-up. She was positive on the identification of Oswald, and he was the No. 2 man in the four-man line-up.

Graves in Larry Sneed's *No More Silence (3184)*: *After I got to headquarters, my first duty was to take a statement from a lady named Helen Markham who was an eyeball witness to the shooting of Tippit. That took a little while because she was quite upset, rather hysterical really, but I finally got a statement from her. She was a terribly upset lady. Under the circumstances her reaction was fairly typical considering she was close by when it happened, had heard the gun and saw him fall. I had no doubt about the validity of her statement because we verified everything she said. She identified Oswald in the line-up, so that pretty well established the fact that he was the one that did it as far as we were concerned. The line-up that Mrs. Markham observed was a typical line-up. The authorization was given by Captain Fritz, and the jail supervisor picked the line-up and brought them down. All those in the line-up were as similar as possible. The only thing different about this one was everybody that could get in got in which, in my opinion, wasn't good. But I didn't have any control over it. Other than just a lot of people being in there, though, that shouldn't have been, it was conducted in the same manner as all others. The witness would stand or sit behind a one-way nylon screen so that they couldn't be seen by those in the line-up. As I recall, and this was the only one I attended on Friday, there was definitely shock or excitement when she saw him. She said something to the effect, "That's him! That's the one that shot Tippit!" She didn't have to be prompted; she knew him. As she identified him, Oswald remained quiet like the rest of them.*

Jim Leavelle's report regarding the circumstances surrounding this particular line-up is interesting, to say the least. After looking around he finds Markham in the hospital emergency room of City Hall (3185) with LC Graves as she was suffering from shock. And as soon as she was able, Leavelle took her down to the showup room and then called upstairs to Fritz's office to let them know they were ready. She identified the #2 man in the line-up, who was Lee Oswald, as the shooter of JD Tippit. Leavelle states that Will Fritz, Jesse Curry and LC Graves were there when the line-up took place. He makes no mention of the frisking by Elmer Boyd and Richard Sims just before the line-up nor of the discovery of the bullets and the bus ticket. He would have seen that happening had it actually happened.

In his WC testimony (3186) Jim Leavelle states:

Mr. Ball. Well, did Captain Fritz instruct you to go out and pick up the witness and come down to a showup, bring her down to a showup?
Mr. Leavelle. Yes; this Helen Markham, the witness, was in such a state of shock she had been unable to view the line-up.
Mr. Ball. Where did you see her the first time?
Mr. Leavelle. She was in the emergency room, in the hospital emergency room, first aid room, whatever you call it in the basement of the city hall, and I went over and talked with her and kind of got her calmed down where she thought she could stand to view the line-up, and when she told me that she felt like she was able to stand it, why, I called the captain and told him that we were ready for the showup, at which time some of the other officers brought Oswald down. I took her into the showup room myself and stood with her while she viewed the line-up.
Mr. Ball. Were you and Helen Markham the only two in what you call the showup room?
Mr. Leavelle. No, Captain Fritz and Chief Curry was in there also and possibly one or two others; I do not recall.
Mr. Ball. How about your partner, C. W. Brown?
Mr. Leavelle. I do not know whether he was there or not.
Mr. Ball. Any other witnesses?
Mr. Leavelle. Now Mr. Graves may have been in there.
Mr. Ball. Were there any other Witnesses in there?
Mr. Leavelle. No.

[And later...]

Mr. Ball. Now, what did Helen Markham say while she was in the showup room?
Mr. Leavelle. Well, she was very nervous and I do not recall what all she did say, but she was able to identify Oswald as the one.
Mr. Ball. What did she tell you?
Mr. Leavelle. She said he was the man that was at the scene she saw do the shooting over there in Oak Cliff.
Mr. Ball. Did you take a statement from her then?
Mr. Leavelle. I took one from her but I do not remember whether--just when I took it.

239

In 1993 Joseph McBride interviewed Leavelle for his book, *Into The Nightmare* (3187), and on page 482, after asking whether she was hysterical, he answered: "*Well she was. See, L.C. Graves took her over to the first aid, to the doctor's office, and they were doing something, I don't know what they were doing because I wasn't there, to kinda calm her down. Finally, when I had the people all set, and she hadn't gotten over there, Cap Fritz told me, 'Well you'd better get over there and see what the holdup is.' I went over there and explained to her – she was calmed down quite a bit. Of course, she was nervous, and understandably so. They had had all kinds of stories that she passed out, and I broke smelling salts under her nose, and all this kinds of stuff. That didn't happen, no. I did have some smelling salts with me, some of the little capsules that you break. And it's possible, I don't remember offhand, but I may have because I know that I asked the doctor for 'em, I said 'I don't think she is going to pass out, but let me have a couple of 'em anyway.' So, I may have given her one, broke one and given it to her, after this.*"

16:50 Second Interrogation

Present:
DPD: Will Fritz, Elmer Boyd and MG Hall.
FBI: James Bookhout.
USSS: Forrest Sorrels.
U.S. Marshalls: Robert Nash.
It is possible that assistant DA Bill Alexander walked in just after 18:00.

After the Helen Markham line-up Oswald is taken back to room 317 and interrogated for another 2 hours. Notes are non-existent of this session.

Elmer Boyd's WC testimony (3188) makes mention of this session:

Mr. Ball. You stayed there, didn't you?
Mr. Boyd. Yes.
Mr. Ball. And you heard what was said?
Mr. Boyd. Yes, sir.
Mr. Ball. Tell us what you heard.
Mr. Boyd. Well, I know Mr. Nash asked him a question or two.
Mr. BILL. What were they?
Mr. Boyd. I don't recall what questions he asked.
Mr. Ball. Who else asked questions?
Mr. Boyd. Captain Fritz talked to him and-let me see-I don't remember if Mr. Bookhout, it seemed like Mr. Bookhout asked a question or two. I believe all of them asked him something.
Mr. Ball. Do you know what they asked?

Mr. Boyd. No, sir.
Mr. Ball. Do you remember what Oswald said?
Mr. Boyd. Well, let me see-no, sir; I can't recall what he said; like I say, I didn't keep notes there because I was sitting right near Oswald.

And with that poor answer, Boyd gets a free pass.

Marrion Baker (3189), while Oswald is being interrogated, having his infamous first statement taken by Marvin Johnson (3190), and only a short distance away from where Oswald is seated and questioned, overhears them and mentions this in his HSCA testimony (3191), saying: *"Did you kill the President? Did you kill the President?"* To which Oswald replied, *"That's absurd! I want a lawyer! I want a lawyer!"*

During these particular interrogations someone else makes his entry, Roger Craig (3192). Dallas Deputy Sheriff Roger Craig was in Dealey Plaza after the shooting. Craig's relevance to this segment of the case is that he claimed he saw Lee Oswald leave the TSBD and run down the grassy slope to get into a Nash Rambler at about 12:42. This, of course, completely contradicts the *official story* of Oswald leaving the TSBD 2.5 minutes after the shooting, taking a bus and a cab back to his room on North Beckley, grabbing a pistol and changing his shirt before making his way to a fateful encounter at 10th and Patton with JD Tippit, and then, finally, to his apprehension and arrest at the Texas Theatre.

When Craig heard of Oswald's arrest over the police radio, he called Will Fritz and told him of the man he had seen running from the scene. After the description, Fritz said, *"That sounds like the man we have in custody. Come down and see if you can identify him."* Fritz met Craig outside his office. He looked through the glass and told Fritz that was the man he had seen escape. Subsequently, the two men entered the little room where Oswald was being interrogated and Oswald was confronted by Fritz: *"This man saw you leave."* Oswald's temper flared and he replied, *"I told you people I did."* Fritz said, *"Calm down, son, we are just trying to find out what happened. What about that car?"* Oswald answered, *"That station wagon belongs to Mrs. Paine, don't try to get her involved in this."* Then he leaned back in his chair. He said in a low voice, *"Everybody will know who I am now."* Craig has emphasized that Oswald made this statement in a dejected tone of voice. He said this as if his cover had just been blown. What is even more important is the fact that Fritz used the word *car*, and that Oswald replied with *station wagon*. Once again, controversy surrounding Oswald's departure from the TSBD as noted by Craig and others.

This exchange is something that was denied by Fritz; that he only could have possibly met with Craig in the *outer* office.

Roger Craig's story is being recited by Police Chief Dallas Curry in the evening of the 22ⁿᵈ (3193) and the FBI James Bookhout, issues a report on the 23ʳᵈ (3194) Bookhout reports the time of Craig going into Fritz's office at 17:18, not 15 or 20 minutes past, but 18 minutes past.

Craig's story also makes the front page of the Fort Worth Star Telegram on the morning edition of the 23ʳᵈ (3195). In this article Craig relays that Oswald was spotted by him leaving the TSBD and whistling down to a Nash Rambler that was driven by a negro. Plus, he confirms going into police HQ and identifying Oswald as the man he saw over there.

Craig's WC testimony (3196) mentions the following on this happening:

Mr. Craig - And---uh---then I kept thinking about this man that had run down the hill and got in this car, so--uh--it was about, oh, I don't recall exactly the time, nearly 5 or something like that, or after, when--uh-the city had apprehended a suspect in the city officer's shooting. And--uh--information was floating around that they were trying to connect him with the assassination of the President--as the assassin.
So--uh, in the meantime, I kept thinking about this subject that had run and got in the car. So, I called Captain Fritz' office and talked to one of his officers and--uh--told him what I had saw and give him a description of the man, asked him how it fit the man they had picked up as a suspect.
And--uh--it was then they asked me to come up and look at him at Captain Fritz' office.
Mr. Belin - All right. Then what did you do?
Mr. Craig - I drove up to Fritz' office about, oh, after 5--about 5:30 or something like that--and--uh--talked to Captain Fritz and told him what I had saw. And he took me in his office---I believe it was his office---it was a little office, and had the suspect setting in a chair behind a desk---beside the desk. And another gentleman, I didn't know him, he was sitting in another chair to my left as I walked in the office.
And Captain Fritz asked me was this the man I saw--and I said, *"Yes, it was."*
Mr. Belin - All right. Will you describe the man you saw in Captain Fritz' office?
Mr. Craig - Oh, he was sitting down but--uh--he had the same medium brown hair; it was still--well, it was kinda wild looking; he was slender, and--uh-- what 1 could tell of him sitting there, he was--uh---short. By that, I mean not--myself, I'm five eleven--he was shorter than I was. And--uh--fairly light build.

Mr. Belin - Could you see his trousers?

Mr. Craig - No; I couldn't see his trousers at all.

Mr. Belin - What about his shirt?

Mr. Craig - I believe, as close as I can remember, a T-shirt--a white T-shirt.

Mr. Belin - All right. But you didn't see him in a line-up? You just saw him sitting there?

Mr. Craig - No; he was sitting there by himself in a chair--off to one side.

Mr. Belin - All right. Then, what did Captain Fritz say and what did you say and what did the suspect say?

Mr. Craig - Captain Fritz then asked him about the---uh---he said, *"What about this station wagon?"* And the suspect interrupted him and said, *"That station wagon belongs to Mrs. Paine"*---I believe is what he said. *"Don't try to tie her into this. She had nothing to do with it."*

And--uh--Captain Fritz then told him, as close as I can remember, that, *"All we're trying to do is find out what happened, and this man saw you leave from the scene."*

And the suspect again interrupted Captain Fritz and said, *"I told you people I did."* And--uh--yeah--then, he said--then he continued and he said, *"Everybody will know who I am now."*

And he was leaning over the desk. At this time, he had risen partially out of the chair and leaning over the desk, looking directly at Captain Fritz.

Mr. Belin - What was he wearing-or could you see the colour of his trousers as he leaned over the desk?

Mr. Craig - No; because he never--he just leaned up, you know, sort of forward--not actually up, just out of his chair like that (indicating) forward.

Mr. Belin - Then, did you say anything more?

Mr. Craig - No; I then left.

Mr. Belin - Well, in other words, the only thing you ever said was, *"This was the man,"*--or words to that effect?

Mr. Craig - Yes.

Mr. Belin - Did Captain Fritz say anything more.

Mr. Craig - No; I don't believe---not while. I was there.

Mr. Belin - Did the suspect say anything more?

Mr. Craig - Not that I recall

Mr. Belin - Did you say anything about that it was a Rambler station wagon there?

Mr. Craig - In the presence of the suspect?

Mr. Belin - Yes.

Mr. Craig - No.

Mr. Belin - You don't know whether Captain Fritz said anything to the suspect about this incident before you came, do you?

Mr. Craig - No; I don't.

Mr. Belin - Is there anything else that you can think of involving this interrogation at which you were present?

Mr. Craig - No. Nothing else was said after that point. I then left and give 'my name to the---uh---Secret Service agent and the FBI agent that was outside the office.

[And near the end of the same testimony...]

Mr. Belin - Do you feel, in your own mind, that the man you saw at Captain Fritz's office was the same man that you saw running towards the station wagon?
Mr. Craig - Yes, I feel like it was.
Mr. Belin - Do you feel that you might have been influenced by the fact that you knew he was the suspect---subconsciously, or do you----
Mr. Craig - Well, it's---it's possible, but I still feel strongly that it was the same person.
Mr. Belin - Okay. That's it. Thank you

Afterwards, Craig claimed that some exchanges during his WC testimony had been changed (3197).

Roger Craig also testifies during the Clay Shaw trial (3198) for Jim Garrison, and once again the matter of Oswald's 'escape' and the subsequent confrontation that very same evening was brought up:

Q: Did you have occasion Mr. Craig, to see the individual that you saw running down the slope and getting in the station wagon, did you have occasion to see him again on that day?
A: Yes, later that evening.
Q: Where did you see him?
A: At Captain Will Fritz's Office who is Captain of Homicide & Robbery in the Dallas Police Department.
Q: What were you doing up there on that occasion?
A: I was filling out a report after the assassination in my office and of course I had known about the officer being killed and I possibly in my mind possibly tied the two together and I called Captain Fritz and gave him a description of the man I saw running down the grassy knoll and he said *"That sounds like --"*
Mr. Dymond: I object, Your Honour.
THE Court: You can't say what he said, Mr. Craig.

By Mr. Alcock:
Q: As a result of this telephone conversation did you have occasion to view anyone?
A: Yes, sir, I went to Police Headquarters.
Q: Did you recognize anyone at Police Headquarters?

A: Yes, sir, in Captain Fritz's office the same man that I had seen running down the hill.

Q: Who was in Captain Fritz's Office at the time you saw the individual?

A: There were two men in the office. The one seating to the left as I walked in, I didn't know, and he was in a business suit with a white Stetson hat and I assumed he was one of Captain Fritz's men and the other man was Lee Harvey Oswald.

Q: Now I show you what has been marked for purposes of identification as State Exhibit 1 and I ask you if you recognize the person in this picture?

A: Yes, sir, that is the man I saw in Captain Fritz's Office.

Q: Is this the man you saw running down the slope?

A: Yes, it is.

Q: The one that got in the station wagon?

A: Yes.

Q: And who is the individual depicted in this picture?

A: Lee Harvey Oswald.

Q: Did you have occasion to go into Captain Fritz's Office at the time Lee Harvey Oswald was in there?

A: Yes, sir, Captain Fritz showed me into his office where the two gentlemen were sitting.

Q: Did you have occasion to confront or speak to Lee Harvey Oswald on this occasion?

A: I did not, Captain Fritz did.

Q: Were you there when he made any responses to anything Captain Fritz asked him?

A: Yes, I was.

Q: What did he say?

A: Captain Fritz, this man was –

Mr. Dymond: I object to what Captain Fritz said.

THE COURT: You can't say what Captain Fritz said but just what Lee Harvey Oswald said.

THE WITNESS: I made an identification of Lee Harvey Oswald as the man I saw running down the grassy knoll.

Q: What if anything did he say?

A: He said *"I told you people I did."*

Mr. Dymond: What?

THE WITNESS: *"I told you people I did."*

BY Mr. ALCOCK:

Q: Did he say anything else?

A: Yes.

Q: What was that?

A: I can't testify in answer to Captain Fritz's comments' cause it was in response –

Q: I am afraid you can't give us what Captain Fritz said 'cause that would be hearsay but what if anything did Lee Harvey Oswald respond to the question of Captain Fritz?
A: He said that the station wagon belonged to Mrs. Paine, but *"Don't try to drag her in this."*
Q: Did he make any other responses?
A: He leaned back in his chair and said *"Everybody will know who I am now."*
Q: Did you hear him say anything else on this occasion?
A: No, sir, I did not.
Q: How long did you stay in the office?
A: Approximately ten minutes.

Will Fritz's testimony in front of the WC (3199):

Ball. Did you ever know a man named Roger Craig, a deputy sheriff?
Fritz: Roger Craig, I might if I knew which one he was. Do we have it here?
Ball. He was a witness from whom you took a statement in your office or some of your men.
Fritz. Some of my officers.
Ball. He is a deputy sheriff.
Fritz. One deputy sheriff who started to talk to me but he was telling me some things that I knew wouldn't help us and I didn't talk to him but someone else took an affidavit from him. His story that he was telling didn't fit with what we knew to be true.
Ball. Roger Craig stated that about 15 minutes after the shooting he saw a man, a white man, leave the Texas State Book Depository Building, run across a lawn, and get into a white Rambler driven by a coloured man.
Fritz. I don't think that is true.
Ball. I am stating this. You remember the witness now?
Fritz. I remember the witness; yes, sir.
Ball. Did that man ever come into your office and talk to you in the presence of Oswald?
Fritz. In the presence of Oswald?
Ball. Yes.
Fritz. No, sir; I am sure he did not. I believe that man did come to my office in that little hallway, you know outside my office, and I believe I stepped outside the door and talked to him for a minute and I let someone else take an affidavit from him. We should have that affidavit from him if it would help.
Ball. Now this man states that, has stated, that he came to your office and Oswald was in your office, and you asked him to look at Oswald and tell you whether or not this was the man he saw, and he says that in your presence he identified Oswald as the man that he had seen run

246

across this lawn and get into the white Rambler sedan. Do you remember that?

Fritz. I think it was taken, I think it was one of my officers, and I think if he saw him, he looked through that glass and saw him from the outside because I am sure of one thing that I didn't bring him in the office with Oswald.

Ball. You are sure you didn't?

Fritz. I am sure of that. I feel positive of that. I would remember that, I am sure.

Ball. He also says that in that office-

Fritz. Yes, sir.

Ball. After he had said, *"That is the man,"* that Oswald got up from his chair and slammed his hand on the table and said, *"Now everybody will know who I am."* Did that ever occur in your presence?

Fritz. If it did, I never saw anything like that; no, sir.

Ball. That didn't occur?

Fritz. No, sir; it didn't. That man is not telling a true story if that is what he said. Do you have any— could I ask a question, is it all right if I ask a question?

Mr. McCloy. All right, go ahead.

Ball. Go ahead.

Fritz. I was going to ask if we had any affidavits from any of our officers that would back that up? If they did, I never heard of it.

Ball. If you are here tomorrow.

Fritz. It is something I don't know anything about.

Ball. If you are here tomorrow, I would like to show you the deposition of the man for you to read it.

Fritz. I am sure I would know that. The only time I saw the man hit the desk was when Mr. Hosty talked to him and he really got upset about that.

[This last bit has been confirmed by Elmer Boyd yet denied by Bookhout in his WC testimony]

Strange how Fritz barely knows the man (3200), when he was also present on the sixth floor when the rifle was found and happened to work with the Sheriff's Office for quite a few years.

Will Fritz's follow-up WC testimony (3201) repeats what he said before during his primary WC testimony and it again contradicts Craig's testimony, but Fritz's account is hard to swallow. It is hard to accept that Will Fritz did not know Roger Craig.

"I don't remember the name Roger Craig, but I do remember a man coming into my outer office and I remember one of my officers calling

247

me outside the door of my private office. I talked to this man for a minute or two, and he started telling me a story about seeing Oswald leaving the building. I don't remember all the things that this man said, but I turned him over to Lt Baker who talked to him. Lee Harvey Oswald was in my office at this time. I don't remember anything about Lee Harvey Oswald jumping up or making any remarks or gestures to this man or to me at this time, and had I brought this officer into my inner office I feel sure that I would remember it. There were other officers in my inner office at the time, and I have found no one who knows about the remarks that you have asked about."

While this interrogation of Oswald was going on, Alan Belmont of the FBI compiled a report which is sent to Clyde Tolson (3202). In this he speaks of having talked to Gordon Shanklin at 17:10. He mentions that the Secret Service is not doing much. That all possible investigative steps should be taken by the Bureau, such as the gun being checked for fingerprints, checking the whereabouts of Oswald during the morning and so forth. And that Shanklin needs to be sure and not assume the police are going to handle this properly. Plus, the FBI must conduct a vigorous and thorough investigation to come up with the answers. Shanklin is also instructed to locate the bullets that hit JFK and governor Connally. And there is more, so please read the document carefully.

18:20 Second Line-up for McWatters, Callaway & Guinyard

Jim Leavelle's line-up notes (3203) for Cecil McWatters, Ted Callaway and Sam Guinyard.

The same three guys, William Perry and Richard Clark from Vice and Don Ables the assistant jailer who participated in the Helen Markham line-up, are again attached to Oswald (who is again in the No. 2 position).

Cecil McWatters was the bus driver allegedly seeing Oswald laugh out loud. From McWatters WC testimony (3204) it becomes clear that he would not pick Oswald out, even though the WC makes it sound that he did. Plus, McWatters points out that overall, everyone looked different of age, size and height. They are supposed to look similar in a line-up:

Mr. McWatters - Yes, sir; when they stopped me over there and took me into the police department there, like I say, it was around 6:15 or 6:20, they took me down before the line-up there and asked me if I could identify anyone in that line-up as getting on my bus that day.
Mr. Ball - Did they take you down and show you a line-up?

Mr. McWatters - Yes, sir.

Mr. Ball - You sat there with police officers and they brought men in there?

Mr. McWatters - They brought four men out. In other words, four men under the lights; in other words, they was all—

Mr. Ball - All the same age?

Mr. McWatters - No, sir; they were different ages, different sizes and different heights. And they asked me if I could identify any man in particular there, and I told them that I couldn't identify any man in particular, but there was one man there that was about the size of the man. Now, I was referring back, after they done showed me this transfer at that time and I knew which trip, that I went through town on at that time, in other words, on the Lakewood trip and just like I recalled, I only put out two transfers and I told them that there was one man in the line-up was about the size and the height and complexion of a man that got on my bus, but as far as positively identifying the man I could not do it.

[Then later during the same testimony...]

Mr. Ball - Anyway, you were not able to identify any man in the line-up as the passenger?

Mr. McWatters - No, sir.

Mr. Ball - As the passenger who had gotten on?

Mr. McWatters - No, sir.

Mr. Ball - You said there was one man who closely resembled in height, weight and colour?

Mr. McWatters - That is right.

Mr. Ball - Do you know who that was?

Mr. McWatters - Just like I told them; I didn't know who was who or anything.

Mr. Ball - Did you ever learn who that person was?

Mr. McWatters - Well, I don't know whether that was really the man or not, I don't know.

Mr. Ball - I see.

[And later...]

Mr. Ball - You didn't--as I understand it, when you were at the police line-up, you told us that you didn't--weren't able to identify this man in the line-up as the man who got off, that you gave the transfer to.

Mr. McWatters - I told them to the best of my knowledge, I said the man that I picked out was the same height, about the same height, weight and description. But as far as actually saying that is the man I couldn't—

Mr. Ball - You couldn't do it?

Mr. McWatters - I wouldn't do it and I wouldn't do it now.

[And later, during the same testimony while the Commission is trying to really pin it all down...]

Mr. Ball - *"This man looks like the No. 1 man I saw in the line-up today."*
Mr. McWatters - Yes.
Mr. Ball - Who was the No. 2 man you saw in the line-up on November 22, 1963?
Mr. McWatters - Well, just like I say, he was the shortest man in the line-up, in other words, when they brought these men out there, in other words, he was about the shortest, and the lightest weight one, I guess, was the reason I say that he looked like the man, because the rest of them were larger men than..
Mr. Ball - Well, now, at that time, when you saw the line-up.
Mr. McWatters - Yes.
Mr. Ball - Were you under the impression that this man that you saw in the line-up and whom you pointed out to the police, was the teenage boy who had been grinning?
Mr. McWatters - I was, yes, sir; I was under the impression—
Mr. Ball - That was the fellow?
Mr. McWatters - That was the fellow.
Mr. Ball - You were not under the impression then that night when you saw the line-up that the No. 2 man in the line-up was the man who got off the bus, to whom you had given a transfer?
Mr. McWatters - That is what I say. In other words, when I told them, I said, the only way is the man, that he is smaller, in other words, he kind of had a thin like face and he weighs less than any one of them. The only one I could identify at all would be the smaller man on account he was the only one who could come near fitting the description.
Mr. Ball - Let me ask you this, though. Did you tell them the man, the smaller man, you saw in the line-up, did you tell them that you thought he was the man who got off your bus and got the transfer or the man who was on the bus who was the teenager who was grinning?
Mr. McWatters - Well, I really thought he was the man who was on the bus.
Mr. Ball - That stayed on the bus?
Mr. McWatters - That stayed on the bus.
Mr. Ball - And you didn't think he was the man who got off the bus and to whom you gave a transfer?
Mr. McWatters - No, sir.
Mr. Ball - At that time you didn't?
Mr. McWatters - That is why I say I pinpointed that transfer on that boy as far as that is concerned. But at first, just like I say, I really thought from the height and weight of the two men, I mean was just like I say,

was both of them were small. In the line-up they had, in other words, bigger men, in other words, he was the smallest man at the line-up.

[And the WC keeps returning to the line-up...]

Mr. Ball - Now, that night of the line-up, when you identified this one short man.
Mr. McWatters - Yes.
Mr. Ball - As being probably the teenager that had been on the bus—
Mr. McWatters - Yes.
Mr. Ball - Was there anything unusual in the conduct of anyone in the line-up?
Mr. McWatters - No.
Mr. Ball - Did any man in the line-up talk more than anyone else?
Mr. McWatters - No, I believe they had a guy that asked them their address, and they said, *"address"* and I don't know, he asked them, I believe he asked some of them where they lived or some of them where they worked, or I don't remember just what, in other words, he asked some enough, every one of them to say some few words.
Mr. Ball - You could hear them talk?
Mr. McWatters - Yes, sir; you could hear them talk.
Mr. Ball - Was any one man boisterous, mean, loud, anything of that sort?
Mr. McWatters - No, not that I could tell any difference. They all talked to me as, in other words, you just asked them their name and address. If they did, I didn't pay any attention to it.

[And clearly the WC cannot let go of this line-up which is nothing short of a mess...]

Senator Cooper - You saw--was any of the men in the police line-up ever identified to you as being Lee Oswald?
Mr. McWatters - Any men in the—
Senator Cooper - Yes, I think you saw the men in the line-up, didn't you?
Mr. McWatters - Yes.
Senator Cooper - Before you were asked to select a man in the line-up, did the police or any officer identify any one of them as bearing the name of Lee Oswald?
Mr. McWatters - No, sir; they never stated anything.
Senator Cooper - Later was he identified to you in any way?
Mr. McWatters - Was he identified to me?
Senator Cooper - As being Lee Oswald?
Mr. McWatters - No, they didn't tell me as far as saying, mentioning any name Lee Oswald, it was never, the name Lee Oswald, I don't believe was ever mentioned while we was back there.

251

Senator Cooper - Did you ever see this same man you call No. 2 in the line-up again--did you ever go back there after that time and see this same person again?
Mr. McWatters - No, sir.
Senator Cooper - Identified as No. 2?
Mr. McWatters - No, sir; I never did go back any more, that was the only time I was ever there was the one on November 22, about 6 something in the afternoon.

From McWatters' handwritten affidavit (3205) one can deduct that this was written after the line-up.

Sam Guinyard and Ted Callaway, both working at the same car repair shop, not far away from the scene of the crime, contradict each other during their WC testimonies by describing the killer walking on *opposite sides of the street*, something Gokay Hasan Yusuf (3206) has already succinctly brought forward in his blog post from 2013.

- Harold Weisberg (3207) is of the opinion that Guinyard was primed before the line-up and his WC testimony, something I tend to agree with. Guinyard mentioned a second person involved with the Tippit shooting.
- Jim Leavelle's report (3208) states he took Galloway's and Guinyard's statements *before* the line-up. Something he reconfirms during his WC testimony (3209). The two men's handwritten statements are taken and the No. 2 ID is added on in the typed statement after. Calloway handwritten (3210) - Calloway typed (3211). Guinyard handwritten (3212) – Guinyard typed (3213) statements.

Guinyard's WC testimony (3214) details the line-up:

Mr. Ball. Later that day, did you go down to the police department?
Mr. Guinyard. Yes, sir; I went down that night.
Mr. Ball. That same night?
Mr. Guinyard. Yes.
Mr. Ball. Whom did you go down with?
Mr. Guinyard. Me and Ted.
Mr. Ball. You and who?
Mr. Guinyard. Ted---Ted Callaway.
Mr. Ball. Ted Callaway?
Mr. Guinyard. Yes.
Mr. Ball. And where did you go when you went to the police station?
Mr. Guinyard. I went to the identifying office.
Mr. Ball. You went into a place where there were police officers?

252

Mr. Guinyard. Yes, sir.

Mr. Ball. And how did you identify him--tell me what happened to you, what you saw?

Mr. Guinyard. Well, I just saw him.

Mr. Ball. Well, were you in a big room?

Mr. Guinyard. Yes--in a big room.

Mr. Ball. With police officers?

Mr. Guinyard. Yes, sir.

Mr. Ball. And what did you see?

Mr. Guinyard. I don't understand you.

Mr. Ball. Did you see some men up ahead of you?

Mr. Guinyard. Yes--four men.

Mr. Ball. Four men?

Mr. Guinyard. Yes--four men--handcuffed together.

Mr. Ball. What did you say?

Mr. Guinyard. They was handcuffed together.

Mr. Ball. They was handcuffed?

Mr. Guinyard. Yes; all four of them.

Mr. Ball. Were they of different sizes?

Mr. Guinyard. Well, they was pretty close together--there wasn't much difference in size.

Mr. Ball. In height--they were about the same?

Mr. Guinyard. About the same.

Mr. Ball. Were they all about the same colour?

Mr. Guinyard. No, sir; they wasn't all about the same colour.

Mr. Ball. All about the same colour?

Mr. Guinyard. No, sir; they wasn't all about the same colour.

Mr. Ball. Did you say anything to any police officer there after you saw them?

Mr. Guinyard. I talked to one---with the detective---after he came out there.

Mr. Ball. What did you tell him--I mean in this room---as you saw these four men up there?

Mr. Guinyard. He just asked me reckon I could identify them and I said I sure could.

Mr. Ball. What did you tell him?

Mr. Guinyard. I just told him I sure could.

Mr. Ball. What did you say to him about it?

Mr. Guinyard. Well, I didn't say anything--I was just waiting on them to bring them in.

Mr. Ball. After they brought them in and after you looked at them, what did you tell the police officers?

Mr. Guinyard. I told them that was him right there---I pointed him out right there. That was him right there.

Mr. Ball. Do you remember where he was standing in the line-up--what number he was?

Mr. Guinyard. I don't know what his number was, but I can tell you where he was standing at.

Mr. Ball. Where was he standing?

Mr. Guinyard. He was standing--the second man from the east side, and that line-up was this way [indicating] and he was the second man from that there end.

Mr. Ball. And did you tell any police officer that you thought that was the man?

Mr. Guinyard. Yes, sir.

Mr. Ball. Whom did you tell; what police officer was it?

Mr. Guinyard. I don't know his name.

Mr. Ball. You don't know his name?

Mr. Guinyard. No, sir; I don't know his name but I know him now if I would see him.

Mr. Ball. Before you went in there, did the police officers show you any pictures?

Mr. Guinyard. No, sir.

Mr. Ball. Did the police officer say anything to you before you went in there?

Mr. Guinyard. No, sir.

Mr. Ball. Did he say that he thought they had the man that killed the police officer?

Mr. Guinyard. No, sir; he didn't tell me that.

Mr. Ball. Did you hear Ted Callaway say anything before you said you thought that was the man?

Mr. Guinyard. No, sir.

Mr. Ball. Were you with Ted at the time?

Mr. Guinyard. Yes, sir.

Mr. Ball. How close was Ted to you?

Mr. Guinyard. Oh--sitting about like that.

Mr. Ball. You mean 3 or 4 feet away from you?

Mr. Guinyard. Yes; something like that.

Ted Callaway has his say during his WC testimony (3215):

Mr. Ball. Did you go down to the police station later?

Mr. Callaway. That evening.

Mr. Ball. What time?

Mr. Callaway. I think it was around 6:30 or 7 o'clock. I remember it was after dark.

Mr. Ball. Did you go down there alone?

Mr. Callaway. No. I went with Sam Guinyard, a coloured porter of ours. He saw him, also.

[At this point, Representative Ford withdrew from the hearing room.]

Mr. Callaway. We drove down. Officer--Detective Jim Leavelle met us, and took us into this room where they showed us the line-up.

Mr. Ball. Now, before you went down there, had you seen any newspaper accounts of this incident?

Mr. Callaway. No, sir; I had been out there on the lot. I hadn't seen a newspaper, hadn't even heard a radio, really.

Mr. Ball. Had you seen any television?

Mr. Callaway. No sir.

Mr. Ball. Had you seen a picture of a man?

Mr. Callaway. No.

Mr. Ball. The officer show you any pictures?

Mr. Callaway. No, sir.

Mr. Ball. You went into a police line-up, in a room where they had a line-up of men?

Mr. Callaway. Yes.

Mr. Ball. How many?

Mr. Callaway. Four.

Mr. Ball. And were they all the same size, or different sizes?

Mr. Callaway. They were about the same build, but the man that I identified was the shortest one of the bunch.

Mr. Ball. Were they anywhere near the same age?

Mr. Callaway. They were about the same age, yes, sir. They looked-- you know.

Mr. Ball. And you say you identified a man. How did you do that?

Mr. Callaway. Well

Mr. Ball. Tell us what happened.

Mr. Callaway. We first went into the room. There was Jim Leavelle, the detective, Sam Guinyard, and then this bus driver and myself. We waited down there for probably 20 or 30 minutes. And Jim told us, *"When I show you these guys, be sure, take your time, see if you can make a positive identification."*

Mr. Ball. Had you known him before?

Mr. Callaway. No. And he said, *"We want to be sure; we want to try to wrap him up real tight on killing this officer. We think he is the same one that shot the President. But if we can wrap him up tight on killing this officer, we have got him."* So, they brought four men in.

[This indicates that Leavelle tipped off the witnesses that the killer of Tippit and The President was in the line-up-BK]

Mr. Callaway. [Continues] I stepped to the back of the room, so I could kind of see him from the same distance which I had seen him before. And when he came out, I knew him.

255

Mr. Ball. You mean he looked like the same man?
Mr. Callaway. Yes.
Mr. Ball. About what distance was he away from you--the closest that he ever was to you?
Mr. Callaway. About 56 feet.
Mr. Ball. You measured that, did you?
Mr. Callaway. Yes, sir.
Mr. Ball. Last Saturday morning?
Mr. Callaway. Yes, sir.
Mr. Ball. Measured it with a tape measure?
Mr. Callaway. Yes, sir.

Then there is the issue of the supposedly grey jacket; and this jacket was found pretty quickly by the police, but by the looks of it, Oswald was never confronted with that jacket, nor were there any fingerprints found on the jacket.

Sam Guinyard's WC testimony (3216):

Mr. Ball. How was this man dressed that had the pistol in his hand?
Mr. Guinyard. He had on a pair of black britches and a brown shirt and a lithe sort of light-gray-looking jacket.
Mr. Ball. A gray jacket.
Mr. Guinyard. Yes; a light gray jacket and a white T-shirt.
Mr. Ball. A white T-shirt?
Mr. Guinyard. Yes; a white T-shirt on under it.
Mr. Ball. Now, he had a light gray jacket on?
Mr. Guinyard. And a brown shirt on.
Mr. Ball. And a white T-shirt on?
Mr. Guinyard. Underneath it, because this brown shirt was open at the throat and the white T-shirt under it like this [indicating].
Mr. Ball. Sam, I'll show you an exhibit here, which is a piece of clothing and which is marked Commission Exhibit No. 150. Have you ever seen this before?
Mr. Guinyard. Yes, sir.
Mr. Ball. When and where?
Mr. Guinyard. In Oak Cliff.
Mr. Ball. Did you ever see anybody wearing it?
Mr. Guinyard. Yes, sir.
Mr. Ball. Who?
Mr. Guinyard. Oswald.
Mr. Ball. Where?
Mr. Guinyard. Oak Cliff.
Mr. Ball. Tell me a little more about it.
Mr. Guinyard. In Oak Cliff and down in the courtroom.

Mr. Ball. Where?

Mr. Guinyard. Down in the examining room.

Mr. Ball. When this man came down Patton Street toward Jefferson with his gun, you have mentioned he had a shirt on?

Mr. Guinyard. Yes, sir.

Mr. Ball. You described that shirt as a brown shirt?

Mr. Guinyard. Yes.

Mr. Ball. Does this look anything like the shirt?

Mr. Guinyard. It looks just like it does.

Mr. Ball. You saw that shirt before?

Mr. Guinyard. Yes.

Mr. Ball. Where?

Mr. Guinyard. Down at the City Hall.

Mr. Ball. At the Police Station?

Mr. Guinyard. Yes.

Mr. Ball. And what did you tell them when they showed you this shirt?

Mr. Guinyard. I told them that that's the shirt he had on.

Mr. Ball. Now, the next exhibit here is Commission Exhibit No. 162; have you ever seen this before?

Mr. Guinyard. That's the jacket.

Mr. Ball. This is a gray jacket?

Mr. Guinyard. Yes; that's the gray jacket.

Mr. Ball. It has a zipper on it?

Mr. Guinyard. Yes.

Mr. Ball. You say that's the jacket?

Mr. Guinyard. Yes; that he had on in Oak Cliff when he passed the lot.

Mr. Ball. That the man with the pistol had on?

Mr. Guinyard. Yes, sir.

Ted Callaway goes through similar motions during his WC testimony (3217):

Mr. Ball. Did he have the same clothes on in the line-up--did the man have the same clothes?

Mr. Callaway. He had the same trousers and shirt, but he didn't have his jacket on. He had ditched his jacket.

Mr. Ball. What kind--when you talked to the police officers before you saw this man, did you give them a description of the clothing he had on?

Mr. Callaway. Yes, sir.

Mr. Ball. What did you tell them you saw?

Mr. Callaway. I told them he had some dark trousers and a light tannish gray windbreaker jacket, and I told him that he was fair complexion, dark hair.

Mr. Ball. Tell them the size?

257

Mr. Callaway. Yes; I told them--I think I told them about 5'10"—

Mr. Dulles. Did you see his front face at any time, or did you only have a side view of him?

Mr. Callaway. He looked right at me, sir. When I called to him, he looked right at me.

Mr. Dulles. You saw front face?

Mr. Callaway. Yes.

Mr. Ball. I have a jacket here Commission's Exhibit No. 162. Does this look anything like the jacket that the man had on that you saw across the street with a gun?

Mr. Callaway. Yes; it sure does. Yes, that is the same type jacket. Actually, I thought it had a little more tan to it.

Mr. Ball. Same type?

Mr. Callaway. Yes.

Mr. Ball. I show you a shirt, No. 150. Does it look anything like the shirt he had on under the jacket?

Mr. Callaway. Sir, when I saw him, he didn't have--I couldn't see this shirt. I saw--he had it open. That shirt was open, and I could see his white T-shirt underneath.

Mr. Ball. He had a white T-shirt underneath?

Mr. Callaway. Yes. That is the shirt he had on in the line-up that night.

In *Accessories After the Fact* (3218) page 258, according to Domingo Benavides, Callaway had to ask him what had happened. And Callaway also had to ask him which way the perpetrator fled so he could chase him.

Domingo Benavides is the biggest absentee during this or any other line-up. He was the witness who was positioned closest to the whole shooting; his pick-up truck was parked 15-20 feet diagonally across from Tippit's patrol car, and refused to ID Oswald as the killer and naturally was not asked to come by LC Graves and Jim Leavelle. LC Graves makes mention of Domingo Benavides in his report (3219). Jim Leavelle's reports on the other hand omits him. The FBI and USSS have not produced any reports at all. This just begs the question why was he *not* used for the line-ups?

His first official record is his WC testimony (3220), four months after the happening.

Here's a snippet which pertains to Oswald's identification:

Mr. Belin - You used the name Oswald. How did you know this man was Oswald?

Mr. Benavides - From the pictures I had seen. It looked like a guy, resembled the guy. That was the reason I figured it was Oswald.

Mr. Belin - Were they newspaper pictures or television pictures, or both, or neither?

Mr. Benavides - Well, television pictures and newspaper pictures. The thing lasted about a month, I believe, it seemed like.

Mr. Belin – Pardon?

Mr. Benavides - I showed--I believe they showed pictures of him every day for a long time there.

19:03 Arraigned for the Murder of JD Tippit

Just after 19:00 Oswald was arraigned for the Tippit murder in Will Fritz's office, which doesn't resemble a court of law at all. An arraignment is defined as *"the formal summoning of a prisoner in a court of law to answer an indictment."*

Will Fritz's WC testimony (3221):

Mr. Ball. What happened at 7:10?

Mr. Fritz. 7:10 we had this arraignment with Judge David Johnston, and present, I was present, and Officers Sims, Boyd, Hall, and Mr. Alexander from the district attorney's office, and that was in my office.

Mr. Ball. How was the arraignment conducted?

Mr. Fritz. Well, the judge gave him a warning, talked to him for a little bit.

Mr. Ball. What warning did he give him?

Mr. Fritz. He advised him of his rights. I believe he had a form; I couldn't repeat it, of course, but I believe he had some forms that he went over with him.

[Later, during the same testimony...]

Mr. Ball. Now, at 7:10, he was arraigned in your office?

Mr. Fritz. Yes, sir.

Mr. Ball. By arraign you mean he was informed of the charge against him?

Mr. Fritz. That is right.

Mr. Ball. He wasn't asked to plea.

Mr. Fritz. Before a judge, before a justice of the peace, a magistrate.

Mr. Ball. It is not your practice to ask for a plea at that stage, is it?

Mr. Fritz. No, sir; we don't.

Mr. Ball. All you do is advise him of his rights and the charge against him?

Mr. Fritz. That is right, I am not a lawyer, you might feel--I don't want to leave a bad impression, I am just telling you what we do.

Mr. Ball. What the practice is in Texas.

Mr. Fritz. Yes, sir.

Mr. Ball. Did Oswald make any reply to Judge Johnston?

Mr. Fritz. He said a lot of sarcastic things to him.

Mr. Ball. What did he say?

Mr. Fritz. Irritable, I can't remember all the things that he said. He was that way at each arraignment. He said little sarcastic things, some of the things were a little impudent things.

Richard Sims' WC testimony (3222):

Mr. Ball. Now, in your report, you mentioned that a murder complaint was signed by Fritz that evening?

Mr. Sims. Yes, sir.

Mr. Ball. Were you present when that happened?

Mr. Sims. Yes.

Mr. Ball. Was Oswald present also?

Mr. Sims. Yes, sir.

Mr. Ball. He was present when the murder complaint was signed?

Mr. Sims. Yes, sir.

Mr. Ball. Where did this take place?

Mr. Sims. In Captain Fritz' office.

Mr. Ball. And who was present?

Mr. Sims. Well, let me see Justice of the Peace Dave Johnston, and Assistant District Attorney Bill Alexander, and I don't know who else was there--I don't know who else was present.

Mr. Ball. Was the judge there--the justice judge--the J.P., Dave Johnston?

Mr. Sims. Yes, sir.

Mr. Ball. And Bill Alexander and Fritz?

Mr. Sims. Yes.

Mr. Ball. And you? And Boyd?

Mr. Sims. Yes, sir.

Mr. Ball. And Oswald was there?

Mr. Sims. Yes, sir.

Mr. Ball. Was anything said to Oswald about the signing of a murder complaint?

Mr. Sims. Yes, sir.

Mr. Ball. What was said, and who said it?

Mr. Sims. I don't remember what was said--I know Judge Johnston talked to him and Captain Fritz talked to him.

Mr. Ball. And did Alexander talk to him?

Mr. Sims. I believe he did, but I'm not positive about that.

Mr. Ball. Do you remember what Judge Johnston said?

Mr. Sims. No, sir; I don't.

Mr. Ball. Do you remember what Oswald said?

Mr. Sims. No, sir.

Mr. Ball. Did anyone tell him that a murder complaint was being filed against him?

Mr. Sims. I believe so; yes, sir.

Mr. Ball. For what murder?

Mr. Sims. For Officer Tippit.

Mr. Ball. Do you remember what Oswald said?

Mr. Sims. No, sir; I don't.

Elmer Boyd's WC testimony (3223):

Mr. Ball. Who was present in Captain Fritz' office at that time?

Mr. Boyd. Well, that was when Justice of the Peace David Johnston [spelling] J-o-h-n-s-t-o-n, and our assistant district attorney, Bill Alexander, William F. Alexander, I believe is his true name they came in with Captain Fritz.

Mr. Ball. Oswald was there too, was he?

Mr. Boyd. Yes.

Mr. Ball. What took place there?

Mr. Boyd. Well, Captain Fritz signed a murder complaint against Lee Harvey Oswald and that was for the murder of J. D. Tippit.

Mr. Ball. Was there some conversation that took place there at that time in front of Oswald?

Mr. Boyd. Yes, sir.

Mr. Ball. What was it that you can remember?

Mr. Boyd. Well, I believe Judge Johnston, I believe, read the charge to Oswald, and--well I don't recall the rest of that conversation.

Mr. Ball. Do you remember what Oswald said?

Mr. Boyd. No, sir.

From the Tippit arraignment the four men present besides Oswald did not remember anything of what the accused man had to say. Nor did the person doing the officiating.

Justice of the Peace David L Johnston, according to his WC testimony (3224):

Mr. Hubert. Were you the Justice of Peace that arraigned Oswald?

Mr. Johnston. Yes; I arraigned Lee Harvey Oswald--let me give you the sequence of them--that's the easiest thing to do. I brought the complete record and I have everything here. The first charge that was filed was for murder with malice of Officer J. D. Tippit of the Dallas Police Department in case No. F-153, The State of Texas versus Lee Harvey Oswald. This complaint was filed at 7:05 p.m. on the 22nd day of November 1963.

Mr. Hubert. By whom?

Mr. Johnston. By Capt. J. W. Fritz, captain of the Homicide Bureau, Dallas Police Department, was accepted by W. F. Alexander, who is William F. Alexander, an assistant criminal district attorney of Dallas County, Tex., which was passed over to me at 7:05 p.m. The actual complaint was signed at 7:04 p.m. and I arraigned Lee Harvey Oswald at 7:10 p.m. on November 22, 1963, advising him of his constitutional rights and that he had to make no statement at all, and that any statement he made may be used in evidence against him for the offense concerning which this affidavit was taken, and remanded the defendant to the custody of the sheriff of Dallas County, Tex., with no bond as capital offense.

Mr. Hubert. Is it within your jurisdiction to do that?

Mr. Johnston. Yes, sir.

Mr. Hubert. Where did that occur?

Mr. Johnston. That was in Captain Fritz' office of the Dallas Police Department.

Mr. Hubert. Who else was present?

Mr. Johnston. Mr. Bill Alexander--William Alexander--an assistant district attorney; Captain Fritz--these are--if I can remember them either two or three of the other homicide detectives; at least one Federal Bureau of Investigation agent (which must have been James Bookhout-BK), and which one I couldn't say at this time because we were just all in and out of there, and I'm almost sure it was one of the FBI agents, and which one, I couldn't say at this time because we were just all in and out of there, and I'm almost sure there was one of the FBI agents in the room and possibly a Secret Service agent.

[And a little later...]

Mr. Hubert. Under Texas law is a man charged with murder required to be brought before a committing magistrate, such as you, right away?

Mr. Johnston. This can be done immediately forthwith before the magistrate or a reasonable period of time within a reasonable period of time of the filing.

Mr. Hubert. What occurs at such time at such a proceeding?

Mr. Johnston. In this particular incident, the complaint--the affidavit-- was read to the defendant, Lee Harvey Oswald, at which time I advised him that this was merely to appraise him of his constitutional rights and what he was charged with.

Mr. Hubert. This was not a court proceeding?

Mr. Johnston. This was not the examining trial; no, sir. It was not the examining trial.

Mr. Hubert. It did not call for a plea?

Mr. Johnston. It required no pleadings whatsoever; no, sir. This was merely to appraise him of what he was charged with and to advise him of his constitutional rights.

Mr. Hubert. Did he make any comment upon that at all?

Mr. Johnston. Yes, sir; but I can't recall what it was. At this particular time, he made some remark. Also, at the second arraignment for the murder of President Kennedy, when he was brought through the door at this time, he said, *"Well, I guess this is the trial,"* was the statement that he made then, but I don't remember what he said at the arraignment regarding Officer Tippit.

Bill Alexander in *No More Silence* (page 537): *"Oswald's demeanour was that of one of the most arrogant people that I have ever run into in a situation like that. He just disclaimed any knowledge of anything."*

Straight after this arraignment for the Tippit murder, there are three videos available showing Oswald as he is being escorted out by Boyd, Sims and Hall. The corridor is filled to the brim with reporters and camera men. The first one is while leaving Room 317 (3225), and so is the second one (3226), without audio. He complains that he has been given a hearing without any legal representation present; he also denies that he has shot anyone. The third video is from an opposite angle alongside the wall (3227) about 20 feet further down and captures Oswald on his way to the door which leads toward the elevator. He is about to have his next line-up for the Davis Sisters. The audio in this video is much better.

It is more than likely that the reporter who asked Oswald the question is Jim Lehrer. In an article for Daily Beast (3228), Lehrer, then a young reporter, recalled the informality in the police station; where they were moving Oswald from one office to another, *"and I went right to Oswald. 'Did you kill the president?' 'I didn't kill anybody,'"* he replied. *"I wrote that down."* Lehrer said.

19:30 Interrogation by Manning Clements

FBI Special Agent Manning Clements (3229) arrived on the evening of November 22nd and asked James Bookhout (3230) if anyone has, to his knowledge, taken a detailed physical description and background information from Lee Harvey Oswald. Bookhout tells him that such description and background data has not been obtained, and suggests that Clements do it. This is captured in Manning Clements' report from November 23rd (3231). In this report, on the first page, set aside especially, the Hidell ID is buried.

Oswald is under guard inside Room 317 of the Homicide & Robbery Bureau of the DPD. Clements talks with Oswald over a period of just about half an hour, during which time Oswald is taken out for the Davis Sister's line-up. During Oswald's absence Clements spends time going through the evidence laid out on a table outside the interrogation room. While going through these exhibits he allegedly notices the Selective Service Card of Alek James Hidell. The fact that not one person of the DPD, FBI or Secret Service makes any mention of this card and its *"Hidell"* alias during the three interrogations prior to his own with Lee Oswald is nothing short of remarkable. What is even more remarkable is that Oswald is interrogated again by Fritz shortly after Clements' questioning and there is not a peep about a Hidell ID at all!

Remember that James Hosty made notes of the evidence just after 16:00 while Oswald is downstairs for the Markham line-up and there is no mention of any Hidell ID in any of his notes.

Will Fritz does not bring the ID up until near the end of the next morning of the 23rd, according to his handwritten notes. James Bookhout's report confirm this. That is a few hours after the name AJ Hidell is 'discovered' by the FBI (3232) during the morning of the 23rd.

In his WC testimony (3233) Clements says that he questioned Oswald at about 22:00, but this is wrong. Thanks to a report by MG Hall (3234) it is determined to be at about 19:40.

Clements indicates that during his WC testimony (3235) Oswald was not at all hostile or resentful. And answered all questions, except when asked about the Hidell ID. That's because it was not there at all (3236):

Mr. Stern. Will you now tell, Mr. Clements, as much as you can recall of your interrogation of Oswald at that time?
Mr. Clements. I informed him of the purpose of my interview. He made no objection. I proceeded to get his name in full. I asked him questions as to his date and place of birth, height, weight, color of his hair and eyes, and as to the existence of any permanent scars or marks. As to the identities of close relatives, their addresses and occupations, and asked him as to his own occupation, residence, attempting to get them in chronological order, and asked as to his past occupations.
Mr. Stern. Did you review with him the contents of his wallet and ask him questions on any of it?
Mr. Clements. I questioned him as to the fictitious, and obviously fictitious Selective Service card, which I found in his wallet. I recognized it as being a fictitious card from the fact that the photograph was mounted on the card, and that there were obvious erasures in typing

of information on the card itself. The card was in the name of an Alek James Hidell, but bore the photograph of Oswald.

Mr. Stern. What did he say about that card?

Mr. Clements. He declined to answer any questions as to the reason of his possession of it.

Mr. Stern. Were there any other questions you put to him that he refused to answer?

Mr. Clements. Toward the conclusion of the interview and after he had been absent and returned, I continued with the questions of past residence and past occupations. He responded to my questions. At a time when I asked him as to his present occupation he hesitated and told me that he thought the obtaining of his description and background information had become somewhat prolonged. He said that he had refused to be interviewed by other law enforcement officers previously, and that he had no intention of being interviewed by me. He continued that he knew the tactics of the FBI. He stated there was a counterpart or a similar agency in Russia, that I was using the soft touch, where the approach of a Russian agency would be different, but the tactics would be the same.

Mr. Stern. At that point did he stop answering questions?

Mr. Clements. No; at that point I asked the same question that I had asked previously, and he answered.

Mr. Stern. Did the interview continue beyond that?

Mr. Clements. That was substantially the end of the interview.

Mr. Stern. Were there other persons present besides the two Dallas police officers who were guarding him?

Mr. Clements. No.

Mr. Stern. At either time, either before or after he had been withdrawn from the line-up?

Mr. Clements. No.

Mr. Stern. Did he seem hostile or resentful or irritated by the fact that you were an FBI agent?

Mr. Clements. He did not state that, if that were the case. He was courteous, responsive as to any question. Volunteered little information.

Mr. Stern. But volunteered very little information. Did he seem a person in command of himself?

Mr. Clements. He seemed to be in command of himself both physically and mentally. He had what appeared to me to be a slightly haughty or arrogant attitude.

Mr. Stern. Did he complain to you about the treatment he was receiving?

Mr. Clements. No.

Mr. Stern. Did he say anything to you about obtaining counsel, whether he had tried to?

Mr. Clements. He said nothing whatsoever in that regard.

Elmer Boyd during his Oral History Interview (3237) in 2006 states: "*After Oswald returned to Room 317 from his line-up, Clements wanted to continue his questioning, but Oswald was not going along with that and said, "Well I think I have answered enough of your questions. You came in for a short interview, it has become rather long. I think I have said all I needed to say."*

19:40 Third Line-up for the Davis Sisters

Jim Leavelle's notes for the Davis sisters' line-up (3238).

Oswald, during this third line-up for the Davis sisters, is accompanied by:

- Don R Ables, a civilian Jail Clerk employed by the DPD at City Hall. Ables was in his mid-20s, 5'9" tall, weighed around 165 pounds, and had dark hair, brown eyes and a ruddy complexion. On each of the three line-ups he attended, he wore a white shirt, a grey-knit sweater and dark trousers.
- Richard Walter Borchardt, a remand prisoner being held on suspicion of firearms, burglary and theft offences. He was 23 years old, 5'9", 161 pounds and had blonde hair, blue eyes and a fair complexion.
- Ellis Carl Brazel, another prisoner, on remand for motoring offences. He was 21 years old, 5'10", weighed 169 pounds also had blonde hair, green eyes and a ruddy complexion.

Even though Barbara Jeanette (3239) and Virginia Davis (3240) point Oswald out, they fail to give a description of the assailant in their affidavits, and again in their Secret Service (3241) / Secret Service (3242) reports. The DPD affidavits were taken after the line-up.

Virginia Davis cites Detective Dhority as the police officer she gave the shell to in her affidavit. During her WC testimony (3243) page 11. She is quoted as, *"I didn't hear the detective's name called."*

The Davis sisters eventually (during their WC testimonies) described the man they saw running across their lawn as a white male, slender, light complexion, with either light brown or black hair. But both fillers Richard Walter Borchgardt and Ellis Carl Brazel had blond hair, and a ruddy complexion. And Don Ables also had a ruddy complexion.

In her March 12th 1964 FBI affidavit (3244), on page 7, Barabara Jeanette states that the killer wore a *dark* jacket and black pants. That creates another issue with the alleged light coloured jacket Oswald wore.

The WC testimony of Barbara Jeanette Davis (3245):

Mr. Ball. Now, did you have some difficulty in identifying this No. 2 man in the showup when you saw him?

Mrs. Davis. Well, they made us look at him a long time before they let us say anything.

Mr. Ball. What about you? I am not talking about what you told them. What was your reaction when you saw this man?

Mrs. Davis. Well, I was pretty sure it was the same man I saw. When they made him turn sideways, I was positive that was the one I seen.

Mr. Ball. I have no further questions.

Mr. Belin. Thank you, Mrs. Davis.

Mr. Dulles. Did your sister-in-law go with you to the line-up?

Mrs. Davis. Yes, sir.

Mr. Dulles. Did she make an identification?

Mrs. Davis. Yes, sir.

Mr. Dulles. At the same time as you did?

Mrs. Davis. Yes, sir.

Mr. Dulles. Did you see her identification?

Mrs. Davis. We didn't discuss it.

Mr. Dulles. I mean, but after she had made it, did you see what identification she had made?

Mrs. Davis. Do you mean--I don't understand what you mean.

Mr. Dulles. Well, let me start over again. Did you identify the man in the line-up before your sister-in-law?

Mrs. Davis. Yes, sir.

Mr. Dulles. Before your sister-in-law?

Mrs. Davis. Yes, sir; I was the first one.

Mr. Dulles. All right. Did your sister-in-law, to your knowledge, make the same identification?

Mrs. Davis. Yes, sir; she was there with me at the same time.

Mr. Dulles. She was standing with you. And she saw the identification you had made?

Mrs. Davis. All I done was just lean over and tell the man.

Mr. Dulles. How did you make your identification? By pointing or holding up your fingers.

Mrs. Davis. The man that was sitting next to me just asked me which one I thought it was, and I leaned over and told him. And then he leaned around me and asked her.

Mr. Dulles. He did what?

Mrs. Davis. He leaned around--he was behind me, and asked her.

Mr. Dulles. I see.

Mrs. Davis. I sort of set up where he could talk to her.

Mr. Dulles. And did you identify the man by number or by pointing?

Mrs. Davis. By number.

Mr. Dulles. Do you remember what number it was?

Mrs. Davis. It was number 2. From the left.

Virginia Davis' WC testimony (3246):

Mr. Belin. All, right, you went with the detective to a dark room?

Mrs. Davis. Yes.

Mr. Belin. What did you do when you got to the dark room?

Mrs. Davis. He told us to sit down.

Mr. Belin. All right.

Mrs. Davis. And then these five boys, or men walked up on this platform, and he was No. 2.

Mr. Belin. You say he was No. 2. Who was No. 2?

Mrs. Davis. The boy that shot Tippit.

Mr. Belin. You mean the man--did you see him shoot Tippit? Or do you mean the man you saw with the gun?

Mrs. Davis. The man I saw carrying the gun.

Mr. Belin. Was he white or a Negro man?

Mrs. Davis. He was white.

Mr. Belin. Were all the men in the line-up white men or some Negroes?

Mrs. Davis. All of them were white.

Mr. Belin. Could you describe any other people in the line-up as to whether they might be fat or thin or short or tall?

Mrs. Davis. Well, one of them was sort, well, he was tall and slim. And then the other one there, he was sort of chubby and he was short. Then this other one, he was about the same height as the other one, the last one I told you about, short and chubby. And the other one was about-- medium tall.

Mr. Belin. Now you identified someone in that line-up?

Mrs. Davis. Yes, sir.

Mr. Belin. Did you hear your sister-in-law identify him first, or not?

Mrs. Davis. No, sir; I identified him first.

Mr. Belin. Where was your sister when you identified him?

Mrs. Davis. She was sitting right next to me.

Mr. Belin. How did you identify him? Did you yell that this is the man I saw?

Mrs. Davis. No; I just leaned over and told the detective it was No. 2.

Mr. Belin. Where was the detective? Was he to your right or to your left?

Mrs. Davis. Let's see, to my right.

Mr. Belin. Where was your sister, to your right or to your left?

Mrs. Davis. Right.

Mr. Belin. As she was to your right, so you leaned over to the detective and told the detective it was No. 2?

Mrs. Davis. Yes, sir.

Mr. Belin. Anything else that you can think of that happened that day?

Mrs. Davis. No, sir.

Mr. Belin. Later did you ever see a picture of Lee Harvey Oswald on television?

Mrs. Davis. Yes, sir.

Mr. Belin. When did you first see it on television?

Mrs. Davis. When they was bringing him out of the jail out here.

Mr. Belin. When?

Mrs. Davis. When they were bringing him out of the jail.

Mr. Belin. You mean Sunday when he got shot?

Mrs. Davis. Yes.

Mr. Belin. Did this look, could you tell whether this was the same man you saw running with the gun?

Mrs. Davis. I wouldn't say for sure.

Mr. Belin. You mean from seeing his picture on television?

Mrs. Davis. Yes, sir.

Mr. Belin. What about the man you identified as No. 2? Would you say for sure that he was the man you saw running with the gun?

Mrs. Davis. I would say that was him for sure.

Mr. Belin. What you are saying is that you couldn't necessarily tell from the television picture?

Mrs. Davis. No, sir. Our television was blurred anyway, so we couldn't hardly tell.

19:50 Oswald Declares, *"I'm Just a Patsy"*

Henry *"Hank"* Moore was mostly occupied with the searches at Beckley and at Ruth Pain's residences, but was also around Oswald on Friday evening, since he was filmed alongside Oswald while in the third-floor corridor. His WC testimony (3247) did not make any mention of it, and his Moore's report (3248) is devoid of any details of it as well.

At 19:50 in the evening of the 22nd, Oswald declared himself a patsy (3249) after being denied legal representation during his arraignment for killing JD Tippit 30-40 minutes prior.

Here is a transcript of what happened during the filmed sequence linked to above:

Oswald: "I'd like to have some legal representation; these police officers have not allowed me to have any. I don't know what this is all about."

269

Reporter: *"Did you kill The President?"*
Oswald: *"No Sir I didn't, people keep asking me that."*
Reporter: *inaudible as another reporter is asking "Did you shoot the President?"*
Oswald: "I work in that building."
Reporter: "Where you in the building at the time?"
Oswald: *"Naturally if I work in that building, yes sir."*
Reporter: *"Did you shoot The President?"*
Oswald: *"No, they are taking me in because of the fact that I lived in The Soviet Union. I'm just a patsy!"*

Henry Wade (3250) does not arrive until early evening at City Hall. He spoke to Chief of Police Curry who showed him the Revill memo about James Hosty and his remarks regarding Oswald's guilt. Then he makes his way towards Captain Fritz's office and, to his surprise, sees Jim Allen there.

Wade refers to James K Allen in his WC testimony (3251)).

Mr. Wade. There was another one of another man there, Jim Allen, who was a former first assistant who is practising law there in Dallas. Frankly, I was a little surprised of seeing him there, he is a real capable boy but he was there in Homicide with Captain Fritz. They were good friends. And I know there is no question about his intentions and everything was good, but he is just a lawyer there, but he had tried many death penalty cases with Fritz, of Fritz's cases.

Later, during the same testimony Wade mentions him again in the context of Oswald assassinating The President.

Mr. Rankin. The conversation you described when Jim Alexander was there and the others?
Mr. Wade. Yes; I first asked Jim Allen, a man whom I have a lot of confidence in, do they have a case and he said it looks like a case you can try.
Mr. Rankin. Is that the case about the assassination?
Mr. Wade. Yes; we are talking entirely about the assassination. On the Tippit thing, I didn't take the charge on that and I think they had some witnesses who had identified him there at the scene, but I was more worried about the assassination of them filing on somebody that we couldn't prove was guilty.

Jim Allen (3251), like Bill Alexander was a former Assistant DA and was known for his hard-core attitude against criminals. He was renowned for his death penalty prosecutions, overseeing at least twenty of them

270

(3252). Allen was a friend of Fritz and had tried many of Fritz's cases and, as mentioned earlier, Wade trusted him. But at that time, he was present as a civilian.

Jim Hosty also writes a report mentioning Allen on December 20th 1963 (3253), and in this communique he states that Allen is someone who has a lot of access inside the Robbery and Homicide Bureau as a private citizen.

19:55 Third interrogation

DPD: Will Fritz
Assistant DA Bill Alexander.
FBI: James Bookhout a.o.
USSS: Forrest Sorrels.

There is not much available about this particular interrogation so it is hard to ascertain who was actually there, what questions were asked and what answers were given. Fritz's notes do not mention this session in detail at all.

Bill Alexander was an Assistant DA to Henry Wade, and along with Jim Allen, tried most Dallas' death penalty cases during the 1950's and 60's. Alexander is said in Larry Sneed's *No More Silence (3254)*, to have been present in the early evening, with Will Fritz, to interrogate Oswald:

As I understand, Oswald had arrived at City Hall around two o'clock in the afternoon. Early that evening Captain Fritz asked me to come in and talk with Oswald. I don't know, but if all the people who have claimed to have interviewed Oswald were put in one group, I doubt if the city auditorium would accommodate them. Every son of a bitch wants to claim he interviewed Oswald, but I know this: I know that Captain Fritz and I were alone with Oswald in Captain Fritz's office the first time that I saw him and Fritz tried to question him. At that time, Fritz tried to get some information from him and Oswald was not responsive. He would answer a question with a question. Fritz asked him if he had a lawyer or wanted a lawyer, and he said yes, that he wanted John Abt. Well, I'd never heard of John Abt, but I found out after I left the office, through a discreet inquiry, that Abt was a Communist lawyer in New York. Captain Fritz said, "We'll pay for the phone call if you want to call him.' Oswald didn't pursue that. So, the Captain said, "Well, do you want us to get you a local lawyer?" But he didn't want a local lawyer. Fritz tried to talk to him about Tippit. 'Who's Tippit?" As I've said, he responded to almost every question with a question.

I had some phone calls to make to find out this and that. When I returned, a couple of FBI agents were there. At that time, FBI agents wouldn't write notes down in front of a suspect. They'd listen until they thought they'd gotten all they could remember, then they'd go outside to write up whatever they heard, then others would come in and out. Throughout these two sessions, Oswald was in command of himself and aware of his surroundings. He seemed intelligent, used good English and expressed himself well. In fact, he almost seemed rehearsed for the questions. He wasn't giving any meaningful answers. Personally, I don't think that he would have ever talked. As time wore on, there was always the question of conspiracy and what next?

Anyway, Captain Fritz wanted a chance to talk about what evidence we had, so we went over to the Majestic Cafe along with Forrest Sorrels, the local head of the Secret Service, an FBI guy, a couple of Dallas police, and I don't remember who else. We went and got a big table, ordered, and then began to talk about the evidence we had and whether we had enough to file. In working closely with Fritz, I had the benefit of whatever information he had, and the case looked solid to me.

20:00 Marina & Marguerite Oswald arrive at City Hall

Carl Day paraded the rifle through the third-floor corridor (3255) at about 20:00. He is asked by Will Fritz to show the rifle to Marina Oswald (3256) in his office. In her statement (3257) taken that day, she is not sure whether the rifle shown to her by Day is Lee's. More importantly, this is not further reflected anywhere during any of the interrogations in Will Fritz's notes, nor in any other report from the FBI (James Bookhout) or the USSS (Thomas Kelley).

In his WC testimony (3258) Carl Day comments about this visit and the rifle ID:

Mr. Belin. Anything else with regards to the rifle?
Mr. Day. I can't think of anything else that I did with it at the time. I don't know whether you are interested in this or not, but about, it must have been about 8:30 I was processing the gun on the fourth floor----
Mr. Belin. Of the police department there?
Mr. Day. Of the Police Department where my office is, The Identification Bureau. And Captain Fritz came up and said he had Mrs. Oswald in his office on the third floor, but the place was so jammed with news cameramen and newsmen he did not want to bring her out into it.
Mr. Belin. Was this the wife or the mother of Lee Harvey Oswald?

Mr. Day. That was Marina, Oswald's wife. She had her baby with her, or babies, and there was an interpreter down there. He wanted her to look at the gun to see if she could identify it, didn't want to bring her in through the crowd, and wanted to know if we could carry it down. He said, *"There is an awful mob down there."* I explained to him that I was still working with the prints, but I thought I could carry it down without disturbing the prints, which I did. We waded through the mob with me holding the gun up high. No one touched it. Several of the newsmen asked me various questions about what the gun was at that time. I did not give them an answer. When I went back to the office after Marina Oswald viewed the gun, they still were hounding me for it. I told them to check with the Chief's office, he would have to give them the information, and as soon as I got back to my office I gave a complete description, and so forth, to Captain King on the gun.

Mr. Belin. Were you there when Marina Oswald was asked whether or not she could identify it?

Mr. Day. Yes, sir. But I didn't understand what she said. I was standing across the room from her where I couldn't understand. The interpreter said something to her and said something to Captain Fritz. I didn't catch what was said. I mentioned that because there was some talk about a Mauser and 30-06 at the time and various other things. That is the reason I mentioned it.

John Adamcik acknowledges Carl Day's presence (3259). Adamcik (seen in the background behind Marina and Marguerite Oswald) in this Darryl Heikes photo (3260) was present while Marina was questioned by Will Fritz at 20:00. This statement makes Day's explanation a bit odd. Adamcik spoke Russian, but there was also an interpreter there.

Will Fritz in his undated and unsigned report (3261) states that Marina did *not* positively ID the rifle. Had Marina given a positive ID then this would have been reflected in the interrogation following shortly after.

20:45 Buell Wesley Frazier is Brought In

Buell Wesley Frazier was first taken into custody by the Irving Police and then Gus Rose and Richard Stovall picked him up and transported him to the Dallas Police station. Once there, they take his mugshot and his finger prints which would indicate he was under arrest. The strange thing is that there is nothing from the DPD to substantiate this.

In the book *Where Were You?* (3262) by Gus Russo and Harry Moses, Buell Wesley Frazier relates his part in this chapter:

Before I got off to Irving, the radio said they had captured a man outside of the Texas Theatre in Oak Cliff, and the more they talked about what went on, I put things together and realized they were talking about Lee. I said, "My gosh. I can't believe what I'm hearing."

Since I'd gotten off early, my mother and my stepfather were up visiting one of my sisters and her husband and three children. He had had a heart attack, so he was in the hospital at Irving Boulevard and Pioneer. I thought, I can stop by and check on him, so that's what I did.

I was in his room, and then a nurse came to the door and said, "I have a phone call for you at the desk." I said, "Just patch it through here to the room." She said, "I'm new; I don't really know how to do that." I said, "OK, I'll be there in just a minute. "Well, I opened the door to go to the nurses' station, and two guys grabbed me and threw me up against the wall; I was totally shocked. I said to them, "What is going on here? Why are you doing this to me?"

They said, "We're arresting you." I said, "For what? I haven't done anything." That was Detective Rose and Detective Stovall. They took me to their car, and we stopped at the Irving Police Station (The paperwork from Irving Police Station (3263) disputes this arrest scenario-BK). *They talked with someone there, and then they took me on to downtown Dallas. They asked about everything you could think of. It was just repetitious—over and over and over for hours.*

Detective Rose and Stovall started off; then they took a break, and two more detectives come in and quizzed me with the same questions, over and over. They just asked me things about Lee and my work and stuff like that. Things I knew I could tell them. They asked about the package Lee had with him. I said, "He did bring a package with him this morning." They asked me about the length of the package, and I told them, "It was roughly two feet, give or take an inch or two either way." Every answer I gave them was the answer I knew.

One time, Captain Will Fritz, who was head of the Homicide Department, brought in a typed statement, and he wanted me to sign it. Now, Captain Fritz, I'm sure, did a lot of good things for the Dallas Police Department, but over the years, I've asked myself: Somewhere along the line did he become like the people he hunted? When he put the paper down in front of me, I started to read it. He wanted me to sign a paper that I was confessing to being part of the assassination and that I knew of it—that I had knowledge of it and that it was going happen. I told him I wasn't signing that. I told him it wasn't the truth. Well, Captain Will Fritz was quite hot-tempered. When I told him I wasn't signing it, he drew back his hand to hit me, and I took my arm up to block. I was sitting there at the table, and all during the questioning, I just had to look straight into a wall. I couldn't look sideways or anything, and when I told him I wasn't going to sign it, I think he really could have struck me. But I told him, 'Outside that door are some policemen, and before they get in here, we're going to have one hell of a fight. I'm going to get some punches in.' He walked out, and I never did see the man again. I don't want to come across as though I hated the man. I just was so unhappy with the way he treated me.

On Saturday morning I was cleared to go home. They cleared me one time, and we were on the way out to Irving when they got a call and turned around and brought me back. That's when they did the fingerprints and a mugshot. I couldn't believe what was going on. This was kind of like a nightmare to me. We went back, and after more questioning and so forth, they finally let me go. I didn't know anything about Lee shooting the policeman, JD Tippit. When I'd tell them something, they'd come back and say, "That's not true." But I knew it was. I knew what I was telling them was the truth, and I didn't deviate from that."

In the Richmond Times Dispatch (3264) Frazier makes mention of those same interrogations which took place over several hours. The Fritz incident is retold there and again in this video (3265): *Capt. Will Fritz came into the room with a typed statement. He handed Frazier a pen and demanded he sign it. It was a confession. Frazier refused. "I said I was not signing that. This was ridiculous," he said. "Captain Fritz got very red-faced, and he put up his hand to hit me and I put my arm up to block. I told him we'd have a hell of a fight and I would get some good licks in on him. Then he stormed out the door."*

Frazier also discusses Fritz and the Lee Enfield (3266) rifle at the AARC Conference at 19:05.

He starts with his arrest while at the hospital visiting his father-in-law. They then go to his home to confiscate his Lee Enfield rifle and a shotgun, then to the police station. He states that two homicide detectives (probably Rose and Stovall) interrogated him for hours in a style that sounds like a military interrogation: telling him where to look and slapping him down and when the first two got tired a new crew would walk in and start all over again with the same questions. At 24:55 he brings up Will Fritz and again states the same as before that Fritz walked in with a prepared statement and wanted Frazier to sign it. He again repeats the same story in this video (3267) to Hugh Aynesworth. *"The way he treated me was totally uncalled for."*

Gus Rose is seen behind Buell Wesley Frazier, filmed (3268) while leaving Homicide & Robbery.

Frazier was taken back home and just when he was about to be dropped off, he was brought back in again and subjected to a polygraph test. This polygraph test has not seen the light of day, and I doubt it ever will. I myself tried to obtain it from the National Archives and got sent a batch of records where they were just passing the buck. From those records (3269), one thing jumps out: Frazier did not believe that the package that the DPD showed him, in which Oswald allegedly transported the rifle to the TSBD, was the one that he had seen on the backseat of his car. Detective RD Lewis was the polygraph operator (3270) during Frazier's examination.

21:00 Paraffin Casts, Fingerprints and Palm Prints Taken

Oswald is being visited in Will Fritz's office by Captain George *"Max"* Doughty, Detective JB *"Johnny"* Hicks and Sergeant William E *"Pete"* Barnes. They arrived to take Oswald's finger and palm prints, but also apply a nitrate test to determine whether he had fired a rifle. I will divide this whole happening and its aftermath in three sections. In this WC draft document (3271) pages 1-3, they present their side of this story. Here's mine.

The Search for the Original Fingerprint Sets

Only a few of the fingerprint sets are available to see publicly in archives and as WC Exhibits. Original sets that have been digitally reproduced are yellow in colour. Some are at The Portal to Texas History.
Further investigation of those sets shows that not one of the Oswald inked & original fingerprint sets seem to be from November 22nd. They only have reproductions of WC exhibits for that date.

One of the first to report on any fingerprints was Nat Pinkston in his late afternoon report of November 22nd. Lt Day has found a partial print and he wished to photograph it before it got lifted.

There is a set of photos (3274) made by Jim Murray of the three above mentioned policemen holding Oswald's fingerprints, palm prints and paraffin test tools. They were paraded around the third floor corridor for the world press to see. The policemen appear out of Room 317, one at a time. WE Barnes holds the palm prints, George Doughty shows two fingerprint cards, and JB Hicks carries an empty tin of wax, a brush, a small jar and a scraper (3275).

Careful study of the fingerprint sets put on display by the DPD in the third floor corridor show these sets in sufficient detail of the prints themselves to ascertain where they are positioned on the fingerprint card. This is based on the comparison with the five rows wide and two rows down squares printed on the cards and the positions of certain fingerprints of Oswald's on these cards (3276).

At first, with just the set of Jim Murray photos that was available, I was under the impression that Doughty showed off just one set of fingerprints (3277).
A video (3278) of this scene in the third-floor corridor shows that there are two cards shown. But I can only see one set due to the angle of the camera. As luck would have it, in Malcolm Blunt's archive (3279), in a folder labeled 'Newspapers,' I came across the second set, photographed up close by a news photographer from that opposite angle (3280). And again, that set of prints cannot be reconciled with any of the known fingerprint cards that are publicly available in any archive, nor are they presented as Commission Exhibits.

I came across another set of fingerprints, also signed by JB Hicks. This set is known as CE 627 (3281), but it is not part of either one of the sets shown that evening to the press.

While the HSCA was active, a record was made on July 7th 1978 (3282). It states that the original fingerprints and palm prints cannot be found in the archives. While scanning documents for Malcolm Blunt, I came across three pages of which two were RIF sheets (ending with 48 and 49), and a cover sheet which states that the files have been withdrawn. After looking at these more carefully I can state that the RIF sheet ending with 49 (3283) is the same as the file stored online at the National Archives. But the RIF sheets are not equal as to the font used; check for yourself and compare the one below with the one at the link. The file with the RIF number ending with 48 (3284) is nowhere to be found. It gets no mention in Google and this is in tandem with the cover sheet stating that the file consisting of four pages has been withdrawn by the FBI (3285).

From there on, a search ensues and some are eventually found (3286). The finding of these fingerprints, shown on the next page, and the palm prints in the FBI archives described in this undated FBI document (3287), is quite something and you might well wonder whether the other two sets suffered a similar fate.

During Carl Day's WC testimony (3288), however, it appears that he had these original sets with him. So, what happened to the originals? Were they eventually pilfered from the evidence?

Mr. Belin. With the permission of Commissioner McCloy, would it be possible to have Xerox copies substituted for these so that the original can go back with Lieutenant Day?
Mr. McCloy. Yes.
Mr. Belin. As I understand it, these are the last original copies you have of palm prints of Lee Harvey Oswald.
Mr. Day. Yes.
Mr. Belin. Were you there when these prints were made?
Mr. Day. No, sir. The prints that were made in my presence, which I compared with these, I can state are his, were sent to the FBI.
Mr. Belin. Would these be the same prints as shown on Commission Exhibit 628 (3290) and 629 (3291)?
Mr. Day. No, sir. They are still not the originals. They had my name on it when I saw them sign it. But I did compare these with ones I saw made personally of Oswald, and I can say this is his left hand, his left palm, and his right palm.
Mr. Belin. So you are saying 735 (3292) and 736 (3293) are his right and left palms. What about 628 and 629?
Mr. Day. 629 is the right palm, and 628 is the left palm of Lee Harvey Oswald.
Mr. Belin. What about 627 (3289), can you state what that is, if you know?
Mr. Day. That is a set of fingerprints, standard set of fingerprints, of Lee Harvey Oswald taken by Detective JB Hicks on November 22, 1963.
Mr. Belin. You have just examined these with your magnifying glass, is that correct?
Mr. Day. Yes, sir.
Mr. Belin. And you so identify these?
Mr. Day. They are the fingerprints of Lee Harvey Oswald, whose palm prints appear in 735 and 736.

The fingerprint cards of Lee Harvey Oswald on November 22nd are signed by JB Hicks as you can see in this undated FBI document (3294) on page 6. Oswald would not sign any of the fingerprint cards, so the DPD did it for him.

WE Barnes in his WC testimony (3295):

Mr. Belin. Did he request that he have an attorney present at all, or not?
Mr. Barnes. He didn't request one. He would not sign the fingerprint card when I asked him. We have a place on this card for the prisoner's

signature, and I asked him would he please sign that, and he said he wouldn't sign anything until he talked to an attorney.

Mr. Belin. Did he ask for an attorney or say anything about an attorney when you took the paraffin test?

Mr. Barnes. None to me.

Mr. Belin. What did you say when he said he would not sign the fingerprint card?

Mr. Barnes. That was all right with me.

Mr. Belin. Did you just take the palm prints, or did you also take fingerprints?

Mr. Barnes. We took both.

Then there are inkless fingerprints, of which there is a set at UNT (3296). Detective Johnny Hicks in his WC testimony (3297):

Mr. Ball. Did you do any identification work on either the assassination of President Kennedy or the investigation of Tippit's murder?

Mr. HICKS. Do you mean as far as fingerprints?

Mr. Ball. Yes; and things of that sort.

Mr. HICKS. Let me see now, I took a set of Oswald's prints from him that night some time. I do not recall.

Mr. Ball. 9 o'clock or so?

Mr. HICKS. It was some time in that area.

Mr. Ball. Where were you when you took the prints?

Mr. HICKS. I was in Captain Fritz' office. In other words, I made those on an inkless pad. That's a pad we use for fingerprinting people without the black ink that they make for the records.

Things got even more peculiar when I came across an inkless set (3298) in the book *First Day Evidence* by Gary Savage & Rusty Livingstone (3299). This set differs from the one at UNT (3300), simply by comparing the positions of Hicks' signature on both. This set is also not known outside of this book; it's unique. It looks like a reproduction of an original to me and, dare I say, this set has been 'taken' from the evidence locker, since there is no other archival / online presence of this set of prints. A souvenir, perhaps.

That set is thought to have been taken at Parkland Hospital when Oswald was in the morgue. We have a DPD set from November 25th at Getty Images (3301).

Paul Groody, a Dallas mortician, in a sworn statement on October 23rd 1979 (3302) pages 26 & 27 states:

Q: While the body was in the prep room did the FBI or the Secret Service come into the prep room?

A: Yes, I am not sure which, but members of those kinds of company, those kinds of departments, did arrive with photographic equipment and finger- printing equipment and go in and fingerprint because we had to clean the fingers off afterwards, and therefore there was that further work done by some authorities.

Q: Did you have to clean each finger on each hand?

A: If I remember correctly, we did. I am not positive on that but at least we know they took fingerprints. We were used to it.

Q: The substance they use is a black, very noticeable substance is that not correct?

A: Yes, that's true. The black ink they use, and all usually. It's quite difficult to get good prints, especially after embalming, and especially this one because they don't come out so good. There is a lot of wrinkling and a lot of drying, you might say, and they wouldn't have been great prints. I am sure of that, but could be distinguishable.

In a video (3303) from the documentary, *The Men Who Killed Kennedy* (3304) in 1988, Groody states that *"agents would come"* early on the 25th and that they had fingerprinting equipment with them and had left ink on Lee Harvey's hands. Showing that they had finger and palm printed him. And they had to remove this ink to make the body be ready for burial.

From Henry Hurt's book *Reasonable Doubt* (3305) page 107: *In 1983 FBI Agent Drain, who was closely involved in the investigation stated in an interview* (with Hurt-BK) *that he could not think of any logical reason that the FBI would want further prints from Oswald, since they had already taken sufficient ones for the case. What was even more puzzling to Drain was the report that the agents went to the funeral home, when there had been ample earlier opportunities.*

In *First Day Evidence* by Gary Savage & Rusty Livingstone (3306) Savage writes on page 111: *Rusty and JB Hicks rolled at least three inkless cards and inked card of Oswald that Sunday night in the Parkland morgue.*

If the FBI or the USSS did take fingerprints besides the DPD then these have not been shared publicly. Why then did they just stick with the same copies shared by the DPD in their documentation? Groody tactfully avoids who *they* were that walked in with fingerprint equipment. My money is on the DPD as they are the ones that created some at that time.

The Trigger Housing of the Carcano

Further in the book *First Day Evidence* by Gary Savage & Rusty Livingstone (3307) Savage writes on page 105: *"Crime Lab detective Barnes was in the office at the time Lieutenant Day photographed the trigger-housing fingerprints. He later compared the trigger-housing photographs himself to a card of Oswald and told us that he found 3 points of identity. Pete told Rusty and me that there was no doubt in his mind that it was Oswald's fingerprint."*
That by itself is nothing short of astonishing as Carl Day had said he had worked on the rifle alone. Barnes never uttered anything of the sort in his WC interview.

It should be noted, three points of identity are not enough in the USA. A minimum of 10-12 would be ok. The FBI, in 1959, aimed for twelve points of identity (3308). So, three points of identity amounts to not very much.

The Media

Dallas newsmen Joe Long and Gary DeLaune of KLIF radio station (RG272 E19 Reel 20 at NARA) both broadcast reports that the rifle contained no fingerprints. *"Once again, that late report from police headquarters. No fingerprints found on the weapon which had been located in the building from which the fatal shots were fired. The...rifle, turned over to the FBI, is being sent to Washington ...but this is a big disappointment to those investigating today's assassination."*

On Saturday, when Captain Fritz was asked by WFAA (RG272 E19 Reel 20 at NARA), *"Were Oswald's prints found on the rifle?"* He replied *"No, Sir."* Both from: *Best Evidence* by David Lifton (3309) page 354.

Vincent Drain

After the press conference Oswald was searched again and has his shirt taken away by the FBI to take to HQ in Washington. It was Vincent Drain who left with the rifle, the pistol, fingerprints, palm prints and some of other Oswald's belongings on a special military plane.

Drain took possession of the evidence after Henry Wade's press conference at about 00:30, and not at 23:45 as officially stated by everyone. At 23:30 Vincent Drain is spotted behind Wade and Fritz (3310), while they spoke to the gathered press in front of Room 317 of Robbery & Homicide. Then there was Oswald's brief press conference at 00:15 and he was still wearing his shirt that became part of the evidence taken by Drain to Washington. Oswald was then moved upstairs to the fourth floor to be processed and hand his shirt over. At the same time, Henry Wade is giving his press conference (3311) with Drain seen standing next to him.

J Edgar Hoover wrote to DPD Chief Jesse Curry (3312) and listed the evidence received in Washington on November 23rd.

Oswald had his finger & palm prints taken again after his press conference, since all fingerprint and palm print cards were taken by Drain. There are two original fingerprint cards at UNT (3313). These sets are marked November 23rd. The signature belongs to Karl P Knight who was the head of the fingerprint division (3314) page 19. The first set below is not dated, but the second one is. Again, it appears that Oswald refused to sign the fingerprint cards.

On November 29th 1963 Vincent Drain (3315) created a report, confirming what Hoover wrote on the 23rd, listing all items of evidence that were taken early on November 23rd. *The latent prints appearing in the photograph taken of the rifle, k1, by the Dallas Police Department, are too fragmentary and indistinct to be of any value for identification purposes. Photographs of this weapon taken by this Bureau also failed to produce prints of sufficient legibility for comparison purposes. The FBI dismantled the rifle when these pictures were taken.*

Carl Day in his WC testimony (3316) is not sure and would need to further investigate when he admits that the standard of quality for fingerprints has, in this case, not been met to a sufficient degree:

Mr. McCloy. Am I to understand your testimony, Lieutenant, about the fingerprints to be you said you were positive---you couldn't make a positive identification, but it was your opinion that these were the fingerprints of LeeOswald?
Mr. Day. Well, actually in fingerprinting it either is or is not the man. So, I wouldn't say those were his prints. They appeared similar to these two, certainly bore further investigation to see if I could bring them out better. But from what I had I could not make a positive identification as being his prints.

So, when Day passed the rifle on to Drain, he had *no* positive ID from what he had found near the trigger guard of the rifle and the fingerprints of Oswald delivered to him that evening by Hicks and

Barnes. Day was not holding back since he was under oath. He also states this in his statement from January 8th 1964 (3317).

The Palm Prints

Oswald's palm prints are of major significance, and that is because eventually they were linked to the rifle, but not before they went through some interesting moves.

JB Hicks who handles two sets of the palm prints was photographed leaving with them from the Homicide & Robbery Bureau.

Sylvia Meagher (3318) page 24, in December 1964, was one of the very first to focus attention and write about the palm print. She was remarkably close in determining what happened, at least, in principle.

The Palm Print Cards

There are two sets of November22nd palm prints known to me. Both are signed by Hicks, and referred to as CE 735 (3319) & 736 (3320). A better quality set may be found at the Malcolm Blunt archive in an FBI report from May 19th 1978 (3321). At UNT, the second set left (3322) & right (3323) is also signed by Hicks and the images are referred to as the Commission Exhibits. This means that these photos come from the WC and are not reproductions from the DPD. The black edging and numbering give that away. These sets are not originals. They differ from each other once you check the annotations and the positions of the printed fingers of the palm prints in the photographic reproductions.

Carl Day

Taking a closer look at Carl Day and his statements about the alleged palm print lift. It was allegedly underneath the barrel and 'protected' by the wood stock. Day was the only person who handled the rifle.

Lieutenant Day is seen in this Helmer Reenberg compilation of various clips (3324) handling the weapon on the sixth floor of the TSBD, near the front entrance and inside the third-floor corridor of the DPD.

In his WC testimony (3325) he explains where he found the print and what happened during the process of developing the palm print:

Mr. Day. I took it to the office and tried to bring out the two prints I had seen on the side of the gun at the bookstore. They still were rather unclear. Due to the roughness of the metal, I photographed them rather than try to lift them. I could also see a trace of a print on the side of the barrel that extended under the wood stock. I started to take the wood stock off and noted traces of a palm print near the firing end of the barrel about 3 inches under the wood-stock when I took the woodstock loose.

Mr. Belin. You mean 3 inches from the small end of the wood stock?
Mr. Day. Right--yes, sir.
Mr. McCloy. From the firing end of the barrel, you mean the muzzle?
Mr. Day. The muzzle; yes, sir.
Mr. Belin. Let me clarify the record. By that you mean you found it on the metal or you mean you found it on the wood?
Mr. Day. On the metal, after removing the wood.
Mr. Belin. The wood. You removed the wood, and then underneath the wood is where you found the print?
Mr. Day. On the bottom side of the barrel which was covered by the wood, I found traces of a palm print. I dusted these and tried lifting them, the prints, with scotch tape in the usual manner. A faint palm print came off. I could still see traces of the print under the barrel and was going to try to use photography to bring off or bring out a better print. About this time, I received instructions from the chief's office to go no further with the processing, it was to be released to the FBI for them to complete. I did not process the underside of the barrel under the scopic sight, did not get to this area of the gun.
Mr. Belin. At what time did these same photographs which are the same as Commission Exhibit 720 (3326) and 721 (3327) of this print.
Mr. Day. About 8 o'clock, somewhere around 8 o'clock, in that neighbourhood.
Mr. Belin. Of what date?
Mr. Day. November 22, 1963.
Mr. Belin. What about the lift which has previously been marked as Commission Exhibit 637?
Mr. Day. About what?
Mr. Belin. When did you turn that over to the FBI?
Mr. Day. I released that to them on November 26, 1963. I did not release this----
Mr. Belin. You are referring now.
Mr. Day. On November 22.
Mr. Belin. You are referring to Commission Exhibit 637?
Mr. Day. Yes.
Mr. Belin. Is there any particular reason why this was not released on the 22d?
Mr. Day. The gun was being sent in to them for process of prints. Actually, I thought the print on the gun was their best bet, still remained

on there, and, too, there was another print, I thought possibly under the wood part up near the trigger housing.

Mr. Belin. You mean the remaining traces of the powder you had when you got the lift, Exhibit 637, is that what you mean by the lift of the remaining print on the gun?

Mr. Day. Yes, sir. Actually, it was dried ridges on there. There were traces of ridges still on the gun barrel.

Mr. Belin. Can you tell the circumstances under which you sent Commission Exhibit No. 637 to the FBI?

Mr. Day. We released certain evidence to the FBI, including the gun, on November 22. It was returned to us on November 24. Then on November 26 we received instructions to send back to the FBI everything that we had.

Mr. Belin. Did you do that?

Mr. Day. Yes, sir; and at that time, I sent the lift marked----

Mr. Belin. 637.

[But then Day admits photographing the rifle again. He had another chance to photograph the rifle but did not bother about that all important lift again!]

Mr. Belin. I am now going to hand you No. 737 (3329) and ask you to state if you know what this is.

Mr. Day. Yes, sir. This is the rifle found on the sixth floor of the Texas School Book Depository November 22, 1963.

Mr. Belin. Who took that picture?

Mr. Day. I took it myself.

Mr. Belin. When?

Mr. Day. About 9 or 9:30 p.m., November 22, on the fourth floor of the City Hall in my office.

[Day will not confirm for 100% that Oswald's palm print is CE 637 without checking it first...]

Mr. Belin. Based on your experience, I will ask you now for a definitive statement as to whether or not you can positively identify the print shown on Commission Exhibit No. 637 as being from the right palm of Lee Harvey Oswald as shown on Commission Exhibit 629 (3330)?

Mr. Day. Maybe I shouldn't absolutely make a positive statement without further checking that. I think it is his, but I would have to sit down and take two glasses to make an additional comparison before I would say absolutely, excluding all possibility, it is. I think it is, but I would have to do some more work on that.

285

[He is questioned about the palm print at the very end by John J McCloy and his statement is very telling...]

Mr. McCloy. Can you restate again for the record what you can positively identify in terms of fingerprints or palm prints and Oswald's----
Mr. Day. The palm print on the box he apparently sat on I can definitely say it is his without being in fear of any error. The other, I think it is his, but I couldn't say definitely on a witness stand.
Mr. McCloy. By the other, you mean the other palm print?
Mr. Day. The palm print and that tracer print aside the trigger housing or the magazine housing.

In an FBI interview from September 9th 1964 (3331) JC Day states on page 4: *It appeared probable these prints were from the right palm and fingers of Lee Harvey Oswald, but the rifle was released to the FBI, to be sent to Washington, D .C. before the examination was completed and positive identification of the prints could be made. The prints were not very good for comparison purposes.*

Later on (3332), he states that after the palm print lift he only told Jesse Curry and Will Fritz about it that evening. He was not able to state the exact time of the discovery nor when he relayed the result to Curry and Fritz. He only knows it is prior Vincent Drain's collection of the evidence. Yet Curry is asked about the fingerprints that same evening and Will Fritz early on the 23rd and both answered negative.

Hard to believe that as Fritz would have used this there and then since he had nothing that tied Oswald to the rifle at that time. On December 23rd 1963 Will Fritz had a report made up (3333) about the evidence and the palm print is briefly summarised. All irregularities are conveniently swept under the carpet.

In Carl Day's HSCA interview (3334) on October 18th 1977 he states that Will Fritz ordered him to bring the rifle downstairs and display it to Marina Oswald. Day could not understand whether she recognised the rifle or not. Only after his return to the fourth floor does he 'discover' part of a print on the metal bit underneath the barrel where it sits on the stock.

Will Fritz tells him twice to stop as the FBI is taking the rifle with them. No mention of Jesse Curry who was originally stated as the man who told Day to cease his work on the rifle.

He did not give the FBI the print lift as he thought the FBI would do a better job. When the rifle returns to Dallas, Day is disappointed that the

FBI did not find the print on the barrel. And once the FBI requires the rifle to be sent back again. Day sent the print lift alongside with the rifle.

He did not make a positive ID with the print he lifted off the barrel as belonging to Oswald. He felt it was Oswald's, but would not have testified that it was, under oath without further examination.

Henry Hurt for his book *Reasonable Doubt* (3335) interviewed Carl Day and Vince Drain in 1984 (page 109): *Day remains adamant that the Oswald print was on the rifle when he first examined it a few hours after the shooting. Moreover, Day stated that when he gave the rifle to Agent Drain, he pointed out to the FBI man both the area where the print could be seen and the fingerprint dust used to bring it out. Lieutenant Day states that he cautioned Drain to be sure the area was not disturbed while the rifle was in transit to the FBI laboratory. Drain flatly disputes this, claiming that Day never showed him such a print. "I just don't believe there was ever a print," said Drain. He noted that there was increasing pressure on the Dallas police to build evidence in the case. Asked to explain what might have happened, Agent Drain stated, "All I can figure is that it* [Oswald's print] *was some sort of cushion, because they were getting a lot of heat by Sunday night. You could take the print off Oswald's card and put it on the rifle. Something like that happened."*

In *First Day Evidence (3336)*, Gary Savage writes: *Captain Doughty came in at about 20:30 – 21:00 hrs and told Day to stop working on the rifle* (p 108). Also on the same page, *"He then placed a strip of 2" scotch tape over the developed print and rubbed it down before finally lifting the tape containing the print off and placed it on a card. He said he then compared the lift to Oswald's palm print card and was certain (!) that it was Oswald's. He also said that after the lift, he could still see an impression of the palm print left on the barrel.*

This is hard to believe when Day previously stated that he did not do such a thing.

Next, Lieutenant Day had intended to photograph the area of the rifle barrel from which the palm print lift had been made, but was again interrupted by Captain Doughty at about 22:00. He was told once again to stop working on the gun and release it to FBI Agent Drain, who would arrive about 23:00. Lieutenant Day did not have time to write any reports about what he had found, but did have time to reassemble the rifle before Drain arrived.

So, we have a third person entering the fold as to telling Day to stop working on the rifle! He was first told by Will Fritz to cease working on the rifle, then Max Doughty tells him twice at 22:00 and then in a statement made by Day to the FBI (3337) page 5 he said that the call from Jesse Curry to get the evidence ready for the FBI to collect came just before midnight! Curry btw does not make any mention of this in his WC testimony_(3338).

In *First Day Evidence*: Day said that a few days after the evidence was turned over, an FBI agent came to his house. He wanted to know when Lieutenant Day had lifted the palm print included in the evidence they had received because they had positively identified it themselves as Oswald's palm print. Lieutenant Day got the impression that they had missed it and he could "envision J Edgar Hoover going into orbit." (pages 109 & 110).

Lieutenant Day believed at the time that he had not completely obliterated the palm print on the barrel after his lift and later stated he had pointed out the area of the palm print to FBI agent Drain when turning the rifle over to him. Drain on the other hand did not recall being show the palm print (page 110).

In this ARRB document from December 19th 1996 (3339) they question the course of the narrative regarding the palm print and the lack of contemporaneous evidence and wonder whether they should question Carl Day again.

Henry Wade

It was Dallas DA Henry Wade who mentioned the alleged palm prints first and that was during the press conference on November 24th (3340), when Oswald is dead.

The FBI

The FBI's Vincent Drain collects the rifle (3341). Day and others reports state that he handed the rifle over to Drain at 23:45. This time is hard to accept as being correct. When Oswald speaks to the press at 00:15 he is still wearing his shirt. That shirt was part of the collection of evidence taken by Drain to Washington. Furthermore, Henry Wade held a press conference (3342) after Oswald's and Drain is seen standing next to Wade. The earliest Drain could have collected it and taken it away with him would have been 00:30.

The FBI (J Edgar Hoover) writes on November 23rd to DPD Chief Jesse Curry (3343) and have found nothing. He states the following on page 7: *The latent prints appearing in the photograph taken of the rifle K1, by the Dallas Police Department, are too fragmentary and indistinct to be*

288

of any value for identification purposes. Photographs of this weapon taken by this Bureau have failed to produce prints of sufficient legibility for comparison purposes.

After processing the rifle, the FBI returns it to the Dallas Police on November 24th (3344).

The FBI could not find anything, but the DPD produced a palm print lift four days after the evidence has travelled back and forth from Dallas to Washington already.

Then the evidence is turned back over to the FBI by Carl Day to Vincent Drain on November 26th (3345). And this time the palm print lift is included with the rest of the evidence. The official report by Day (3346).

The FBI states in a report, titled *"LATENT FINGERPRINTS EXAMINATIONS"*, from November 28th (3347) that fingerprints and palm prints have been discovered on certain items, but there is no mention of any found on the rifle.

On November 29th 1963 (3348) the rifle is back in FBI custody after it had been in DPD custody from November 24th.

In this report by the ARRB (3349) all rifle transportations are logged.
The FBI on February 23rd 1964 questions the initial missing photographs of the palm print (3350) page 2.

Sebastian Latona

Sebastian Latona, who is the FBI's supervisor of the latent fingerprint section of the identity division, in his WC testimony (3351) states the following about the quality of the weapon and its connection to fingerprints:

Representative BOGGS. Now, does a weapon lend itself to retaining fingerprints?
Mr. Latona. This particular weapon here, first of all, in my opinion, the metal is very poorly finished. It is absorbent. Believe it or not, there is a certain amount of absorption into this metal itself. It is not finished in the sense that it is highly polished.
Representative BOGGS. So, this would be conducive to getting a good print, or would it?
Mr. Latona. It would not.
Representative BOGGS. I see-because it would absorb the moisture.

Mr. Latona. That's right. Now, there are other guns-for example, Smith and Wesson, which have exceptionally nice finishes, the blue metal finishes are better surfaces for latent prints. Where you have a nickel-plated or silver-plated revolvers, where it is smooth-they are much more conducive to latent prints than some of these other things, say like the army type, the weapons used in wartime that are dull, to avoid reflection;   things   of   that   type.

[Latona had various photographs taken of the rifle and also looked for any other prints...]

So, I made arrangements to immediately have a photographer come in and see if he could improve on the photographs that were taken by the Dallas Police Department. Well, we spent, between the two of us, setting up the camera, looking at prints,... highlighting, side lighting, every type of lighting that we could conceivably think of, checking back and forth in the darkroom-we could not improve the condition of these latent prints. So, accordingly, the final conclusion was simply that the latent print on this gun was of no value, the fragments that were there. After that had been determined, I then proceeded to completely process the entire rifle, to see if there were any other prints of any significance or value any prints of value. I would not know what the significance would be, but to see if there were any other prints. I completely covered the rifle.

[Then he is asked whether he dusted the rifle himself...]

Mr. EISENBERG. We will get other evidence in the record at a subsequent time to show those were the prints of Oswald. Mr. Latona you were saying that you had worked over that rifle by applying a grey powder to it. Did you develop any fingerprints?
Mr. Latona. I was not successful in developing any prints at all on the weapon. I also had one of the firearms examiners dismantle the weapon and I processed the complete weapon, all parts, everything else. And no latent prints of value were developed.

[When it comes to the palm print, Latona's testimony confirms that they had no knowledge of it until seven days after the murder. They only knew of the trigger guard prints wrapped in cellophane. Nor did he see any trace of markings of a lifting on the gun...]

Mr. EISENBERG. Now, Mr. Latona, as I understand it, on November 23, 'therefore, the FBI had not succeeded in making an identification of a fingerprint or palm print on the rifle, but several days later virtue of the receipt of this lift, which did not come with the weapon originally, the FBI did succeed in identifying a print on Exhibit 1303?

Mr. Latona. That is right.

Mr. EISENBERG. Which may explain any inconsistent or apparently inconsistent statements, which I believe appeared in the press, as to an identification?

Mr. Latona. We had no personal knowledge of any palm print having been developed on the rifle. The only prints that we knew of were the fragmentary prints which I previously pointed out had been indicated by the cellophane on the trigger guard. There was no indication on this rifle as to the existence of any other prints. This print which indicates it came from the underside of the gun barrel, evidently the lifting had been so complete that there was nothing left to show any marking on the gun itself as to the existence of such even an attempt on the part of anyone else to process the rifle.

Mr. Dulles. Do I understand then that if there is a lifting of this kind, that it may obliterate-

Mr. Latona. Completely.

Mr. Dulles. The original print?

Mr. Latona. That is right.

Mr. EISENBERG. So that you personally, Mr. Latona, did not know anything about a print being on the rifle which was identifiable until you received, actually received the lift, Exhibit 637.

Mr. Latona. On the 29th of November.

Mr. EISENBERG. Seven days after the assassination. And in the intervening period, correspondingly, the FBI had no such knowledge?

Mr. Latona. As far as I know.

The WC and the FBI Try to Iron out the Creases

On August 28th 1964 Wesley Liebeler reported to J Lee Rankin (3352) and refers to Carl Day's WC testimony pointing out issues regarding the lift of the palm print. He refers to FBI agent Sebastian Latona who makes contradicting statements about the barrel, the fingerprint powder, the prints and the lack thereof.

On August 28th 1964 in a FBI document to Alan Belmont (3353) it is noted that the WC has some questions about the timing of the actual lift of the palm print. They also wonder aloud whether Day had taken actual photographs of the lift or the barrel and this is something he had not done.

In WC Exhibit 2637, a letter from J Edgar Hoover on September 4th 1964 (3354) to J Lee Rankin. Hoover states that the attached photos of the palm print are the ones that were found under the barrel of the rifle.

In a DOJ document of September 11th 1964 (3355) Day is mentioned as having lifted the palm print, that it belonged to Oswald, and that the FBI also tested it and came to the same conclusion. This record is based on the September 9th interview of Carl Day by the FBI.

When the WR is published (3356), the whole 'discovery of the palm print' is rubber stamped.

The Paraffin Casts

Joseph L Thimes on gunshot wounds and their residue tests (3357). This four-page summary is a great way to familiarise yourself with the subject matter at hand. Here are some article and book excerpts on the paraffin casts and its tests (3358).

At the Weisberg Archive is a chronology (3359) of some of the reports and DPD statements released by Dallas Police. Jesse Curry (3360) and CW Brown (3361) seem to be most vocal about the tests.

The WR (3362) states on page 561: *In fact, however, the test is completely unreliable in determining either whether a person has recently fired a weapon or whether he has not.*

A positive reaction is, therefore, valueless in determining whether a suspect has recently fired a weapon. Conversely, a person who has recently fired a weapon may not show a positive reaction to the paraffin test, particularly if the weapon was a rifle. A revolver is so constructed that there is a space between the cylinder, which bears the chambers, and the barrel. When a revolver is fired, nitrate-bearing gases escape through this space and may leave residues on the hand. In a rifle, however, there is no gap between the chamber and the barrel, and one would therefore not expect nitrates to be deposited upon a person's hands or cheeks as a result of his firing a rifle.

An agent of the FBI, using the C2766 rifle, fired three rounds of Western 6.5-millimeter Mannlicher-Carcano ammunition in rapid succession. A paraffin test was then performed on both of his hands and his right cheek. Both of his hands and his cheek tested negative. The paraffin casts of Oswald's hands and right cheek were also examined by neutron-activation analyses at the Oak Ridge National Laboratory. Barium and antimony were found to be present on both surfaces of all the casts and also in residues from the rifle cartridge cases and the revolver cartridge cases. Since barium and antimony were present in both the rifle and the revolver cartridge cases, their presence on the casts were not evidence that Oswald had fired the rifle.

In short, the WC wasn't too impressed with the paraffin tests from an evidentiary point of view.

Oswald, while working at the TSBD that morning, definitely had gotten into contact with printing ink (nitrates), which would have been enough to have contaminated the paraffin test from the beginning.

WE 'Pete' Barnes, who had been doing these tests for quite a few years, had not applied this test to a suspect's face ever before. He did this test on orders of Will Fritz. Unfortunately, it would not have made *any* difference in determining whether Oswald had fired a rifle that day! For this I refer you to Barnes' WC testimony (3363):

Mr. Belin. Well, let me ask you this. Of the paraffin tests that you have made, how many have you made of a cheek or cheeks?
Mr. Barnes. One.
Mr. Belin. Was that with Lee Harvey Oswald?
Mr. Barnes. It was.
Mr. Belin. Other than that, you have never made a paraffin test of anyone's cheek?
Mr. Barnes. No.
Mr. Belin. Any particular reason why you might not have in any other case?
Mr. Barnes. It has never been requested of me before.
Mr. Belin. Based on your knowledge and information about the science of paraffin tests, do you know whether or not it is a common practice or not a common practice to make it of one cheek?
Mr. Barnes. It is not a common practice.
Mr. Belin. Any particular reason it is not a common practice that you can think of or know of?
Mr. Barnes. Firing a revolver, should he fire a revolver, I would say the revolver most likely would be far enough away where powder residue wouldn't reach his cheek.
Mr. Belin. What about a rifle?
Mr. Barnes. Firing a rifle, you get your chamber enclosed with steel metal around it, and the chances of powder residue would be very remote.
Mr. Belin. Have you fired a bolt-action rifle at all before?
Mr. Barnes. Many times.
Mr. Belin. How close would the chamber be to the cheek as you would be looking through the sight of the gun?
Mr. Barnes. Be several inches to the rear of the chamber.
Mr. Belin. Would this have any effect on the paraffin test at all?
Mr. Barnes. It sure would.

Mr. Belin. What about telescopic sights? Would that push your face back further or not?

Mr. Barnes. Push it even further back.

Mr. Belin. Would this have an effect on the paraffin test?

Mr. Barnes. The further you get from the chamber, the less possibility of getting powder residue on it would be.

[A little later during the same testimony...]

Mr. Belin. Did Lee Harvey Oswald say anything to you as you were removing these casts, that you remember?

Mr. Barnes. Very little, other than what I repeated to you before, that he knew what I was trying to do, and that I was wasting my time that he didn't know anything about what we were accusing him of.

Barnes is also quoted in a summarisation of a DPD/WC document (3364) that taking a paraffin cast of Oswald's hand was ok with him.

Carl Day says pretty much the same during his WC testimony (3365):

Mr. Day. I directed them to make it, and also paraffin casts or just of a piece of paraffin on the left side of the face to see if there were any nitrates there.

Mr. Belin. On the left side or right side of the face?

Mr. Day. Right side.

Mr. Belin. Do you know what the results of the paraffin tests were?

Mr. Day. The test on the face was negative.

Mr. Belin. Had you ever done a paraffin test on a face before?

Mr. Day. No; actually--had it not been for the particular type of case and this particular situation here we would not have at this time. It was just something that was done to actually keep from someone saying later on, *"Why didn't you do it?"* Actually, in my experience there, shooting a rifle with a telescopic sight there would be no chance for nitrates to get way back or on the side of the face from a rifle.

Detective Johnny Hicks in his WC testimony (3366):

Mr. Ball. Is it usual to find any trace of nitrate on the face if a rifle has been fired?

Mr. HICKS. That is the first time that I had the opportunity to make a paraffin test on a person's face.

Mr. Ball. You never made one before?

Mr. HICKS. Never before.

Mr. Ball. The other tests were always on the hands?

Mr. HICKS. Yes, sir.

Mr. Ball. Was there some reason for that?

Mr. HICKS. I had never had the occasion arise that I know of where anyone had that suggested, that a paraffin test be made of a cheek. On other occasions they were only interested in the hand. The facial paraffin test was ordered by Will Fritz. The admissions during the WC testimonies of Barnes and Day mean that the paraffin cast of Oswald's right cheek was not going to give them the confirmation of Oswald's connect to the rifle.

An Empty Tin

When WE Barnes is photographed in the corridor after applying the casts it becomes clear that he has an empty tin of wax (3367) in his hands (a close-up can be seen 3368), but there are no paraffin casts on display. Allegedly Barnes dropped these off on the fourth floor, as per his WC testimony (3369), and the three of them did their appearance in the corridor with the evidence afterwards.

Mr. Belin. At the time you carried back the paraffin casts?

Mr. Barnes. No. We came back and got the palm prints after I delivered the paraffin tests upstairs.

Paraffin Test Before or After the Fingerprints?

Then there is the small, but pivotal matter of whether the fingerprints and palm print were taken before the paraffin tests. During Barnes' testimony something jumps out. And that is whether the finger prints and palm prints were administered before or after the paraffin tests. If they did them before then these paraffin tests would have been useless from the beginning due to the nitrates from the ink being present.

Mr. Belin. Sergeant, did you make any other tests or obtain any other evidence or information from Lee Harvey Oswald other than the paraffin that you made?

Mr. Barnes. I obtained palm prints from Lee Harvey Oswald.

Mr. Belin. When did you do this?

Mr. Barnes. Immediately before we made---no, immediately after, I am sorry, immediately after we made the paraffin test.

Mr. Belin. I would assume you did it afterwards?

Mr. Barnes. That is right. It was after we made the tests.

According to Ramparts Magazine (3370) page 4, Oswald had his palm prints and finger prints taken before those paraffin tests. In a report submitted by Richard Sims and Elmer Boyd (3371) it states that the fingerprints were taken *before* the paraffin casts.

Barnes is also interviewed for the HSCA on April 17th 1978 (3372). And he does not misspeak again and sticks to the order of the paraffin casts being taken first on Oswald and then having his finger and palm prints taken. At the end of the statement, it says that JB Hicks was not present to be interviewed since he had left town to go fishing.

The paraffin casts are sent in three envelopes (3373) to DCCCIL at Parkland hospital (3374) by George Doughty (3375) page 5. The results from these tests are not obtained until the next day (3376). In this ten-page report it is brought forward that the results are showing nitrate patterns consistent with the subject having discharged a firearm on exhibits #2 and #3. A pattern on exhibit #3 is typical of the patterns produced in firing a revolver. None of these point to Oswald firing a rifle. The Dallas Times Herald on November 24th (3377) claims the paraffin tests show positive results on Oswald's hands and cheek!

They are not able to differentiate the powder residues, after a Neutron Activation Analysis (3378), to see which particles are from a revolver or from a rifle. There is more additional technical info from Vincent Guinn and contains more articles (3379). Guinn himself defends the work he and others have done in a newspaper article on October 13th 1964 (3380).

The FBI also releases a report in the afternoon of November 23rd (3381) which states the same. The FBI earlier that day is keen to obtain the test results (3382) for section Chief Jim Handley. The second page is peculiar as it states the paraffin tests were taken at 10:45 and that a doctor was present who conducted it!

The findings get repeated in another FBI document (3383) alongside the mention of Louie L Anderson, of the Dallas City Council Criminal Investigative Laboratory who had washed and taken the paraffin casts home since they were marked to be discarded.

Norman Redlich writes to Warren Commissioner Allen Dulles on July 2nd 1964 (3384) and states rather concisely what the Neutron Activation Analysis had managed to achieve. Which is not much.

Marrion Johnson of NARA confirms on February 3rd 1966 (3385) page 2 that he has examined seven pieces of paraffin cast and an empty wax tin among the FBI evidence exhibits.

In conclusion, there was not a shred of evidence that tied Oswald to the rifle, not the fingerprints, the palm prints nor the nitrate tests. Add to that the DPD had no clue about the Hidell ID on the 22nd (3386): What did they *actually* have, to charge Oswald with the murder of John Kennedy?

21:00 Killing JFK as Part of an International Communist Conspiracy

Bill Alexander (3387), after his return from the Beckley address attends Oswald's third interrogation. He then has a meeting with Will Fritz and Jim Allen and others in the Majestic Café to talk things over. Alexander wants to charge Oswald with the murder of JFK as part of an international communist conspiracy with malice and forethought (3388).

Ronald Duggar, editor of the Texas Observer, did an interview (3390) with Bill Alexander and noted that he put out the story that Oswald was a communist to offset any talk of Oswald being a right-winger.

Barefoot Sanders and others work hard that evening to make that phrase disappear from the up-and coming charge sheet. In a Waggoner Carr Interview with William Manchester on September 22nd 1964 (3391) on page 14 Carr states that he speaks with Gordon Shanklin to dissuade Bill Alexander and was also in contact with Nicholas Katzenbach and also talked to Henry Wade. Nicholas Katzenbach in an interview with William Manchester (3392) on page 47, said that he was in contact with Barefoot Sanders, and also with Bill Moyers and George Reedy to ask whether they had any contacts in Texas to kill this indictment. And later on, they called Katzenbach and told him it was taken care off.

Henry Wade, in an interview with Melissa Johnson in 1993 (3393), shares that Cliff Carter had called him three times to get the indictment annulled.

Barefoot Sanders in an interview with William Manchester (3394) on page 7, states that he got the whole thing called off, only for Jesse Curry to re-ignite the whole thing again. Sanders thought that Wade was not taking the whole thing seriously and that with the help of Gordon Shanklin it was called off at about 23:30 which is the time of Oswald being charged with killing the President with the conspiracy charge taken out.

Look at Oswald's case report (3395) and note that Bill Alexander's name is stricken through and Henry Wade's faded name is inserted instead.

David Johnston speaks to Earl Golz (3396) as well, on November 18th 1975. Golz's handwritten notes mention that Alexander and Jim Allen were involved in doing this. But he also indicates that Alexander may have been influenced by the Beckley address search to which Johnston was also present to bring the conspiracy charge forward.

21:30 Howard Brennan Line-up

Howard Brennan, a steam pipe fitter who sat opposite the TSBD became an important witness.

In his statement for the Sheriffs Department on November 22nd (3397) he states that the man was in his early 30s, slender, nice looking, weighing about 165-175 pounds and wearing light colored clothing. No suit.

During Brennan's WC testimony (3398) a few things jump out:
- He has seen Oswald's face on TV twice before going to City Hall.
- He cannot remember how many people he was looking at during the line-up.
- He does not remember whether there were people of a different race present either.
- He mentions talking to Fritz and Sorrels after the line-up.
- He could not identify Oswald.

There are no DPD records present for this line-up besides a little card (3399) which states: *"Failed to identify."*

Initially the Secret Service had difficulty finding him, but William Patterson manages to locate him and brings Brennan in and has him attend a line-up. A line-up that is nothing short of a huge let down for the Secret Service. Let's have a look at a part of his WC testimony regarding this during the evening of November 22nd. Howard Brennan the star witness in identifying Oswald as the sixth-floor shooter:

Mr. Belin. Now, taking you down to the Dallas Police Station, I believe you said you talked to Captain Fritz. And then what happened?
Mr. Brennan. Well, I was just more or less introduced to him in Mr. Sorrels' room, and they told me they were going to conduct a line-up and wanted me to view it, which I did.
Mr. Belin. Do you remember how many people were in the line-up?
Mr. Brennan. No; I don't. A possibility seven more or less one.
Mr. Belin. All right. Did you see anyone in the line-up you recognized?
Mr. Brennan. Yes.
Mr. Belin. And what did you say?
Mr. Brennan. I told Mr. Sorrels and Captain Fritz at that time that Oswald--or the man in the line-up that I identified looking more like a closest resemblance to the man in the window than anyone in the line-up.
Mr. Belin. Were the other people in the line-up, do you remember--were they all white, or were there some Negroes in there, or what?

Mr. Brennan. I do not remember.

Mr. Belin. As I understand your testimony, then, you said that you told him that this particular person looked the most like the man you saw on the sixth floor of the building there.

Mr. Brennan. Yes, sir.

Mr. Belin. In the meantime, had you seen any pictures of Lee Harvey Oswald on television or in the newspapers?

Mr. Brennan. Yes, on television.

Mr. Belin. About when was that, do you believe?

Mr. Brennan. I believe I reached home quarter to three or something of that, 15 minutes either way, and I saw his picture twice on television before I went down to the police station for the line-up.

Mr. Belin. Now, is there anything else you told the officers at the time of the line-up?

Mr. Brennan. Well, I told them I could not make a positive identification.

Mr. Belin. When you told them that, did you ever later tell any officer or investigating person anything different?

Mr. Brennan. Yes.

Mr. Belin. When did that happen?

Mr. Brennan. I believe some days later--I don't recall exactly--and I believe the Secret Service man identified himself as being Williams, I believe, from Houston. I won't swear to that-whether his name was Williams or not.

Mr. Belin. All right.

Mr. Brennan. And he could have been an FBI. As far as I remember, it could have been FBI instead of Secret Service.

But I believe it was a Secret Service man from Houston.

And I--

Mr. Belin. What did he say to you and what did you say to him?

Mr. Brennan. Well, he asked me he said, *"You said you couldn't make a positive identification."*

He said, *"Did you do that for security reasons personally, or couldn't you?"*

And I told him I could with all honesty, but I did it more or less for security reasons--my family and myself.

Mr. Belin. What do you mean by security reasons for your family and yourself?

Mr. Brennan. I believe at that time, and I still believe it was a Communist activity, and I felt like there hadn't been more than one eyewitness, and if it got to be a known fact that I was an eyewitness, my family or I, either one, might not be safe.

Mr. Belin. Well, if you wouldn't have identified him, might he not have been released by the police?

Mr. Brennan. Beg pardon?

Mr. Belin. If you would not have identified that man positively, might he not have been released by the police?

Mr. Brennan. No. That had a great contributing factor--greater contributing factor than my personal reasons was that I already knew they had the man for murder, and I knew he would not be released.

Mr. Belin. The murder of whom?

Mr. Brennan. Of Officer Tippit.

Mr. Belin. Well, what happened in between to change your mind that you later decided to come forth and tell them you could identify him?

Mr. Brennan. After Oswald was killed, I was relieved quite a bit that as far as pressure on myself of somebody not wanting me to identify anybody, there was no longer that immediate danger.

Mr. Belin. What is the fact as to whether or not your having seen Oswald on television would have affected your identification of him one way or the other?

Mr. Brennan. That is something I do not know.

Mr. Belin. Mr. Brennan, could you tell us now whether you can or cannot positively identify the man you saw on the sixth-floor window as the same man that you saw in the police station?

Mr. Brennan. I could at that time I could, with all sincerity, identify him as being the same man.

Brennan also wrote a book, *Eye Witness to History (3400)*, about the happenings of that day. In it he describes the situation inside the DPD and the line-up.

While we were discussing this latest news, I saw something on the television that made me quake. I'm not certain of the exact time, but I believe it was about 5:30 PM that the first picture of Lee Harvey Oswald was flashed on the screen. I remember thinking, "It's him! He's the one who did it!" But I never said a word at the time, not even to Louise. Showing the picture of Oswald before any identification was made seemed very strange to me. Millions of people were seeing Oswald before I, the one person who could positively identify him, had been taken to an official line-up. I felt a sense of resistance within myself. How is this man going to get a fair trial?" I thought. "He is already guilty in the minds of everyone who is seeing him?"....

[And later...]

The officer walked over to me sticking out his hand to shake. He greeted me by name and I knew if he knew who I was and what my connection with the case was, then others must know. He asked me, "Does the second man from the left look most like the man you saw?" He was talking about Oswald and I knew what he wanted me to say.

I felt even more angry and betrayed. I hadn't agreed to make an identification to the local authorities. I knew that there were ways my identity could become known though the leaks in the police department and I didn't want any part of it. I knew that they had Oswald on enough charges that he wasn't going anyplace. He had been charged with resisting arrest and carrying a firearm without a permit. There was overwhelming evidence that he had killed Officer Tippit and so my identification in that moment wasn't absolutely necessary. If they needed me later, I knew I could identify him.

I said brusquely, "He looks like the man, but I can't say for sure!" I needed some time to think. I turned to Mr. Lish, who had detected my resentment and said, "Let's go back to the office. We have some talking to do." As we went, I commented that the man in the line-up wasn't dressed the same way the man in the window had been.

"We forgot to tell you that he changed his clothes immediately after leaving the Depository," Lish said. When we reached the office I responded angrily, "You promised me anonymity. You people haven't kept your word."   Sorrels looked genuinely puzzled. "What do you mean?" "If this Detective knows who I am and what my connection with the assassination is, then it won't be long before everybody finds out." Sorrels tried to be reassuring, "We'll do everything we can to protect your identity, Mr. Brennan, but this isn't entirely our jurisdiction." I wasn't sure just what he meant, and said so. "There isn't anything we could do about it," Sorrels explained. "The law is clear that murder, even assassination, is a state offense and must be turned over to local officials for investigation and prosecution!"

So, it was out and I had to deal with it. No matter how hard they might try, it was only a matter of time before people would find out that the unidentified witness whose description had helped catch Oswald was really Howard Brennan. Suddenly, I didn't feel very good. I felt very vulnerable, exposed to naked light, and I didn't like it one bit. I knew I was going to be sorry that I decided to become involved.

While we were talking, Captain Fritz came in and asked me, "Can you make a positive identification of any of those we showed you in the line-up?" *Having felt betrayed in my quest for anonymity, I was in no mood to hurry the process of exposure. I said, "You already have your man on enough charges to hold him for a long time. I'm not going to make a positive identification at the moment. If and when the time comes and you need it or have to let him go, we'll deal with it then." I wasn't saying, "Yes, Oswald is the man," nor was I saying, "No, he isn't the one."....*

In a WC memo from Samuel Stern and John Hart Ely to J Lee Rankin April 7th 1964 (3401) concerning Will Fritz's statements whether Brennan had attended a line-up. Neither he nor TL Baker could attest to that and they would attempt to find out....

Fritz's 'amnesia' regarding his attendance during Brennan's line-up in his WC testimony (3402):

Mr. McCloy. Were you present at the show-up at which Brennan was the witness?
Mr. Fritz. Brennan?
Mr. McCloy. Brennan was the alleged----
Mr. Fritz. Is that the man that the Secret Service brought over there, Mr. Sorrels brought over?
Mr. McCloy. I don't know whether Mr. Sorrels----
Mr. Fritz. I don't think I was present but I will tell you what, I helped Mr. Sorrels find the time that that man--we didn't show that he was shown at all on our records, but Mr. Sorrels called me and said he did show him and he wanted me to give him the time of the show-up. I asked him to find out from his officers who were with Mr. Brennan the names of the people that we had there, and he gave me those two Davis sisters, and he said, when he told me that, of course, I could tell what showup it was and then I gave him the time.
Mr. McCloy. But you were not present to the best of your recollection when Brennan was in the showup?
Mr. Fritz. I don't believe I was there. I doubt it.

In an Interview of Forrest Sorrels by William Manchester. RG 233, BOX 290-JFK Task Force, Numbered File (3403) on page 7. Sorrels had high hopes on Brennan to ID Oswald as the shooter. But Brennan backed off and was terrified. He refused to identify Oswald.

In a Preliminary interview of Forrest J Sorrels by Samuel A Stern for the WC April 10th 1964 (3404) Sorrels stated *"but could not give a positive identification."*

And of course, this very same matter is discussed during Sorrell's WC testimony (3405), but he is not as forthcoming with the fact that Brennan did *not* ID Oswald as the shooter:
Mr. Hubert. Now, were you present at a meeting at which the news media were present and Oswald was brought into an assembly room, in which the news media were assembled?
Mr. Sorrels. I was present when Oswald was brought into what is called the line-up room, which is also the assembly room. They have the line-up section at one end of it. That was on the evening of November 22. At that time, it was my request, because a witness who had been interviewed by me, and who had seen the person fire the-third shot from the window of the Book Depository Building, I had gotten in touch with him through one of our agents, and he was brought down there for the specific purpose of being able to see Oswald, because when he

302

was first interviewed by me he stated that he thought he could identify him.

Mr. Hubert. That was in fact, however, a true line-up for the purpose of identification.

Mr. Sorrels. I am sorry--I did not understand the question.

Mr. Hubert. I said that was a true line-up for the purpose of identification.

Mr. Sorrels. Yes, sir.

Mr. Hubert. I was speaking of another meeting where the assembly room usually used for the line-up was used to give the press an opportunity to see Oswald.

Mr. Sorrels. I was not present. That is the only time I saw Oswald in the line-up.

Winston Lawson of the Secret Service, during his WC testimony (3406):

Mr. Stern. When did you next see Oswald?

Mr. Lawson. I recall seeing him in another room in homicide headquarters with a couple of plainclothes people and their talking to him. I saw him later in the evening, perhaps 9:30, 10 o'clock, when he was brought down to a showup room, because we had information that a gentleman had seen someone at a window, and so----

Mr. Stern. Do you know who that was, the witness?

Mr. Lawson. I do not know; no, sir.

Mr. Stern. Could it have been someone named Brennan?

Mr. Lawson. The name doesn't mean anything to me. Mr. Sorrels had sent an agent out to bring him down to police headquarters to talk to him, and he informed us he had seen someone in the window, but he had also seen Lee Oswald on television in the meantime, and he didn't know of how much, value he would be.

Mr. Stern. Did he say anything about whether he thought----

Mr. Lawson. He could not say yes or no, whether Oswald was the individual or not.

Mr. Stern. Did you notice any irregularity in the way the showup was conducted?

Mr. Lawson. No, sir.

Mr. Stern. Did it seem like a normal one to you, the size of the people?

Mr. Lawson. I didn't notice any irregularity.

Mr. Stern. And their dress?

Representative Ford. Had Oswald had any additional physical damage done?

Mr. Lawson. No, sir.

23:00 Interrogation by John Adamcik

Detective John P Adamcik (3407) talks to Oswald as well, this is while Fritz is gone.
John Adamcik on the right while Lee Oswald is being escorted (3408).

Adamcik's WC testimony (3409):

Mr. Belin. What did you do when you got back to the office?
Mr. Adamcik. Went to the office and I stayed there a while, and I guess it was around 11 o'clock, I mean the interrogation room in the captain's office, and spent about 15 minutes.
Mr. Belin. Why did you go in the interrogation room?
Mr. Adamcik. Well, at that time I think somebody else just finished talking to him, and I think the captain had to go see somebody or something, and nobody was in the room at the time, and he told us to go on in there for a little while and see whether we could talk to Oswald. I think Detective Montgomery went in there with me, I am not sure.
Mr. Belin. Were you the only two in there at that time?
Mr. Adamcik. Yes; I think so. The ID Bureau came in there and either fingerprinted him or done something. When they came in there, I left. It was just a short period of time.
Mr. Belin. Do you remember any conversation that took place there?
Mr. Adamcik. No; except I asked him whether he drove a car. I did ask him that. And I remember him saying something that he didn't.
Mr. Belin. That he did or did not?
Mr. Adamcik. That he did not. And I asked him how long he was in Russia and whether he liked it there, and I remember him telling me how long he was there. I think it was two years, or something like that.
Mr. Belin. Well----
Mr. Adamcik. I don't remember exactly what he said, and he liked it okay, and that is just about it.
Mr. Belin. Did you talk about the assassination at all?
Mr. Adamcik. No; it wasn't anything at all concerned with the assassination.
Mr. Belin. Did you ask him any questions?
Mr. Adamcik. We did.
Mr. Belin. Like what kind of questions?
Mr. Adamcik. Like where were you at the time this assassination occurred; and he just wouldn't say anything.
Mr. Belin. Did he just keep quiet?
Mr. Adamcik. He just sat there and stared straight ahead.
Mr. Belin. Didn't talk at all?
Mr. Adamcik. No.
Mr. Belin. Did he ask for an attorney while you were there?

Mr. Adamcik. Not in my presence.

Mr. Belin. Did you ask him any questions about Officer Tippit's murder?

Mr. Adamcik. No; I don't believe that I did.

Mr. Belin. Anyone else there that did?

Mr. Adamcik. I didn't hear anybody.

Mr. Belin. All right, then what happened?

Mr. Adamcik. Well, I just stayed at the office until about 2 o'clock in the morning.

Mr. Belin. Ever see Oswald again?

Mr. Adamcik. I seen him being led out of the office from the interview, I believe. I didn't go down there.

Mr. Belin. What interview?

Mr. Adamcik. I think they had--I don't know whether it was an interview or some kind of press conference down in the assembly room.

Mr. Belin. When would that have been?

Mr. Adamcik. It would have been about midnight.

Mr. Belin. Do you know if Oswald requested it or if someone else did?

Mr. Adamcik. I don't recall.

Mr. Belin. Then what happened?

Mr. Adamcik. I stayed in the office after Captain Fritz and the other men came back. He told us to go on home and come back the next morning about 10 o'clock.

Adamcik, who spoke Russian (3410), spends 15 minutes with Oswald and he barely remembers what was being said.

23:00 Greg Olds, Greer Raggio, Otto Mullinax & LND Wells Arrive at DPD

According to Ronnie Duggar (3411) it was Brandon L Lovely (3412) from the Austin ACLU who had heard about Oswald being denied legal representation, and Lovely rang Greg Olds for him to find out whether Oswald had anyone representing him at all. Olds then gets in contact with Will Fritz who relays to him that Oswald was offered legal assistance and that he had refused any, which is very strange since Oswald does nothing but ask for legal help. Even asking *"someone to come forward"* about an hour later during his press conference.

Greg Olds (3413), gathered Greer Raggio (3414), Otto Mullinax (3415) and LND Wells (3416) and made their way towards the DPD. Olds then, at first, tries to get hold of Chief Jesse Curry or Will Fritz. As you can see in their internal communique ACLU document (3417). "*Captain Fritz reported that Oswald had not asked for council to that time, offered the partial explanation that Oswald had been pretty busy with paraffin tests, questioning and the like."* Partial explanation indeed.

One of the group of ACLU lawyers and Charles Webster are trying to talk with Justice of the Peace David Johnston (3418) who relays to them that while Oswald is being arraigned just after 19:00 and that he has been advised about his legal rights regarding an attorney's service, yet shortly after midnight Oswald is heard complaining to the press about not having any legal representation (3419).

Greg Olds' WC testimony (3420):

Mr. Olds. Yes. I got a phone call about 10:30 that night from one of our board members saying they had been called by the President of the Austin affiliate who was concerned about the reports that were being circulated on the air. I think Oswald was directly quoted as saying he had not been given the opportunity to have counsel, and the suggestion was made that it might be well to check into this matter, and I believe I called this--I first called the police department to inquire about this, and finally talked to Captain Fritz, Capt. Will Fritz, and was--raised the question, and he said, *"No--"* that Oswald had been given the opportunity and declined. And I called--then I called the board member back who had called me----
Mr. Stern. Excuse me. Did Captain Fritz say that Oswald did not want counsel at that time, or that he was trying to obtain his own counsel?
Mr. Olds. What I was told, that he had been given the opportunity and had not made any requests. So, I called our board member back and conferred with him and he suggested that we go down and see about it at the police department, in person, to get further assurances.

They go down there and try to get hold of Mayor Earle Cabell on the phone, to no avail as he is too busy! Then they encounter Professor Charles Webster (3421) who has been there for most part of the day. Webster is a professor of law at SMU.

The ACLU lawyers wish to get some better assurances, and accompanied by Charles Webster their first port of call is Captain Glen D King.

Mr. Olds. We went-first, we talked-- conferred with Captain King, I believe is the right name, who is, I believe, assistant to the chief of police. I'm not sure on that. We all went in with Mr. Webster, and this was shortly after 11:35, or 11:40, and Captain King was, at this time, talking to somebody and said that Oswald had just been charged with the assassination of President Kennedy. He had here--earlier been charged with the assassination-I mean the murder of the policeman,

Tippit, and we told Captain King what we were there for, and he said, he assured us that Oswald had not made any requests for counsel. And we went outside of the office and went downstairs, at least I didn't, but two of the others, I believe, went downstairs to the basement where Justice of the Peace David Johnston was. He was the one that had held then believe an arraignment, I believe is the right term, at 7:30 when the first charge of murder was filed against Oswald, and he also assured us that there had been an opportunity of-Oswald's rights had been explained, and he had declined counsel. Said nothing beyond that. I think that was the extent of our inquiry.

[How could this possibly be true when Oswald did nothing but request legal representation? -BK]

Mr. Olds. Also, we were, I believe Chief Curry was quoted to us as having said some-also that Oswald had been advised of his rights to counsel. I am not sure who told me that. I believe that it was Mr. Webster. That was about all. We felt fairly well satisfied that Oswald probably had not been deprived of his rights, so, we then broke up.

Will Fritz's WC testimony (3422) regarding Oswald's rights to an attorney:

Mr. Ball. What rights did he advise him of; do you know?
Mr. Fritz. Of his rights for an attorney, and everything that he told was supposed to be voluntary and things of that kind.
Mr. Ball. He was advised that he had a right to an attorney, was he?
Mr. Fritz. Yes, sir; I am sure he was; I advised him on that on two or three different occasions.
Mr. Ball. Did---you have a rule in Texas, do you, that whatever a witness, a person in custody, says cannot be used against him unless he is warned?
Mr. Fritz. We do have; yes, sir. We have to warn them before we can use the testimony. We have to warn them in the beginning before he is questioned.
Mr. Ball. Before he is questioned you must warn him?
Mr. Fritz. Yes.
Mr. Ball. Before you questioned Oswald the first time, did you warn him?
Mr. Fritz. Yes, sir.
Mr. Ball. What did you tell him? What were the words you used?
Mr. Fritz. I told him that any evidence that he gave me would be used against him, and the offense for which the statement was made, that it would have to be voluntary, made of his own accord.
Mr. Ball. Did he reply to that?

307

Mr. Fritz. He told me that he didn't want a lawyer and he told me once or twice that he didn't want to answer any questions at all. And once or twice he did quit answering any questions and he told me he did want to talk to his attorney, and I told him each time he didn't have to if he didn't want to. So, later he sometimes would start talking to me again.

Mr. Ball. Do you remember when you warned him again?

Mr. Fritz. Yes, sir; I warned him two or three different times; yes, sir.

Mr. Ball. Do you remember when those times were?

Mr. Fritz. No, sir; but during the afternoon.

Mr. Ball. They were you were more or less continuously questioning through the afternoon, were you?

Mr. Fritz. Yes, sir.

The New York Times, on December 6th 1963 (3423) writes an article about this chapter. Oswald declined his right to a lawyer (a bald face lie), the ACLU attorneys could not see Oswald because they were not retained by him. The DPD would not comment on whether Oswald had been given his right to a telephone call (he had not) and not comment on the duration and the intensity of the interrogations.

23:30 The Press Ask to See Oswald

Vincent Drain in Larry Sneed's *No More Silence* (3424):

At the police department, I was with Henry Wade, the district attorney, and the chief of police during the rest of the afternoon. There it was a three-ring circus because the White House Press Corps was there and, if you've ever dealt with them, you've really got something to deal with. Later that evening Oswald attended a so-called press conference. The reason that he was brought to the show-up down in the basement was really more for the purpose of demonstrating to the press that the allegations that the police had beaten up Oswald were untrue. I first knew about it when the District Attorney Henry Wade and I were talking to the Chief of Police, Jesse Curry, and Curry said, "Let's go down to the show-up."

How this happened can be explained much easier with this video (3425). Drain was right in the midst of how this came together. The reporters asked them for it:

So, Wade, Curry, and I walked down to the basement where it was being held and stood partially in the doorway. The press was already there including Jack Ruby, who was sitting on the second row. That was on Friday night, the night of the assassination. I can't recall just what all he was saying other than his shouting some remarks and throwing his fist in the air and that sort of thing. It's hard to say what kind of opinion you'd have of a fellow that you'd just observed there, but considering the stress he must have been under, he seemed pretty cool and not overly excited. He seemed to be very sure of himself with a feeling of a sense of accomplishment.

This final part of this paragraph above is utter rubbish. If one were to study the videos of Oswald's press conference then one could only conclude that he was humble, did not shout during the event and did his utmost to stay composed after being told he was being charged with killing JFK. As far as *"throwing his fist in the air,"* Oswald showed his cuffs when questioned by photographers in the corridor many hours before the press conference.

23:45 Alfred D Hodge Arrives at the DPD

Alfred D Hodge (3426) was a Dallas based gun shop owner, and also owned a bar next to his shop. Will Fritz rang him just after 23:00 and asked him to come over to the Robbery & Homicide Bureau and have a look at the revolver and the rifle. There are discrepancies that show up between his FBI reports, WC testimony and his HSCA interview. Most of the paperwork mention his altercation with Jack Ruby while being in the elevator going down, this is while Hodge is being escorted down by two DPD detectives whose names to this day are not known. Nothing too serious but it does indicate that no one wants to be associated with Ruby. Hodge himself is called in to check the hand gun and the rifle and takes down the serials to check whether they have been purchased at his store, which they have not.

In his WC testimony (3427) he states:
Mr. Hubert. Who was in Captain Fritz' office when you went in first?
Mr. Hodge. Well---
Mr. Hubert. Was Oswald there?
Mr. Hodge. I didn't see Oswald. I have never seen him except on TV, but Captain Fritz has one office I don't know which office is his, but the one on the left has a glass window in it, and when I went in this hallway, out in the hallway where all the TV cameras was, there was another hallway, and Captain Fritz waved at me--he seen me through this glass and there was several people in there with him, and I went on in a little office not quite as big as this and sat down. But in his HSCA interview (3428), he mentions three (!) sightings of Oswald, alone with Fritz no less. There has been no recording of Fritz being alone with Oswald at all.

November 23rd

00:15 Oswald's Press Conference

From Retired Dallas Police Chief Jesse Curry Reveals His Personal JFK Assassination File by Jesse Curry (3429) page 76:

"After discussion of this problem with District Attorney Henry Wade, a news conference was arranged shortly before midnight. Press representatives from all over the world were carefully screened and brought to the Police Assembly Room. Oswald was then escorted to the Assembly Room to allow photographs to be taken by newsmen. The press had agreed to only photograph and observe Oswald's physical condition. The minute Oswald entered the room newsmen caused an uproar and tried to get statements from him. Oswald was taken from the room and returned to his cell after only a few minutes with the newsmen. He seemed to rather enjoy the attention."

That last sentence is not true. Oswald's appearance was one of humility and at the end of complete shock after being told he *was* being charged with murdering President JFK. See how composed he is for the follow-up question, *after* he has been told that *"he had been charged......"*

Please pay careful attention to this footage (3430) and make yourself aware of Oswald's silence while he is moving inside the corridor to the room where the press conference is about to be held. Earlier during that day on the 22nd, Oswald used every opportunity to speak to the press yet in this instance he kept quiet until he was *"lined-up"* for them. Here is another version shot from a different angle with poorer audio from Four Days in November (3431).

Oswald: I positively know nothing about this situation here. I would like to have legal representation.
Reporters: [unintelligible]
Oswald: I was questioned by a judge. However, I protested at that time that I was not allowed legal counsel ... [noise] ... during that short and sweet hearing. I really don't know what the situation is about. Nobody has told me anything except I'm accused of murdering a policeman. I know nothing more than that.
Someone from the crowd: At ease!
Oswald: I do request someone to come forward to give me legal assistance.
Reporter: Did you kill the President?

Oswald: No. I've not been charged with that: In fact, nobody has said that to me yet. The first thing I heard about it was when the newspaper reporters in the hall asked me that question.

Reporter (1): You have been charged with killing The President.
Reporter (2): Nobody said what?
Oswald: Sir?
Reporter (1): You have been charged with killing The President.
Reporter (2): Nobody said what?
Reporter (3): We can't hear anything.

This creates an unforgettable expression of shock by Oswald of that particular moment. The press conference is abruptly stopped by Jesse Curry who signals Lt Baker who tells the escort of detectives (Boyd, Sims and Hall) to take Oswald away. The reporters try to squeeze in a few more questions.

Reporter: What did you do in Russia? [Oswald is led away and does not answer that question]
Reporter: Mr. Oswald, how did you hurt your eye?
Oswald: A policeman hit me.

What ought to be observed here is how composed Oswald is answering that last question, a few seconds after being charged for murdering JFK.

Winston Lawson during his WC testimony (3432) on the Oswald Press Conference:

Representative Ford. [Was that] the last time you saw him?
Mr. Lawson. No; he had not. That was not the last time I saw him, however. Then I later, approximately 11:30, or around midnight, it was announced that there would be a press conference again down in the showup room, and Inspector Kelley had arrived by that time, not too long before that, and Inspector Kelley and I and another agent or two went down to this press conference where it was just completely packed. Everyone couldn't get in the room, the cameramen, reporters, broadcasters, and so forth. Upon a signal----
Mr. Dulles. Who conducted that meeting?
Mr. Lawson. I believe it was the assistant district attorney and Chief Curry and perhaps Captain Fritz. We were just there watching.
Mr. Stern. Tell us more about what----
Mr. Lawson. He was brought in through the crowd and through a side door there, through the corridors, brought in, and I believe the chief and the district attorney each gave statements, and Oswald was asked

a few questions then by the press, but I don't recall of it except that he was whisked out again fairly rapidly after that.

Mr. Stern. Do you remember what any of the questions were and his responses?

Mr. Lawson. No, I don't.

Mr. Stern. How many people were in this room?

Mr. Lawson. It was overflowing. You could hardly hear because everyone was shouting questions. That is why I don't remember what the specific questions were and what his responses were.

Mr. Stern. Do you have any impression why this interview was conducted?

Mr. Lawson. No; I do not.

Mr. Stern. Do you recall anything else that was said by the eyewitness that Mr. Sorrels had arranged to be brought in for the showup, anything else that he said while he was standing talking to you or Mr. Sorrels or while Oswald and others were on the----

Mr. Lawson. No; I don't

Mr. Stern. Then shortly after this show up, or shortly after this interview in the showup room, you left for Washington, I take it?

Mr. Lawson. Yes; there had been quite a bit of discussion during the evening as to what evidence they had up to this time, the rifle, clothing, et cetera, would be brought to Washington to the FBI lab to be worked on, or whether the police would keep it in their custody for a little while longer for their investigation, and there was quite a-bit of discussion by various people all evening long.

And when it was finally decided it would be released by the Dallas Police, the rifle and other evidence to return to Washington, Inspector Kelley told me to return on the special plane that was flying the evidence and the accompanying FBI agent back to Washington.

Mr. Dulles. Was the evidence turned over to you or the FBI?

Mr. Lawson. To the FBI, sir. I just returned on the plane.

Greg Olds' WC testimony:

Mr. Olds. I think the other men went home, and I went downstairs. I heard that there was going to be a press conference, so I thought I could stand in on that and-do you want me to go ahead and detail that?

[Later, during this testimony...]

Mr. Olds. He looked remarkably 'composed and determined. He had a - I remarked afterwards that I would have been very much distraught, and he seemed very well self-contained and determined and maintained his innocence. I heard that, and beyond that scratch above--on his forehead and the eye that was swollen and the little-he looked all right.

312

He looked a little tired, of course, and I think his clothes were dirty, but he looked remarkably in good shape, I thought.

Mr. Stern. Did this give you any further assurance that-about the right to counsel question?

Mr. Olds. Possibly so, it was.

Mr. Stern. I don't want to put the idea in your head.

Mr. Olds. Well, I know, but we had the idea that Oswald was not being accurate when he said he had been denied, because in our dealings with the police here, we have had reason to believe that they are very careful of this sort of thing. And certainly, in a case of this notoriety, certainly, our tendency was to believe that, but I have always been sorry that we didn't talk with Oswald, because it was not clear whether we would be permitted to see him that night or not.

Mr. Stern. But you did not ask to see him?

Mr. Olds. NO; we did not, which I think was a mistake on my part.

Mr. Stern. Did anything transpire on Saturday, November 23?

Mr. Olds. Not so much. I was watching television most of the day.

Ronald Dugger does a fantastic job in an article for the Texas Observer in December 1963 (3434) pages 5 & 6. This, in my opinion, is the best article to date describing Oswald's lack of rights and his press conference at that time.

00:23 Oswald is Booked in Jail

Oswald is officially booked in jail at 12:23 (3435) by GR Hill. Oswald was not officially booked in for more than ten hours and this document by itself is a good give away that Oswald had no phone calls allowed and recorded all the time he was inside. And he had to wait another thirteen before he was given the chance to do so.

00:25 Henry Wade's Press Conference

Henry Wade photographed during his press conference (3436). After Oswald has been led away and is booked in jail Henry Wade is holding his press conference (3437). While watching the video at the link above it abruptly ends, but not before the reporters ask Wade whether Oswald has been charged yet.

Then the following exchange takes place: Justice of the Peace Johnston watched with fascination. The questioning turned a corner when the reporters reminded Wade that Oswald said he didn't know he had been charged with the assassination of the President. Wade said he had been filed on. Which was right? *"I do not know,"* the DA replied. *"He has just been charged. I know he has been advised of the other and taken before the magistrate."* One of the newspapermen put the question to Johnston: *"Did he answer that question whether the man had been advised that he's been charged? The man said here that he didn't know he had been, Dave. How about that?"* David Johnston thought it over. *"He has not been advised that the charge of the murder of the President, because he is on capital offense on the other."* The reporters could not decipher the sentence. *"He has not been advised?"* one asked. The judge said: *"He has not been advised."* *"When will the arraignment be for the President?"* Wade reclaimed his press conference. *"I imagine in—tonight sometime."* The interviewers could not seem to let go of the question.

"He has not been arraigned on the assassination?"
"No." (*The Day Kennedy Was Killed* by Jim Bishop (3438), chapter 12 Midnight). Bishop is a little too close for comfort with the FBI as can be seen in a report from July 17th 1968 (3439).

Hugh Aynesworth mentioned in a recent interview for BBC History Magazine (3440) that: *"The District Attorney, Henry Wade, was asked at a press conference how Oswald got from the Book Depository to the place he killed a cop. Wade said, "he got a cab", and said a man named Deryl Click was the cab driver.* To this day, there has never been a cab driver in Dallas named Deryl Click. Aynesworth later asked Wade why he said that, and he told me, *"it just popped out."*

During Wade's press conference another person appears in the picture (3441), who stands rather close by him, David Johnston and Vincent Drain. His name: James K Allen, a *former* assistant DA and a close friend of Captain Will Fritz.
Wade refers to James K Allen in his WC testimony:

Mr. Wade. *Bill Alexander. There was another one of another man there, Jim Allen, who was a former first assistant who is practising law there in Dallas, frankly I was a little surprised of seeing him there, he is a real capable boy but he was there in homicide with Captain Fritz. They were good friends. And I know there is no question about his intentions and everything was good, but he is just a lawyer there, but he had tried many death penalty cases with Fritz, of Fritz's cases.*

00:40 Oswald's Mugshot and Fingerprints

After the press conference Oswald is being searched again and has his shirt taken away for analysis by the FBI. It is Vincent Drain who leaves

314

with the rifle, the pistol and some of Oswald's belongings on a special plane towards Washington. And while undergoing all this he has his mug short taken in b&w (3442) and colour (3443) and is also photographed in between two police officers (3444). And he has his finger and palm prints taken again.

01:35 Oswald's Arraignment for the Murder of JFK

Oswald's jail release slip (3445) shows he arrived at 12:35 after the press conference and was subsequently, so it seems, taken out again at 01:10. Sylvia Meagher in her first reaction to the WR in September 1964 (3446) already states her doubts on Oswald ever being arraigned.
David Johnston, a Dallas Justice of the Peace, is being interviewed by ABC's Roger Sharp (3447) on the 23rd, after the Wade press conference and states that *'the complaint'* was *not* read out to the accused at 01:17. Since Oswald was locked back into his cell at 01:10, he had been 35 minutes 'out' according to the slip. It would be technically possible to arraign Oswald even though Wade gave his press conference and Johnston gave an interview after that press conference and Oswald at the same time was photographed, allegedly fingerprinted and had his shirt taken. But let's have a closer look at this.

David Johnston's WC testimony (3448):

Mr. Hubert. Now, let's pass to the arraignment concerning President Kennedy, and I wish you would dictate into the record the same information you did as to the first one.
Mr. Johnston. All right, sir. This was the arraignment of Lee Harvey Oswald for the murder with malice of John F. Kennedy, cause No. F-154. The State of Texas versus Lee Harvey Oswald. The complaint was filed at 11:25 p.m., was accepted by me at 11:26 p.m. It was filed at approximately 11:25 p.m. by Capt. J. W. Fritz, Homicide Bureau of the Dallas Police Department, and was accepted by Henry Wade, criminal district attorney, Dallas County, Tex., and was docketed as cause No. 154, F-154 at 11:26 p.m.
Shortly after this is when the defendant was taken to the detail room or the assembly room.
Mr. Hubert. What happened at this arraignment--was it the same as before?
Mr. Johnston. He was not arraigned at this time. He was then arraigned after he was removed to the detail room where the press was allowed to have their first interview with the defendant, with Lee Harvey Oswald. Subsequently in a conference between Captain Fritz, Mr. Wade, and two or three of his assistants and myself, and Chief Curry--it was decided to go ahead and arraign him and that arraignment was held at 1:35 a.m.,

November 23, 1963, in the identification bureau of the Dallas Police Department, and once again I appraised him of his constitutional rights, read the affidavit, and advised him again that I remanded him to the custody of the sheriff, Dallas County, denying bond as capital offense. He was also told at both of these instances that he would be given the right to contact an attorney of his choice.

Mr. Hubert. Did he ask this at either of these occasions?

Mr. Johnston. Yes, sir; that was one of the first things he said--that he wanted this man from New York of the Civil Liberties Union.

Mr. Hubert. He said that to you?

Mr. Johnston. Yes [spelling] A-b-t; however, that's pronounced. He said he would like to have this gentleman and I told Oswald when he made that statement that he would be given the opportunity to contact the attorney of his choice.

Mr. Hubert. Whose duty was it to see that he was given that opportunity?

Mr. Johnston. The telephone would be made available to him to make any call he wished to make and that would have been advanced to him through the normal routine. He possibly could have been given this permission at the city jail and also had he ever made it to the county jail, here again he would have been given the opportunity to contact a lawyer.

Mr. Hubert. In any event, you made it clear to him that he had a right to contact a lawyer?

Mr. Johnston. That he had a right to be represented by counsel, that he had the right to make a telephone call to contact any person of his choice, and the assault to murder complaint, alleging the assault to murder of John B. Connally in cause No. F-155, The State of Texas versus Lee Harvey Oswald, this complaint was filed by Lt Robert E. McKinney of the forgery bureau of the Dallas Police Department. This complaint was filed in my office at Richardson, Tex., at 6:15 p.m., on November 23, 1963, and the defendant was not arraigned in this case because he was already being held for two capital offenses. He would have been arraigned in this probably the following week had he lived.

Jesse Curry in his WC testimony (3449) on those arraignments, has another case of that particular amnesia:

Mr. Rankin - Do you know when Lee Harvey Oswald was arraigned?

Mr. Curry - It was about 1:30 in the morning. That would be on the morning of the 23d, I believe.

Mr. Rankin - How long did he, how long had he been in your custody then?

Mr. Curry - About 11 hours. That was on the Tippit; yes, sir.

Mr. Rankin - When you say that he was arraigned the following day early in the morning, did you mean for the Tippit murder or for the assassination?

Mr. Curry - No; that was for the assassination of the President.

Mr. Rankin - All right, will you tell us when he was arraigned for the Tippit murder?

Mr. Curry - I was not present but I believe it was about 7:30.

Mr. Rankin - That same evening?

Mr. Curry - Yes; that would be about 5 hours afterwards.

Mr. Rankin - Do you recall whether he was arrested first for the assassination or for the Tippit murder?

Mr. Curry - For the Tippit murder. There were some witnesses to this murder and they had observed him as he left the scene, and this was what he was arrested for.

The Chairman - May I interrupt Just to ask the chief a question?

Chief, on your arraignments does the magistrate advice the petitioner as to his right to counsel?

Mr. Curry - Yes, sir; he does.

The Chairman - Does he ask him if he has counsel?

Mr. Curry - I don't recall him doing that. I am not customarily present when a person is arraigned.

The Chairman - You were not present at the arraignment?

Mr. Curry - I was present when he was arraigned for the assassination of the President. I was not present when he was arraigned for the murder of Tippit.

The Chairman - I suppose they make a stenographic record of that, do they not?

Mr. Curry - Yes, sir; I am sure they do.

The Chairman - That is all I have.

Mr. Rankin - Chief, our people made an inquiry whether there was a stenographic record. They don't believe there was any.

Mr. Curry - I am not sure of that. I know at the time he was arraigned for the assassination of the President I was present there at the time. It was decided that we should, district attorney was there at the city hall. He was there during most of the evening.

Mr. Rankin - Will you just describe for the Commission what happened during the arraignment for the assassination, who was present, what you saw.

Mr. Curry - As I recall, I know the Justice of the Peace David Johnston was there. It seemed like Sergeant Warren, but I couldn't be positive but some of the jail personnel brought him out into the identification bureau.

Mr. Rankin - How was he taken out? Were there several people around him, what was the security arrangements?

Mr. Curry - At that time there was only, we were inside the offices of the criminal identification section. He was brought out through a door that opens from the jail into the criminal identification section. There was only about a half dozen of us altogether there, I don't recall who all was there.

Mr. Rankin - What do you mean by the criminal identification section. Could you describe what that is?

Mr. Curry - That is the identification bureau.

Mr. Rankin - Does that have a room that this meeting occurred in?

Mr. Curry - It is not a room such as this. It was in the little foyer or lobby, and it is separated from the jail lobby.

Mr. Rankin - Did the justice of the peace sit or stand or what?

Mr. Curry - He stood. He stood on one side of the counter and Oswald on the other side of the counter.

Mr. Rankin - What floor is this on?

Mr. Curry - The fourth floor.

Mr. Rankin - That is nearest the place where there are some filing cabinets?

Mr. Curry - Yes; it is.

Mr. Rankin - And besides the people that you have described, I assume that you yourself were there as you have said?

Mr. Curry - Yes; I was.

Mr. Rankin - Was there anyone else that you recall?

Mr. Curry - Not that I recall, other than the justice of the peace.

Mr. Rankin - Will you describe what happened?

Mr. Curry - Lee Harvey Oswald was brought in and the complaint was read to him, and here again he was very arrogant and he said, *"I don't know what you are talking about. That is the deal, is it?"* and such remarks as this, and the Justice of the Peace very patiently and courteously explained to him what the procedure was and why it was.

Mr. Rankin - What did he say about that?

Mr. Curry - I don't recall his exact words.

Mr. Rankin - Just tell us in substance.

Mr. Curry - He didn't--as I recall, he didn't think much of it. He just said, *"I don't know what you are talking about."*

Mr. Rankin - What did the Justice of the peace say about the procedure and any rights and so forth?

Mr. Curry - As I recall it, he read to him the fact that he was being charged with the assassination of the President of the United States, John Kennedy on such and such day at such and such time.

Mr. Rankin - Did he say anything about his right to plead?

Mr. Curry - I don't recall, sir.

Mr. Rankin - Did he say anything about counsel?

Mr. Curry - I don't recall whether he did or not.

Mr. Rankin - What else happened at that time that you recall?

Mr. Curry - That is about all. After it was read to him, he was taken back to his cell.

From Jesse Curry, Retired Dallas Police Chief Jesse Curry Reveals His Personal JFK Assassination File by Jesse Curry (3450): *"Oswald stood with a sullen look on his face as the charges against him were read, in order to inform him that he was charged with the slaying of the President. Oswald's response was typical. He said, I don't know what you're talking about. What's the idea of this? What are you doing this for?"* (Page 80).

Joseph McBride in his book, *Into the Nightmare* (3451), manages to interview Jim Leavelle in the early nineties, and at this interview he lets his guard down a tad. *"Now the thing was, the Captain (Will Fritz, the Head of Homicide, who was running the interrogation of Oswald) asked me if I had enough to make a case on him for the Tippit killing. And I said, 'OH yeah. I got plenty on that.' I had him identified by about three or four people. And so, Cap said, 'Well go ahead and make a tight case on him in case we have trouble making this one on the presidential shooting.' So that was one reason he was arraigned early on the Tippit shooting. But I was thinking that we also arraigned him somewhere down the line on the shooting of the president. But I wouldn't swear to that offhand."* (pages 235-236).

- Deputy Chief of DPD MW Stevenson on Oswald's arraignment to NBC's Tom Petit (3452). Just before midnight. He can also be seen in this photo (3453) talking to reporters on the third floor of City Hall.
- MG Hall states in his report (3454) that Oswald was placed in his cell after the press conference.
- And on April 11th 1964 a document by Wilson F Warren (3455) has been created to show Oswald was taken out of his cell at 01:35 to be arraigned on the fourth floor.
- There is a listing of all individuals present while Oswald is being filed on for the murder of JFK in this December 5th USSS report by Thomas J Kelley (3456). Someone who has not been mentioned as of yet is Maurice (real name: Morris) Harrell (3457), who is also an assistant DA. He was also mentioned by David Johnston in his WC testimony (3458):

Mr. Johnston. No, sir. As I say, the only thing he said was when he was brought in for the arraignment on President Kennedy, and he says to me, *"Is this the trial?"* I said, *"No, sir; I have to arraign you again on another offense."* And, there was some seven or eight officer witnesses to that arraignment and an assistant district attorney, and that assistant district attorney at that time was Mr. Maurice Harrell [spelling] H-a-r-r-e-l-l.

Other than that, I have not managed to source anything else of Harrell's involvement.

Henry Wade's WC testimony (3459):

Mr. Wade. Yes, sir; so, they said, *"Have you filed on him?"* At that stage, started yelling has he been filed on, and I said yes, and filed on for murder with malice, and they asked Judge Johnston, is there-they asked him something. Then they started asking me questions everywhere, from all angles.
Mr. Rankin. Under your practice, what do you mean by file on him? Is that something different than an arraignment?
Mr. Wade. Well, of course, it is according to the terminology and what you mean by arraignment. In Texas the only arraignment is when you get ready to try him. Like we arraigned Ruby just before we started putting on evidence. That is the only arraignment we have, actually.
Mr. Rankin. I see. You don't bring him before a magistrate?
Mr. Wade. Well, that is called-you can have an examining trial before the magistrate to see whether it is a bailable matter. At that time, I don't believe he had been brought before the magistrate, because I told David Johnston as we left there, I said, "You ought to go up before the jail and have him brought before you and advise him of his rights and his right to counsel and this and that," which, so far as I know, he did. But at that meeting you had two attorneys from the American Civil Liberties Union.
Is Wade saying that two ACLU lawyers were present when he and Johnston were conferring about bringing Oswald in front of a magistrate? Or present when Oswald was actually brought in front of one? Both scenarios are rather peculiar as this did not happen.

Timothy Cweik (3460) starts digging deeper into this shortly after and finds out that only four newspapers were reporting about the alleged arraignment that Saturday morning; the Philadelphia Bulletin here & here (3461), the Dallas Times-Herald, The New York Times and the Washington Evening Star. Of those, only the Bulletin and the Times actually used the word *"arraignment."* Cweik found no follow-up stories in any of the four papers, including in *"wraps-ups"* of the entire weekend. Stranger still; no other publications picked up the story. In an effort to find out more, Cweik contacted the reporter for the Bulletin who had landed this apparent major scoop, John McCullough. McCullough declined an interview. He did appear before the WC, but did not offer information about the arraignment, nor was he asked about it. The story got even stranger when Cweik looked more closely at the other three papers. The Times article appeared in the microfilm records of the newspaper, but not in any actual hard copies that were tracked down. And the Evening Star reporter was Jeremiah O'Leary. O'Leary was once described by Carl Bernstein as having, *"a valuable personal relationship"* with the CIA during the 1960s.

The James Hosty affidavit in WC Document 5, page 400 (3462) states that since Oswald was already arraigned for the Tippit murder there was no need to do this again in relation to JFK's slaying.

In chapter three of *Assignment Oswald (3463)*, he states on November 23rd at 6 AM, *I was interrupted by Shanklin for the morning briefing and update. I took a seat on the corner of Bookout's desk. The agents had arrived in virtual silence, all of us in shocked mourning, whispering hesitantly about yesterday's event as we congregated. Our office had taken on the air of a funeral parlor. "While you've been sleeping there have been some important developments," Shanklin said. "Last night at about 1:30 A.M., the county prosecutor filed first-degree murder charges against Oswald for the killing of the president. Our agents in Chicago were able to trace the ownership of the rifle found on the sixth floor of the depository to Oswald. And one of our agents in New Orleans, DeBrueys, discovered that one of Oswald's aliases was AJ Hidell. This alias was given to all FBI offices yesterday. Someone found out that rifles like the one found in the depository are advertised in certain magazines and can be mail ordered from Chicago. By using both Oswald's true name and his alias, the Chicago agents made a hit and traced the ownership to Oswald. "This trace apparently tipped the balance for the prosecutor and they filed on Oswald after you all left last night," Shanklin added. He pointed out that as much as the FBI wanted to take over the investigation, the Dallas police had jurisdiction over all matters.*

So according to Hosty/Shanklin, it was the trace of the ownership of the rifle that tipped the balance for the Dallas DA office to press charges for the murder of JFK. That is a whole different tune compared to the document on the previous page. Plus, the ownership was not established until the morning of the 23rd which is hours after the alleged arraignment of Oswald.

In the Cuero Record from November 24th 1963 (3464), showing pages 1 & 12 together. Oswald allegedly said during his arraignment, *"This is ridiculous."* During an earlier charge Oswald responded with *"I don't know what this is all about."* This article is an excellent example that the police leaked almost everything.

There is a well-researched segment on this whole matter inside a larger article in the Mattoon Journal Gazette on December 13th 1968 (3465). Its detail is really something. Start at the bottom of the sixth column.

And here is another DPD statement by Elmer Boyd (3466), which clearly states when they dropped Oswald off at 00:23 and at 10:25 they picked him up again.

Here is MG Hall's statement (3467) that he took Oswald from the press conference to his cell.

Finally Lt TL Baker in his WC testimony (3468):

Mr. Ball. You are up here with Captain Fritz?
Mr. Baker. Yes, sir.
Mr. Ball. And you are the man who prepared Commission Document 81-B; is that correct?
Mr. Baker. I assisted in it, sir.
Mr. Ball. You were sort of the editor, is that right?
Mr. Baker. Something like that.
Mr. Ball. The question we addressed to Captain Fritz was where was Oswald between the 12:35 and, I believe, 1:10 in the evening, 1:10 a.m., on Saturday, November 23, that is right after midnight.
Mr. Baker. Yes, sir; at 12:35 a.m. Lieutenant Knight of the I.D. bureau took him out of the jail on the fifth floor and with the assistance of Sergeant Warren and one of the jailers brought him to the fourth floor where the I. D. bureau was located.
Mr. McCloy. The I. D. bureau is the identification bureau?
Mr. Baker. Yes, sir. There in the presence of Sergeant Warren and this jailer, one of his assistants, he was processed through the I. D. bureau, which consists of taking his pictures and fingerprints and making up the different circulars that go to the FBI and so forth. When they had finished processing him, he returned him to the jail. Lieutenant Knight released him. He was placed back in the jail at 01:10. Approximately 01:30 Sergeant Warren received a call from Chief Curry, advising him to bring him back to the identification bureau the same place, for arraignment. Sergeant Warren and the same jailer returned him to the ID bureau, where he was arraigned by Judge Johnston at approximately 01:35. This arraignment took approximately 10 minutes, and he was returned to the fifth-floor jail by Sergeant Warren at approximately 01:45.

TL Baker's Report (3469) states pretty much the same. That after Oswald's press conference he is taken upstairs to the fourth floor for booking, and another search. Then taken to the fifth floor and then back to the fourth for his arraignment for killing the President.

In Robert Oswald's WC testimony (3470) the following is told by him:

Mr. Jenner. Did you go to your room?

Mr. Oswald. Yes, sir.

Mr. Dulles. Approximately what time was this?

Mr. Oswald. Approximately 10:30 p.m., that night, sir.

Mr. Jenner. After registering, did you retire for the evening, or did you go somewhere?

Mr. Oswald. No, sir; I did not retire for the evening. I did, in fact, go into the coffee room of the Statler Hilton Hotel in Dallas, and have a ham sandwich and some milk, and shortly after completing this, I walked across the street, which was approximately a half a block down the street, to the Dallas police station again.

Mr. Jenner. All right. Now, up to that moment, other than was necessary for you to register and your conversation with a waitress, in connection with you're having some evening lunch, did you have any contact with anybody?

Mr. Oswald. No, sir; I did not.

Mr. Jenner. Did you have any contact at all of any kind or character up to this moment with anybody in connection with the events of the day?

Mr. Oswald. No, sir; I had not.

Mr. Jenner. All right. You went across the street to the Dallas City police station?

Mr. Oswald. Yes, sir, I did.

Mr. Jenner. Had you had an appointment?

Mr. Oswald. No, sir, I did not.

Mr. Jenner. What was your purpose in going across the street for that visit?

Mr. Oswald. I wanted to speak to Captain Fritz, if possible.

Mr. Jenner. You record on page 8 that you entered the Dallas police station, you were interviewed or consulted by some FBI agents in a small office.

Mr. Oswald. That is correct.

Mr. Jenner. Do you recall their names?

Mr. Oswald. No, sir; I do not.

Mr. Jenner. I take it in any event, however, that they questioned you, did they?

Mr. Oswald. That is correct.

Mr. Jenner. And were all the answers that you gave the truth and nothing but the truth to the best of your information, recollection, and belief, at that time?

Mr. Oswald. It most certainly was, sir.

Mr. Jenner. All right, sir. When did you learn, if you ever learned, that your brother, Lee Harvey Oswald, had in fact been charged with the assassination of President Kennedy?

323

Mr. Oswald. At approximately midnight or a few minutes before midnight, November 22, 1963.

Mr. Jenner. And is that recorded on page 8 of your memorandum?

Mr. Oswald. Yes, sir, it is.

Mr. Jenner. What was your reaction when that information was conveyed to you? What were your thoughts?

Mr. Oswald. I do not recall if I had any thoughts at that particular time, sir. I did not make any comment that I recall. I believe I just shook my head.

Mr. Jenner. I was going to ask you in connection with page 8, your opinion respecting the possible involvement of your brother, Lee Harvey Oswald, in the assassination of President Kennedy, but Mr. Dulles this morning in his questions has covered that subject, so I will skip it. Now, did you see Captain Fritz that evening?

Mr. Oswald. No, sir, I did not.

Mr. Jenner. Did you attempt to see him?

Mr. Oswald. Yes, sir; I did.

Mr. Jenner. Did you inquire further with respect to an opportunity on your part that you wished to see your brother?

Mr. Oswald. No, sir; I had been told so many times that Captain Fritz was quite busy, and I realize, of course, he was, and I let it go at that.

Mr. Jenner. Now, following your visit to the police station, which you do record there, and therefore I won't go into it further, what did you do that evening?

Mr. Oswald. I returned to my hotel, sir.

10:30 Joe Molina Arrives at the DPD

Joe Molina (3471) worked in the credit department of the TSBD on the second floor. He stood on the Easterly side of the landing on the front steps of the building. Joe Molina's house has been searched early in the morning of the 23rd by Bill Alexander, Captain Pat Gannaway and Lieutenant Jack Revill, quite a heavy presence for a house search, which does not yield anything to nail Molina with for being a subversive. Yet he is still ordered to come into the DPD later that same morning to give a statement. Molina is kept there almost all day and spends most of the time waiting around.

Molina's statement is taken by detective Billy Senkel (3472).

Chief of Police and blabbermouth, Jesse Curry stating Molina's name on national radio and TV, and mentioning subversive activities in the same sentence. That being said without a shred of evidence of Molina being involved with anything of the kind. The damage has been done and 21 days after the assassination Molina is let go from the TSBD under the

324

guise of modernisation, but the real reason is people calling and writing in complaints and threatening not buying from a company that harbours commie sympathisers.

The FBI report, CE 2036 from July 20th 1964 (3473) gives a very good description of what happened.

In Molina's WC testimony (3474), which he insisted upon giving, the visit to the DPD on November 23rd is discussed:

Mr. Ball. Did you go down to the police department?
Mr. MOLINA. Well, they asked me if I would go down the next morning and I said yes, I would go down the next morning. I would rather go down the next morning than now. It was already past 2, so the next morning my wife drove me down. I got there about 11. My wife drove me down and I got there about 10:30. The place was full of television people and reporters swarming all over the place and they told me to wait in the room there and then I went into Chief Gannaway's office or whatever his name is.
He said I was supposed to be questioned by Mr. Fritz down there but that he wanted to talk to me after they questioned me up there because they wanted to know more about the GI Forum so I said, *"I will come back when they get through questioning me."* So, I went up there and they told me to wait in an office and so I waited there for about 30, 40 minutes and, oh, must have been longer than that, they finally questioned me and they put me in a room and there was a man from the FBI or Secret Service, I don't recall which one it was.
He was sitting on my right and there was a fellow from the Dallas Police Department taking a statement and a fellow from the FBI introduced himself, said I'm so and so, showed me his badge and so forth. The other fellow didn't say who he was or anything, just sat there and so then they told me to wait there in that room and I did.
I was there for about 45 minutes and then the fellow came back from the FBI, said *"My God, are you still in here?"* I said *"Yes,"* he said *"How long you been here?"* Here it was about 2 or 3 o'clock. I said *"I have been here since about 11; I haven't eaten lunch or haven't had a drink of water."* You know, I was just there and he told this fellow, said, *"Can't you let him go; he has been here. He has already given his testimony statement, whatever he is going to give; you should let him go."* This fellow said *"No, he got to wait in there,"* so I had to go back in there; about 10 or 15 minutes later, they came back and I went up to the office of Lieutenant Revill and he started asking a lot of questions about the GI Forum, did I know such and such fellow--some I knew, they had been in the club. Naturally, I knew them though we weren't intimate friends, some were, some weren't. Then he gave me a bunch of names, I imagine

they were in their so-called subversive files that they claim they have; of course, I didn't know a lot of them. In fact, I didn't know most of them. Knew some of the names. I didn't know some of the names they mentioned are kept in their files or not. Anyhow, they asked me---I had to---they didn't ask me---I had to just ask to sign a statement I belonged to the forum and certain members were charter members of the forum and I said yes, I would sign it. I didn't see anything wrong with it so I signed it and they told me I could go home. It was 4:30 or 5 and they asked me if I had a ride home and I said no. They said *"Well, we'll give you a ride home,"* so one of the officers there, plainclothes man, drove me home.

When I got home, of course, there were about three or four cars at the house. My wife was all shook up and she said, *"My God,"* she said, *"Don't you know what they been saying about you?"* I said *"No, I don't know what they are saying about me."* She said, "*Don't you know you been on TV and the news media across the nation saying you are on the so-called list with the Dallas Police Department claiming that you associate with persons of…"*--see if I can quote it right--I was known to "*associate with persons of subversive background."*

Listen carefully to what Chief of Dallas Police Jesse Curry (3475) has to say about Molina while on the third floor at the same time. It made Molina so angry that he wanted to take Curry to court because of his name being thrown out all over the airwaves.

10:35 Fourth Interrogation

Oswald has his breakfast which consists of oatmeal, apricots, bread and coffee. He eats this with a guard present who has handed him a spoon. As Captain Glenn D King relates to journalist Holland McCombs (3476) it was possible that he could choke himself with that spoon. Then Oswald is taken down for that day's first interrogation.

Oswald's jail release slip (3477) shows he is picked up again between at 10:25 and locked up again upstairs at 11:33.

Present:
DPD: Will Fritz, Elmer Boyd and MG Hall.
US Marshal: Robert Nash.
FBI: SA James Bookhout.
Secret Service: David B Grant, Forrest Sorrels and Thomas J Kelley
US Marshals: Robert Irvine Nash (3478). I still have yet to find any of his reports.

Will Fritz's notes (3479) regarding this interrogation show the bus ride and the ticket transfer as part of Oswald's escape with more clothes changes than reported the day before.

On a second page of notes (3480) we find the quote: On the morning of the *22nd* *"says two negr. came in. One Jnr. + short negro."*

Will Fritz's WC testimony (3481) on the *"Junior"* matter, shows that he never properly investigated it himself or had others do it for him so he would provide an adequate answer.

Mr. Ball. And you asked him again, didn't you, what he was doing at the time the President was shot?
Mr. Fritz. Yes, sir.
Mr. Ball. What did he say?
Mr. Fritz. Well, he told me about the same story about this lunch.
Mr. Ball. He mentioned who he was having lunch with, did he not?
Mr. Fritz. Yes, sir; he told me he was having lunch when the President was shot.
Mr. Ball. With whom?
Mr. Fritz. With someone called Junior, someone he worked with down there, but he didn't remember the other boy's name.
Mr. Ball. Did he tell you what he was eating?
Mr. Fritz. He told me, I believe, that he had, I am doing this from memory, a cheese sandwich, and he also mentioned he had some fruit, I had forgotten about the fruit until I looked at this report.
Mr. Ball. Did he say that was in the package he had brought from home?
Mr. Fritz. Yes, sir; there was one reason I asked him about what was in the package, we had had a story that had been circulated around the meantime about some chicken bones, I am sure you heard of that, and I wanted to find for sure what he did have in his lunch and he told me about having--he told me they did not have any chicken out there and I also talked with the Paines and they told me they didn't have any chicken in the icebox, they did have some cheese.
Mr. Ball. But he said he had had lunch with Junior?
Mr. Fritz. Yes, sir; and with someone else.
Mr. Ball. Did you find out that there was an employee named Junior, a man that was nicknamed Junior at the Texas School Book Depository?
Mr. Fritz. Probably we have it here, some of the officers probably did we had all these people checked out. I didn't do it myself probably.

Fritz did nothing about checking Oswald's alibi.
James Bookhout in his dodgy November 25th report (3482), which is being used as a cover up for the joint November 22nd Bookhout & Hosty report (3483) pages 1 & 2, three days prior and which also inserts the

second-floor lunchroom encounter mentions this aforementioned event as well:

"Oswald stated that on November 22, 1963, he had eaten lunch in the lunchroom at the Texas School Book Depository, alone, but recalled possibly two Negro employees walking through the room during this period. He stated possibly one of these employees was called 'Junior,' and the other was a short individual whose name he could not recall, but whom he would be able to recognize.
He ate lunch by himself and he possibly saw two other employees walking through the room."

The domino room is a tiny room for the labourers to eat lunch or play dominoes in. How do you walk through that small space with just one entry and exit door (3484) without getting noticed? Check out the photographs 14-20 (3485). The statement also says that, *"possibly one was called 'Junior.'"* That is twice the mention of 'possibly'.

J Edgar Hoover wanted to know more about this aspect of the case and remarked *"handle promptly"* seen in the document, from January 3rd 1964 (3486). What Secret Service report is Hoover talking about?
By January 14th (3487) page 15, the outstanding matter seems to be 'dealt with.'

"He said that Ray and Norman were with him all the time he was on the first floor and they did not see Lee Harvey Oswald at any time between 12 noon until they returned to the first floor after the shooting."

This is not the only change of Oswald's 'escape' as he also added the alleged cab ride on Saturday, according to Fritz. See his notes for the first interrogation on the 23rd.

Check out the last section of this Fritz notes page (3488) and compare to Kelley's November 24th report (3489). Upon being shown the bus transfer ticket Oswald revised the story that he had told on the 22nd in which he said that he had taken a bus to his rooming house, now admitting that he left the bus *"because the traffic was heavy"* and that he then took a taxi to his rooming house.

It seems that this interrogation report and the next when compared to each other have been blended together by Fritz and Bookhout. It is thanks to Thomas Kelley's reporting that we can differentiate which info came from which interrogation.

USSS inspector Thomas Kelley (3489) wrote a report on November 24th entitled *"First interview with Lee Harvey Oswald."* (3490) In this, Kelley claims that Oswald stated he had NOT seen the parade, an assertion which only comes from Kelley and is not supported by anyone else present, such as Bookhout and Fritz.

The passage is on page 2: *"I asked him if he viewed the parade and he said he had not. I then asked him if he had shot the President and he said he had not. I asked him if he has shot governor Connally and he said he had not."*

Will Fritz's notes corroborate everything above except the pivotal bit *"I asked him if he viewed the parade and he said he had not."* This particular insert cannot be corroborated by Fritz's and Bookhout's report of the same interrogation. It is also in direct contradiction to Oswald's claim stating that he was watching the Presidential Parade in James Hosty's first interrogation pre-report.

Kelley's report confirms Fritz's notes with regards to eating lunch in the Domino Room and the mention of 'Junior' Jarman and a short little Negro boy (which in all likelihood is Harold Norman). And furthermore, Oswald's lunch description coincides with Fritz's notes as well.

Consider a 'gem' like that in Kelley's report. Surely it would have had a mention in Fritz's handwritten notes and Bookhout's report as well, but neither of them fail to do so. This interrogation has another mention of Oswald seeing the parade go past which Bookhout and Fritz kept quiet about and Kelley did mention and falsified its answer to.

James Bookhout's solo report from the same interrogations is almost an exact copy of Will Fritz interrogation notes. Or is it the other way around?
In the second paragraph there is a slight mistake, since Oswald's bus ticket allegedly appeared just before his first line-up and not during his arrest which was 2.5 hours earlier!

In the fourth and final paragraph the bus ride home story is being changed with the inclusion of a cab ride, which Fritz also included.

In James Bookhout's November 25th 1963 report (3492), Oswald apparently changed his shirt and trousers because they were dirty. Fritz makes mention of 'shirts' in the handwritten notes, Bookhout on the other hand mentions just 'shirt'. Typo material.

In the third paragraph John Abt is mentioned for the first time during this interrogation on the 23rd. And so is the Hidell ID in the 9th paragraph. This matter coincides with Thomas Kelley's report and Will Fritz's handwritten notes. Roughly 22 hours after his arrest.

James Bookhout's WC testimony (3493) states:

Mr. Stern - When did you next see Oswald?

Mr. Bookhout - Well, it would be on the morning of November 23, 1963, in the homicide and robbery bureau.

Mr. Stern - This was another interrogation?

Mr. Bookhout - Yes.

Mr. Stern - Conducted by Captain Fritz?

Mr. Bookhout - That's correct.

Mr. Stern - Do you recall who else was present, and you may refer any time to your reports to refresh your recollection.

Mr. Bookhout - All right; that will be the interrogation that was in the presence of myself, T. J. Kelley of the U.S. Secret Service, David B. Grant U.S. Secret Service, Robert I. Nash, U.S. marshal, and Detectives Billy L. Senkel and Fay M. Turner from the homicide and robbery bureau, Dallas Police Department. This interview was conducted, primarily, by Captain Fritz.

Mr. Stern - Did you ask any questions in the course of this interview?

Mr. Bookhout - Yes.

Mr. Stern - What were they, and what were the responses, if you recall?

Mr. Bookhout - One specific question was with regard to the Selective Service card in the possession of Oswald bearing a photograph of Oswald and the name Alek James Hidell. Oswald admitted he carried this Selective Service card, but declined to state that he wrote the signature of Alek J. Hidell appearing on same. Further declined to state the purpose of carrying same, and---or any use he made of same.

Mr. Stern - Did Oswald say anything in the course of this interview with regard to obtaining a lawyer?

Mr. Bookhout - Yes, it was in this interview that he mentioned he wanted to contact Attorney Abt [spelling] A-b-t, New York City. I recall Captain Fritz asked him if he knew Abt personally and he said he did not, but he explained that he knew that Abt had defended the Smith Act cases in 1949, or 1950, and Captain Fritz asked him if he knew how to get ahold of Mr. Abt, and he stated that he did not know what his address was, but he was in New York.

I recall that Captain Fritz explained to him that he would allow him to place a long-distance call for Abt, and he explained to Oswald how to ask the long-distance operator to trace him down and locate him, even though Oswald didn't even know his address or telephone number.

Mr. Stern - Did he actually make the call in your presence?

Mr. Bookhout - No; he didn't make the call in my presence. The next interview that we had with him, I recall that Captain Fritz asked him if he had been able to contact Mr. Abt. Oswald stated that he had made the telephone call and thanked Captain Fritz for allowing him to make the call, but actually he had not been able to talk to Abt. He wasn't available. Wasn't in his office or something----

Mr. Stern - Was he complaining about not having counsel furnished, or did he seem satisfied with the effort to reach Abt?

Mr. Bookhout - No; he made no complaint about not being furnished an attorney. Actually, there was a good deal of conversation on that point, and he stated that he did not want any Dallas attorney representing him, and said that if he couldn't get in touch with Mr. Abt, that he would probably contact someone with the Civil Liberties Union, and have them furnish an attorney.

I recall sometime during November 22 or 23, I believe it was, the head of the Dallas Bar Association appeared at the homicide and robbery bureau and requested permission to talk to Oswald. Captain Fritz gave him that permission, and when he got through talking to Oswald and came back in and told Captain Fritz that he had seen him, and that Oswald did not want anybody from Dallas to represent him.

Mr. Stern - You heard this?

Mr. Bookhout - Yes; that was in my presence. I don't recall the name of the attorney, but I was there at the time or during that conversation.

Mr. Stern - Can you tell us approximately how long this Saturday morning interview took?

Mr. Bookhout - Well, that would be approximately an hour. No interview that I participated in lasted over an hour, and I think roughly this one probably started around 10:35 in the morning and lasted for approximately an hour.

Mr. Stern - All right. What was his physical appearance at this time?

Mr. Bookhout - His appearance was no different than it was on the 22d.

Mr. Stern - You saw no other bruises?

Mr. Bookhout - No.

Mr. Stern - Did he seem rested, or tired?

Mr. Bookhout - I saw no difference in his appearance on the 23rd than it was on the 22nd.

Mr. Stern - How about the way he handled himself? Was he any calmer, any more communicative Saturday morning than he had been Friday afternoon?

Mr. Bookhout - Well, I think that he might not have been quite as belligerent on the 23d as he was on the 22nd. But he still refused to discuss certain points indicated above, Selective Service card being one point that I recall. I remember he was asked if he would take a polygraph, and he said he would not, that it had always been his practice not to agree to take a polygraph.

Mr. Stern - Did he suggest that he had been asked before to take a polygraph?

Mr. Bookhout - He made some comment along the line that it had never been his policy--before, to take a polygraph.

Mr. Stern - But he didn't elaborate on it?

Mr. Bookhout - He didn't elaborate on it.

Mr. Stern - Did he make any further comment at this interview about his interviews with the FBI, or their interviews of his wife?

Mr. Bookhout - I think probably this is the one I referred to a while ago. Yes, it would be in this interview that he made further comment that on the interview of Ruth Paine by the FBI, regarding his wife, that he felt that his wife was intimidated. Also, in this interview that he made mention as previously stated above that he had arrived about July 19, 1962, from Russia, and was interviewed by the FBI at Fort Worth, Tex.

He stated that he felt that they had overstepped their bounds and used various tactics in interviewing him.

Mr. Stern - Did he specify what the tactics were?

Mr. Bookhout - No; he did not.

Mr. Stern - In your report before this interview you mentioned that he again denied shooting President Kennedy, and apparently said that he didn't know until then that Governor Connally had been shot?

Mr. Bookhout - That's correct. That was his statement, that he denied shooting President John F. Kennedy on November 22, 1963, and commented that he did not know that Governor John Connally had been shot.

Mr. Stern - Did you form any impression about whether he was genuinely surprised? Did he look genuinely surprised to you, or how did you feel about that? I am just asking for your impression. If you don't have one, say so.

Mr. Bookhout - No; I have no impression on that. I arrived at no conclusion.

Mr. Stern - What did he say at this interview with respect to the purchase of a rifle, or possession of a rifle?

Mr. Bookhout - Generally, he stated that he didn't own a rifle, hadn't ever made any mail order purchase of one.

Mr. Stern - Now, did anything transpire that you observed concerning Oswald between the end of that morning interview on Saturday, and the next interview of Oswald?

Mr. Bookhout - No.

Forrest Sorrels' WC testimony (3494):

Mr. Stern - Did you participate in or observe any other interrogation of Oswald following your own brief interrogation?

Mr. Sorrels - Yes, sir.

Mr. Stern - When was that?

Mr. Sorrels - On the following day----

Mr. Stern - That is Saturday, the 23d?

Mr. Sorrels - Yes, sir; I sat in on part of an interview with him, with Captain Fritz. And then, again, on Sunday the 24th, just before he was shot.

Mr. Stern - Did the question of counsel come up again--that is, a lawyer for Oswald?

Mr. Sorrels - Yes. During the interview with Captain Fritz, when I was in there, he mentioned the fact that he wanted to get a man by the name of Abt, or some similar name like that. I never had heard of him before. Apt, or some similar name.

And Captain Fritz said, *"Well you can use the phone and you can call him."*

Mr. Stern - When was this?

Mr. Sorrels - That was Saturday morning. And it is my understanding that Oswald did attempt to reach this man on the phone.

Mr. Stern - But you didn't observe it?

Mr. Sorrels - I did not observe that; no.

Mr. Stern - Did you hear him mention at any time a lawyer from the American Civil Liberties Union?

Mr. Sorrels - Yes. He said if he could not get this man--I wish I could remember his name a very short name, Apt or something like that.

Mr. Stern - A-b-t?

Mr. Sorrels - Yes, A-b-t. Yes--if he couldn't get him, he wanted a lawyer supplied by the Civil Liberties Union.

Mr. Stern - What else occurred at the interview on Saturday that you can remember?

Mr. Sorrels - He was questioned about the rifle, because, at that time, as I recall it, it had been determined that the rifle had been purchased from Kleins in Chicago, and shipped to a person using the name of A. Hidell. And he was questioned by Captain Fritz along those lines. And he denied that the rifle was his. He denied knowing or using the name of A. Hidell, or Alek Hidell.

He was, of course, questioned about his background and he at that time still maintained an arrogant, defiant attitude. The questions were, of course, directed towards getting information. A lot of them he would not answer. And a lot of the answers, of course, were apparent falsehoods.

And he gave me the impression of lying to Captain Fritz, and deliberately doing so, maybe with an attempt to get Captain Fritz to become angered, because he, Oswald, would flare up in an angry manner from time to time.

Mr. Stern - But you think that was acting--not genuine?

Mr. Sorrels - That is the impression I got, that he was just deliberately doing that, possibly to agitate Captain Fritz and maybe get him to become angry, and maybe do or say something that he shouldn't do. That is just the impression I gained from him. And the reason--I guess one reason I gained that impression is because on the last interview, on Sunday morning, Oswald seemed to have taken a little bit different attitude. In other words, he was talking a little bit freer--he wasn't giving out any information of any value particularly, but he wasn't flaring up like he did before.

The Hidell ID

Towards the end of that fourth interrogation, the Hidell name is mentioned for the very first time on record. So where is the evidence for the Hidell ID on the day before?

Oswald was arrested at about 13:50 and is searched while inside the car transporting him to City Hall, where they arrive at around 14:00. During that journey, they radio the DPD dispatch starting at 13:51. A full transcript is on pages 107-110 (3495).

Let's have a closer look at these five lawmen and their statements and interviews during that weekend and thereafter. Paul Bentley, the DPD detective who sprains his ankle during the scuffle to arrest Oswald inside the Texas Theatre speaks to gathered press in the third-floor corridor (3496). There is no mention of any Hidell ID.

On the 23rd Bentley is interviewed on WFAA TV (3497) and asked about the identification cards he pulled from Oswald's wallet while they were on their way to City Hall. At 08:39 Paul Bentley explains this in detail. Is there any mention of the Hidell ID? No; as a matter of fact, there is not.

On December 3rd 1963 Paul Bentley wrote up his report (3498), rather late if I may add, but even then there is no mention at all of a Hidell ID. And that makes it even stranger since the Hidell ID has already, by then, been in play.

Bob Carroll, -- *and I am starting to repeat myself here* -- not a whiff of any Hidell ID in his December 3rd 1963 statement (3499) pages 41 & 42. Carroll is also known for allegedly taking the gun from Oswald and handing it over to Gerald Hill. He also drove the car that took Oswald and the others to City Hall (3500).

Then during Bob Carroll's WC testimony (3501), the Hidell name is not uttered, but he does manage to come up with something that no other policeman in that car managed to do:

Mr. Belin. Was he ever asked his name?
Mr. CARROLL. Yes, sir; he was asked his name.
Mr. Belin. Did he give his name?
Mr. CARROLL. He gave, the best I recall, I wasn't able to look closely, but the best I recall, he gave two names, I think. I don't recall what the other one was.
Mr. Belin. Did he give two names? Or did someone in the car read from the identification?
Mr. CARROLL. Someone in the car may have read from the identification. I know two names, the best I recall, were mentioned.

Another one of the arresting DPD officers was Sergeant Gerald Hill (3502). He spoke to the press shortly after arriving at City Hall, just as Paul Bentley did, and supplied incriminating details; yet not once did he mention the name Hidell. Perhaps Gerald Hill could have forgotten to mention this during that interview, but when he is interviewed for a second time, as mentioned In the supplementary volumes of the WR, Hill states to the newsmen, *"The only way we found out what his name was, was to remove his billfold and check it ourselves; he wouldn't even tell us what his name was." Later in the interview a reporter asks, "What was the name on the billfold?"* Hill replies, *"Lee H. Oswald, O-S-W-A-L-D."* Once again, no mention at all of the name Hidell. In another filmed interview (3503) at 02:55, Hill makes no mention of the billfold at all. This video is rather poorly edited and looks incomplete.

Four months later, Gerald Hill was interviewed by the WC (3504), and, by a miracle, the Hidell ID appears:

Mr. Belin. Now after, from the time you started in motion until the time you called in, do you remember anyone saying anything at all in the car?
Mr. HILL The suspect was asked what his name was.
Mr. Belin. What did he say?
Mr. HILL. He never did answer. He just sat there.
Mr. Belin. Was he asked where he lived?
Mr. HILL. That was the second question that was asked the suspect, and he didn't answer it, either.
About the time I got through with the radio transmission, I asked Paul Bentley, *"Why don't you see if he has any identification."*
Paul was sitting sort of sideways in the seat, and with his right hand he reached down and felt of the suspect's left hip pocket and said, *"Yes, he has a billfold,"* and took it out.

I never did have the billfold in my possession, but the name Lee Oswald was called out by Bentley from the back seat, and said this identification, I believe, was on the library card.

And he also made the statement that there was some more identification on this other name which I don't remember, but it was the same name that later came in the paper that he bought the gun under.

Mr. Belin. Would the name Hidell mean anything? Alek Hidell?

Mr. HILL. That would be similar. I couldn't say specifically that is what it was, because this was a conversation and I never did see it written down, but that sounds like the name that I heard.

Mr. Belin. Was this the first time you learned of the name?

Mr. HILL. Yes; it was.

He repeats this years later in an interview with George O'Toole in his book *The Assassination Tapes* (3505), page 157: *"As I say, in the car on the way downtown he was belligerent, he was surly, he wouldn't tell us who he was. We took his billfold out of his pocket, we found the ID in both names, Oswald and Hidell, that he later was proved to have ordered the gun under. He had library cards and draft cards in one name, and he had identification cards from various organizations in the other name."*

That is not what the evidence pointed to.

Gus Rose and Richard Stovall question him for about 10-15 minutes after which Will Fritz arrives and sends them to go to Irving and takes over. In the joint report by Richard Stovall, Gus Rose and John Adamcik (3506), there is only the briefest mention of this 'interrogation.' Not a word in that statement about an ID with the name Hidell. You'd think something like that would be reported, no?

Months later on April 8th 1964 Richard Stovall's WC testimony (3507) mentions the following before he was sent out by Fritz:

Mr. Ball. Do you remember what was said to him and what he said to you?

Mr. Stovall. I don't recall exactly--I went in and asked him for his identification, asked him who he was and he said his name was Lee Oswald, as well as I remember. Rose and I were both in there at the time. He had his billfold and in it he had the identification of *"A. Hidell,"* which was on a Selective Service card, as well as I remember.

Mr. Ball. That's [spelling] H-i-d-e-l-l, isn't it?

Mr. Stovall. I'm not positive on that--I believe it was [spelling] H-i-d-e-l-l, I'm not sure. And he also had identification of Lee Harvey Oswald, and I believe that was on a Social Security card, and at that time Captain Fritz opened the door to the office there and sent Rose and I to go out to this address in Irving at 2515 West Fifth Street in Irving.

[Later during the same testimony...]

Mr. Ball. Now, did you do anything else on this investigation?
Mr. Stovall. No, sir; that's all I can recall that I did on the investigation. I might add, there was--well, you have that on the list--some property.
Mr. Ball. What is that?
Mr. Stovall. When we took this identification off of Lee Oswald that had this Selective Service card, the name Hidell, and he also had his own identification--at the time we were in the garage we found some negatives out there that appeared that he had made a snapshot of a Selective Service card, and on the back of the negatives it was where the name would have been typed in--there was some stuff on the back of the negatives to block out the name when it was reprinted, and there were some Selective Service cards that he had printed himself out there from a negative that were blank and which appeared to be the same that he had on him at the time, on the 22nd of November, that had the name of *"A Hidell"* typed in on it.

Gus Rose, who submitted his findings in the same report (3508) mentioned just above with Richard Stovall and John Adamcik. These three also released a supplemental report (3509) and even then not a peep on any negatives or the Hidell ID. The handwritten report by Gus Rose (3510). I assume it was him since it is the first name of the three at the bottom of this document and it does not help either.

Gus Rose's WC testimony (3511) states:

Mr. Rose. There were some people in the office from the Book Depository and we talked to a few of them and then in just a few minutes they brought in Lee Oswald and I talked to him for a few minutes?
Mr. Ball. What did you say to him or did he say to you?
Mr. Rose. Well, the first thing I asked him was what his name was and he told me it was Hidell.
Mr. Ball. Did he tell you it was Hidell?
Mr. Rose. Yes; he did.
Mr. Ball. He didn't tell you it was Oswald?
Mr. Rose. No; he didn't, not right then--he did later. In a minute--I found two cards--I found a card that said, *"A. Hidell."* And I found another card that said, *"Lee Oswald"* on it, and I asked him which of the two was his correct name. He wouldn't tell me at the time, he just said, *"You find*

out." And then in just a few minutes Captain Fritz came in and he told me to get two men and go to Irving and search his house.

Mr. Ball. Now, when he first came in there--you said that he said his name was *"Hidell"*?

Mr. Rose. Yes.

Mr. Ball. Was that before you saw the two cards?

Mr. Rose. Yes; it was.

Mr. Ball. Did he give you his first name?

Mr. Rose. He just said *"Hidell"*; I remember he just gave me the last name of "Hidell".

Mr. Ball. And then you found two or three cards on him?

Mr. Rose. Yes; we did.

Mr. Ball. Did you search him?

Mr. Rose. He had already been searched and someone had his billfold. I don't know whether it was the patrolman who brought him in that had it or not.

Mr. Ball. And the contents of the billfold supposedly were before you?

Mr. Rose. Yes.

From their statements to the WC about this short interview session with Lee Oswald on the 22nd it becomes apparent that Rose and Stovall, despite the fact that they had been in the same room, contradict each other about Lee Harvey Oswald telling them what his name was. They mention the Selective Service card found on Oswald only during their WC testimonies, four months *after* the assassination.

In 1998, in an article from D Magazine, Gus Rose (3512) mentions the card again: *On the table lay the two identification cards. Rose looked down at them. One read, "Alec Hidel." The other: "Lee Oswald."*

If that were the case, it should have been easy to spot for the people involved in the interrogation of Lee Harvey Oswald, no?

Gus Rose and Richard Stovall could have mentioned the Hidell ID to Fritz, but they did not share it with him. Fritz does not mention anything about the ID during this first interrogation. James P Hosty (3513) and James W Bookhout (3514) join Fritz at about 15:15. Within that timespan the Hidell ID is not brought up by either FBI agent at any time during this first interrogation. It is not found in Fritz's interrogation notes nor his subsequent undated typed report, nor is it in Hosty's handwritten interrogation notes, nor in the typed joint Bookhout-Hosty FBI report.

During James Bookhout's WC testimony (3515) the Hidell name gets brief mentions, but only in the vaguest terms:

Mr. Stern - What sort of question would he refuse to answer? Was there any pattern to his refusing?

Mr. Bookhout - Well, now, I am not certain whether this would apply then to this particular interview, the first interview or not, in answering this, but I recall specifically one of the interviews asking him about the Selective Service card which he had in the name of Hidell, and he admitted that he was carrying the card, but that he would not admit that he wrote the signature of Hidell on the card, and at that point stated that he refused to discuss the matter further. I think generally you might say anytime that you asked a question that would be pertinent to the investigation, which would be the type of question he would refuse to discuss.

[And later during the same testimony when they do discuss the first interrogation of the 23rd]

Mr. Stern - Did you ask any questions in the course of this interview?
Mr. Bookhout - Yes.
Mr. Stern - What were they, and what were the responses, if you recall?
Mr. Bookhout - One specific question was with regard to the Selective Service card in the possession of Oswald bearing a photograph of Oswald and the name Alek James Hidell. Oswald admitted he carried this Selective Service card, but declined to state that he wrote the signature of Alek J. Hidell appearing on same. Further declined to state the purpose of carrying same, and---or any use he made of same.

That is nothing short of remarkable since none of this is reflected in his reports made about that first interrogation.

Robert E Jones of the 112th INTC contacts the DOJ at 15:15 (3516) while Oswald is being interrogated by Will Fritz. In this document Oswald is already marked as the guilty man for the Tippit murder. Jones provides plenty of information on Lee Harvey Oswald and his previous endeavours in Russia and New Orleans, the majority coming from newspaper clippings. The timing and the sharing of this is most interesting when Oswald is still being interrogated and Hosty and Bookhout have only just walked in. But the hammer, of course, is that Jones already knows that Oswald was carrying a Selective Service card bearing the name of AJ Hidell. This is quite remarkable as well when not one of the arresting officers attested to having found this card that day. Not until months later!

A report by the Secret Service on December 5th 1963 (3517) clarifies that *"Ana J Hidell"* is a typo.

The HSCA investigated and interviewed Jones on three occasions over the period of a year. The first time was on April 4th 1977 (3518). The next document is Robert Jones' HSCA interview from April 20th 1978 (3519). This session is filled with some good details. In a nutshell: Jones got his information from someone inside the DPD at about 13:30-14:00 and that is quite interesting since no DPD officer was on record about the Hidell ID or name at that time.

Forrest Sorrells (3520) got about ten minutes to talk to Oswald before he was taken down for his first line-up with Helen Markham at 16:05. Not a word about Hidell.

Then at 16:25 the San Antonio office of the FBI sent a report (3521) to its director and to the Dallas office. Again, Oswald is declared the guilty man for murdering Tippit, which is remarkable since the timing of the cable is ten minutes before Oswald's first line-up with the hysterical Helen Markham.

Jim Hosty takes notes of the *so-called* Oswald evidence which has been laid out on a table after the first interrogation has ended at 16:00. In *Assignment Oswald* (3522), Hosty states "*I decided nonetheless that I would remain at the police station. Just because I couldn't talk to the police didn't mean I couldn't learn things from them. I headed back to Fritz's office, where I knew the police were keeping Oswald's personal belongings. Nothing there, but in the second inner office, which belonged to Lieutenant Walter Potts, I spotted Oswald's things, which had been removed from his person and from his apartment at the Oak Cliff rooming house.*" Hosty then describes Oswald's address book and the entry of his name in it. Was there anything about Hidell? No! You'd think that if there was a Selective Service Card with that name amongst the evidence Will Fritz and James Bookhout would have mentioned this in the following interrogartion on the 22nd and not at the end of the morning the next day.

Here is the Church Committee testimony that Hosty gave on December 13th 1975 (3523). On page 138 he mentions the same as above; that he had walked into the adjoining office and went through the evidence. And again, the attention moves immediately towards the address book: No mention of the Hidell ID. It is reasonable to suppose that Hosty would have mentioned that if there was one.

Manning Clements (3524) arrived at about 19:30, saw James Bookhout (3525), and asked him if anyone has, to his knowledge, taken a detailed physical description and background information from Lee Harvey Oswald. Bookhout tells him that such description and background data had not been obtained, and suggests that Clements do it. In his WC testimony (3526) Clements says that he questioned Oswald at about 10 PM, but this is wrong. Thanks to a report by MG Hall (3527), who is very precise with his time recordings. He makes mention of Clements' arrival at 19:40. Which is very close to the *"I'm just a patsy"* scene in the corridor. Clements talks with Oswald over a period of just about half an hour, and his questioning of the suspect gets interrupted during which time Oswald is taken out for a line-up, which would be the one with the Davis Sisters. While Oswald is gone, Clements has a look at the evidence and he, allegedly, sees the Selective Service card with the Alek James Hidell name on it. In his report made the next day on the 23rd (3528), he becomes the first person to make an official mention of seeing, the day before, the Hidell Selective Service card. He makes no further references to any of the other items taken from Oswald's wallet. What boggles the mind even more is that he makes no mention of this 'fact' to James Bookhout or Will Fritz who start their third interrogation at 19:55!

This FBI report (3529), from its director, is from 22:21 on the 22nd of November and it deals predominately with the Hidell link to the FPCC.

Don Stringfellow of the DPD Crime Intelligence Division sends a cable (3530) to the 112th INTC that Oswald is a card carrying communist. Robert E Jones of the 112th INTC shares his thoughts about this during an HSCA interview on December 28th 1978 (3531).

On November 23rd, near the end of the first interrogation just before 11:30, Will Fritz mentions in his notes (3532) that FBI agent James Bookhout asks him about the Hidell ID. This handwritten note is the first trace of anyone of the DPD asking Oswald about this. James Bookhout (3533) and Thomas J Kelley (3534) confirm this at the end of their reports. This took place *after* the mail-order for the rifle has been discovered in Chicago earlier that morning.

On the morning of the, 24th Harry Dean Holmes has joined Will Fritz, Jim Leavelle and Forrest Sorrels for a last interrogation before Oswald is to be transported to the Dallas Jail. Holmes authors a report in which he stated that Fritz asked Oswald about the Hidell ID card, and Oswald *"flared up and stated 'I've told you all I'm going to about that card. You took notes, just read them for yourself, if you want to refresh your memory.'"* Oswald could have been referring to anyone in that room.

Harry Dean Holmes' WC testimony (3535):

Mr. Holmes. In his billfold the police had found a draft registration card in the name of A. J. Hidell on his person at the time of his arrest, and I had seen it.

[And later, during the same testimony...]

"Well, who is A J Hidell?" I asked him.
And he said, *"I don't know any such person."*
I showed him the box rental application for the Post Office box in New Orleans and I read from it. I said, *"Here, this shows as being able to receive, being entitled to receive mail is Marina Oswald."* And he said, *"Well, that is my wife, so what?"*
And I said also it says *"A J Hidell."*
"Well, I don't know anything about that."
That is all he would say about it.
Then Captain Fritz interrupted and said, *"Well, what about this card we got out of your billfold? This draft registration card,"* he called it, *"where it showed A. J. Hidell."*
Well, that is the only time that I recall he kind of flared up and he said, *"Now, I have told you all I am going to tell you about that card in my billfold."* He said, *"You have the card yourself, and you know as much about it as I do."* And he showed a little anger. Really the only time that he flared up.

The last part of Holmes' testimony clearly points out Oswald's denial of carrying the Hidel ID. Walter E Potts' report (3536) states that he had gone to the Beckley address on the 22nd and claims that they checked for the Oswald and Hidell names and then finds out that Oswald was registered under the name O. H. Lee. The issue with this report is that it is made after the 25th.

There is no report from the DPD dated the 22nd of November that points to the Hidell name and ID at all. No one from that group interviewed by the press makes any mention of this either. The first real evidence that Oswald was asked about the Hidell name is at the end of the first interrogation, close to 11:30 on November 23rd 1963. This is confirmed by reports of Will Fritz, James W Bookhout and Thomas J Kelley. Shortly before, in Chicago, an order for the alleged murder weapon, a Mannlicher-Carcano in the name of Alek J Hidell is found and reported to the FBI.

On November 23rd 1963 Richard Sims of the DPD (3537) submits the wallet contents to the Identification Bureau and requests four copies of photographs of each item. The description of them is very generic.

On November 29th 1963 the FBI (3538) creates a report on the wallet contents sent from the DPD to the FBI. Is there a mention of the Hidell Selective Service card? No there is not. On top of that, according the Feds, it appears the DPD had failed to photograph this content and requests the FBI to do so.

In a document dated December 19th 1963 (3539) the FBI states that it had received Oswald's wallet and that it did *not* contain the US Marines Certificate of Service and the Selective Service Card in the name of Hidell; and that these were subsequently sent as such at a later date; and that the SSC was a complete forgery.

This FBI document from November 23rd 1963 (3540) is also not online anywhere else. I have highlighted the Hidell related matters. This document provides a good insight that the Hidell name and rifle order came not in play until Saturday morning the 23rd.

Then there is the alleged sighting of a Hidell ID in a wallet at the Tippit murder scene.

William Westbrook's report from December 3rd 1963 (3541) makes no mention of the find of a wallet near that scene. Then, during Westbrook's WC testimony (3542) again there is not a word about a wallet let alone any mention of Oswald and Hidell IDs at all! Westbrook's HSCA report in 1978 (3543) makes not one mention of that find either.

Robert Barrett of the FBI in his November 22nd statement (3543) does not make a mention of a wallet or a Hidell ID.

In this book excerpt (3544) on page 4, Barrett is quoted when Westbrook, *"looked up and saw me and called me over. He had this wallet in his hand. Now I don't know where he found it, but he had the wallet in his hand. I presumed they had found it on or near Tippit. Westbrook asked 'Do you know who Lee Harvey Oswald is?' and 'Do you know Alek Hidell is?'"*

11:30 Oswald Wants John Abt to Represent Him

After the first interrogation that day Oswald is being transferred back from room 317 to the jail elevator. While Oswald is being moved towards the jail elevator. He manages to stop for a couple of seconds and speak into Bob Clark's microphone. Neither Oswald nor Clark know that the microphone is dead and does not record Oswald's request.

In this video starting at 5:25 (3545) you can see the above mentioned occur, and you see that someone else is moving a microphone into the frame, but by that time Oswald has already been pulled towards the jail elevator and is moved on his way back to his cell.

In 2003, Bob Clark is part of a 40th Kennedy Assassination Anniversary panel as he talks about that moment in this PBS video (3546) at 46:00. Oswald spoke into Clark's dead microphone "*I want to contact Mr. Abt of New York City, to serve as my attorney.*"

This is not the first time Oswald voiced his request to speak to Abt. He had already done so during his first interrogation according to the interrogation reports by Will Fritz, James Hosty and Thomas Kelley.

This then begs the question as to how Oswald found out about Abt. He asked for someone to come forward at 00:30 that same morning during that ultra-short press conference. He did not get interrogated until after that at 10:30, so who planted the idea in his head? One can only speculate.

12:30 Harold McDervid Offers Counsel to Oswald

Harold E McDervid (3547), a lawyer from Chicago, offered his services by sending a telegram on November 23rd. That was after trying to call the DPD first.
In a report by FBI agent Richard Harrison from November 23rd (3548) he refers to Will Fritz who was making excuses for not passing McDervid's message to Oswald. This may have been a deliberate strategy, a clever way of trying to blend things together and makes it sound that it was Oswald who put up the barriers with respect to who was going to represent him. That could explain why no lawyer showed up initially.
Because Oswald had not requested McDervid's services, but Abt's only, this telegram was not forwarded to him. But the telegram was sent at 12:29 CST on the 23rd. This FBI statement was made up in the evening of the 23rd, a few hours after H Louis Nichols had a chat with Oswald at about 18:00 hrs, and Oswald that morning had already mentioned Abt. Fritz did his best to keep *any legal assistance* away from Oswald. This we know since he did not offer any on the 22nd while Oswald was asking for legal representation in the corridor on the first day and for, "*someone to come forward*" at the press conference very early on the 23rd!

12:35 Fifth Interrogation

Present:
DPD: Will Fritz, BL Senkel and FM Turner
FBI: James Bookhout
Secret Service: Thomas Kelley.
There is only a report of this interrogation available from Thomas Kelley (3549). Neither Fritz nor Bookhout made separate reports and, from the looks of it, blended both interrogations into one report or set of notes. This report states that the DPD tried to ascertain Oswald's places of residence and resulting in the DPD obtaining a search warrant to enter Ruth Paine's residence again and find the backyard photos. Oswald would be interrogated about these during this next session.

13:00 Marina and Marguerite Oswald Visit Lee

This visit lasts approximately twenty minutes (3550). MG Hall issues the two ladies a visitors pass per the instructions of Will Fritz. Jailer JR Stacey (3551) confirms this.
From Marina Oswald's WC testimony (3552):

Mr. Rankin. When you saw your husband on November 23d, at the police station, did you ask him if he had killed President Kennedy?
Mrs. Oswald. No.
Mr. Rankin. Did you ask him at that time if he had killed Officer Tippit?
Mrs. Oswald. No. I said. *"I don't believe that you did that, and everything will turn out well."* After all, I couldn't accuse him--after all, he was my husband.
Mr. Rankin. And what did he say to that?
Mrs. Oswald. He said that I should not worry, that everything would turn out well. But I could see by his eyes that he was guilty. Rather, he tried to appear to be brave. However, by his eyes I could tell that he was afraid. This was just a feeling. It is hard to describe.
Mr. Rankin. Would you help us a little bit by telling us what you saw in his eyes that caused you to think that?
Mrs. Oswald. He said goodbye to me with his eyes. I knew that. He said that everything would turn out well, but he did not believe it himself.
Mr. Rankin. How could you tell that?
Mrs. Oswald. I saw it in his eyes.
Mr. Rankin. Did your husband ever at any time say to you that he was responsible or had anything to do with the killing of President Kennedy?
Mrs. Oswald. After Kennedy--I only saw him once, and he didn't tell me anything, and I didn't see him again.

Mr. Rankin. And did he at any time tell you that he had anything to with the shooting of Officer Tippit?

Mrs. Oswald. No.

Mr. Rankin. Did you ever ask your husband why he ran away or tried to escape after the assassination?

Mrs. Oswald. I didn't ask him about that.

13:40 Oswald Has Lunch and Calls New York

He consumes dried beans, mixed vegetables, coffee and bread. Relayed by Captain Glenn D King to Holland McCombs on November 26th (3553).

Oswald makes a phone call to New York as per the statements from Buel T Beddingfield (3554) and Arthur E Eaves (3555). The timing of this call is almost 24 hours after his arrest.

14:15 Oswald's Line-up with W Whaley and W Scoggins

Line-up notes, William Whaley and William Scoggins, by Jim Leavelle (3556).

Oswald is 'sharing' this line-up with two teenagers and a Mexican, all prisoners.

- John Thurman Horne, on remand for motoring offences. He was 18 years old.
- David Edmond Knapp, another prisoner, on remand on suspicion of burglary and theft. Also 18 years of age.
- Daniel Gutierrez Lujan, another prisoner, arrested on 21st November on suspicion of narcotics offences. He was 26 years old, 5'8", 170 pounds and had black hair, brown eyes and an olive complexion. He confirmed that he was of Mexican descent. This man was an inch shorter than Oswald but nearly 40 pounds heavier!

Detective Charles Dhority escorted Oswald on his way down to this particular line-up.

From his WC testimony (3557):

Mr. Ball. Now, on the next day, November 23, you took part in a showup, didn't you?

Mr. Dhority. I didn't take part in the one on the cab driver there.

346

Mr. Ball. Were you present?

Mr. Dhority. I was present--what it was--they wanted me to take the cab drivers--me and Brown, to take the cab driver back down to the station, and I believe we walked into the showup room while there was a showup--the showup had just started or was going on and we walked in there and Mr. Alexander from the district attorney's office was also there.

Mr. Ball. Did you talk to Whaley?

Mr. Dhority. No; I did not.

Mr. Ball. Was there a cab driver there named Scoggins [spelling] S-c-o-g-g-i-n-s also?

Mr. Dhority. I believe there was--there was two cab drivers there and I know Mr. Alexander, down at the district attorney's office, told us they identified him.

Mr. Ball. Did Whaley ever tell you he identified him?

Mr. Dhority. No, sir.

Mr. Ball. Did you take an affidavit from Whaley?

Mr. Dhority. No, sir.

Oswald is seen protesting against the unfair line-up while wearing his dirty white T-shirt (3558). Detective CW Brown is on the right.

And this video (3559), from the same instance, shows Oswald closer but fuzzier and from a different camera angle. He can be clearly heard saying: *"I've been photographed in a t-shirt and now they are taking me in front of a line-up along these men and that way I will be picked out. Right?"* To which a detective in the background replies: *"That's right."*

Walter Eugene Potts was present at that line-up and he testified to the following during his WC testimony (3560):

Mr. POTTS. Well, he was complaining all during the show up. He had on a t-shirt and the rest of them didn't have on T-shirts, and he was complaining, *"Well, everybody's got on a shirt,"* and everything, and rest of them didn't have on T-shirts, and he was complaining, *"Well, everybody's got on a shirt and everything, and I've got a T-shirt on"*- he was very belligerent about the show up. He wouldn't cooperate in any way. He was just making all kinds of commotion out there and he was doing more of the talking than anybody.

Mr. Ball. What kind of commotion was he making?

Mr. POTTS. Well, he was doing a lot of talking about him being in a T-shirt, and *"nobody else has got on a T-shirt and I've got on a T-shirt, this is unfair,"* and all that-just generally talking and after the showup was over, we just accompanied them back from the stage out to the

347

anteroom door and just walked along with them and the elevator-took them on the elevator, and that's all we had to do with the show.

And Jim Leavelle confirms it during his WC testimony (3561):

Mr. Ball. How were these men dressed?
Mr. Leavelle. That I do not recall either.
Mr. Ball. Do you remember whether they had coats on?
Mr. Leavelle. I know in all cases we usually try to have them dressed as alike as possible, the same as each other.
Mr. Ball. What is your memory of this incident? Were they dressed anywhere near similar?
Mr. Leavelle. In one instance--now, I am not positive which one it was, Oswald was in a T-shirt, having the other shirt removed upstairs where they were going to send it to the FBI laboratory for tests, and the rest of them, I believe, had on shirts. He was the only one that had on a T-shirt and I recall--I am not sure but I think it was the last one where he was raising Cain about being up there with a T-shirt and wouldn't be quiet
Mr. Ball. What did he say?
Mr. Leavelle. He said it wasn't fair, him being showed up in a T-shirt and being photographed in a T-shirt and all that. I don't know what he didn't say; he went on all the time.

William Whaley describes this 'event' in his WC testimony (3562):

Mr. Ball. They brought you down to the Dallas police station?
Mr. Whaley. Yes, sir.
Mr. Ball. What did you do there?
Mr. Whaley. Well, I tried to get by the reporters, stepping over television cables and you couldn't hardly get by, they would grab you and wanted to know what you were doing down here, even with the detectives one in front and one behind you. Then they took me in an office there and I think Bill Alexander, the Assistant District Attorney, two or three, I was introduced to two or three who were FBI men and they wanted my deposition of what happened. So, I told them to the best of my ability. Then they took me down in their room where they have their show-ups, and all, and me and this other taxi driver who was with me, sir, we sat in the room awhile and directly they brought in six men, young teenagers, and they all were handcuffed together. Well, they wanted me to pick out my passenger. At that time he had on a pair of black pants and white T-shirt, that is all he had on. But you could have picked him out without identifying him by just listening to him because he was bawling out the policeman, telling them it wasn't right to put him in

348

line with these teenagers and all of that and they asked me which one and I told them. It was him all right, the same man.

Mr. Ball. They had him in line with men much younger?

Mr. Whaley. With five others.

Mr. Ball. Men much younger?

Mr. Whaley. Not much younger, but just young kids they might have got them in jail.

Mr. Ball. Did he look older than those other boys?

Mr. Whaley. Yes.

Mr. Ball. And he was talking, was he?

Mr. Whaley. He showed no respect for the policemen, he told them what he thought about them. They knew what they were doing and they were trying to railroad him and he wanted his lawyer.

Mr. Ball. Did that aid you in the identification of the man?

Mr. Whaley. No, sir; it wouldn't have at all, except that I said anybody who wasn't sure could have picked out the right one just for that. It didn't aid me because I knew he was the right one as soon as I saw him.

A CBS cameraman captured Scoggins in the far distance, inside City Hall (3563).

Both Scoggins and Whaley admitted they had seen Oswald's face in the morning paper. Yet Scoggins tells the FBI on November 25th (3564) that he looked at a photograph of Lee Harvey Oswald on the 22nd, he could not be sure he was identical with the person he had seen in Oak Cliff.

Whaley made some monumental mistakes, one of them being identifying the killer as the wrong man. He pointed out the No. 2 man in that line-up, whereas Oswald was in the No. 3 position. Whaley needed to correct himself during his WC testimony. He also admitted signing a statement *before* he was taken to the line-up and again had to correct himself as to saying he had the statement written down before he went down for the line-up and then have it signed.

There are two handwritten statements by Whaley. The first one (3565), written by detective LD Montgomery (who was Marvin Johnson's partner), and in this version the ID of the No. 3 man is missing and so is the story of the elderly lady. The second one (3566), written by Whaley, contains the ID of the No. 3 man, who in that line-up was Oswald.

Whaley did not read the statement before signing it, as indicated in his WC testimony. His testimony concerning what Oswald was wearing is enough to disqualify him as a reliable witness.

Read Whaley's first WC testimony (3567) and see for yourself what a complete mess this is and that Whaley did not pick out Oswald at all and that he was told what to do when it came to his signature on 'his statement':

Mr. Ball. Later that day did you--were you called down to the police department?
Mr. Whaley. No, sir.
Mr. Ball. Were you the next day?
Mr. Whaley. No, sir; they came and got me, sir, the next day after I told my superior when I saw in the paper his picture, I told my superiors that that had been my passenger that day at noon. They called up the police and they came up and got me.
Mr. Ball. When you saw in the newspaper the picture of the man?
Mr. Whaley. Yes, sir.
Mr. Ball. You went to your superior and told him you thought he was your passenger?
Mr. Whaley. Yes, sir.
Mr. Ball. Did the Dallas police come out to see you?
Mr. Whaley. Yes, sir.
Mr. Ball. Or FBI agents?
Mr. Whaley. The Dallas police came down and took me down and the FBI was waiting there.
Mr. Ball. Before they brought you down, did they show you a picture?
Mr. Whaley. No, sir.
Mr. Ball. They didn't?
Mr. Whaley. No, sir.
Mr. Ball. They brought you down to the Dallas police station?
Mr. Whaley. Yes, sir.
Mr. Ball. What did you do there?
Mr. Whaley. Well, I tried to get by the reporters, stepping over television cables and you couldn't hardly get by, they would grab you and wanted to know what you were doing down here, even with the detectives one in front and one behind you. Then they took me in an office there and I think Bill Alexander, the Assistant District Attorney, two or three, I was introduced to two or three who were FBI men and they wanted my deposition of what happened.

So, I told them to the best of my ability. Then they took me down in their room where they have their show-ups, and all, and me and this other taxi driver who was with me, sir, we sat in the room awhile and directly they brought in six men, young teenagers, and they all were handcuffed together. Well, they wanted me to pick out my passenger.
At that time, he had on a pair of black pants and white T-shirt; that is all he had on. But you could have picked him out without identifying him by just listening to him because he was bawling out the policeman, telling them it wasn't right to put him in line with these teenagers and

350

all of that and they asked me which one and I told them. It was him all right, the same man.

Mr. Ball. They had him in line with men much younger?

Mr. Whaley. With five others.

Mr. Ball. Men much younger?

Mr. Whaley. Not much younger, but just young kids they might have got them in jail.

Mr. Ball. Did he look older than those other boys?

Mr. Whaley. Yes.

Mr. Ball. And he was talking, was he?

Mr. Whaley. He showed no respect for the policemen, he told them what he thought about them. They knew what they were doing and they were trying to railroad him and he wanted his lawyer.

Mr. Ball. Did that aid you in the identification of the man?

Mr. Whaley. No, sir; it wouldn't have at all, except that I said anybody who wasn't sure could have picked out the right one just for that. It didn't aid me because I knew he was the right one as soon as I saw him.

Mr. Ball. You don't think that that in any way influenced your identification?

Mr. Whaley. No, sir; it did not. When you drive a taxi, sir, as long as I have, you can almost look at a man, in fact, you have to, to be able to tell whether you can trust or whether you can't trust him, what he is. Now, like you got in my taxicab and I looked you over and you told me just wait for me here and went in the building, well, I will have to know whether I could just say, *"OK, sir."* Or say, *"Will you leave me a $5 bill, sir?"* When you drive a taxi that long you learn to judge people and what I actually thought of the man when he got in was that he was a wino who had been off his bottle for about two days, that is the way he looked, sir, that was my opinion of him.

Mr. Ball. What was there about his appearance that gave you that impression? Hair mussed?

Mr. Whaley. Just the slow way he walked up. He didn't talk. He wasn't in any hurry. He wasn't nervous or anything.

Mr. Ball. He didn't run?

Mr. Whaley. No, sir.

Mr. Ball. Did he look dirty?

Mr. Whaley. He looked like his clothes had been slept in, sir, but he wasn't actually dirty. The T-shirt was a little soiled around the collar but the bottom part of it was white. You have to know those winos, or they will get in and ride with you and there isn't nothing you can do but call the police, the city gets the fine and you get nothing.

Whaley's second WC testimony (3568):

Mr. Ball. Now, in the police line-up now, and this man was talking to the police and telling them he wanted a lawyer, and that they were trying to, you say he said they were trying to, frame him or something of that sort-

Mr. Whaley. Well, the way he talked that they were doing him an injustice by putting him out there dressed different than these other men he was out there with.

Mr. Ball. Now, did anyone, any policeman, who was there, say anything to him?

Mr. Whaley. Yes, sir; Detective Sergeant Leavelle, I believe it was, told him that they had, would get him his lawyers on the phone, that they didn't think they were doing him wrong by putting him out there dressed up.

Representative Ford. Did the man you identified have any reaction when they brought the group out, did he have any reaction that you noticed at the time you identified him?

Mr. Whaley. Only that he was the only one that had the bruise on his head, sir. The only one who acted surly. In other words, I told this Commission this morning you wouldn't have had to have known who it was to have picked him out by the way he acted. But he was the man that I carried in my taxicab. I told them when I identified him. I didn't identify him as the man who shot the President. I identified him as the man who rode from the Greyhound to 1500 North Beckley with me.

Representative Ford. Did you point him out with your hand?

Mr. Whaley. No, sir; I did not. They asked me which number he was standing under and he was standing under No. 2.

Representative Ford. Could he hear you make this identification?

Mr. Whaley. No, sir; he couldn't see me.

Representative Ford. He couldn't see you?

Mr. Whaley. No, sir; they had the black silk screen that keeps the prisoners from seeing the people who show up.

Whaley's third WC testimony (3569):

Mr. Belin. Then you went down to the police station to identify this man?

Mr. Whaley. Yes, sir.

Mr. Belin. You saw a line-up?

Mr. Whaley. Yes, sir.

Mr. Belin. Do you remember what number he was in the line-up at all?

Mr. Whaley. There was four of them, sir, and from the right to the left, he was No. 3. [That means No. 2-BK]

Mr. Belin. Starting from the right to the left, from his right or your right.

Mr. Whaley. From your right, sir, which would have been his left. There were numbers above their heads, sir.

Mr. Belin. Mr. Whaley, what number did you say the man was in the line-up?

Mr. Whaley. No. 2.

Mr. Belin. From the right or from your right?

Mr. Whaley. From my left.

Mr. Belin. No. 2?

Mr. Whaley. They brought out four of them and stood them up there, and he was under No. 2. I mentioned he was the third one that come out. There were four and all handcuffed together.

Mr. Belin. Did you sign an affidavit for the Dallas Police Department?

Mr. Whaley. Yes, sir.

Mr. Belin. I will hand you a document which I am calling Whaley Deposition Exhibit A, and ask you to say if your signature appears on there?

Mr. Whaley. Yes, sir; that is my signature.

Mr. Belin. Now I notice in the statement there it says that you travelled Wood Street to Houston Street, turned left and went over the viaduct to Zangs Boulevard. You see that statement there?

Mr. Whaley. Yes.

Mr. Belin. *"Travelled Zangs to Beckley and turned left and travelled on Beckley until I reached the 500 block of North Beckley. When I got in the 500 block of North Beckley, he said this will do and I stopped."*

Now is that what you told them on that day?

Mr. Whaley. Yes, sir; that is what I told them on that day.

Mr. Belin. Well, was that the fact that you drove until you reached the 500 block, or not?

Mr. Whaley. No, sir, I didn't drive until I reached the 500 block. I drove until I reached Beckley and Neely. If you would be in my place when they took me down there, when they had to force their way through the reporters to get me in the office, they wrote that up, and I signed it, because I told them that the man said he wanted to go to the 500 block of North Beckley.

Mr. Belin. All right. Now in here it says, *"The No. 3 man who I now know is Lee Harvey Oswald was the man who I carried from the Greyhound Bus Station"*

Was this the No. 3 or the No. 2 man?

Mr. Whaley. I signed that statement before they carried me down to see the line-up. I signed this statement, and then they carried me down to the line-up at 2:30 in the afternoon.

Mr. Belin. You signed this affidavit before you saw the line-up.

Mr. Whaley. Well, now, let's get this straight. You are getting me confused.

Mr. Belin. Now, I will put it this way. There was an FBI reporter, FBI interviewer with you?

Mr. Whaley. Yes, sir; there was.

Mr. Belin. And there was an interview with the Dallas Police Department?

Mr. Whaley. Yes. And Bill Alexander from the district attorney's office was there, also.

Mr. Belin. All right, now, the last sentence.

Mr. Whaley. Let me tell you how they fixed this up. They had me in the office saying that. They were writing it out on paper, and they wrote it out on paper, and this officer, Leavelle, I think that is his name, before he finished and before I signed he wanted me to go with him to the line-up, so I went to the line-up, and I come back and he asked me which one it was, which number it was, and I identified the man, and we went back up in the office again, and then they had me sign this. That is as near as I can remember.

My recollection for that afternoon in that office was very disturbed because every time they would open the door, some flash camera would flash in your face and everybody coming in and out and asking you questions.

Mr. Belin. You mean reporters?

Mr. Whaley. I made this statement more to Bill Alexander, because I tried to talk to him more. Everybody was trying to talk to me at once.

Mr. Belin. When you saw the statement the first time, did you see the statement before you went down to see the line-up?

Mr. Whaley. No; I didn't see the statement. I don't think I did. I am not for sure.

I think I signed it after I came back. It was on paper. They were writing it up on paper.

Mr. Belin. They were writing?

Mr. Whaley. Before I left there, I signed this typewritten, because they had to get, a stenographer typed it up. I had to wait.

Mr. Belin. But was this before or after you saw the line-up.

Mr. Whaley. After she typed it up. It was after.

Mr. Belin. It was after?

Mr. Whaley. That is when I signed it, after.

Mr. Belin. Now, when you signed it--what I want to know is, before you went down, had they already put on there a statement that the man you saw was the No. 3 man in the line-up?

Mr. Whaley. I don't remember that. I don't remember whether it said three or two, or what.

Mr. Belin. Did they have any statements on there before you went down to the line-up?

Mr. Whaley. I never saw what they had in there. It was all written out by hand. The statement I saw, I think, was this one, and that could be writing. I might not even seen this one yet. I signed my name because they said that is what I said.

Mr. Belin. Well, Mr. Whaley---

Mr. Whaley. I know, sir, but I don't think you can understand what I had to put up with that afternoon.

Mr. Belin. You mean with the press?

Mr. Whaley. Yes, sir; with everything.

And later on, when everyone needs to be re-assured that Whaley picked No. 2 and not No. 3 as the whole thing has become a really bad joke already. Even more so than when the four participants in the line-up entered the area, they entered from left to right, with No. 4 entering first, then No.3, No. 2 and the last being No. 1. So, there could not be any confusion with mixing 2 and 3 up at all.

Mr. Belin. Now when you saw a line-up down at the police station----

Mr. Whaley. He didn't have on the same clothes. He had on a white T-shirt and black pants, and that is all he had on.

Mr. Belin. Do you remember now whether the man that you saw there was the No. 2 or the No. 3 man?

Mr. Whaley. I will admit he was No. 2.

Mr. Belin. No. 2 from your left, or from your right?

Mr. Whaley. He was the third man out in the line of four as they walked out in a line. They put the first man out on the right, and the last one on my left, and as near as I can remember, he was No. 2, but it was the man I hauled.

Mr. Belin. It says here the No. 3.

Mr. Whaley. Well, I am not trying to mix nobody up. I'm giving it to you to the best of my ability.

Mr. Belin. Your memory right now is that it was the No. 2 man?

Mr. Whaley. That is the way it is right now. I don't think it will change again. But on that afternoon, all I saw was the man that I hauled up there, and they asked me which number he was, and I said No. 2. I am almost sure I did, but I couldn't get up to swear to it that I did, sir.

Mr. Belin. Just one more minute, if you would, please? Mr. Whaley, earlier in your testimony here you said that Lee Harvey Oswald was No. 3. Do you remember saying that?

Mr. Whaley. Yes, sir; but I meant that he was the third one out when they walked out with him. I said from my right.

Mr. Belin. From your right he was No. 3?

Mr. Whaley. Yes, sir.

Mr. Belin. What number was over his head?

Mr. Whaley. Well, they--when they walked over the line and they stopped him, No. 2 was over his head, but he was pulling on both of the other men on each side and arguing with this detective, so he didn't stay under any certain number.

He was moving like that.

Mr. Belin. Did you ever see him later on television?

Mr. Whaley. No, sir; I didn't.

Mr. Belin. You never did see his picture in the paper?

Mr. Whaley. I saw his picture in the paper the next morning, sir.

Mr. Belin. That would have been Sunday morning, the 24th?

Mr. Whaley. I guess it was, if you say it was, sir.

Mr. Belin. I don't want to---

Mr. Whaley. I don't want to get you mixed up and get your whole investigation mixed up through my ignorance, but a good defence attorney could take me apart. I get confused. I try to tell you exactly what happened, to the best of my ability, when they brought Oswald out in the line-up of four. He was the third man out. I don't know which way they count them.

Mr. Belin. We don't want you to be concerned about affecting the investigation one way or the other by what you say. What we want you to say is tell us what you know, to the best of your recollection.

Mr. Whaley. That is exactly what I am doing, sir.

Mr. Belin. Let me ask you this. What day of the week did you take this cab passenger, on a Friday or Saturday?

Mr. Whaley. I would have to see my trip sheet.

Mr. Belin. You don't remember?

Mr. Whaley. No, sir.

Mr. Belin. Was it the day of the motorcade?

Mr. Whaley. The day of the President's parade, yes, sir.

Mr. Belin. Now, was it that day that you went down to the police station to see the line-up?

Mr. Whaley. No, sir.

Mr. Belin. Was it the next day?

Mr. Whaley. Yes, sir.

Mr. Belin. The next day you went down to the Dallas Police Station and saw a line-up of how many people?

Mr. Whaley. Four people.

Mr. Belin. These men came out and there were numbers above their heads?

Mr. Whaley. The numbers were stationary. Looked through a black silk screen at them. In other words, they were very dim, the numbers.

Mr. Belin. What did you see as the number over the man that you identified as having been in your cab that day?

Mr. Whaley. No. 2.

Mr. Belin. Did you see a picture of that man in the paper at any time?

Mr. Whaley. Saturday morning, sir; following the event on Friday.

Mr. Belin. You saw his picture in the paper?

Mr. Whaley. Yes, sir.

Mr. Belin. Was that the same man that you identified as No. 2 in the line-up?

Mr. Whaley. Yes, sir.

Mr. Belin. Did you ever see his picture in the paper again?

Mr. Whaley. No, sir; I take that back, sir. I saw the picture in the paper when they had, when Ruby killed him at the time between the two detectives.

Mr. Belin. Was the man in connection with the Ruby matter with the two detectives, did it have his name in the paper as Lee Harvey Oswald? Was his name in the paper then when you saw his picture?

Mr. Whaley. Well, I don't think they had it that way. I think they just had it Oswald. I am not sure what they had under it. I am not for sure, but I did see the picture.

Mr. Belin. Was that the same man you carried in your cab on Friday?

Mr. Whaley. Yes, sir.

Mr. Belin. Was that the man you identified at the police station?

Mr. Whaley. Yes, sir.

Mr. Belin. It is your best recollection, if I understand it, that this was the No. 2 man in the line-up?

Mr. Whaley. That's right, sir. That was from the left now. No. 2 from my left. I was facing him.

Mr. Belin. Right. I mean correct. Now, your affidavit which is Whaley's Deposition Exhibit A, the last sentence says, *"The No. 3 man who I now know as Lee Harvey Oswald was the man who I carried from the Greyhound bus station to the 500 block of North Beckley."* Now you say it was the No. 2 man from your left, is that correct?

Mr. Whaley. From my left. No. 3 from my right.

William Scoggins was another cab driver, who was called in for the very same line-up. He was another witness to the Tippit shooting. He had seen a picture of Oswald in the paper before he went down to City Hall. Scoggins also gave no description in his affidavit, but said he would recognise the assailant if he saw him again. In Scoggins' affidavit (3570) he described the assailant going West before the murder, this would exclude Oswald being the killer as this contradicts Helen Markham who said the assailant was travelling East.

On November 25th Scoggins had his statement taken by the FBI (3571) and I'd like you to look at the final paragraph in the document below. As a witness to Oswald's guilt in the Tippit slaying, it renders this guy utterly useless.

William Scoggins' WC testimony (3572):

Mr. Belin. You say you went down to the police station when, Mr. Scoggins, approximately?

Mr. Scoggins. You mean the time of day it was?

Mr. Belin. Was it the same day of the shooting or the next day?

Mr. Scoggins. No, it was the next day.

Mr. Belin. Morning, afternoon, or evening, if you remember?

Mr. Scoggins. Well, the best I can remember, they called me down from the cab stand, the police came down to the office and picked me up. Well, the other guy--I was close to the downtown area, and it didn't take me long to get there, and I waited quite a while before the other man, he was quite out a ways, and it was before dinner.

Mr. Belin. It was before dinner?

Mr. Scoggins. Yes, whenever they called me in.

Mr. Belin. Would it have been on the afternoon of November 23, to the best of your recollection?

Mr. Scoggins. When they took me down there it was along about dinner time.

Representative Ford. What do you mean by dinner time? In various parts of the country dinner and supper get confused a little bit. Was it the noon meal or the evening meal?

Mr. Scoggins. Yes.

Representative Ford. Yes what? It was the noon meal?

Mr. Scoggins. Yes.

Mr. Belin. They took you down about the time of the noon meal, is that correct; they took you to the police station?

Mr. Scoggins. I would think that would be about the time.

Mr. Belin. Sometime after you got there after the noon meal you saw the line-up, is that correct?

Mr. Scoggins. Yes.

Mr. Belin. How many people were in the line-up, if you can remember?

Mr. Scoggins. Four.

Mr. Belin. Four? Did any one of the people look anything like strike that. Did you identify anyone in the line-up?

Mr. Scoggins. I identified the one we are talking about, Oswald. I identified him.

Mr. Belin. You didn't know his name as Oswald at that time, did you, or did you not?

Mr. Scoggins. Yes, the next day I did. But, of course I didn't know what his name was the day that I picked him out.

Mr. Belin. You saw a man in the line-up?

Mr. Scoggins. Yes.

Mr. Belin. Did anyone tell you any particular man was Oswald in the line-up?

Mr. Scoggins. No.

Mr. Belin. Well, describe what happened in the police station with regard to the line-up, what they did to you, what they said to you, and what you said to them, and so on.

Mr. Scoggins. Well, they had the four men up there in the line-up, and before they brought them in they told us what they wanted us to do, to look them over and be sure we was, in our estimation, we was right on the man, and which one it was, the one that we saw, the one that I saw.

Mr. Belin. Did they tell you one of the men was the man you saw or not, or did they tell you *"See if you can"*--just what did they say? Did they say *"Here is a line-up, see if you-can identify anyone,"* or did they say, *"One of the men in the line-up"*--

Mr. Scoggins. Yes, I believe those are the words they used. I am not--

Mr. Belin. Did all of these men look different to you? Were most of them fat, or were most of them thin, or some fat, some thin, some tall, some short?

Mr. Scoggins. There were two of them--the one that I identified as the one I saw over at Oak Cliff, and there was one I saw similar to him, and the other two was a little bit shorter.

Mr. Dulles. Had you been looking at television or seeing television prior to your appearance here at the line-up?

Mr. Scoggins. No.

Mr. Dulles. You had not?

Mr. Scoggins. No, sir.

Representative Ford. Had you been working this Saturday morning with your cab?

Mr. Scoggins. Yes, sir.

Representative Ford. In other words, you went to work Saturday morning at the regular time?

Mr. Scoggins. Yes.

Representative Ford. And were working when they asked you to come down to the cab stand to go over to the police station?

Mr. Scoggins. Yes, sir.

Representative Ford. All right.

Mr. Belin. Had you seen any pictures of Lee Harvey Oswald in the newspapers prior to the time you went to the police station line-up?

Mr. Scoggins. I think I saw one in the morning paper.

Mr. Belin. Do you subscribe to the morning or evening paper?

Mr. Scoggins. I take the evening paper myself.

Mr. Belin. You went down and bought a morning paper?

Mr. Scoggins. No; I didn't go out. I was looking at one of the--some of the cab drivers had it.

Mr. Belin. Did you see any television picture on the morning of November 23 of Lee Harvey Oswald?

Mr. Scoggins. I have never until this day seen it.

Mr. Belin. On television?

Mr. Scoggins. I never have.

Representative Ford. Do you have a television in your home?

Mr. Scoggins. Yes sir; I do. But I don't--when I get home I will read the paper, and after you work about 12 hours you don't feel like fooling around with television too much.

Mr. Belin. What number man in the line-up did you identify as having seen on November 22?

Mr. Scoggins. Number 3.

Mr. Belin. Did you have the man turn around, or could you--

Mr. Scoggins. Yes, they turned him around.

Mr. Belin. Did they turn just one man around or all of them?

Mr. Scoggins. No; they had them all.

Mr. Belin. Do you remember if the number 3 man in the line-up was wearing the same clothes that the man you saw at the Tippit shooting wore?

Mr. Scoggins. He had on a different shirt, and he didn't have a jacket on. He had on kind of a polo shirt.

Mr. Belin. Before you went to view the line-up, did any of the police officers show you a picture of this man?

Mr. Scoggins. No.

Mr. Belin. Sometime later, after the line-up, did any of the police officers show you with a picture of anyone and ask you if you could identify him?

Mr. Scoggins. Yes.

Mr. Belin. Do you remember if he was an FBI man or a Dallas policeman or a Secret Service agent?

Mr. Scoggins. He was an FBI or a Secret Service.

Mr. Belin. What did he ask you and what did you tell him?

Mr. Scoggins. He gave me some pictures, showed me several pictures there,, which was, some of them were, pretty well resembled him, and some of them didn't, and they looked like they was kind of old pictures, and I think I picked the wrong picture. I am not too--

Mr. Belin. What did he say to you and what did you say to him, if you remember?

Mr. Scoggins. I don't really--I know he showed me his credentials.

Mr. Belin. Did he say to you something like *"These are pictures we have of Lee Harvey Oswald"?* Did he use that name in front of you, or did he say, *"Here are some pictures. See if you can identify them"*--if you remember?

Mr. Scoggins. I don't remember, but after I got through looking at them and everything, and I says, I told them one of these two pictures is him, out of this group he showed me, and the one that was actually him looked like an older man than he was to me. Of course, I am not too much on identifying pictures. It wasn't a full shot of him, you know, and then he told me the other one was Oswald.

360

Representative Ford. Had you narrowed the number of pictures from more than two to two?

Mr. Scoggins. Yes.

Representative Ford. In other words, they showed you pictures of how many people altogether, how many different people, your best estimate?

Mr. Scoggins. I would say 4 or 5.

Representative Ford. And you narrowed the number of 4 or 5 down to 2?

Mr. Scoggins. Down to two; yes.

[Later, during the same testimony...]

Mr. Belin. Those are all the questions I have. Just a second. When you saw a picture in the morning paper of Lee Harvey Oswald, did this look similar to the man you saw at the Tippit shooting, or did it look different?

Mr. Scoggins. I would say similar; yes.

Mr. Belin. Did it look like the same man?

Mr. Scoggins. Yes.

[Later, again during the same testimony...]

(Discussion off the record.)

Mr. Belin. Mr. Scoggins, when you identified the man in the line-up at the police station on November 23rd, was there any other person who at the same time was asked to identify a man in that line-up?

Mr. Scoggins. Yes, one other.

Mr. Belin. Do you know-one other person?

Mr. Scoggins. Yes.

Mr. Belin. Do you know what that man's name is or what his occupation is?

Mr. Scoggins. Yes, he drives a taxicab.

Mr. Belin. Do you know his name?

Mr. Scoggins. Yes; his name is Bill Whaley.

Mr. Belin. Whaley?

Mr. Scoggins. I think it is Whaley. I didn't know him from Adam until that day, you know, and he said his name was Whaley.

Mr. Belin. When you were there and identified a man, had Whaley already identified that man or not? I mean, did you hear Whaley or see Whaley identify that man?

Mr. Scoggins. No. He was sitting over on my left.

Mr. Belin. He was on your left?

Mr. Scoggins. Yes. It was dark. They turned the lights out where we were sitting. We could see the man with lights up there.

361

Mr. Belin. Could you see Mr. Whaley at the time he made the identification?

Mr. Scoggins. Well, I suppose if I would have looked over there I could have seen that there was a man there, that I could have recognized him.

Mr. Belin. Were you looking at Mr. Whaley at the time?

Mr. Scoggins. No.

Mr. Belin. Did you make your identification by your voice or by your hands?

Mr. Scoggins. By my hands, using--I put up three fingers.

Mr. Belin. Did they tell you ahead of time to hold up the number of fingers for the man that you saw?

Mr. Scoggins. Yes, sir.

Mr. Belin. How many fingers did you hold up?

Mr. Scoggins. Three.

Mr. Belin. At the time you held up your three fingers, did you know how many fingers Mr. Whaley was holding up?

Mr. Scoggins. No.

Mr. Belin. Then did you know whether or not Mr. Whaley had identified the man?

Mr. Scoggins. No, I sure don't.

Mr. Belin. Was there any person or were there any persons standing between you and Mr. Whaley?

Mr. Scoggins. That I don't know because I did not look over there.

Mr. Dulles. Could Mr. Whaley, in your opinion, see you holding up these fingers?

Mr. Scoggins. No, no. I made sure of that because I had my hand down like this.

Mr. Belin. When you had your hand down you are putting it in front of your belt?

Mr. Scoggins. As well as I could remember I had it down kind of like this here. I don't know whether I used my right or my left hand, but I didn't hold up three fingers like this, but I held them down just about like this.

Mr. Belin. You are pointing to your right hand and putting it somewhat about a few inches above the buckle of your belt; it that about where you held up your fingers?

Mr. Scoggins. About as well as I could remember.

Mr. Belin. What happened after you held up your fingers, did someone see you holding your fingers up there?

Mr. Scoggins. Yes.

Representative Ford. Where were they standing beside you so that they could see your fingers?

Mr. Scoggins. Well, this gentleman was standing over back a piece to my left, sir.

Representative Ford. Was it close to you, sir?

362

Mr. Scoggins. There was one man on my right. He was Secret Service or FBI, I think FBI; and the other man was a policeman, Dallas policeman.

Mr. Dulles. Do you know whether Mr. Whaley was making his identification at the same time that you did or did he make it before or after?

Mr. Scoggins. No. All I know is that we viewed them at the same time.

Mr. Dulles. He viewed them at the same time?

Mr. Scoggins. Yes.

Mr. Dulles. You don't know at what time Mr. Whaley made his identification?

Mr. Scoggins. Yes.

Mr. Dulles. You didn't see him make the identification?

Mr. Scoggins. I didn't even see him.

Mr. Dulles. You don't know what his identification was?

Mr. Scoggins. No. I never asked him which one or nothing, because I never did discuss it with him at all after that.

14:45 Hair and Nail Samples & Paraffin Casts Delivered

In this DPD report from November 24th (3573) it is stated that Captain Doughty and Detective BG Brown delivered the paraffin casts of Oswald's hands and right cheek to Parkland hospital. In addition, multiple hair and nail samples had been taken and were also delivered. This was provided at FBI Agent Ray Hall's request. There is also a handwritten report (3574) confirming this.

15:30 Robert Oswald Visits Lee

After waiting two hours to be given a pass by MG Hall, as ordered by Captain Fritz, Robert Oswald was allowed to talk for around ten minutes with his brother, Lee.

Robert Oswald's WC testimony (3575):

Mr. Jenner. Now, following that conversation that you do record on that page, did you see your brother?

Mr. Oswald. Yes, sir; I did.

Mr. Jenner. Where?

Mr. Oswald. Dallas police station.

Mr. Jenner. Will you describe the surroundings?

Mr. Oswald. I was taken up on the elevator by a Dallas police officer--Mr. Tom Kelley, inspector from Washington, D.C., U.S. Secret Service joined us, and one agent Mr. Mike Howard. On arrival to the floor where Lee was being held, the police officer passed through a glass slot in the window to another police officer the pass, I believe signed by Captain Fritz, which authorization was for me to see Lee Harvey Oswald. Two or three minutes went by, and I was added that he was now ready to see me, and I was taken to a small room to the left of the elevators on this floor, and no one else was in this room on his side, or my side of the glass partitions that separated the locked side from the unlocked side. And Lee was standing there before me on the other side of the glass.

Mr. Dulles. Did you have the impression that the officers had told your brother that you were the one who was coming to see him?

Mr. Oswald. No, sir; I did not.

Mr. Dulles. Because you just said that the officer said he was ready to see you, and I gained the impression from that----

Mr. Oswald. Yes, sir--whether or not I meant by that that--I do not believe that was my full meaning on that statement because I was not aware that they had actually told Lee that it was me he was about to see.

Mr. Jenner. Did you converse with your brother?

Mr. Oswald. Yes, sir; I did.

Mr. Jenner. By what means?

Mr. Oswald. By telephone, while looking at him through the glass partition.

Mr. Dulles. How far apart were you, roughly?

Mr. Oswald. Just a matter of inches.

Mr. Jenner. How long were you in that room, conversing with your brother?

Mr. Oswald. Approximately 10 minutes.

Mr. Jenner. And as near as you can recall, what did he say to you and what did you say to him?

Mr. Oswald. I do recall to the best of my ability, his first statement to me was, *"How are you?"* My reply was, *"I am fine."* I asked him how he was; I observed the cuts and bruises on his face. He said he was just fine, and that they were treating him okay. I believe his next statement was at this time *"I cannot or would not say anything because the line is apparently tapped."* I did not comment on that, and he rather carried the conversation for 2 or 3 minutes.

Mr. Jenner. Would you repeat it to us as best you can recall it, please?

Mr. Oswald. Sir, I do not recall this particular part of the conversation.

Mr. Jenner. Just do your best.

Mr. Oswald. I am sorry, sir, I just cannot recall that particular part of the conversation. I might comment on that particular part to this extent. That I felt that it was rather a mechanical conversation from his standpoint. He seemed to be speaking very fast, and there was approximately 2 or 3 minutes of him speaking in this nature. Then I took the initiative and-started speaking to him about the family.

364

Mr. Jenner. His family?

Mr. Oswald. About the family, including his family, my family. And also, at this time, when we talked about his family in particular--I believe my question to him was *"What about Marina and the children?"* His reply to me at that time was *"Don't worry about them. The Paines will take care of them"*--that his friends, the Paines, would take care of them satisfactorily.

Mr. Jenner. That Lee's friends, the Paines, would take care of them satisfactorily?

Mr. Oswald. That is correct. My reply to him on that was what he considered to be his friends were not mine.

Mr. Jenner. Did he respond to that?

Mr. Oswald. Not to my recollection, sir.

Mr. Dulles. Were you the first member of the family to see him, or had Marina seen him the day before?

Mr. McKenzie. Both Marina and Marguerite had seen him before.

Mr. Oswald. Earlier that afternoon, sir. I was the last member of the family to see him.

Mr. Jenner. Did you say anything about the new child, Rachel?

Mr. Oswald. Yes, sir; I did.

Mr. Jenner. Did you raise that, or did he?

Mr. Oswald. I believe I did, sir.

Mr. Jenner. What did you say?

Mr. Oswald. I simply stated that I had seen the new baby and was not aware of it at that time.

Mr. Jenner. Not aware that the baby had been born?

Mr. Oswald. That is correct.

Mr. Jenner. Did he respond to that?

Mr. Oswald. Yes, sir, he did.

Mr. Jenner. What did he say?

Mr. Oswald. He smiled and stated he had hoped for a boy rather than a gift. His further comment was, *"Well, you know how that goes."*

Mr. Jenner. He said nothing, I take it, then, by way of apology or otherwise that you had not theretofore been informed of the birth of this child?

Mr. Oswald. That is correct.

Mr. Jenner. You record on page 13 of your memorandum---you use this expression: *"I was not talking to the Lee I knew."* Do you find that?

Mr. Oswald. Yes, sir; I do.

Mr. Jenner. Would you read that full sentence?

Mr. Oswald. *"He talked about the Paines as his friends and that they would take care of Marina and the children."* Excuse me--I started too soon.

Mr. Jenner. That is all right.

Mr. Oswald. *"I stated who he considered to be his friends were not necessarily mine. I did this to try to get through to him. To me his answers were mechanical and I was not talking to the Lee I knew."*

Mr. Jenner. Were you able to get through to him? Did you feel you got through to him?

Mr. Oswald. No, sir; I was not.

Mr. Jenner. And would you elaborate, please, on your expression *"I was not talking to the Lee I knew"?*

Mr. Oswald. I was referring more specifically to the first part of our conversation, where his conversation seemed to me, as previously stated, very mechanical.

Mr. Jenner. You had the feeling he was not exposing himself fully to you?

Mr. Oswald. That is correct.

Mr. Jenner. Was this the last time you ever saw your brother?

Mr. Oswald. Alive, sir?

Mr. Jenner. Yes.

Mr. Oswald. Yes, sir; it was.

Mr. Jenner. On page 14 you record a later conversation after you had left your brother--you have an expression there along the lines that you agreed with someone that if the conversation had been person to person, that things might have been different. Do you find that?

Mr. Oswald. Yes, sir; I do.

Mr. Jenner. Would you please elaborate on what you meant by that?

Mr. Oswald. By *"we"* in that paragraph, sir, on page 14, I am talking about Mr. Tom Kelley, Inspector from Washington, D.C., United States Secret Service, and agent, Mr. Mike Howard. Our discussion was of the nature I related to them as best I could remember my entire conversation with Lee Harvey Oswald on that afternoon of November 23, 1963, and I was of the opinion, or perhaps expressed, either by Mr. Kelley or Mr. Mike Howard, that had we been placed in a room facing each other, perhaps more could have been learned or something could have been learned about whether or not he was actually guilty or how much he was involved in the assassination of the President of the United States.

[Later during his testimony...]

Mr. McKenzie. Now, you have testified this afternoon following our lunch break that you visited Lee Oswald in the Dallas County Jail. Do you recall that testimony--the testimony of just a few minutes ago?

Mr. Oswald. Yes, sir; I do.

Mr. McKenzie. Have you previously testified to that before the Commission, to your recollection?

Mr. Oswald. To my recollection, I believe we at least touched on that during our first session on February 20, 1964.

Mr. McKenzie. When you were in the jail--and I believe it is in the sixth floor of the Dallas County Jail--I mean the Dallas City Jail--talking with your brother, Lee Harvey Oswald, did you ask him at that time if he had committed the crime?

Mr. Oswald. Yes, sir; I had.

Mr. McKenzie. You did ask him that question?

Mr. Oswald. Yes, sir; I did.

Mr. McKenzie. And what did he say?

Mr. Oswald. I put it to him as stated in my diary, sir.

Mr. Jenner. Identify the page, please.

Mr. Oswald. On page 12, *"I do not recall everything he said. I did try to point out to him that the evidence was overwhelming that he did kill Police Officer Tippit and possibly the President. To this he replied do not form any opinion on the so-called evidence.'"*

Mr. Jenner. Is that all he said? He said nothing else?

Mr. Oswald. To that----

Mr. Jenner. In response to you?

Mr. Oswald. That is correct.

Mr. Jenner. At no time when you interviewed him over the telephone while you were in that--the sixth floor--did he affirmatively deny either that he had shot Officer Tippit or that he shot the President?

Mr. Oswald. He did not admit to anything whatsoever.

Mr. Jenner. Nor did he deny it affirmatively--other than the remark that you have recorded in your memorandum?

Mr. Oswald. That is correct, sir.

Mr. McKenzie. In other words, Mr. Oswald, when you were talking there with your brother, in the city jail of Dallas, he did not deny that he had killed Officer Tippit, nor did he deny that he had assassinated President Kennedy?

Mr. Oswald. He did not admit to anything, sir.

Mr. McKenzie. And he didn't deny anything?

Mr. Oswald. That is correct.

Mr. McKenzie. Have you, or haven't you told this Commission that you believed a denial?

Mr. Jenner. Excuse me, Mr. McKenzie, I don't understand that question.

Mr. McKenzie. It says in this article that he told the Commission that he believed the denial. Since there was no denial, there was nothing for you to believe.

Mr. Oswald. That is correct.

Mr. Jenner. Up to this moment he has never testified as to that, to my recollection.

Mr. McKenzie. That is correct. Again, based on the evidence that you have read or heard in newspaper articles, whether it be evidence or not, but based on everything that you have heard or read, you now believe that your brother, Lee Harvey Oswald, did kill Mr. Tippit and assassinated President Kennedy, is that correct?

Mr. Oswald. Purely on the circumstantial evidence that has been brought to my attention or that I have read.

In his book *Portrait of Lee Harvey Oswald by his Brother* (3576) pages 142-145. He recounts pretty much the same of his WC testimony. Except that Lee stated to Robert that he had no idea what they were talking about. And also stated that Lee said *"Don't believe all this so-called evidence"*.

16:00 Oswald Makes another Call

JL Popplewell states in his August 20th 1964 (3577) affidavit that at 16:00 Lt Lord called and instructed to put Oswald on the phone. Oswald asked the operator for two numbers then asked Popplewell for a pencil and paper. He wrote down a telephone number and returned the pencil. At about 20:00 Lt Lord told me to let Oswald use the phone.

The log sheet with Oswald's phone calls is gone. How inconvenient.

James Bookhout wrote a report on Popplewell and Oswald's calls on February 5th 1964 (3578). According to Popplewell, nothing happened without Fritz's approval. Oswald requested jail clothes to be provided for him to wear which they refused and, at that particular time, would not allow him. That seems rather odd as Ruby was provided a jail uniform quite quickly after killing Oswald.

Ruth Paine's WC testimony (3579):

Mrs. Paine - Then about 3:30 or 4 I got a telephone call.
Mr. Jenner - The phone rang?
Mrs. Paine - The phone rang; I answered it.
Mr. Jenner - Did you recognize the voice?
Mrs. Paine - I recognized the voice but I don't recall what he said?
Mr. Jenner - What did the voice say?
Mrs. Paine - The voice said: *"This is Lee."*
Mr. Jenner - Give your best recollection of everything you said and if you can, please, everything he said, and exactly what you said.
Mrs. Paine - I said, *"Well, Hi."* And he said he wanted to ask me to call Mr. John Abt in New York for him after 6 p.m. He gave me a telephone number of an office in New York and a residence in New York.
Mr. Jenner - Two telephone numbers he gave you?
Mrs. Paine - Yes.

Mr. Jenner - One office and one residence of Mr. John Abt. Did he say who Mr. John Abt was?

Mrs. Paine - He said he was an attorney he wanted to have.

Mr. Jenner - Represent him?

Mrs. Paine - To represent him. He thanked me for my concern.

Mr. Jenner - Did he tell you or ask you what you were to do or say to Mr. Abt if you reached him?

Mrs. Paine - I carried the clear impression I was to ask him if he would serve as attorney for Lee Oswald.

Mr. Jenner - All right.

Have you given the substance of the conversation in as much detail, of the entire conversation, as you now can recall?

Mrs. Paine - There is a little more that is.

Senator Cooper - Why don't you just go ahead and tell it as you remember it, everything that he said and you said?

Mrs. Paine - I can't give the specific words to this part but I carry a clear impression, too, that he sounded to me almost as if nothing out of the ordinary had happened.

I would make this telephone call for him, would help him, as I had in other ways previously. He was, he expressed gratitude to me. I felt, but did not express, considerable irritation at his seeming to be so apart from the situation, so presuming of his own innocence, if you will, but I did say I would make the call for him.

Then he called back almost immediately. I gather that he had made the call to me on the permission to make a different call and then he got specific permission from the police to make a call to me and the call was identical.

Mr. Jenner - This is speculation?

Mrs. Paine - This is speculation but the content of the second call was almost identical.

Mr. Jenner - The phone rang?

Mrs. Paine - He asked me to contact John Abt.

Mr. Jenner - He identified himself and he asked you to make the call?

Mrs. Paine - Yes.

Mr. Jenner - What did he say?

Mrs. Paine - He wanted me to call this lawyer.

Mr. Jenner - Did you express any surprise for him to call back almost immediately giving you the same message that he had given previously?

Mrs. Paine - I think somebody must have said, that the officers had said he could call, make this call.

Mr. Jenner - Did you say anything about the fact that he had already just called you about the same subject matter?

Mrs. Paine - He may have added.

Mr. Jenner - Did you, please?

Mrs. Paine - No. I was quite stunned that he called at all or that he thought he could ask anything of me, appalled, really.

Mr. McCloy - Did he say he was innocent, or did he just have this conversation with respect to the retention of a counsel?

Mrs. Paine - That is all.

Mr. Jenner - At no time during either of these conversations did he deny that he was in any way involved in this situation?

Mrs. Paine - He made no reference to why he was at the police station or why he needed a lawyer.

Mr. Jenner - He just assumed that you knew he was at the police station, did he?

Mrs. Paine - That is right,

Mr. Jenner - That was your impression?

Mrs. Paine - That is right,

Mr. Jenner - He didn't say where he was?

Mrs. Paine - No.

Mr. Jenner - He just started out saying what you now say he said?

Mrs. Paine - That is right.

Mr. Jenner - But in no respect did he say to you that he was entirely innocent of any charges that had been made against him?

Mrs. Paine - He did not say that.

Mr. Jenner - Did he mention the subject at all of the assassination of the President or the slaying of Officer Tippit?

Mrs. Paine - No; he did not.

Mr. Jenner - What you have given is your best recollection of the entire conversation?

Mrs. Paine - That is correct.

Representative Ford - This was Saturday afternoon, November 23?

Mrs. Paine - Yes.

Representative Ford - About what time?

Mrs. Paine - Four, perhaps in the afternoon.

Representative Ford - Had you seen him the day before?

Mrs. Paine - No.

Mr. McCloy - Who was in the house with you when that call came in?

Mrs. Paine - Just my children.

Mr. McCloy - Just your children.

And later on:

Mr. Jenner - All right. The phone rang, you answered it.

Mrs. Paine - Yes.

Mr. Jenner - Did you recognize the voice?

Mrs. Paine - I recognized the voice.

Mr. Jenner - Whose was it?

Mrs. Paine - It was Lee Oswald's.

Mr. Jenner - What did he say and what did you say?

Mrs. Paine - He said, *"Marina, please,"* in Russian.

Mr. Jenner - Please, Mrs. Paine, did he speak to you in English in the conversations in the afternoon or in Russian?

Mrs. Paine - He spoke in English the entire conversation.

Mr. Jenner - The two in the afternoon?

Mrs. Paine - Yes.

Mr. Jenner - Now, however, he resorted to Russian, did he?

Mrs. Paine - Yes. He planned to speak to Marina.

Mr. Jenner - I beg your pardon?

Mrs. Paine - He planned to speak to Marina, and this opening phrase was one he normally used calling, as he had many previous times to speak to her.

Mr. Jenner - He was under the assumption, you gathered, that Marina was in your home?

Mrs. Paine - He certainly was.

Mr. Jenner - All right.

Mrs. Paine - And I would be fairly certain that I answered him in English. I said she was not there, that I had a notion about where she might be, but I wasn't at all certain. That I would try to find out. He said, he wanted me to--he said he thought she should be at my house. He felt irritated at not having been able to reach her. And he wanted me to--

Mr. Jenner - Did he sound irritated?

Mrs. Paine - Yes; he sounded just a slight edge to his voice. And he wanted me to deliver a message to her that he thought she should be at my house.

Mr. Jenner - And he so instructed you?

Mrs. Paine - Yes.

Mr. Jenner - That is what he said?

Mrs. Paine - Yes. That was so far as I remember, the entire conversation.

Mr. Jenner - What response did you give to his direction?

Mrs. Paine - I said I would try to reach her.

Mr. Jenner - His direction--

Mrs. Paine - And tell her his message.

Mr. Jenner - All right.

Mrs. Paine - In the meantime, had you sought to reach John Abt?

Mrs. Paine - I had, after 6 o'clock, thank you. I had dialled both numbers and neither answered.

Mr. Jenner - Neither answered. Was there any conversation between you and Lee Oswald in the evening conversation to which you reported to him your inability to reach Mr. Abt?

Mrs. Paine - I do not specifically recall.

Mr. Jenner - Or the subject of Mr. Abt at all?

Mrs. Paine - I don't want to get in, to rationalization. I can judge that something was said but I do not recall it specifically.

Mr. Jenner - Now, have you given the full extent of that conversation?

Mrs. Paine - To the best of my recollection.

Mr. Jenner - At any time during that conversation with Lee Harvey Oswald did he assert or intimate in any form or fashion his innocence of any charges against him?

Mrs. Paine - No; he did not.

Mr. Jenner - Was the assassination mentioned at all?

Mrs. Paine - No; it was not.

Mr. Jenner - Was the shooting or murder of Officer Tippit mentioned?

Mrs. Paine - No.

[Later, continuing...]

Mr. Jenner - Tell us what your activities--you are a member of the American Civil Liberties Union?

Mrs. Paine - I am.

Mr. Jenner - What have been your activities in connection with that organization?

Mrs. Paine - Primarily to send in my membership fee each year. I have been a member for some years prior--that is to say, going back to the time prior to my marriage. I have recently, perhaps a year ago, became on the membership committee for the local chapter in Dallas. That chapter, I might say, only just opened a year and a half ago.

Mr. Jenner - And have you, as part of those activities, sought to enlist others to become members of the American Civil Liberties Union?

Mrs. Paine - I have talked to perhaps half a dozen people, to encourage them; yes.

Mr. Jenner - Did you ever discuss this organization with Lee Oswald?

Mrs. Paine - Yes; I did.

Mr. Jenner - Have you told us in your testimony up to this moment all of your discussion of that organization with Lee Oswald?

Mrs. Paine - Yes; I have. I call your attention to my testimony of a conversation with Lee over the phone saying that I thought that if he was losing his job because of his political views, that this would be of interest to the Civil Liberties Union.

Mr. Jenner - Did any of those discussions embrace the question of what possible help this organization might be to him if he got into trouble eventually?

Mrs. Paine - My judgment is that he took that statement I have just referred to as an implication of the possibility of help from that organization to him personally.

Mr. Jenner - With reference particularly to the possible need at any time for counsel?

Mrs. Paine - He may have assumed such a thing. My understanding of the Civil Liberties Union is that they are not interested in just defending people, but in defending rights or entering a case where there is doubt that a person's civil liberties have been properly upheld.

Mr. Jenner - Or might be?

Mrs. Paine - Or there might be such doubt; yes. I wouldn't know whether Lee understood that.

Mr. Jenner - At least your discussions with him do not enable you to proceed to the point at which to enable you to voice any opinions in this area or subject than you have now given?

Mrs. Paine - No.

Mr. Jenner - Were you aware of the name John Abt before you received the telephone call you testified about from Lee Oswald?

Mrs. Paine - No; I had not heard that name.

Mr. Jenner - And, therefore, you never suggested it to Lee Oswald?

Mrs. Paine - No; that is right.

[And later...]

Mr. Jenner - Nobody reported to you anything about any conversation they might or did have with Lee Oswald either on the 22d or 23d or even on the 24th of November 1963?

Mrs. Paine - No. I am of the impression I again tried the home telephone of John Abt on Sunday morning, but I am not certain, and there was no answer. That I certainly remember.

Mr. McCloy - Did you ever reach Abt?

Mrs. Paine - No.

Mr. Jenner - Did you ever attempt to report to Lee Oswald that you had been unable to reach Mr. Abt?

Mrs. Paine - Not unless such transpired in our 9:30 conversation Saturday evening, but I made no effort to call the police station itself.

Mr. Jenner - Excuse me?

Mrs. Paine - I made no effort to call the police station.

17:15 H Louis Nichols Visits Oswald in Jail

H Louis Nichols, president of the Dallas Bar Association, was allowed to meet with Oswald in his jail cell late Saturday afternoon (November 23rd). It was Bob Storey (3580) who got into contact with Nichols and have him check to see whether Oswald was provided legal assistance. It may be that Storey got a call from Nicholas Katzenbach (3581), on page 48, since he was most concerned as well.

Nichols gets involved about 16 hours after Greg Olds and his three colleagues from the Dallas ACLU had made their way to the DPD already shortly before Oswald's press conference.

In his talks with Oswald at about 17:00 Nichols is told that he wanted to be represented by John Abt or an ACLU member. Nichols said that he did not know any ACLU members (a strange thing to say really).

He asked if Oswald wanted him or the Dallas Bar Association to get him an attorney. Oswald said he would wait until he could see Abt, an ACLU attorney, or at least someone who believed in his innocence.

In his WC testimony (3583) H Louis Nichols mentions that he was no criminal lawyer and he talked to a friend who was one and was told by him that the obligation was only to appoint counsel after a man had been indicted, and that, as he understood it, since Mr. Oswald had not been indicted there was no legal obligation to appoint an attorney. Yet he was already arraigned for Tippit and supposedly for the murder of JFK as well.

He then speaks to Henry Wade over the phone and asks him whether or not either he or anybody in his office had been advised that Oswald wanted a lawyer, or had made a request for a lawyer, and he said as far as he knew he had not asked for a lawyer. Since this phone call happened on the 23rd and Oswald had made quite a few public calls for legal representation on the 22nd and early on the 23rd we can deduct that Wade was spinning a tall tale....

Nichols knows a fair amount of people inside the DPD and he decides to call Captain Glen King and asks him the same questions he put forward to Henry Wade, and King pretty much answers in the same vein as Wade did: *Oswald was not represented by anyone, he did not ask for anyone to represent him nor ask for the right for a phone call to call one.* That is another strange thing to say, as Oswald was granted his phone call earlier on the 23rd about 24 hours after his arrest.

From Jesse Curry's book Retired Dallas police chief, Jesse Curry reveals his personal JFK assassination file (3584) on page 75: "*By mid-evening I was concerned that every attempt be made to see that Oswald's civil rights were not being violated. I escorted Louis Nichols, president of the Dallas Bar Association, into the jail to confer with the prisoner. Oswald at that time spurned an offer by the Dallas Bar Association for legal assistance, but Mr. Nichols did discuss Oswald's right for legal counsel with him. Oswald indicated that he wanted Attorney John Abt of New York City to defend him. If that failed his second choice would have been a member of the American Civil Liberties Union. Oswald seemed well informed of his rights and had definite ideas about how he would seek legal counsel. Attorney Louis Nichols left completely satisfied that*

Oswald had not been denied council and that his civil rights were not being violated."

In his WC testimony Jesse Curry says (3584):

Mr. Rankin - Chief Curry, you said that Mr. Nichols came that afternoon. I call to your attention that we have information that he came there on the Saturday afternoon.
Mr. Curry - Perhaps it was, not the Friday. That perhaps was on Saturday.
Mr. Rankin - Yes.
Mr. Dulles - I wonder if you could just summarize briefly where we are. (Discussion off the record.)
Mr. Rankin - Back on the record.
In regard to Mr. Nichols, did you know whether or not he offered to represent or provide counsel?
Mr. Curry - Yes; he did.
Mr. Rankin - What did he say about that?
Mr. Curry - He said he didn't care to at this time.
Mr. Rankin - What did Mr. Nichols say about providing counsel?
Mr. Curry - He said the Dallas Bar would provide counsel if he desired counsel.
Mr. Rankin - That is to Mr. Oswald?
Mr. Curry - Oswald.
Mr. Rankin - What did Mr. Oswald say?
Mr. Curry - He said, *"I don't at this time,"* he said, *"If I can't get Mr. Abt to represent me or someone from Civil Liberties Union I will call on you later."*
Representative Ford. - Did Nichols and Oswald talk one to another?
Mr. Curry - Yes; he was taken to see Oswald and he talked to him.
Mr. Rankin - And this all occurred at the meeting you have already described?
Mr. Curry - Yes, sir.
Mr. Rankin - Between Mr. Nichols and Mr. Oswald?
Mr. Curry - That is correct.

From Nichols' WC testimony (3585):

...call from another friend of mine, and that I had made some inquiry, and at this time I did not know whether Oswald had a lawyer or was getting a lawyer, but that I was going to make some inquiry to find out about it. After talking to the second friend about it who called, I then called Mr. Henry Wade, the district attorney, to see whether or not he knew whether or not Oswald was represented by a lawyer or not.
I did not know for sure at that time whether he was, simply because I had no way of knowing whether he was represented or not. I hadn't

talked to anybody who was really informed, and I called Mr. Wade. He said he didn't know for sure whether he was or not, as far as he knew he hadn't been contacted by any lawyer who purported to represent Oswald. I asked him whether or not either he or anybody in his office had been advised that Oswald wanted a lawyer, or had made a request for a lawyer, and he said as far as he knew he had not asked for a lawyer. I asked him too, as he was going up there, and I asked him if Oswald requested a lawyer and didn't have a lawyer would he tell him that the Dallas Bar Association would get a lawyer if he needed one.

By that time, I had time to think about what I thought my obligation should be, and realizing that under the circumstances maybe some people might overlook the fact that Oswald had rights that needed to be protected at the same time, and if he didn't have a lawyer, regardless of what the legal obligation was to appoint him a lawyer, we, the bar association, ought to look into the matter.

Mr. Wade said he was going to go up there later on in the evening and he would talk to his assistants who were in closer contact than he was, and if Oswald wanted a lawyer--asked for a lawyer or wanted a lawyer appointed--he would tell him of my conversation. I then called Glen King, and a captain on the police force that I knew. I used to work for the city attorney's office, and still represent, the city credit union and have a brother on the police force, so, I have known many of these people for many years. I called Captain King and asked him whether or not Oswald was represented by an attorney, if he knew if there was an attorney up there, or anybody who had been up there representing him, and Captain King said that as far as he knew there had been no one representing him, and as far as he knew, Oswald had not asked for a lawyer. He had not asked for the right to call a lawyer, and or had not asked that a lawyer be furnished to him---and Captain King said, *"If he does, I am certainly going to call you and let you know, because we want to be sure if he wants a lawyer, he gets one. We don't want it to be a situation of anybody saying that we deprived him of the right to have a lawyer."*

About that time Chief Curry looked up and saw me, and he knew me and motioned me in, and I went in there and he introduced me to one of the FBI agents who was there, and I told him I was up there as president of the bar association looking for Captain King. I had talked to him earlier and I had come up: there to see whether or not Mr. Oswald had a lawyer, or needed a lawyer, or wanted the Dallas Bar Association to do anything. The chief said that he was glad to see me and would take me up to see Oswald himself and, so, we immediately left his office and started to another part of the building, and he asked me where I wanted to talk to him. If I wanted to be taken to a room or some place, or what would be convenient with me, and I told him that any place would be all--I just wanted to visit with the man and see what his situation was with regard to him having a lawyer. So, we then went through a door on the third floor and got into the elevator and went up to the sixth floor, and the chief again asked me where I wanted to talk to him. I said, *"Well, just any place."*

By that time, we had gotten to a portion of the jail that was separated by bars and a door. Beyond that door were three separate cells, and there was an officer seated outside one, and then we went through the first door and got to that point and Mr. Oswald was in the centre of the three cells, no one being in the other two, and there was an officer seated outside there. The chief had the officer open the door, and he introduced me to Oswald, and told him my name and said that I was the president of the Dallas Bar Association and had come up to see him about whether or not he needed or wanted a lawyer, and then the chief stepped back and--I don't really know how far away. He was at least--he was far enough removed where I couldn't observe him or see him there in the cell. The officer stayed just right outside the door there. I reintroduced myself to Oswald and told him my name, and that I was president of the Dallas bar, and that I had come up to see him about whether or not he had a lawyer, or needed a lawyer, or wanted a lawyer, and suggested that he sit down.

So, he sat on one bunk and I sat on the other. Maybe 3 or 4 feet apart. When I got there he was lying on a bunk, and then he stood up when I came in and then he sat on one bunk and I sat on the other, much as you and I are seated here, only actually, a little bit closer, and I asked him if he had a lawyer, and he said, *"Well, he really didn't know what it was all about, that he was--had been incarcerated, and kept incommunicado,"* and I said, *"Well, I have come up to see whether or not you want a lawyer, because as I understand--"* I am not exactly sure what I ,said there, or whether he said something about not knowing what happened to President Kennedy, or I said that I understood that he was arrested for the shot that killed the President, and I don't remember who said what after that. This is a little bit vague. I had covered that point in detail, and I don't recall exactly, but in any event, our conversation was such that I informed him that I was there to see whether or not he had a lawyer, or wanted a lawyer, and he said--he asked me first did I know a lawyer in New York named John Abt and I don't know if it is A-b-t, or A-p-t.

Mr. Stern. I believe it is A-b-t.

Mr. NICHOLS. I believe it is. In New York City, I said I didn't know him, and he said, *"Well, I would like to have him to represent me,"* and at some period I believe prior to that, either in talking to the police, or talking to--must have been talking to either Captain King or the chief---I had been told that some effort had been made to get hold of Mr. Abt, and that he was in Connecticut at his home, and maybe, and I have forgotten who said who was trying to get ahold of him. At least, I did vaguely know

377

that someone was trying to get ahold of him, but I told Mr. Oswald I didn't know him. He said, *"Well, that is the man he would like to have represent him."* Then he asked me if I knew any lawyers who were members of the American Civil Liberties Union, and he said, *"Well, I am a member of that organization, and I would like to have somebody who is a member of that organization represent me."* And I said, *"I'm sorry, I don't know anybody who is a member of that organization."*

Although, as it turned out later, a number of lawyers I know are members. Two or three of them called me later. He said, *"Well, if I can't get either one of those, and if I can----"*

Mr. Stern. That is either----

Mr. NICHOLS. *"Either Mr. Abt or someone who is a member of the American Civil Liberties Union, and if I can find a lawyer here who believes in anything I believe in, and believes as I believe, and believes in my innocence"-*then paused a little bit, and went on a little bit and said, *"as much as he can, I might let him represent me."*

I said, *"What I am interested in knowing is right now, do you want me or the Dallas Bar Association to try to get you a lawyer?"*

He said, *"No, not now."*

He said, *"You might come back next week, and if I don't get some of these other people to represent me, I might ask you to get somebody to represent me."*

I said, *"Well, now, all I want to do is to make it clear to you, and to me, whether or not you want me or the Dallas Bar Association to do anything about getting a lawyer right now."*

And he said, *"No."* As I left the chief asked me whether or not I wanted to make a statement to the press, and I said, *"Well, I don't know whether I do or not. I don't know whether it is the thing to do or not."*

And he said, *"Well, they are going to be right outside the door there, and if you want to say anything this would be an opportunity to do it. Incidentally, I am very glad you came up here. We don't want any question coming up about us refusing to let him have a lawyer. As far as I know, he has never asked for one. He has never asked to call one."* Evidence presented earlier shows that this is utter rubbish.

Curry lasts for just over five minutes and then makes his exit. You can view this H Louis Nichols interview on YouTube (3586).

The H Louis Nichols' obituary in the Dallas Morning News (3587) includes a few interesting bits. Esteemed law school deans from, *"back East"* were calling to express concern that only a legal backwater would deny an attorney to a murder suspect, Mr. Nichols' friends told him. Nichols described Oswald, who was dressed in a white T-shirt and slacks, as calm and rested. He had a bruise over one eye but appeared to be in good health. He said that police were holding him *"incommunicado"* and that he did not know what had happened to the president, Mr. Nichols told the Warren Commission. Oswald said he wanted a New York lawyer named John Abt or a lawyer associated with the American Civil Liberties Union to represent him. Oswald also wanted a lawyer *"who believes as I believe, and believes in my innocence." "What I am interested in is knowing right now, do you want me or the Dallas Bar Association to try to get you a lawyer?"* Mr. Nichols asked Oswald. *"No, not right now,"* he replied.

H Louis Nichols remembers that day in this edited video, by Jessica Smith (3588).

In the Dallas Times Herald of December 16th 1963 (3589) Nichols retells the story again with some additional bits on Oswald's rights. Nichols saw Oswald on Saturday evening around 6 PM and not on Friday evening as the article implies.

18:25 Oswald Demands Hygienic Rights

In this video of Oswald entering the corridor taken Saturday the 23rd at about 18:25 (3590), Oswald is on his way to Fritz's office for another interrogation. He is heard demanding *basic fundamental hygienic rights*, such as a shower. This is after he has been seen by H Louis Nichols, who was seen talking to the press around the same time.

In this video (3591) as Oswald is being transferred Saturday evening from his cell to Room 317, from the documentary The Lost JFK Tapes. Oswald is being taken into the corridor and low and behold Marrion Baker (wearing his white helmet) stands a few feet in front of him and averts his eyes and ducks away. Oswald does not seem to recognise Baker at all.

18:30 Sixth Interrogation

Present are:
DPD: Will Fritz, Gus Rose.
FBI: James Bookhout.
Secret Service: Thomas Kelley.

In this Jailer's Release form of the DPD (3592), it states the suspect was released at 18:00 and signed back in at 19:15.

During this session the backyard photos (BYP) are shown and brought up. Oswald denies it is him and states that he has been superimposed in these photographs. He complains about the Whaley & Scoggins line-

up earlier for being in just a T-shirt and denies he bought the rifle at Kleins.
Here are Will Fritz's interrogation notes (3593).

"Shows photo of gun would not discuss photo. Denied buying gun from Kleins. Comp of wanting jacket for line-up, says I made picture super imposed"

James Bookhout, sat with Fritz and in his report, he states the same as what Fritz wrote down in his notes; that Oswald denies the backyard photos are of him, denies that he had purchased a rifle at Kleins and that he complained of his appearance during the Whaley & Scoggins line-up. All this is in Bookhout's November 25th report (3594).

Gus Rose sat in on the sixth Oswald interrogation session with Captain Fritz on Saturday the 23rd. This is after the 'find' of the backyard photographs.

Gus Rose's WC testimony (3595):

Mr. Ball. Did you find some pictures?
Mr. Rose. Yes; I found two negatives first that showed Lee Oswald holding a rifle in his hand, wearing a pistol at his hip, and right with those negatives I found a developed picture--I don't know what you call it, but anyway a picture that had been developed from the negative of him holding this rifle, and Detective McCabe was standing there and he found the other picture--of Oswald holding the rifle.
Mr. Ball. What color were the sea bags?
Mr. Rose. I believe they were kind of an off white--I would call them-- more of a greyish-white.
Mr. Ball. What about the suitcases?
Mr. Rose. I don't remember the color of those suitcases. I know one of them was real worn.
Mr. Ball. But you brought that property back here into town, did you?
Mr. Rose. Yes; we did.
Mr. Ball. Now, you say you sat in on the interrogation of Oswald later that day?
Mr. Rose. Yes; we did.
Mr. Ball. Now, you say you sat in on the interrogation of Oswald later that day?
Mr. Rose. On Saturday evening--that Saturday evening.
Mr. Ball. What time?
Mr. Rose. I don't remember--it was late--it seemed like it was around 9 or 10 o'clock, I don't remember.
Mr. Ball. Who was present?

Mr. Rose. Well, Captain Fritz, Detective Sims, and myself--I don't remember--there was an FBI agent and a Secret Service agent there, but I don't remember their names.

Mr. Ball. Do you remember what was said?

Mr. Rose. Do I remember what was said?

Mr. Ball. That this took place in Captain Fritz' office?

Mr. Rose. In Captain Fritz' office--yes. Well, the occasion was--I got back to the office and I took this small picture of Oswald holding the rifle, and left the rest of them with the Captain and I took one up to the I.D. bureau and had them to make me an enlargement of it, and they made an almost 8" by 10" enlargement of this picture and I brought it back to the captain and Oswald was brought in and the captain showed him this picture, and Oswald apparently got pretty upset when he saw the picture and at first he said, *"Well, that's just a fake, because somebody has superimposed my face on that picture."* Then, the captain said, *"Well, is that you face on the picture?"* And he said, *"I won't even admit that. That is not even my face."* I remember that part of it distinctly. I remember him volunteering some information about when he was in Russia.

Mr. Ball. What did he say?

Mr. Rose. Well, he talked about how life was better for the colored people in Russia than it was in the United States. I don't remember--he just rambled on--he liked to talk about that, but he wouldn't talk about anything to do with the assassination or the killing of Tippit.

Read Gus Rose's HSCA testimony (3596) especially pages 9, 10, 13-15 from an interview on April 13th 1978. On the find of the BYP and him participating during Fritz's interrogation on Saturday evening.

Thomas Kelley of the USSS in his third report (3597) on the interrogations mentions the backyard photos and Oswald's demeanour.

Even Dallas Police Chief Curry makes a mention of them during his WC testimony (3598):

Mr. Dulles - Could I ask a question? What was Oswald's attitude toward the police? Have you any comment on that?

Mr. Curry - The only things I heard him say, he was very arrogant. He was very--he had a dislike for authority, it seemed, of anyone. He denied anything you asked him. I heard them ask once or twice if this was his picture or something, he said, *"I don't know what you are talking about. No; it is not my picture,"* and this was a picture of him holding a rifle or something. I remember one time they showed him and he denied that being him.

Check this video where upon leaving the Homicide & Robbery Bureau (3599) and having been interrogated for the sixth time by Captain Fritz. Oswald is being escorted down the corridor again and this time he emphatically denies the charges being levied on him. Oswald is closely followed by Charles Dhority (dark hat). On the left with the youthful face is detective Fay Turner.

In this video Will Fritz is seen in front of the cameras on the 23rd (3600) and gives the following statement: *"There is only one thing I can tell you. Without going into evidence. This case is cinched. This man killed the President. There is no question in my mind about it."* He brushed aside all other questions. Overall, this was a false claim since the evidence at that time was very weak. Better yet, there was nothing present that could put Lee Oswald on the sixth floor at that time while the motorcade passed by. If one thing was certain it was that Fritz did nothing to investigate Oswald's alibi, in which he clearly stated he was on the first floor when it all went down.

20:00 Oswald Makes A Phone Call

JL Popplewell states in his August 20th 1964 (3601) affidavit that Oswald made a long call at 20:00. No further details are available at this time.

22:15 The Raleigh Call

The alleged Raleigh Call is an overblown affair that doesn't deserve the coverage it has had all these years. Oswald made no such call. John David Hurt made the phone call while drunk and did not get very far. It is regrettable that this non-story escalated inside the conspiracy theorist community.

The reasons I believe that there is not much to this story include the available evidence of:
- Louise Swinney, Alveeta Treon and Sharon Kovac contradict each other (3602) to such an extent that there are very few areas of agreement of the Raleigh call actually happening.
- All other calls by Oswald were reported by the jailers Arthur E Eaves (3603), JE Popplewell (3604) & 2 and Thurber T Lord (3605) and there is no such report present when Oswald allegedly made that call. This is also confirmed by Will Fritz (3606).
- There is not a single trace of the original calling card. All we have is a bad quality photocopy.
- Louise Swinney denies it is her signature (3607) on the calling card.

- Sharon Kovac was not there, *at the time of the so-called call (3608);* she heard it from Alveeta Treon at a later time.
- The FBI reports on the piece of paper that was found on Oswald (3609), after he has been murdered by Jack Ruby. On it were several numbers, yet not one refers to John Hurt let alone anyone in Raleigh (3610).
- John Hurt denies the whole thing during the HSCA (3611).
- After his death *his wife told the author 4* (3612) *that John Hurt had admitted the truth before he died. Terribly upset on the day of the assassination, he got extremely drunk—a habitual problem with him—and telephoned the Dallas jail and asked to speak to Oswald. When denied access, he left his name and number. Mrs. Hurt said her husband told her he never had any earlier contact with Oswald and had been too embarrassed to admit that he got drunk and placed the call.*

November 24th

09:30 Seventh Interrogation

According to the release slip from the jailer (3613), it shows that Oswald was being picked up at 09:30.

Present for the DPD are Will Fritz, Jim Leavelle, LC Graves, LD Montgomery and Charles Dhority. Chief Jesse Curry also attends.
FBI: James Bookhout.
Secret Service: Forrest Sorrels and Thomas Kelley.
USPS: Harry Dean Holmes.

Jim Leavelle during his WC testimony (3614) talks about the interrogation on Sunday morning the 24th, the interrogation he was actually present. Ask yourself this: Had he interrogated Oswald at the very beginning, wouldn't he have said something about this? And also, wouldn't he have asked additional follow-up questions that morning about it? Yet there is no mention of this anywhere to be read in his testimony. And it gets juicier!

Mr. Ball. Now, on November 24, on Sunday morning, did you return to work about the same time, 8 o'clock, or so?
Mr. Leavelle. Little before 10, I believe, or something.
Mr. Ball. And, were you ordered by Captain Fritz to get Oswald?
Mr. Leavelle. Yes; I don't-I see here it says 9:30 whatever the official time was, I think it probably was maybe about that time.
Mr. Ball. Where did you go to get Oswald?
Mr. Leavelle. I had to go to the fourth-floor jail.
Mr. Ball. Did you handcuff him?
Mr. Leavelle. Yes; I did.
Mr. Ball. Were his handcuffs in the front or in the rear?
Mr. Leavelle. In front.
Mr. Ball. Where were you taking him?
Mr. Leavelle. Took him down the inside elevator to the third floor into Captain Fritz's office.
Mr. Ball. Who was present at that meeting in Captain Fritz's office?
Mr. Leavelle. Well, I can recall, I believe during that time I was there, there were several people in and out. I believe primarily myself and Mr. Graves and Dhority and L.D. Montgomery were in there most of the time, I don't know. We were in, probably might have stepped outside the door at one time or another but primarily we were around and also Mr. Kelley, Secret Service, and a man from the postal inspector's office. I cannot recall his name at this time. He should be on here--oh, yes, Mr.

Sorrels and Holmes of the postal department. So, those people and Chief Curry came in once or twice. All those people may not have stayed in there constantly during the time but they were in there at some time or other.

Mr. BILL. Did these various people ask questions of Oswald?

Nr. Leavelle. I know Mr. Sorrels did and I know Mr. Kelley did. I do not recall whether Mr. Holmes asked any questions or not and Captain Fritz asked him some.

Mr. Ball. Do you remember what Mr. Sorrels asked him?

Mr. Leavelle. No; I don't.

Mr. Ball. Remember what Mr. Kelley asked him?

Mr. Leavelle. I can only remember one question Mr. Kelley asked him and that was whether or not he thought the attitude of the U.S. Government toward Cuba would be changed since the President has been assassinated. To my knowledge, that is the only one I can recall.

Mr. Ball. What did Oswald say?

Mr. Leavelle. Oswald turned and asked Captain Fritz, said *"I am filed on for the President's murder, is that right?"* And, Captain Fritz told him yes and he told Mr. Kelley, he said *"under the circumstances. I don't believe that it would be proper."* That might not be the words he used, but wouldn't he right, anyway, for him to answer that question because whatever he said might be construed in a different light than what he actually meant it to be, but he went on to say he felt like when the head of any government died or was killed, whatever, there was always a second in command who would take over and he said in this particular instance it would he Johnson. He said *"So far as I know, Johnson's views and President Kennedy's views are the same,"* so, he would see no particular difference in the attitude of the U.S. Government toward Cuba. That's about the main-the only one, because he went into such detail on it, the only one I thought was a little elaborate for him to go into that type of answer, the reason I remembered it.

Mr. BALI. Do you remember any question Captain Fritz asked him?

Mr. Leavelle. I remember that the captain asked him about the shooting of the President and the shooting of the officer: I know he did ask him that and I know Oswald did deny it, both times.

Mr. Ball. That he had shot President Kennedy and Tippit?

Mr. Leavelle. Yes; he denied shooting either am? He did say this *"If you want me to 'cop' out to hitting or pleading guilty to hitting a cop in the mouth when I was arrested,"* he said *"Yeah. I plead guilty to that,"* but he.., I do know that he denied the shooting of both the President and Tippit.

Mr. Ball. Can you remember any other questions asked Oswald by Captain Fritz?

Mr. Leavelle. No. not offhand; I would probably remember them if I heard the questions but I don't remember offhand.

Mr. Ball. Did anybody talk to him about the post office box?

Mr. Leavelle. Yes; Sir. Kelley asked him several questions and probably Mr. Sorrels about the post office box. Both here and one he had in Shreveport wherever it was.

Mr. Ball. New Orleans?

Mr. LEATE. New Orleans, yes.

Mr. Ball. Do you remember what Oswald said?

Mr. Leavelle. Since you mentioned it, I do remember them talking to him about the New Orleans and he's asking him about this other name, this

Mr. Ball. Alek Hidell?

Mr. Leavelle. Yes; and he asked him if he knew Alek Hidell; said he didn't know if he ever heard of the name. He never heard of that and asked him several questions along that line and then after he had denied all knowledge of Alek Hidell. Mr. Kelley asked him, said, *"Well, isn't it a fact when you were arrested you had an identification card with his name on it in your possession."* He kind of grunted, said, *"Yes that's right,"* and he said, *"How do you explain that?"* And, as best my knowledge, he said, *"I don't explain it."*

Mr. Ball. Anybody ask him about a gun. Whether or not he bought a rifle?

Mr. Leavelle. I am sure they did. I remember some of them asking about the rifle and about it being sent to the box here in Dallas but I do not recall. I am not sure he denied it but I do not recall what his exact denial was.

Mr. Ball. You say he denied it. Do you remember whether or not he denied that he had bought a rifle?

Mr. Leavelle. To the best of my knowledge, I do. He did deny it but I would not swear to it.

Mr. Ball. Was anything said about a revolver?

Mr. Leavelle. I am sure they asked him something about the revolver, too, but I do not recall what it was.

Mr. BallL. Did he say whether or not he had a revolver in his possession at the time of his arrest?

Mr. Leavelle. I do not recall what the questions was along that line or even what the answers was. Like I say. I am sure that they did. It seems as though my memory tells me that he did not deny taking the revolver but, there, again. I would not want to say definitely.

Mr. Ball. Did you make any notes of the conversation?

Mr. Leavelle. So, I did not myself. That was the only time I ever sat in on the interrogations of him by Captain Fritz or anyone.

[Oswald's legal representation did come up once again...]

Mr. Ball. In that meeting did he ask for a lawyer?

Mr. Leavelle. No; I know Captain Fritz asked him if at one time, if-he handed him a telegram-in fact. I believe it was sent by some attorney, if my memory serves me right, and he said he did not particularly want him but he would take that and if he didn't do any better, he would contact him at a later time. I do not recall what lawyer it was. It seems like some lawyer in the East sent the telegram volunteering his services to Oswald. [This is the telegram from Chicago lawyer Harold McDervid-BK]

Mr. Ball. That is there on Sunday morning, the 23rd? [24th-BK]

Mr. Leavelle. Yes.

Mr. Ball. In the course of this meeting which you have been describing--

Mr. Leavelle. Yes.

Mr. Ball. What did Oswald say?

Mr. Leavelle. He said that he preferred-he never had gotten in touch with this lawyer in New York City that represented the American Civil Liberties Union and he wanted to get in touch with him and said if he didn't do any better, or could not get him, he would like to talk with this man about it.

From the PBS Documentary Who Was LHO-1993 (3615) Leavelle says: *While he didn't admit anything and he didn't confess to anything, he was the type of individual that you had to prove to him that we could make a case on him and this is not unusual. This is very common among people that commits a crime.*

Forrest Sorrels (3616) took notes during the interrogations and they were buried inside the WR, for everyone to see yet no one picked up on them until researcher Larry Haapanen brought it to light in the late nineties (3617).

The top half of his written notes concerns Oswald, the bottom half deals with Ruby as he interviewed Ruby shortly after he had smoked Oswald. There is nothing of value in these few sentences scribbled down by Sorrels regarding this particular segment of the case. One has to wonder whether there was not another page in front of that page inside the notebook with more on Oswald's interrogations.

Forrest Sorrels' WC testimony (3618):

Mr. Stern - Was that Sunday interview extended beyond any time that you know of that it was scheduled to end?

Mr. Sorrels - Yes; it was, because the papers seemed to have gotten the impression that he was going to be moved at exactly 10 o'clock in the morning, and Captain Fritz was talking to him even after 11 o'clock in the morning--we were still there. And I recall that Chief Curry came around and asked Captain Fritz how long he was going to be, or what was holding it up, or something like that, that they wanted to go ahead and get him moved as quick as they could.

Mr. Stern - Did he indicate or did you understand that they wanted to move him at 10 o'clock?

Mr. Sorrels - It was after 10 o'clock then, considerably. As a matter of fact, it was after 11 at that time. Captain Fritz remarked to me afterwards, he said, *"Well, as long as it looks like he might talk, I hesitate to quit, or move him out at that time,"* and he told Chief Curry, *"We will be through in a few minutes."*

And shortly after that, Captain Fritz asked if anyone wanted to ask him any questions, and, at that time, the postal inspector had obtained a change of address card which Oswald had apparently filled out in which one of the names shown on that change of address card that was to receive mail at that particular address in New Orleans was named A. Hidell. And I desired to question Oswald about that thing, because he had denied purchasing this rifle under the name of A. Hidell, and he denied knowing anybody by the name of A. Hidell.

So, I showed Oswald this change of address card and said to him, *"Now, here is a change of address card that you filed in New Orleans,"* and he looked at it.

He did not deny that he had filed the card, because it was apparently in his handwriting, and his signature. And I said, *"Now you say that you have not used the name of A. Hidell, but you show it on this card here as the name of A. Hidell, as a person to receive mail at this address. If you do not know anyone by that name, why would you have that name on that card?"*

He said, *"I never used the name of Hidell."*

Mr. Stern - That was the last question he was asked?

Mr. Sorrels - As far as I know.

Mr. Stern - And then what happened?

Mr. Sorrels - He was told that they were going to move him to the county jail, and he requested that he be permitted to get a shirt out of his--the clothes that had been brought in, that belonged to him, because the shirt he was wearing at the time he had been apprehended was taken, apparently for laboratory examination. And so, Captain Fritz sent and got his clothes and, as I recall it, he selected a dark-colored kind of a sweater type shirt, as I recall it. And then he was taken out, and, at that time, as I recall it, Inspector Kelley and I left and went up to---I say up---down the hall to the executive office area of the police department, and to the office of Deputy Chief Batchelor.

And we remained in that vicinity. I looked out the window, and saw the people across the street, on Commerce Street, people were waiting there. And I saw an individual that I know by the name of Ruby Goldstein, who is known as Honest Joe, that has a second-hand tool and pawnshop down on Elm Street, and everyone around there knows him. He was leaning on the car looking over in the direction of the ramp there at the police station. And we were just waiting around there.

And for a few minutes I was talking to one of the police officers that was on duty up there in that area. And he had made the remark, *"talking about open windows, I see one open across the street over there"* at a building across the street.

I looked over there. I didn't see any activity at the window. And we had walked out into the reception area of the executive office of the Chief of Police there when this same police officer said that he just heard that Oswald had got shot in the stomach in the basement by Jack Rubin, as I understood at that time, R-u-b-i-n--who was supposed to run a night club. Inspector Kelley and I then went just as hurriedly as we could to the basement.

[And later during that same testimony...]

Mr. Hubert. You did see Oswald, I think, on Sunday morning, November 24?

Mr. Sorrels. Yes, sir.

Mr. Hubert. Could you tell us where and at what time?

Mr. Sorrels. That was in the office of Capt. Will Fritz of the Homicide Division of the Dallas Police Department. It was somewhere around 11 o'clock in the morning, and he was removed from Captain Fritz' office at approximately I guess about 11:15.

There is the Griffin and Hubert memo to J Lee Rankin from March 23rd 1964 (3619) on Forrest Sorrels' account of that particular interrogation of Sunday morning where he thought that Oswald was loosening up, more cooperative attitude-wise.

Thomas J Kelley made a three-page report (3620) on this particular session as well, but not until almost a week later. According to Kelley, Oswald was willing to talk to the USSS provided he had the assistance of counsel. A repeat of what Forrest Sorrels had reported.

Harry Dean Holmes (3621), a Postal Inspector, and informant of the FBI was present on Sunday morning the 24th. Holmes makes it sound that he was there Friday and Saturday as well, but no paperwork or statement is present to support that.

The USPS was involved with the interrogations of Lee Oswald, because of the mail order of the rifle (which no one at the USPS could recollect ever handing it to Oswald) and his PO Box. After leaving his wife at church, Holmes was present on Sunday the 24th, to offer assistance and see whether he could be of any help. Low and behold, Will Fritz called him in for the interrogation of Oswald.

Charles Dhority in his WC testimony (3622), testified that Holmes took notes during the interrogations and of course his memory deserts him when asked what questions were put forward to Oswald:

Mr. Ball. Now, were you present at some time on the 24th when Oswald was in Captain Fritz' office?
Mr. Dhority. Yes, sir.
Mr. Ball. That would be Sunday, November 24.
Mr. Dhority. Yes, sir.
Mr. Ball. Tell us about what you did that day, on the 24th of November.
Mr. Dhority. Well, on--I went up to jail along with Leavelle and Graves and got him and brought him down to Captain Fritz' office that morning.
Mr. Ball. Who was present in Captain Fritz' office that day?
Mr. Dhority. Well, Captain Fritz and Mr. Kelley and Mr. Sorrels.
Mr. Ball. Mr. Sorrels of the Secret Service?
Mr. Dhority. And Mr. Holmes.
Mr. Ball. And Holmes is what?
Mr. Dhority. Of the Post Office Department.
Mr. Ball. What time did you bring him into Fritz' office?
Mr. Dhority. About 9:30 in the morning.
Mr. Ball. What time did you leave there?
Mr. Dhority. Oh, I imagine it was shortly after 11 o'clock when Captain Fritz gave me the keys to his car and told me to go get it down there in front of the jail office to move Oswald down to the County in.
Mr. Ball. What was said there in Fritz's office that day---do you remember any of the conversations?
Mr. Dhority. There was a lot of conversation.
Mr. Ball. What did they talk about--the people in there?
Mr. Dhority. Well, they were talking to Oswald and Mr. Kelley talked to him and Mr. Sorrels talked to him--I don't think Mr. Holmes talked to him too much. I think he recorded most of the interviews, as well as I remember.
Mr. Ball. Do you remember what was said?
Mr. Dhority. I couldn't remember all that was said.
Mr. Ball. Did you make any notes?
Mr. Dhority. No, sir; I didn't.

LC Graves makes mention of Holmes and the happenings around the Sunday morning interrogations of Oswald in Larry Sneed's *No More Silence (3623)*: "*Around 9:30 Leavelle and I were sent upstairs and brought Oswald down to Captain Fritz's office which was rather small, probably about nine feet by twelve. I don't remember all that were in on the questioning, but Mr. Holmes of the postal service was there and probably Mr. Bookhout with the FBI and Captain Fritz. There may have been others but I don't recall offhand. We just went on out and started looking through our papers and whatever because we knew they weren't going to be in there long, and we didn't want to clutter the room any more than necessary. Besides, you could never get a word in edgeways anyway, so we just left out. I never entered the room during the questioning. We could see in the room and when everybody got up and left, we went back in."*

The second-floor lunchroom encounter is 'killed off' on page 5 in Holmes' report from November 24th and handed to the FBI (SA Charles T Brown Jnr.) on December 17th (3624).

Holmes, in his affidavit he stated that Fritz asked Oswald about the Hidell ID card, and Oswald "*flared up and stated 'I've told you all I'm going to about that card. You took notes, just read them for yourself, if you want to refresh your memory'.*

In the San Francisco Chronicle January 19th 1978 (3625), Holmes repeats that Oswald *emphatically denied having any knowledge of the Kennedy shooting.*

Holmes' WC testimony (3626) contains some important clues. Actually, he gives the game away regarding Oswald's whereabouts and actions during and just after the shooting, in the sense that he was not as tight lipped as Fritz and co. were. And that Holmes must have missed the 'memo' regarding DPD's collective amnesia when it came to Oswald's interrogations and more importantly his alibi.

- Oswald talked about the commotion and went out to see what this was about.
- Holmes places Oswald's encounter with the policeman and Roy Truly near the front door of the building.
- Upon persistent re-questioning where Oswald was during the encounter Holmes describes the encounter happening in the vestibule.
- Holmes also fails to uphold the coke story to such an extent that no one is able to determine where Oswald bought it and what he actually did with it. It is as shady as Roy Truly's multiple story varieties of where exactly Oswald was standing when encountered by Baker (sitting down in a booth drinking a coke, standing next to the vending machine and so on).
- In his WC testimony the police man asked Oswald to *"step aside"* which rings more true for something happening near a front

door than inside a lunchroom as Baker and Truly said that they turned around and made their way upstairs. This exact phrase was also used by Holmes in his own report.

Mr. Belin. Did anyone say anything about Oswald saying anything about his leaving the Texas School Book Depository after the shooting?

Mr. Holmes. He said, as I remember, actually, in answer to questions there, he mentioned that when lunchtime came, one of the Negro employees asked him if he would like to sit and eat lunch with him, and he said, *"Yes, but I can't go right now."* He said, *"You go and take the elevator on down."* No, he said, *"You go ahead, but send the elevator back up."* He didn't say up where, and he didn't mention what floor he was on. Nobody seemed to ask him. You see, I assumed that obvious questions like that had been asked in previous interrogation. So, I didn't interrupt too much, but he said, *"Send the elevator back up to me."*

Then he said when all this commotion started, *"I just went on downstairs."* And he didn't say whether he took the elevator or not. He said, *"I went down, and as I started to go out and see what it was all about, a police officer stopped me just before I got to the front door, and started to ask me some questions, and my superintendent of the place stepped up and told the officers that I am one of the employees of the building, so he told me to step aside for a little bit and we will get to you later. Then I just went on out in the crowd to see what it was all about."*

And he wouldn't tell what happened then.

Mr. Belin. Did he say where he was at the time of the shooting?

Mr. Holmes. He just said he was still up in the building when the commotion-- he kind of----

Mr. Belin. Did he gesture with his hands, do you remember?

Mr. Holmes. He talked with his hands all the time. He was handcuffed, but he was quiet--well, he was not what you call a stoic phlegmatic person. He is very definite with his talk and his eyes and his head, and he goes like that, you see.

[Here, Belin asks about an alleged incident involving journalist Robert MacNeil's accidental interaction with Lee Oswald...]

Mr. Belin. Did Oswald say anything about seeing a man with a crewcut in front of the building as he was about to leave it? Do you remember anything about that?

Mr. Holmes. No.

Mr. Belin. You don't remember anything about that. Did he say anything about telling a man about going to a pay phone in the building?

Mr. Holmes. Policeman rushed--I take it back---I don't know whether he said a policeman or not--a man came rushing by and said, *"Where's your telephone?"*

And the man showed him some kind of credential and I don't know that he identified the credential, so he might not have been a police officer, and said I am so and so, and shoved something at me which I didn't look at and said, *"Where is the telephone?"*

And I said, *"Right there,"* and just pointed in to the phone, and I went on out.

Mr. Belin. Did Oswald say why he left the building?

Mr. Holmes. No; other than just said he talked about this commotion and went out to see what it was about.

[Later, during Holmes' testimony...]

Mr. Belin. By the way, where did this policeman stop him when he was coming down the stairs at the Book Depository on the day of the shooting?

Mr. Holmes. He said it was in the vestibule.

Mr. Belin. He said he was in the vestibule?

Mr. Holmes. Or approaching the door to the vestibule. He was just coming, apparently, and I have never been in there myself. Apparently, there is two sets of doors, and he had come out to this front part.

Mr. Belin. Did he state it was on what floor?

Mr. Holmes. First floor. The front entrance to the first floor.

Mr. Belin. Did he say anything about a Coca Cola or anything like that, if you remember?

Mr. Holmes. Seems like he said he was drinking a Coca Cola, standing there by the Coca Cola machine drinking a Coca Cola.

[And a little later...]

Mr. Belin. Now, Mr. Holmes, I wonder if you could try and think if there is anything else that you remember Oswald saying about where he was during the period prior or shortly prior to, and then at the time of the assassination?

Mr. Holmes. Nothing more than I have already said. If you want me to repeat that?

Mr. Belin. Go ahead and repeat it.

Mr. Holmes. See if I say it the same way?

Mr. Belin. Yes.

Mr. Holmes. He said when lunchtime came, he was working in one of the upper floors with a Negro.

The Negro said, *"Come on and let's eat lunch together."*

Apparently, both of them having a sack lunch. And he said, *"You go ahead, send the elevator back up to me and I will come down just as soon as I am finished."*

And he didn't say what he was doing. There was a commotion outside, which he later rushed downstairs to go out to see what was going on. He didn't say whether he took the stairs down. He didn't say whether he took the elevator down.

But he went downstairs, and as he went out the front, it seems as though he did have a coke with him, or he stopped at the coke machine, or somebody else was trying to get a coke, but there was a coke involved. He mentioned something about a coke. But a police officer asked him who he was, and just as he started to identify himself, his superintendent came up and said, *"He is one of our men."* And the policeman said, "Well, you step aside for a little bit."

Then another man rushed in past him as he started out the door, in this vestibule part of it, and flashed some kind of credential and he said, *"Where is your telephone, where is your telephone?"* and said, *"I am (so and so), where is your telephone?"*

And he said, *"I didn't look at the credential. I don't know who he said he was, and I just pointed to the phone and said, 'there it is,' and went on out the door."*

In Larry Sneed's *No More Silence* (3637), Holmes says the following about the necessity of an interrogator being able to rely upon an exceptional memory: *There was no tape recording of the interrogation or stenographer or anyone taking notes. That was the way that Fritz operated. The interrogation itself was rather informal with Captain Fritz being in charge. He would ask Oswald various questions and pull-out different things such as the map with the X's on it and the card that had been taken out of Oswald's billfold that had AJ Hidell on it and things like that. Then he would say, "Well, Sorrels, do you have anything you want to ask him?" But Kelley and Sorrels had very little to ask; they didn't have the documentation that I had. We were free to ask or interject anything we wanted. Of course, we were all experienced interrogators, and when you went to trial in those days, especially in Federal Court, you had to show any notes you took to the defence. So, they got to look at every note that you had against their client. But we old-time investigators would just do it by memory. I could still quote nearly every word that boy said to this day and that's been over twenty years ago. That's the way I was trained to interrogate anybody, and so was Fritz. If they're telling the truth, you'd talk to them by the hour, and if they couldn't tell it the same way twice or a third time, or a tenth time, you'd catch them because you'd know exactly what he had said the first time. You didn't need notes; you didn't need a secretary or a stenographer.*

Of course, you do now, but back then you really had to use your own wits to convict people.

LD Montgomery was the partner of Marvin Johnson, who took the dodgy Marrion Baker report on November 22nd. The third page of his report from the Dallas Police JFK Assassination Archives (3628) lists his participation and that of all others present during this interrogation.

From Montgomery's first WC testimony session (3629), about the interrogations:

Mr. Ball Were you ever present at any time when Oswald was questioned?
Mr. Montgomery. Yes, sir.
Mr. Ball. Where was that?
Mr. Montgomery. That would be the Sunday morning of the 24th, just prior to transferring him.
Mr. Ball. Where was that?
Mr. Montgomery. That would be in Captain Fritz' office in the city hall.
Mr. Ball. Who was present, if you remember?
Mr. Montgomery. Well, there was Detective Leavelle, Detective Graves, Detective Dhority, Captain Fritz, and Mr. Sorrels, and Mr. Kelley.
Mr. Ball. Do you know what was said?
Mr. Montgomery. Yes, sir; they just asked him several questions there as to why he shot the President and he said he didn't shoot the President, and Captain Fritz asked Mr. Sorrels if he would like to ask him a question and Mr. Sorrels would ask him one and then Mr. Kelley would ask him one--they would ask him about life in Russia.
Mr. Ball Do you remember anything else?
Mr. Montgomery. No, sir; that's about all the questions I recall.

Montgomery's second WC testimony (3629) gives a small insight into Oswald's Sunday interrogation:

Mr. GRIFFIN. What did you do after Oswald was brought down and while he was in Fritz' office?
Mr. Montgomery. Well, when they brought him down, we stepped into this office there and there was a--I was standing up there listening to the interview----
Mr. GRIFFIN. Did you remain in Fritz' office while he interviewed Oswald?
Mr. Montgomery. Yes.
Mr. GRIFFIN. Who was in Fritz' office at that time?
Mr. Montgomery. At that time, there was, of course, Captain Fritz, and there was Oswald, and I was there, Leavelle was there and Graves.
Mr. GRIFFIN. Was he in Fritz' office?

Mr. Montgomery. Sir?

Mr. GRIFFIN. Was Graves in Fritz' office?

Mr. Montgomery. Uh-huh; I believe, Dhority, I believe Dhority was in there. I am not sure, but Dhority was another one of our officers. I believe he was in there and, of course, he had Inspector Holmes.

Mr. GRIFFIN. Is he the postal inspector?

Mr. Montgomery. Yes. Inspector Holmes, and I forget the man's name for--from the Secret Service.

Mr. GRIFFIN. Mr. Sorrels?

Mr. Montgomery. Mr. Sorrels was there, yes; and a--one other man name--was what--who was that----

Mr. GRIFFIN. Were there any FBI agents there?

Mr. Montgomery. I was trying to think if Mr. Bookhout was there, but I can't remember if he was inside.

Mr. GRIFFIN. Do you remember about what Oswald said and what was to Oswald during that period?

Mr. Montgomery. I remember they asked him why he shot the President, and of course, he said he didn't do it.

Mr. GRIFFIN. Uh-huh.

Mr. Montgomery. And, I don't recall the exact questions. Just asked him several questions there.

Mr. GRIFFIN. How long did this questioning last?

Mr. Montgomery. Seemed like it was about 25 minutes or an hour that he was in there.

Mr. GRIFFIN. All right.

Mr. Montgomery. Captain Fritz, you know, asking him questions, and he would ask Inspector Holmes or Mr. Sorrels if they would like to ask him a question, and, of course, they would ask him one.

Mr. GRIFFIN. Had you been present at any of the earlier interrogations of Oswald?

Mr. Montgomery. No; I wasn't.

Mr. GRIFFIN. Why was it you happened to be present at this interview?

Mr. Montgomery. I think I just got lost in the office. I was in there talking to the captain when they brought Oswald in, and, of course, the captain said shut the door there, and some of the officers shut the door.

Mr. GRIFFIN. What did you happen to be talking to Fritz about?

Mr. Montgomery. I don't recall. I know I was in his office when they brought Oswald down there.

Mr. GRIFFIN. You were there for the entire period of the interrogation of Oswald?

Mr. Montgomery. That morning; yes, sir.

Mr. GRIFFIN. Do you remember during that period anybody coming into the office with respect to the movement of Oswald down to the county jail?

Mr. Montgomery. The chief came in.

Mr. GRIFFIN. How many times do you recall the chief coming in?

Mr. Montgomery. Just recall one time.

Mr. GRIFFIN. How long before the end of the interrogation was it?

Mr. Montgomery. I imagine it was about--well, it was right there at the end, you know, when they was still talking, and the chief came in and wanted to know if we were ready to move him.

From Larry Sneed's *No More Silence* (3631): *I only recall sitting in on one of them. On that occasion, Bill Senkel and I were there when the Cap and others were looking at Oswald's little address book which contained the license number of the FBI agent who had been following him. It was rather comical! Oswald looked up at Mr. Hosty, the FBI agent, and said, "You're the one that's been harassing me and following my family!"*

I doubt this actually happened since this scenario already occurred on Friday afternoon when Hosty was present and he was not involved with any of the interrogations on Saturday nor Sunday.

11:20 Oswald is Being Transferred and Shot by Jack Ruby

Jim Leavelle 'remembers': *"I told him on the way down, 'Lee, if anybody shoots at you, I hope they're as good a shot as you are.' Meaning they'd hit him and not me. And he kind of laughed, and he said, 'Ah, you're being melodramatic,' or something like that. 'Nobody's going to shoot me.'"* There is no corroboration for any of this from anyone else who was inside that elevator.

LC Graves who rode the elevator down with Leavelle and Oswald cannot remember anything being said of significance on that ride down as he says during his Oral History interview for the 6FM (3632): *"I did not say anything to him. Jim might have said something to him. I don't feel it was significant, if he said anything at all."*

From Seth Kantor's *Who Was Jack Ruby* (3633): *Lieutenant Richard E Swain of the Burglary and Theft Bureau, who had known Ruby for several years, then went ahead first into the garage area. Someone in the crowd shouted, "Here he comes!" Swain, who was never questioned by the Warren Commission, surveyed the confused scene quickly and then looked back to the inside corridor where Fritz waited. Everything was in good shape, he indicated. Come ahead. Nothing was in good shape. Dhority was frantically trying to move the car, gunning the motor, honking the horn, but blocked by detectives and reporters who weren't where they were supposed to be. There was no protective corridor of detectives through which Oswald was to walk to the car that wasn't there. Reporters mixed among the police instead of being held behind the railing.*

Homicide detective James R Leavelle, handcuffed to Oswald's right wrist, asked Cutchshaw inside the jail hallway if everything was all right. Cutchshaw, like almost all of the cops down there at 11:21, had no idea what the plan was supposed to be. But Leavelle was assured by Cutchshaw that there were no problems. Chief Curry, ludicrously, was upstairs in his office, responding to a phone call from Dallas mayor Earle Cabell, and had not checked for himself to see if orders were being carried out properly in the basement. Curry told me he had detailed Assistant Chief Batchelor and Deputy Chief Stevenson to set up the corridor of detectives so that Oswald would be shielded, and to move the news people behind the railing so Oswald's transfer car could move.

"There were several higher, supervisory officers in the basement," Curry said, "and 70 detectives, which should have been enough, you know, to guard against any kind of assault that might be attempted to come into the basement. I was trying to let them (reporters and cameramen) have all the freedom they could. I knew this was something the American people were interested in. They were watching it by the millions. But I had told Batchelor and Stevenson to keep them behind the iron railing." Fritz followed Swain and was promptly blinded by the bright television lights that came from behind Ruby to illuminate the target. Oswald came out next, flanked by Leavelle and Detective LC Graves. Billy H Combest, a detective from the vice section, saw Ruby lunge past Blackie Harrison. Combest shouted, "Jack, you son of a bitch!" as the shot went off point blank at Oswald's stomach.

Forrest Sorrels' WC testimony (3634):

Mr. Hubert. You did see Oswald, I think, on Sunday morning, November 24?
Mr. Sorrels. Yes, sir.
Mr. Hubert. Could you tell us where and at what time?
Mr. Sorrels. That was in the office of Capt. Will Fritz of the homicide division of the Dallas Police Department. It was somewhere around 11 o'clock in the morning, and he was removed from Captain Fritz' office at approximately I guess about 11:15.
Mr. Hubert. What was the purpose of your interviewing him that morning?
Mr. Sorrels. We, of course, were interested in any statement that Oswald might make relating to any phase of the assassination of the President. Particularly, I was interested in trying to obtain an admission from him

that he had used the name of A. Hidell as an alias, because information had been developed that he had purchased the rifle which was found on the sixth floor of the Book Depository under the name of A. Hidell. There was a change of address card which he had filed in New Orleans, as I recall it, on which it was shown that persons to receive mail at the address given the name of A. Hidell appeared. And after Captain Fritz got through questioning him on the morning of November 24, he asked if any of the officers present in the room desired to ask him any questions. And I said, *"Yes; I would like to ask him a question."*

In the meantime, Chief of Police Jesse Curry had come to Captain Fritz' office, and inquired about the delay in moving him out. And Captain Fritz informed that he was still talking to him.

Mr. Hubert. Captain Fritz informed----

Mr. Sorrels. Informed Chief Curry----

Mr. Hubert. That he was or you were?

Mr. Sorrels. That he was. And a very short time after that is when I had an opportunity to ask Oswald some questions. I showed Oswald the change of address card----

Mr. Hubert. Let me ask you this: Was your interrogation of him cut off, as it were, by the transfer?

Mr. Sorrels. By the transfer?

Mr. Hubert. Yes.

Mr. Sorrels. No.

Mr. Hubert. Had you finished with him?

Mr. Sorrels. I had finished----

Mr. Hubert. As to that point?

Mr. Sorrels. As to that point; yes, sir.

Mr. Hubert. As a matter of fact, you would have had access to him, I think, at the county jail, anyhow, would you not?

Mr. Sorrels. I had certainly planned on having access to him, and I am sure I would have. As a matter of fact, I had in my mind to start talking to him that afternoon.

Mr. Hubert. What I wanted to clarify is whether or not your effort to interrogate him was interrupted. But I gather that it was not.

Mr. Sorrels. No, I would say not. Possibly, had he remained there, I might have attempted to ask him more questions. But he was not giving out much information.

Mr. Hubert. Well, now, during the whole time that Oswald was in custody of the Dallas Police Department, did you find that any obstacles or hindrances were put in your way of examining him?

Mr. Sorrels. No, sir; except had he been in our own custody, there would have been a chance to have questioned him without others being present, or so many others being present.

Charles Dhority in his WC testimony (3635):

Mr. Ball. After they questioned Oswald, what did you do?

Mr. Dhority. Well, I believe we gave him a sweater to put on. I think it was kind of cool--one of his sweaters.

Mr. Ball. Was he handcuffed?

Mr. Dhority. Yes; Leavelle handcuffed himself to Oswald just before I left the office.

Mr. Ball. Had he been handcuffed during the questioning in Fritz' office that morning?

Mr. Dhority. I don't recall--I didn't have my handcuffs on him.

Mr. Ball. Just before you left the office, Leavelle handcuffed him--did he put one cuff on Oswald and one on Leavelle; is that it?

Mr. Dhority. Yes.

Mr. Ball. Fritz gave you instructions to do what?

Mr. Dhority. He gave me the keys to his car and told me to go down and get his car and back it up front of the jail door to put Oswald in.

Mr. Ball. Is that what you did?

Mr. Dhority. I went downstairs and got his car, unlocked his car, and was in the process of backing it up there in fact--I was just about ready to stop, when Captain Fritz came out and Leavelle and Oswald and Graves and Johnson and Montgomery came out the jail door.

Captain Fritz reached over to the door of the car and I was turned around to see backing it up--still had the car moving it along and I saw someone run across the end of the car real rapid like. At first, I thought it was somebody going to take a picture and then I saw a hand come out and I heard the shot.

Mr. Ball. Graves and Leavelle were there beside Oswald, were they?

Mr. Dhority. Yes; beside Oswald.

Mr. Ball. Oswald was between Graves and Leavelle?

Mr. Dhority. That's right.

LD Montgomery mentions James Bookhout in Larry Sneed's *No More Silence* (3636):

SA Bookhout asked me, "What did you do?" I told him, "You were right there, Bookhout. We handcuffed Oswald; we walked around to the elevator, got on the elevator to go down. Where'd you go? You were right there with us?" He got a little funny and said, "I walked back to the squad room and turned up the squawk box." I said, "Why?" I don't remember the exact wording of his response, but it was something to the effect--"to hear the shooting. Didn't you know that the Chief had received a call during the night that Oswald was going to be shot?" "Hell, no," I said, "I didn't!" I was pretty angry at the time. His whole response, I thought, was very odd.

Oswald was removed from the area and taken to a room where he was attended by Fred A Bieberdorf who later rode in the ambulance that transported Oswald, Leavelle (3637) and Graves (3638) to Parkland Hospital where he was declared dead at 13:07.

The FBI was quick to respond and while Oswald is inside Parkland (3639) being operated upon there are a few agents who have gowned and masked-up just to see if there is any opportunity to question Oswald. Obviously, they waited in vain for Oswald to regain consciousness.

After Oswald had passed away, an FBI report from February 2nd 1964 (3640) states that a piece of paper was found on him with a list of phone numbers. This piece of paper was given to him by the jailer the day before. What is interesting is the telephone number CH-7-3110, which is not a working number at that time and had been disconnected since 1956.

Interrogation of Lee Harvey Oswald Report by Will Fritz

Will Fritz produced an undated report called *"Interrogation of Lee Harvey Oswald"* (3641).

Steve Thomas (3642) mentioned that there are seven different copies of this undated report. These reports come with annotations in shorthand; due to this and it being retyped a few times, the number of pages is affected. I just picked one for comparison reasons regarding what Fritz stated and what really happened based on actual documentation.

The main reason for the chronological approach of this book is that you can place certain specific happenings in a specific time frame and, with the help of the reports/notes/testimonies of Fritz, Hosty, Bookhout, Sorrels and Kelley, hopefully, a bigger picture starts to appear. Compare these with this report and you will see that certain aspects of the interrogations were brought forward in particular ways as to make Oswald look guiltier than he actually was. And this is not once or twice, but quite a few times.

The first page is already a mess, but since this does not concern any interrogation, I have decided to skip it. Pages 2-4 are about Oswald's interrogations on November 22nd.

On page 2 Fritz designates Oswald as the suspect in The President's killing, yet the suspect's description was very generic when sent out. It boggles the mind that Fritz had designated Oswald as the prime suspect without any additional info and he had only been at the TSBD for less than an hour.

On that same page 2, Fritz already makes a mistake by saying that Oswald usually worked on the second floor, whereas that should have been the first floor. He corners Oswald as a suspect with that wrong assertion. This does not rhyme with his own and Hosty's notes or the joint Bookhout and Hosty report at all.

Furthermore, Fritz refers to the back stairway when Marrion Baker supposedly apprehended Oswald, then the Truly and Baker lunchroom encounter is woven in. This particular incident was not concocted until later that day of the 22nd when Truly had given a affidavit to the FBI. Fritz makes it sound as if Truly had told him before he even sat down with Oswald. If that were the case, Fritz would have mentioned the incident in his notes. And so would Hosty and Bookhout, but the opposite was proven instead. Marrion Baker did not give an affidavit until later in the afternoon, and when he did, he mentioned an altercation on the third or fourth floor. There was no talk of a lunchroom at all in his first affidavit.

Fritz also stated that Oswald was in the lunchroom having a coke when Baker encountered him, which of course contradicts the backstairs scenario. This did not happen at all; even Baker and Truly said that he was not holding anything in his hands. Fritz is rhyming this with Mrs. Robert Reid's false statement that Oswald had a coke in his hands after the second-floor encounter with Baker and Truly.

On page 3, according to Fritz, while at Beckley, Oswald only changed his trousers and picked up his pistol which he took from a holster that no one ever bothered to check for fingerprints, btw! The phrase uttered by Oswald to Fritz *"You know how boys do when they have a gun. They just carry it."* Is not supported by anyone from the FBI or USSS in their reports.

Oswald's request for an attorney is brought up on page 4. Fritz is economical with the truth here as it has become more than evident that he did his best not to provide Oswald with an attorney on the 22nd. John Abt's name was not written down until the 23rd in Fritz's handwritten notes (page 4). Oswald made his first attempt to contact Abt with his first permitted phone call at around lunch time on the 23rd.

Then on page 4, the rifle is brought up and it shows that Fritz had been talking with Marina Oswald, but that she *could not* ID the rifle as belonging to her husband. Further down Fritz, along with Bill Alexander and Jim Allen (a *former* Assistant DA, and now private citizen) drew up charges to arraign Oswald for the murder of JFK without a shred of evidence on November 22nd.

On page 6, the bus and cab rides are mentioned. It takes up to the fourth interrogation (morning of the 23rd) to bring all this up. In one version of this report the bus transfer is nowhere to be seen, but it has been added to other copies. Then the document 'progresses' to the long package Oswald supposedly took with him while being driven by Buell Frazier to the TSBD. A package Jack Dougherty did not see Oswald carrying while he asked where his rider was on that morning of the 22nd.

On pages 6 & 7 the clothes exchange is mentioned. You have to ask yourself why Oswald changed his shirt and pants, but not his T-shirt. That dirty sweaty T-shirt he was actually working in whereas his shirt would normally be hanging up during working hours.

Then Oswald's lunch in the Domino Room is introduced on page 7 and the two fellow employees, James 'Junior' Jarman and another person, who were there at some point as well. Fritz made no discernible attempt to verify this. You have to ask yourself how did Oswald know that James Jarman and possibly Harold Norman were inside or passing through on their way up to the fifth floor if he was the shooter?!

Page 8 deals largely with John Abt, but also at the top of the page brings up the pistol again; the gun Oswald supposedly had on him inside the Texas Theatre.

On page 9 Oswald is quoted as indicating that he did not dislike Kennedy at all, and he refuses to submit to a polygraph test.

Fritz places the confrontation over the backyard photos forward by about five hours. Other reports point to this happening in the early evening of the 23rd at the 18:35 interrogation. James Bookhout confirms this in his WC testimony (3643) on page 9.

On page 10 Fritz brings the backyard photo up again, and this time it is at the correct interrogation.

This document (3644) by Martha J Stroud (Barefoot Sanders' assistant and worked as a liaison between Dallas and the WC) states that Will Fritz wishes to make changes to his deposition, before signing off on it. The original deposition and the amended one are to be sent to the WC. What has happened to the original is anyone's guess.

The Aftermath

On the 24th Wade gave another press conference (3645). This is after Oswald was murdered by Ruby and never had a chance to defend himself with any type of legal defence at any time before his death. Wade starts listing the many items of evidence in a spectacle of how badly informed he was. He continues, like the others, with his trial by media method. First item of evidence are the many witnesses who have seen Oswald in the window of the sixth floor of the TSBD which is quite an opening statement since no one was ever able to do this! Not to this day!

As Chief Curry would say in 1969. *"We don't have any proof that Oswald fired the rifle and never did. Nobody's yet been able to put him in that building with a gun in his hand. Why Oswald was nevertheless blamed for the crime seems difficult to explain – but it is what happened."*

Then Oswald's palm print was found on the box in the sniper's nest. What Wade did not mention was that Oswald's was found among about 23 fingerprints and 11 palm prints unaccounted for.

Then the rifle is attributed to him by purchasing it thru mail order under the name Hidell, of which evidence shows it did not exist until the morning of the 23rd at DPD. That same rifle no USPS officer can attest to handing it over to Oswald.

The backyard photographs are mentioned. The package is next. And the list goes on with a lot of so-called evidence that can be disputed one way or another.

Regarding the interrogations, Wade says he did not participate in any; and that Oswald did not admit to any of the killings at all. And that Oswald was bitter at all the law enforcement officers present, so he had been told. Well, who wouldn't be after being kept in the dark, being falsely accused, and being prevented from contacting any legal representation for more than 24 hours? And, adding the ultimate poison cherry on top, to finish it all off by getting murdered while being under protection of the DPD.

Henry Wade in his WC testimony (3646):

Mr. Wade. And then I went out to dinner and got to thinking, I said well now, the Dallas police did have a breakdown in security here, and they are taking a beating and I am taking a beating, but they did have the right man according to my thinking, so I went down to the police station and got all the brass in there but Chief Curry and I said this stuff, people are saying on there: you had the wrong man and you all were the one who killed him or let him out here to have him killed intentionally, I said somebody ought to go out in television and lay out the evidence that you had on Oswald, and tell them everything. It had been most of it laid out but not in chronological order.

Mr. Rankin. When was this now?

Mr. Wade. This was 8 o'clock roughly on the 24th. Sunday night. I sat down with Captain Fritz and took a pencil and pad and listed about seven pieces of evidence from my own knowledge and I was going to write it down. They got hold of Chief Curry and he said no, that he had told this inspector of the FBI that there would be nothing further said about it. I asked Chief Batchelor and Lumpkin, they were all there, I said you all are the ones who know something about it, I said, if you have at least got the right man, in my opinion the American people ought to know. This is evidence you can't use actually, because he is dead. You can't try him. And the upshot of that was the police wouldn't say a word and refused actually to furnish me any more of the details on this.

In 1975 The Richmond Times Dispatch (3647) published an article which puts doubt on whether the evidence would convict Oswald.

In October 2017 on the day of some of the documents being released, I managed to find this unredacted Hoover FBI document (3648) from November 24th.

On November 24th 1963 J Edgar Hoover reports (3649): [same document but from Malcolm Blunt's archive] *"There is nothing further on the Oswald case except that he is dead."* (page 1). On the next page it is rather telling when it comes to the security of Oswald's transfer: *"Oswald having been killed today after our warnings to the Dallas Police Department was inexcusable. It will allow, I am afraid, a lot of civil rights people to raise a lot of hell because he was handcuffed and had no weapon. There are bound to be some elements of our society who will holler their heads off that his civil rights were violated — which they were."*

But, of even greater significance, how shaky the case against Oswald was from a legal point of view. Not only was Hoover praising his own FBI investigative and analytical capabilities above the DPD's: *"They did not have much of a case against Oswald until we gave them our information",* but he also says, *"Oswald had been saying he wanted John Abt as his lawyer, and Abt with only that kind of evidence could have turned the case around, I'm afraid."* May I suggest you read the entire thing, as it gives good insight as to what Hoover was up to on the day Oswald was killed.

No wonder this document had been hidden from public view until late 2017, as it is nothing short of a bombshell. One can only wonder what is still kept hidden from us.

Index

413

Printed in Great Britain
by Amazon

36333145R00231